The Universal Dream Key

ALSO BY PATRICIA GARFIELD

Creative Dreaming

Pathway to Ecstasy: The Way of the Dream Mandala

Your Child's Dreams

Women's Bodies, Women's Dreams

The Healing Power of Dreams

*The Dream Messenger: How Dreams of the
Departed Bring Healing Gifts*

The
Universal
Dream
Key

The Twelve Most

Common Dream Themes

Around the World

Patricia Garfield, Ph.D.

Cliff Street Books
An Imprint of HarperCollinsPublishers

THE UNIVERSAL DREAM KEY: THE TWELVE MOST COMMON DREAM THEMES AROUND THE WORLD.
Copyright © 2001 by Patricia Garfield, Ph.D. All rights reserved. Printed in the United States of
America. No part of this book may be used or reproduced in any manner whatsoever without written
permission except in the case of brief quotations embodied in critical articles and reviews. For information, address HarperCollins Publishers Inc., 10 East 53rd Street, New York, NY 10022.

HarperCollins books may be purchased for educational, business,
or sales promotional use. For information please write:
Special Markets Department, HarperCollins Publishers Inc.,
10 East 53rd Street, New York, NY 10022.

FIRST EDITION

Designed by Jo Anne Metsch

Printed on acid-free paper

Library of Congress Cataloging-in-Publication Data

Garfield, Patricia L.
    The universal dream key : the twelve most common dream themes around the
world / Patricia Garfield.
        p. cm.

    Includes bibliographical references and index.
    ISBN 0-06-095364-0
    1. Dreams.   2. Dream interpretation.   I. Title.

BF1078.G176 2001
154.6'32—dc21   00–060113

        01   02   03   04   05   RRD   10   9   8   7   6   5   4   3   2   1

In memory of my mother,
Evelyn,
who taught me to love dreams:
the past

With special thanks to
Worldwide dreamers,
who share their dream tales:
the present

For my grandson,
Nicholas,
whose dreams are still growing:
the future

Contents

Acknowledgments

THE IDEA OF a universal dream key has been simmering in the back of my mind for years. I was glad when my colleagues in the Association for the Study of Dreams (ASD) asked me to be president for the 1998–99 year, providing the impetus to pull together my thoughts for the presidential address in Hawaii.

These same professional colleagues have helped move the project forward. I'm particularly appreciative of the small group that participated in the first panel on Universal Dreams at the 1999 ASD conference held at the University of California in Santa Cruz. Rita Dwyer shared her insights on wedding dreams and reminded me of the importance of the spirit; Mena Potts applied the new approach to predictive car trouble dreams; Robert Hoss explored the role of color in the Universal Dream themes; and Monique Lortie-Lussier discussed all with her customary good judgment.

Curtiss Hoffmann, in particular, offered an exceedingly helpful critique of the concept of classifying dreams. G. William Domhoff consistently pointed out errors that enabled me to make improvements. Those mistakes that remain are my own. Alan Siegel, in his role as editor of ASD's *Dream Time* newsmagazine, published material on the idea of universal dreaming, and was extremely fair in mediating discussions about it. I found Jill Gregory's Dream Archives in Novato, California, to be an invaluable resource. ASD board meetings and informal chats—with, among others, Kelly Bulkeley, Stephen LaBerge, Fariba Bogzaran, Keelin, Cynthia Pearson, Charla Van Koten, Carol Schoneberg, Arlyn Zones, Una Nakamura, Li Ping, and Amy Ma—provided ingredients for the stew.

French-Canadian dream worker Nicole Gratton shared her perspective on dreams; Peter Elting sent me relevant material from Switzerland; Roger Ripert sent books and his newsletter from France. Annie Ovedoff contributed from Australia; "Mirjana" from Yugoslavia; and Alfio Maggiolini sent his material on typical dreams from Italy. Gloria Sturzenacker shared her Inner Guide Mapping. I'm indebted to these and many other colleagues and friends who have enriched my understanding of dreams.

My artistic advisers and friends—Evelyn Simon, Phyllis Clark Harvey, and Jain McFettridge—provided intriguing notions and drawings related to icons for the Universal Dreams. Even though these ideas did not end up in the finished book, they were thought-provoking and useful.

Computer advisers were essential to this project. Richard Wilkerson was a walking dictionary of computer know-how, as well as a good-natured helper. His skills in designing and managing my website [www.patriciagarfield. com]—without which this book would not have been complete—deserve a special debt of gratitude. Condon Brown also contributed mind-expanding ideas concerning the world of the Internet.

I appreciate the interest Diane Reverand of Cliff Street Books took in the book idea early on, and editor Janet Dery's careful attention in readying it for publication. My agent, Candice Fuhrman, of San Francisco, was a pleasure to work with; she also provided moral support. My favorite local bookstore, Book Passage, in Corte Madera (owned by Elaine and Bill Petrocelli), supplied many of the volumes I needed at just the right time.

In addition to Jung, whose influence will be apparent in my own work, I found the writings of folklorists Stith Thompson, Vladimir Propp, and my contemporary Alan Dundes to be inspiring; the structuralist writings of Claude Lévi-Strauss were also beneficial.

My dear friends Thomasine and Mal Kushner and Laura and Gil Avery were a great comfort during my mother's illness and subsequent death. They read early drafts of the book, checked completed sections, volunteered dreams, and provided general encouragement. Jordan and Mona Beyer also related their dream tales, and Alice Kales has entrusted me with her dreams for many years. I'm so thankful for these good friends.

Members of my family, too, related their dream stories and made me smile. My brother, Fred Goff, has been a wonderful mainstay in dealing with the repercussions of our mother's death—the same year that my dear godmother, Kathryn Keep, died. I value his companionship as well as his computer knowledge. Daughter Cheryl is a source of much delight, along with her son, Nicholas, and husband, Bill. Stepdaughter Wendy makes me laugh with her latest adventures in dreamland as well as those of her husband, Rudy; their children, Ryan and Madison, are just beginning to confide their nighttime tales. Stepson Steven and his wife, Elaine, and their sons, Joey and

Sean; stepdaughter Linda and her husband, Fred—all have recounted their dream stories, which I appreciate.

My beloved husband, Zal, mate and companion for more than thirty years, has never failed me. I love him more than I can tell. Rarely too tired or too busy to hear my ideas or listen to descriptions of my dreams, he offers sound advice, a shoulder to cry on, and a loving cuddle.

Last, I want to thank the many dreamers around the world who related their dreams—the oldest of stories—by means of the newest technology, the Internet. This book wouldn't be complete without you. My thanks go out to all of you.

Perhaps those of you who read this book will carry these ideas into the future. In any case, I hope you find it enhances your life. May your journey be blessed.

Introduction to Using the
Universal Dream Key

EVERY NIGHT YOU tell yourself stories. Tales of adventure and love, narratives of strife and woe arise in your sleeping mind. This nocturnal collection of fables is richly illustrated, presenting your dearest hopes and your worst fears in bright pictures. We call these sleep stories "dreams."

The illuminated storybook of your dreams may reveal a single image—a perfect blue flower or a starving kitten; it may unfold movies of the mind, complete with plot, dramatic action, characters, and dialogue. These film clips and still shots are all about you, every one of them. Their images are your emotions in visible form, your feelings shaped into dream flesh and spirit.

And yet these most personal of tales are also epics that have been told since the dawn of the thinking mind. They are sagas of humanity, repeated a hundred thousand times across the sweep of millennia. The intimate stories that you tell yourself tonight when you go to bed have flowed across the centuries from cave dweller to condo dweller. These tales, repeated by dreamers throughout time, are teaching tales. They unveil not only your most intimate secrets but also the dreads and desires of humankind.

Each sleeper in every bed around the globe reports a variation of the same story line in a local dialect. Persons who grew up in Florida, having heard about incidents of alligator attacks, may dream about being chased by the creature, its jaws spread, sharp teeth ready to snap. Others asleep in India, having seen birds of prey perched in trees near the "towers of silence" where dead bodies are placed to be picked clean, may dream of a vulture swooping down to assault them with talons and beak. Indeed, I have collected these very dreams. The plot is the same: the dreamer is chased or attacked by a wild creature. The local variation in beast—alligator or vulture or one of myriad others—is the regional accent.

Certain dream plots recur so often that I have termed them "Universal Dreams." Whether you live in Poland or Malta, New Zealand or Argentina, you are likely to have experienced one or more of the Universal Dreams. This book will help you understand your individual version of them. You will learn the twelve most common dream themes that occur in every culture. You'll discover their frightening and their uplifting forms, and what these usually mean for the dreamer. You will see the most frequent variations of these Universal Dreams, and what the motifs that compose them probably signify in your own life.

DREAM STORIES MIRROR LIFE CHANGES

YOUR NIGHTLY DREAM tales register changes in your daily life. Your brain, like that of all humans, has evolved to identify change. When you notice the subtle odor of smoke permeating the air, you may be warned of a fire nearby and be able to get out of danger or help others. When you taste something strange in a bite of food, you may be alerted to spoilage and so avoid food poisoning. Observing small shifts from the usual state of affairs may save your life.

So, too, your dreams highlight emotional shifts in your daily life. These can also be subtle, such as recognizing behavior of an aggressive new coworker who may eventually cause you trouble, or perceiving the presence of a potential new love interest. Your dreams also reflect dramatic changes in your waking life, like having a quarrel with a sweetheart or being fired from a job. Your dreaming brain, like your waking one, detects different qualities in your environment and portrays your feelings about them in exaggerated images. The aggressive coworker might become a poisonous snake in your dream desk; the intriguing love prospect might be depicted as a playful puppy in tonight's dream. The breakup with a lover might shape-shift into a violent dream earthquake; being fired might result in a dream of being cast adrift in a wobbly canoe. Changes, subtle or strong, are expressed in your dream pictures.

Too Much, Too Little, or Just Right?

IN PARTICULAR, YOUR dreams will inform you whether your waking conditions, and your feelings about them, are too much, too little, or the perfect amount. As in the fairy tale when Goldilocks tests the size of three chairs, three porridge bowls, and three beds belonging to the Three Bears, some situations fit us and others do not. Feeling overwhelmed? You may dream of being engulfed by a tidal wave; things seem to be too much for you at the moment. Feeling deprived of emotional support? You may dream of falling through space; your loving props feel too weak at the time of the dream.

Some things in life make us feel as if they are too much to endure; other things give us a sense of having too little of what we yearn for; still others give us pleasure because they meet our needs so precisely. As human beings, people throughout Earth share many responses to life's predicaments, ambitions, and satisfactions that are portrayed in the Universal Dreams.

The Universal Dream Themes Apply to You

EACH UNIVERSAL DREAM theme conveys a particular set of feelings, your personal reaction to the too-muchness or too-littleness or just-rightness in your current life. As you learn to understand the basic Universal Dreams, you'll be better equipped to grasp what emotions are expressed in your version of the dream. Your dream images sometimes correspond to ongoing changes in your body functioning. Here I provide a brief preview of twelve Universal Dreams. You'll explore them in greater depth throughout the book. I'll be showing you how to use the Dream Key that appears at the end of this book to help you quickly unlock the doors to the meaning of your version of a Universal Dream.

First you'll want to know how I gathered the material on which this book is based to determine the meanings of Universal Dreams. I used four sources:

1. My personal dream journal, containing more than fifty years of dreams. I started it when I was fourteen and I'm now sixty-six, so it has more volumes than the *Encyclopaedia Britannica's* twenty-nine tomes.

2. Dreams collected from other people, described in detail by the dreamers, along with their life situation at the time of the dream. As a professional dream collector for thirty-five years, I have a large assortment of these as well.

3. Dreams contributed to my website (www.patriciagarfield.com) by dreamers around the world. More than 500 dreamers participated, 325 dreamers from within the United States and 175 dreamers from elsewhere. Each dreamer contributed at least one dream; many described a dozen or so. More material poured in than I could possibly calculate, but the five hundred I counted are ample to show the trend of Universal Dream patterns (both groups yielded almost identical percentages and age and gender distribution). People in more than thirty-six countries participated, from America, Australia, Austria, Belgium, Canada, the Caribbean, Catalonia, China, the Czech Republic, Estonia, France, Guatemala, Germany, India, Ireland,

Israel, Italy, Japan, Kuwait, Malaysia, Malta, Mexico, the Netherlands, New Zealand, Norway, Poland, Puerto Rico, Saudi Arabia, South Africa, Spain, Sweden, Switzerland, Turkey, and the United Kingdom (England, Scotland, and Wales). Speakers of more than twenty different native languages, including Arabic, Bulgarian, Catalan, Czech, Danish, Dutch, English, Estonian, Filipino, French, German, Hindi, Italian, Malaysian, Maltese, Norwegian, Polish, Punjabi, Spanish, Swedish, Telugu, and Urdu, took part. Several lived in countries other than their native land. Three times as many women as men participated.

4. The professional literature on dreams.

Although my resources consist of thousands of dreams, the percentages I mention later are based on the analysis of dreams contributed by people who participated in my website survey (numbers are rounded off). You will probably recognize at least one of these scenarios from your own dreams. If you're not sure, take a glance at the definitions given at the beginning of each chapter.

See how your dream experience matches those of the five hundred study participants. The following are the most common five negative dreams reported around the world.

Being chased or attacked (80%)
Falling or drowning (64%)
Being lost or trapped (58%)
Being naked or inappropriately dressed in public (52%)
Being accidentally injured, ill, or dying (48%)

The next three most frequent dreams were

Being in a natural or man-made disaster (42%)
Having trouble taking a test or other poor performance (40%)
Having trouble with a car or other transport (38%)

The least often reported negative Universal Dreams were

Missing a boat or some other transportation (31%)
Having a house or property lost or damaged (30%)
Having trouble operating a telephone or machine (24%)
Being menaced by a spirit (12%)

Dreams of being chased or attacked were reported by over 80 percent of the study participants. The smallest category—dreams of being menaced by a spirit—was cited by only about 12 percent of the participants, but these people regarded the dreams as extremely significant. The important point here is that a great number of people in various cultures share the same Universal Dream patterns. Since that is so, you can learn from others what these dreams usually signify in the dreamer's lives and, therefore, what they are likely to mean in yours.

Each of the nightmarish dreams listed has positive versions. We'll be looking at these, too, in the chapters ahead. Delightful dream adventures are explored, including being loved, having magical animal friends, having new babies, getting healed, traveling with pleasure, exploring a house, receiving gifts, giving great performances, flying joyfully, wearing wonderful clothes, taking fantastic trips, operating machines with ease, witnessing marvels of nature, discovering new spaces, and being guided by the dead. Negative dreams are more frequent than positive ones because they are a major way of trying to solve our problems—it's no wonder they top the dream chart.

Your first step in gaining fuller understanding of your dreams is to identify those Universal Dreams that you sometimes have. Take a moment to glance over the list and notice which ones are most characteristic of your dream tales. You'll want to know this in order to use the Dream Keys effectively.

BASIC BUILDING BLOCKS

I SUGGEST THAT the Universal Dream themes are among the basic building blocks of all dreams. You may protest that your dreams are more complex than the ones listed, that more happens than a single scene, that your dreams are far fancier, more imaginative and elaborate. This is probably true. Here is where the concept of motifs will help you to make the best use of the information in this book.

What Is a Dream Motif?

IN MUSIC, A motif is a series of notes that form a pattern that identifies a specific character or emotion in the musical selection. In dreams, a motif is a smaller unit of the Universal Dream pattern.

For instance, the Universal Dream about having trouble with a car or some other form of transportation is fairly common (about 40 percent of the participants in my study said they have had it). Each Universal Dream pattern is general (such as having trouble with a car), whereas each dream motif is specific. For example, in the instance of car trouble, you may lose your brakes, you may be driving too fast, a crazy person may grab the steering wheel, you may collide with another vehicle—these and many other motifs may occur. What do you do in response to the trouble? What happens next? What is the condition of the road? What kind of car are you operating? All these specific motifs modify the meaning of your version of the Universal Dream of having car trouble.

Dream motifs, as I define them, have three elements: a subject, a verb, and an object (the order will be different in some languages). In the example just cited, one motif is "I (or whoever is driving) cannot operate the brakes." The motif of lost brakes, I found, was the most common of the dozens of motifs that the Universal Dream of car trouble may occur in.

In general, the motif of losing the brakes indicates that you are having difficulty controlling some situation in waking life when this dream occurs. You feel a lack of control ("too little" control). Each separate motif that makes up a Universal Dream pattern subtly alters the meaning of your personal variation, as you'll see in the chapters ahead.

By monitoring the motifs in your Universal Dreams, you'll gradually come to understand yourself better. You'll develop the ability to activate the uplifting motifs in the positive version of the same Universal Dream. Your improved dream life will in turn lead to greater satisfaction in your waking life. Your nightly dream stories will show you how to empower your waking hours; your fuller life will enrich your dreaming.

KEEPING YOUR OWN DREAM JOURNAL

PERHAPS YOU ALREADY keep a dream journal. If so, you can get the most from this book if you begin identifying the Universal Dreams that you now have. When you record one of the Universal Dreams, underscore the motifs that you observe in it. As you read about that particular Universal Dream, or consult the keys in the back of the book, you'll derive more and more understanding of how these meanings apply to your personal dream.

If you don't keep a dream journal, I suggest starting one tonight. You need very little to do so.

1. Before you go to sleep, place a notepad with a pen clipped to it within easy reach of your bed. Some people prefer to keep a laptop computer at bedside for entering dreams; others like to use a tape recorder—whatever works for you is fine. You'll want to have a written record eventually, as it's easiest to examine.

2. Set aside a special journal to record your dreams in a permanent form; I like to use a three-ring binder so that I can add pages of analysis or material

related to the dream later. The journal can be handwritten pages or computer printouts.

3. Before you turn out the light, take just a few minutes to write a short paragraph, or enter it into your computer, or tape it, describing what you did during the day and how you feel about it. Your activities and feelings often stimulate images that appear in the dreams of that night. By knowing what actually happened, you'll be better able to sort out the scenario in your dreams.

4. During the night or in the morning when you awaken, make brief notes of any dreams you recall. No image is too unimportant to jot down. As you write or speak, try to keep your eyes shut and remain in the body position in which you awoke. Dream recall is much easier with eyes closed. If you have no dream recall, or if you've finished recording whatever you remember, roll gently into any other sleep position you use and relax there a moment. This will often trigger fresh dream memories because—strange as it may seem—the dream appears to be related to a specific sleeping posture.

5. When you have time, then or later, copy over your rough dream notes into your permanent record, whether this is in journal or electronic form. I like to leave wide margins. I use the right-hand margin to jot associations to various images or words, especially names of people or places I might not recall months or years later. I use the left-hand margin to make quick sketches of odd or strange images, peculiar headdresses, or weird creatures that have appeared in the dream. You are creating a historical record—the chronicle of your inner life. It can become your most valuable resource.

6. If you're a person who never developed easy dream recall, I suggest planning a weekend or holiday when you can focus on your dreams. Let yourself sleep in, so that you'll be awaking directly from a dream. All of us dream approximately 20 percent of the time we're asleep; the final dream period lasts about a half-hour or so. You'll have plenty to remember if you wake up naturally rather than to an alarm clock or domestic duties. Keep your eyes closed a few minutes and reach for the last thing you remember. It may be a single image or simply a feeling or thought. Write it down, whatever it is. It'll help start the new habit of dream recall. Some people find that naps yield their best dream memories. Set aside a time to concentrate on gathering your dreams.

7. Working with your dreams has a monumental payoff. Your journal can teach you when you need to be extra-careful of your health, alert you to danger on the horizon, and reveal how you *really* feel about some person or situation. It can confirm when you are on the right path and become a reference for creative, artistic projects—to name just a few of the potential benefits. Start your dream journal tonight, the sooner to gather its rich harvest.

HOW TO USE THIS BOOK

IF YOU ARE an experienced dreamer, you may want to turn directly to Appendix B, "The Key to Universal Dreams," in the back of the book and begin exploring your dream journals with this guide in hand before going through the text. Although some material will be familiar, you're likely to find some precious nuggets to add to your dream treasures.

If you are a newcomer to dream exploration, you can approach the book either by reading it straight through, learning about the types of Universal Dreams and the motifs that compose them, or by going directly to the chapters that deal with dream themes that have been problems for you. Either way, you're bound to discover things about yourself that can improve your life.

Once you have a collection of your own dreams under way and have read the text, consult the Dream Key for each Universal Dream, using the motifs that occur in your dream to extract the most meaning for you. Exploring your inner world of dreams can lead to exhilarating discoveries. It's an adventure as boundless as trekking outer space.

Of course, you're certain to have dreams that don't fit the Universal Dream category. In this case, the material presented in Appendix A, "How to Unlock Any Dream Image," is an invaluable guide. In the body of the book, the material you'll be learning about the motifs in each Universal Dream will be useful for many other kinds of dream themes. There are more Universal Dreams than I have described here.

We human beings are complex creatures. Our capacity to dream is limitless. I would like to create a complete classification of dreams, but I realize such a project cannot be done within my lifetime. It is a task that requires thousands of dreamers working on it, worldwide, perhaps over many lifetimes. But together, we can begin to create the foundation. Your dreams can help.

Your Contribution to the Understanding of Dreams

BECAUSE THIS APPROACH to dreaming is so new, you can contribute to the mission to document the dreams experienced by people around the world. Just as scientists struggled for years using vast numbers of massive computers to map the human genome (the entire genetic structure of a human), we can gather our efforts to chart the cosmos of dreams. Harder to see and measure than stars or genes, dreams are shared with all humanity every time we go to sleep. If people can decipher the intricate code of human genes; if they can map the starry skies, document the plants and animals of Earth, and make a typology of all the folktales of mankind, surely a global network of dreamers can create a classification of our common dream stories.

By keeping track of our personal versions of Universal Dreams, by recording their infinite variety of motifs, you are assembling material that may help everyone better comprehend the grandest mystery of all: the operation of the human mind. At the very least, by exploring your dreams you'll learn about yourself. You can start with your head on the pillow tonight and your pen on your dream pad tomorrow. What story will you tell yourself next? Listen to your dreams; they're talking to you.

The Universal Dream Key

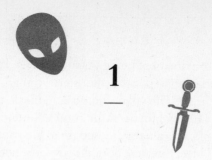

Being Chased or Attacked
Versus Being Embraced or Loved

"HELP! SOMETHING'S AFTER ME!" Around the world, alarming dreams of being pursued and threatened with death are the most common universal nightmares. People from Estonia to New Zealand flee down the corridors of their dreams, pursued by something ghastly. Children are often victims of Chase or Attack dreams, but even competent adults sometimes suffer these frightening nightmares. You've surely had them. We all have.

THE UNIVERSAL NIGHTMARE

ASLEEP UNDER EIDERDOWN or lying on straw pallets, beneath hand-stitched quilts or under ragged blankets, in hammocks at sea or in cradles at home, the pattern is the same. In every bed in every land, we dream that we see or hear or sense the dread aggressor, we run or try to escape, we hide and it finds us; it comes after us, gains on us, until at the most terror-stricken moment, we awaken. This is the Universal Dream of being chased or attacked.

Your dreams about being chased or attacked are bound to have elements of this universal pattern. More than 80 percent of the first five hundred people from around the world who visited my website said they had experienced dreams about being chased or attacked. These dreams are very common, so don't be surprised if you have one now and then. This chapter will help you understand and cope with them.

If the pattern of your Chase or Attack dreams is universal, the variations are local. In this global dream theme, the "thing" in pursuit differs. We run

1.0 BEING CHASED OR ATTACKED

Description:	You dream of being pursued or attacked by a wild animal, evil person, monster, "thing," or some other threat. The villain may catch, harm, eat, or kill you.
Frequency:	This nightmare is the most common among all people. It is a natural response to life stress.
Usual Meaning:	"I feel threatened," either by some person in your environment or by some strong emotion within you. "I'm scared," "I feel attacked," "I feel hounded," "I'm in danger." Occasionally this dream is a replay of an actual event you have experienced.

away from a vast range of frightening beasts and monsters in our dreams. A roll call of creatures from the zoo chase dreamers. The evil stranger, the supernatural horror, and the vague menace inhabit our nightmares.

We will see how each of these dreadful dream enemies has something to tell us. We can learn from our encounters with dream villains and turn the tables on these predators, making their powers beneficent rather than destructive. They can help us rather than harm us.

Before we examine how this transformation can be accomplished, let's look at the components of our dreams. We'll see who the horrific figures of your Chase or Attack dreams are, and how adult fears emerge from childish ones.

The Basic Components of Dreams:
Themes, Variations, Motifs

UNIVERSAL PATTERNS ARE all around us in the natural world, yet each is affected by the local environment. Trees branch in a consistent way, leaves take their genetic form, rivers carve a sinuous route, snowflakes fall in their basic hexameter shape. However, a tree on the coast, exposed to a constant wind from the sea, bends away from the blast. Leaves turn to the direction that provides the best local light, so they may flourish. Rivers break their banks under seasonal downpours and carve new paths. Each snowflake—a variation of the six points—is nonetheless unique.

So, too, are your dreams. The Universal Dream patterns are bent and molded by local forces in your life. Your every dream is influenced by four broad sources of influence:

1. Your biological heritage
2. Your general cultural heritage
3. Your local subculture
4. Your personal experience

As we explore Universal Dream themes, you need to be aware of all four levels that shape your variation of the universal and its features—the motifs—your dream theme contains.

INFLUENCES ON YOUR DREAMS ABOUT BEING CHASED OR ATTACKED

1. Biological

NIGHTMARES ABOUT BEING chased or attacked by wild animals or violent people doubtless originated in primitive times when the threat of being pursued and attacked by a wild beast or an enemy was a part of daily life. The "fight or flight" response people around the world share as human beings is triggered during this Universal Dream, and we awake, shaken, with a pounding heart.

For eons our ancestors fought with predatory beasts to protect themselves and their families, as well as to provide food. From an evolutionary point of view, humankind has had to compete with wild animals and hostile tribes for survival. Our intelligence and ability to communicate allowed us to develop weapons, cultivate food plants, and cooperate with the members of our society, so as to dominate our environment.

Yet, the ancient memories of combat with wild animals and human adversaries are retained in our brains. The monsters, beasts, and other foes we clash with in dreams replay the age-old fight for life. We are genetically programmed to find food, to establish territories, to mate, and to reproduce. Our battle with the beasts of the night is, in part, our reconquest of that primitive world.

Most of us no longer need to fight animals or other human beings for our basic needs of food, water, and shelter, although we still compete for territories and mates. The foes and monsters that assault us in dreams are monsters of the mind—fear, anxiety, anger, hatred, envy. These emotional monsters may be reactions to people in our environment or strange goblins in our own thoughts. The impulse to flee these foes or fight to the death is inborn.

2, 3. *Cultural and Subcultural*

The Bogeyman Creeps into Childhood Dreams

WHATEVER YOU WERE taught and experienced as a child is likely to persist in your dream fears. The bogeyman, or bugbear, of English tales is a monster used to frighten children into obedience. Most cultures have evolved scary figures to curb childish behavior. The words *bogey* and *bugbear* derive from *bugge*, a Middle English word meaning "terror." Depicted as a black male, the bogeyman may shift into various forms, like the Devil (who is said, sometimes, to take the shape of a goat, a snake, or a predatory bird). In dreams, he takes various guises, influenced by our cultural heritage.

The black man figures in many European lullabies as the bogeyman who will steal away naughty children. Italian mothers, for instance, sometimes threaten the infant in sweet songs about *"l'omo nero"* (literally, "the black man"; figuratively, the bogeyman). Yet the black mothers in the plantations of Gran Canaria may lull their black babies to sleep with threats of *"el diablo blanco"* (the "white devil"), who "will come and eat the foot of the little one." An outsider, especially a foreigner or person of a different race or religion, is most often cast as the bogeyman.

People who have heard warnings about "the black man" as bogeyman or devil are likely to dream of such a figure to represent their fears. In contrast, people who were cautioned against "the white devil" tend to shape their fears into this nightmare form. Racism and fear of foreigners are bred in, and they become reinforced in bad dreams. The costs for society can be grievous, as well as for the dreamer.

Is the Devil Black, White, or Red?

WHETHER YOU PICTURE your worst fears—your personification of evil—as being black, white, or red depends upon your own coloration as well as your cultural heritage. Each culture grows its own monsters.

Color symbolism, like other symbolism, differs from culture to culture, although night and darkness are generally associated with dangerous spirits. One anthropological scholar, Victor Turner, claims that the basic triad of black, white, and red used by most cultures derives from their universal existence as fluids, secretions, and waste products of the human body. Red is a worldwide symbol of life, because it is the color of blood. White is the color of semen and of breast milk, so it is linked to mating between man and woman, and the connection between mother and child. Black is more or less the color of excreta and of body dissolution, so it is allied with the transition from one state of being to another. All three colors are associated with heightened states of emotion and are frequently used in initiation rites.

Europeans, predominantly composed of white-skinned people, came to use the term *black* as a symbol for weird, ugly, or evil things, so monsters and wicked persons are often described in their folklore and mythology as dark-colored or black. Black is associated with death and mourning for many Caucasians. Black people, too, sometimes depict danger in black form, as do the followers of voodoo in portraying "Dr. Death" as a black man in black tails and top hat, yet they may refer to Caucasians as "ghosts."

White, for Europeans, is usually associated with the quality of purity, as in christening robes for newborns, or wedding gowns for brides. White magic is used to heal, not harm. Angels and cherubs are said to be garbed in dazzling white, supernatural good guys who wear white wings rather than white hats. The Chinese, in contrast, sometimes call Caucasians "white ghosts" or "foreign devils" and wear white during mourning

The two extremes of white and black are sometimes used together in costumes to represent the struggle between good and evil. In Balinese dance dress, black-and-white checkered scarves signify this underlying struggle. Clothing like Arab headdresses and perhaps even British bobbies' cap bands express this ancient symbolism of the war between good and evil, the eternal struggle enacted in your dreams.

Fiery red, associated with life's blood and danger, often clothes the Devil in European folktales, as it does the many devils and demons appearing in people's dreams. Chinese dreamers, in contrast, consider the color red "lucky."

Whatever your culture's ideas about color are, your dreams will echo them, dressing your dream foes in outfits you have learned are appropriate to their nature.

4. Personal

WHEN YOU ARE coping with life-threatening situations, such as a terminal illness in yourself or in someone you love, or when you are existing under conditions of war, catastrophe, or other emergencies, nightmares about being chased and attacked are apt to increase in direct response to the crisis, portrayed directly or symbolically in your dreams.

When the conditions of your life are less severe—when you are not in actual physical danger from illness or injury or in a situation of imminent destruction—your dreams about being chased or attacked portray your daily problems with family or colleagues, or minor ailments with which everyone struggles to cope. Their exact form is a blend of your biological and cultural heritage, as well as your past experience and your immediate life circumstances.

UNDERSTANDING YOUR DREAMS
ABOUT CHASE OR ATTACK

REGARDLESS OF YOUR culture, the universal pattern of your Chase or Attack dreams will be roughly the same. The shape, clothing, and color of the dream enemies vary, but their behavior is consistent. How can you make sense of these regional and personal variations? What can you do to cope with these dreams? To find out, you need to ask yourself questions about your dream aggressors.

Key Questions to Understanding Your Dream Villains

1. Who or what is chasing or attacking you? What shape is it?
2. What is the size of X (the thing or person after you)?
3. What is the color of X?
4. What is its outstanding characteristic? (Odd hair, head, clothing, and so on)
5. Whom does this remind you of? Who or what has similar elements?
6. What happens in the dream?
7. How does the dream end?

Who or What Is After You?

YOU ARE MOST likely to be attacked by a strange man in your dreams. Your opponent may be wildly different, but a dark stranger is the most common assailant in dreams around the globe. Men and women, teens and children from widely separated cultures—all try to escape from the dread bad guy prowling dreamland.

Your assailant in Chase or Attack dreams is almost certain to be a stranger, an animal, a supernatural being, an unknown "thing," a personal enemy, or an odd object. (Any of these may appear as a group.) We'll look at what these dream foes mean to you in a minute. Among the first five hundred respondents to the survey on Universal Dreams on my website, people from around the globe reported the numerous attackers in their dreams in this order (percentages are rounded off):

Strangers, mostly "a man" or "men" (40%)
Animals (25%)
Supernatural or imaginary beings (15%)
"Something" frightful (10%)
A known person (6%)
An odd object (5%)

You may find yourself dreaming about any or all of them.

The Evil Stranger

OKAY, YOU'VE HAD this awful nightmare about being chased by a man with a knife, or men with rifles, or any other of the weird strangers that populate bad dreams. You are not alone. Listen to these planetary voices:

Australian woman:	A man (serial killer) with a knife was invading my home.
German man:	A man was chasing me or members of my family.
American woman:	A man dressed in black (burglar or rapist) was chasing me.
Irish woman:	I was being chased by soldiers.
Canadian woman:	I was chased by a psychotic ax murderer.
Dutch woman:	A burglar with a knife was chasing me.

These are just a sample of the many dreams about being pursued by a man or men, or, more generally, people, with or without weapons, dressed in black or masked.

Why do men and women worldwide have such fear of strangers in their dreams? I suggest that the stranger in our dreams, masked or armed, seen or "sensed," represents any unknown danger in the dreamer's life. Whatever it is that frightens you in your waking environment is apt to shape itself into the form of an evil stranger pursuing you in your dreams. You may have a vague idea of what it is that you fear, but not be ready to face it fully. For the moment, danger wears the mask of a stranger.

Evil stranger chasing or attacking you in dream = Waking feeling of threat

---

What is it you are afraid of? It depends on your life circumstances. A teenaged girl who has not yet experienced sexual intercourse may feel both fascination and fear about the physical act of sex. In my dream diary from age fifteen I have recorded the dream of seeing a man in a black mask and cape walking down the street I lived on, flourishing his whip. One does not need to be a psychoanalyst to get the impression of my attraction to the masked stranger in romantic garb, and my hesitancy about the damage his "whip" could inflict. Indeed, many of the dreams of young women who run from men with knives, swords, batons, rifles, and so forth are symbolic depictions of their ambivalence about sexual intercourse. The weapons—as Freud has so eloquently pointed out—represent the male genital. Such dreams, of course, may have other meanings, depending upon the dreamer's associations and life circumstances. The threat symbolized by the armed attacker may be more general, and men also experience the dream.

The attacking stranger may symbolize a fear of death. When the late American comedienne Gilda Radner dreamed that her husband and pet poodle were about to be bludgeoned to death by a "very thin and hollow-eyed man in a hospital gown" armed with a hammer, she was not expressing a fear of sex in her dream. This talented woman in her late thirties had been diagnosed with ovarian cancer and was being treated for it. Her struggle to fend off the hammer man was successful in the dream, and it paralleled her battle to survive in the waking state. Her efforts succeeded for a while, but she ultimately succumbed and died of her illness at age forty-two. Although Radner did not comment on her dream imagery, it's quite likely that the evil stranger in her dream represented the specter of illness and death.

Whatever area of your life seems unknown, dark, and threatening may take the form of an evil stranger or strangers in your dream. When you are ready or able to confront this fear, the mask drops and the mysterious danger becomes identifiable.

Threatening Animals

YOU'RE ALSO APT to encounter a menacing animal in your Chase or Attack dreams. Wild animals loom large as pursuers, although they rank second to the male stranger in adults' dreams. These beasts of the night may hunt us singly or in packs, be rabid or mad.

Judy Garland, in the role of Dorothy, sang about lions, tigers, and bears as she followed the Yellow Brick Road through the woods in the film version of The Wizard of Oz. We might add "Snakes, and spiders, and bees—ay-yi!" After "wild animals," bears and wild dogs were the most common dangerous creatures mentioned in my survey. Large black or brown bears pursued dreamers worldwide. The details varied: some dreamers were only chased, others also got mangled, and still others protected children. Lions, tigers, mutated gorillas, hyenas, wolves, snakes, spiders, bees, a skunk, an alligator, an elephant, horses, a shark, a giant ant, and an eagle-like monster also appeared in the role of dangerous animal assailant. Dragons and dinosaurs roamed the dream landscape. The threatening animal you dream about may be among this sample, or it may be totally different.

Who are these creatures that stalk your dreamscape? What do they represent? Like the evil stranger, the dream animal sometimes symbolizes sex, as it did for the young American woman who was being chased by a gigantic rooster. She confided feeling at risk in a romantic relationship. In American slang, the word *cock* refers to a penis; *cock* is also a common synonym for rooster. Thus, dreaming of a giant "cock" hot on her "tail" indicated this woman's fear of being overwhelmed in some waking, potentially sexual, relationship. Your dreams often contain similar puns on words, so watch for them.

Your dream animal may stand for a fear of death. A woman who had recurrent nightmares about dogs tearing at her stomach and fires burning her flesh was diagnosed a few months later with stomach cancer. The wild dogs in her dream depicted the pains she felt in her stomach, and also the dread of death gnawing at her. When you feel actual pain *during* a dream, it is a clue to a possible physical problem. Of course, few dreams about animal attacks are so ominous.

You are the only one who can tell what element is making you feel threatened at the time you have a dream about a wild animal in pursuit. The spectrum of possibilities is wide. The energy, the force, and the impulsive action of animals sometimes portray your own wild impulses, or the chaotic emotions you sense in people around you. Very frequently, the attacking animal of your dream will turn out to be your lover, spouse, parent, teacher, coworker, boss, or some other figure near—and sometimes dear—who has behaved in a biting or wounding way toward you.

Animal chasing or attacking you in a dream = Wild waking impulses or emotions

---

The lover who made you cry may turn into a nasty cat who scratches your eyes in a dream. The mother or wife who's been overly rough on a child may morph into a devouring bear in a dream. The spider in a drawer in your dream may represent a venomous colleague. The dream horse that bit your hand may prove to be a restrictive boss who prevented you from doing something. How can you sort out these possible meanings when they're not quickly obvious? We'll explore that process soon. First, these weird dream foes.

Supernatural Beings in Pursuit

YOU MAY BE one of the dreamers who clash with supernatural creatures in your dreams. These are not realistic people or animals, but beings from other worlds, legends, fantasies, or fairy tales. Supernatural beings were the third most common subcategory of attacker in my study of Universal Dreams. Vampires, zombies, mummies, aliens, witches, ogres, devils, demons, and monsters appeared in the dreams of folk worldwide. Other dreamers tried to escape from Godzilla, King Kong, Darth Vader, Dracula, Frankenstein, or another fantasy figure from film and literature. Again, the details varied, with some dreamers simply running, others being stabbed or kidnapped, still others managing to evade their attackers.

If you dream about the supernatural category of assailant, you are emphasizing the sense of evil or dread you have about the thing you fear.

Supernatural being chasing or attacking you in dream = Waking sense of fear of evil

---

In these dreams of aliens and other supernatural creatures, you are keeping the nebulous threat of danger vague. The spooky aspect of the unknown haunts you. At the moment, you are unready or unwilling to confront whatever it is in your life that lurks in the shadows.

The "Thing" in Pursuit

THE MOST AMORPHOUS of all dream assailants is "something." Numerous dreamers cannot even give shape to the thing that makes them anxious. A woman from Malaysia dreamed "Something surrounded by black energy is chasing me"; a woman from Bulgaria said, "I don't see who it is who is chasing me"; a man from England stated, "I never know what is actually chasing me, but it's behind me." Most dreamers are sure that whatever or whoever it is, it is evil.

If the "something" in pursuit is clearly evil and dangerous, everything else in these dark dreams is murky. Who or what remains totally unknown at the time of the dream. If you have such a dream attacker, you will sense it, perhaps feel it clutch at you, but you'll not see its face or form. These are the dreams you might have when you feel great anxiety while awake but can't explain why, even to yourself.

> Vague "thing" pursuing you in dream = Waking anxiety that is not yet clear

Like the supernatural beings haunting us in dreams, the dim "thing" that chases us represents some fear we are not ready to face directly. If you dream about this kind of assailant, you will need to be patient until you feel strong enough to cope with the threat. Perhaps the threat itself is amorphous, such as danger of war, or of criminals. Trying some of the suggestions in the last section of this chapter may help you to disclose the source of your anxiety, and even to dispel it.

If "things" after us in dreams leave us wondering what's going on, dreams about known enemies make that all too clear. You may recognize the attacker in your dream at once.

Known Enemies in Pursuit

WHEN DARK STRANGERS remove their masks in your dreams, you will see them revealed as everyday assailants, people you know. We usually understand full well why we fear or hate these familiar folk, although sometimes their direct depiction in a dream startles us. "Known person" was the fifth most common category of dream enemy: a Mexican man dreamed he was attacked by a friend; an American girl dreamed a boy from school chased her, trying to stab her; an English woman dreamed that her former best friend's mother was trying to hit her with a frying pan; an American woman dreamed her "ex" hunted her down and found her; a Spanish man dreamed that someone he knew tried to kill him with a sword.

When you dream that you are being chased or attacked by someone you know, the feelings you have of fear, resentment, anger, or hatred toward the person are very close to the surface. One teen told me her horrifying dreams that her mother stood at her bedroom door and smiled, revealing vampire teeth; another dreamed her mother turned into a black octopus that struck her with one of its eight arms; yet another said that her mother and her aunt looked normal in her dream, but she could see that although they wore dresses and masks, underneath they were wolves waiting to attack her; still another dreamed of her mother in the guise of a devil, with her sister as her winged minion, trying to murder her.

In a study I did of the dreams of sexually abused teenaged women, the young victims often dreamed about the abuser's attacking them further. People who have betrayed us, people with whom we have a hostile or conflicted relationship, and people who are open enemies in our daily life sometimes appear in bad dreams as themselves.

You may find yourself confronting similar familiar assailants in dreams. If so, you are ready to deal with your feelings about them. No more witches or black bears or strangers in shadows. You can identify the person you need to improve your relationship with in waking life, or else dismiss from your life, possibly with therapy. You can learn to confront the person, or relate differently, in your dreams and in your waking space—this is good for your psychological health.

> Known attacker in your dream = Waking negative feelings you feel able to face

The Bizarre Attacker in Pursuit

WHAT ARE YOU to make of dreams in which you are chased by something that does not normally evoke fear? You may be one of the few dreamers who are pursued by an unusual object or person. Instead of vague threats, these are specific, seemingly senseless ones, such as clowns or older people. These persons don't ordinarily evoke terror. For instance, an American girl dreamed "I was fleeing from a giant napkin"; a man from the Czech Republic said, "A large rolling orange was after me"; a young English woman was chased by a "bubble"; an American woman stated, "A car with no one in it chased me." These odd objects produced as much horror in dreams as men with rifles in close pursuit.

You can be sure that these bizarre attackers make sense in the dreamer's life. I have heard dreams about being chased by a wobbly, gooey poached egg (the dreamer had been force-fed as a child); being chased by a giant dust-ball (the dreamer was obsessed with cleanliness); being pursued by a tortilla (representing the mother who cooked them); being chased in and out of buses and all over town by a large white paper (the dreamer was having trouble with a master's thesis); being stalked by a pair of disembodied hands trying to strangle her (the dreamer connected this to threats of punishment for masturbation). Each weird attacker has proved to make perfect sense within the dreamer's life circumstances.

If you have a dream with a bizarre aggressor, you'll need to do some dream detective work. Consider the following section about outstanding characteristics of the dream assailant. You'll also want to consult "How to Unlock Any Dream Image," Appendix A. Strange as they seem, these odd dream enemies are important for you to understand. They, like other dream aggressors, often turn out to be the people closest to us.

What Is Your Dream Foe's Outstanding Characteristic?

WHAT IS THE main thing or things you noticed about your dream enemy? Was it the size of the attacking figure? Its color? Its hair? Its weapon? Whatever it is that gets your attention about the assailant is a clue to its identity. Who has a similar characteristic? Remember, first ask yourself, "What was special or unique about the thing or person chasing me?" Then ask, "Who or what does this remind me of?"

Here's an overview of a few of the remarkable characteristics—the motifs—of the villains in Chase or Attack dreams:

Outstanding Characteristic: The Color of the Dream Attacker's Clothing

YOU HAVE ALREADY seen that many of the attacking strangers and animals are described as dressed in black or having black elements in the dreams of adults around the world. Rooted in European culture, as discussed in the section on cultural influences, the dreams of Americans are filled with threatening figures dressed in black. A study I did of the dreams of boys and girls in San Francisco included "A lady in black with two-inch-long fingernails chopped my head off with a sword," "A man in black in a black car drove up to my house and came to the door," and "Darth Vader fought with me."

Darth Vader, the figure from George Lucas's *Star Wars* saga, has become a staple character in scary dreams. With his dark armor, dark visor, and black cape, he epitomizes the dangerous bogeyman for many people. Followers of the saga eventually learn that Vader is the hero's father, who went over to "the dark side." In the new "prequel" to the *Star Wars* saga, the villain is called Darth Maul, cloaked and hooded in black, his face tattooed in fiercely pointed black shapes. The similarity between the word *death* and the name *Darth* is registered by the movie watcher, perhaps only subliminally. The father as villain in this modern myth is paralleled in nightmares when the dreamer's father—or mother—takes, at times, a threatening role as despot or all-powerful enemy.

Adults recalling their most frightening childhood dreams report this same association of parents with dangerous dream figures. This trend is especially clear in dreams in which the parent transforms during the dream into the evil enemy. Remember the black octopus-mother? An American woman in her fifties recalled her most vivid childhood dream, a recurrent one about being chased by a "black widow man," wearing a black trenchcoat and black cap, who pursued her through the streets of her childhood town and into the school cloakroom, where she managed to elude him.

Black occurs most often in negative dreams, but sometimes black represents the unknown in a positive sense. A general rule regarding black is

Black color in your dream = Waking feeling of danger or mystery

An American boy dreamed of his classroom's being covered by a "big red glob like ketchup" that engulfed his classmates. Ketchup, because of its color, is often used to simulate blood in dramatic productions. Blood flowing from wounds, lolling red tongues of monsters, red globs, fiery deaths—these images fill Chase or Attack dreams with crimson.

Other dreamers dress their pursuers in "slimy green" rather than devilish red or black, as did a Swiss boy. He dreamed of slimy green aliens who stuffed green chewing gum into his mouth, rendering him incapable of human speech. A Swiss girl dreamed of being hemmed in by a giant, ugly old toad with a slimy green body; another Swiss girl reported scary figures that appeared to be made of rubber in "very unreal colors" who chained her onto big boulders. When he was a child, an American man dreamed about being followed by the head of a green vampire. Clearly, black is not the only color that may represent evil.

Outstanding Characteristic: The Bad Guys Are (Usually) BIG

YOUR NIGHTMARES ABOUT being chased or attacked are likely to have aggressive characters that are big, as well as being black or dark and most often male. Large size in dreams often represents importance of the character, just as it often does in children's drawings. With negative dream characters, the emotion associated with large size is frequently that of overwhelming fear of an irresistible power.

Giants in folktales and fairy tales are generally thought by mythologists and folklorists to represent the parents in their mean, angry mode. So, too, in a child's dream the threatening ogre or greedy giantess is likely to portray an overbearing parent. Indeed, to a little child, a parent is giant-sized—gigantic—and has unlimited power. Children from India dreamed "A Satan-like giant attacked me with a sword"; "a strange giant with wings chased me"; "a giant goddess scowled at me"; "big, aggressive birds [presumably vultures] ate a dead cow"; "big birds chased me on my way to school"; "a big bird stole my brother." Children from Switzerland dreamed "A huge, old, fat brown spider crawled on me," and "two big pieces of goulash were chasing me." Likewise, children from America spoke of large-sized menacing creatures: "Two giants chased me"; "a monster fifty feet tall with no legs came after me"; "a large dog bit me." Big and bad often go together in dreams. Some adults still have bad dreams about giants; worldwide, dreamers depict big enemies.

If you dream of a huge assailant, you will probably be picturing overwhelming fear; at times big dream images portray a towering feeling of awe. In positive dreams, mammoth characters convey a sense of supreme importance, as does a giant goddess who hands the dreamer a gift.

```
Big figure in your dream = Overwhelming fear or awesome importance
```

If your dream assailant is not gigantic, it may be multiple, such as the "horde of tiny skeletons, swarming and restraining me, Lilliputian-style," that one dreamer reported. Many small creatures in a dream are equivalent to one large one—the sensation is still one of being overwhelmed. Voltaire is said to have seen "little difference between being eaten by a single tiger or a hundred rats."

```
Many small threatening figures in your dream = One gigantic threat-
                                              ening figure
```

Outstanding Characteristic: Hair on the Attacker

DOES THE ASSAILANT in your dream have something odd about its hair or head? If so, it's a clue to the attacker's identity. For example, an American woman in her twenties told me, "I dreamed that a rat with golden, curly hair bit me." Listening to her dream, I found myself recalling my teenaged dream of being in bed when I discovered a tick with red curly hair crawling in the bedcovers.

In my case, the tick was easily connected to the older man in his twenties whom I was then dating, called "Red" for his curly red hair. I'd fancied myself in love with him, yet the dream warned of danger in the relationship. Indeed, not long after this dream, I learned that Red was married and had children. Still a virgin, I was lucky to escape unscathed—unbitten by the tick, so to speak.

With my own dream in mind, I asked the woman, "Who has golden, curly hair?" Her reply confirmed my hunch that the one with blond curls was her boyfriend. This led to a discussion of how she felt that they must soon either break up the relationship or get married. She felt wounded by his behavior toward her. He was being, in her dream language, "a rat."

Odd hair on assailant in your dream = Clue to identity of waking person

---

Happily for this young woman, she and her boyfriend soon became officially engaged, married, and had several children. My dream of the tick with curly red hair, and this young woman's dream of the golden-haired rat, along with others like these, led me to formulate this dream rule:

Wounds in your dream = Emotional wounds in waking life

Note that ticks do not grow red curly hair; nor do rats grow golden curls. The dream image in both cases depicts a threatening, naturally aggressive small creature. Yet the hair formation and color are unnatural. This idiosyncratic element, what dream worker Lillie Weiss calls "the focal point," is the clue to the meaning of the dream. Stay alert for similar odd characteristics.

Outstanding Characteristic: Sharp Teeth, Beak, and Claws on the Attacker

YOUR ASSAILANT MAY bare its teeth, beak, or claws in your Chase or Attack dream. These body parts scratch, cut, and bite; they are the original weapons. Their presence in a dream usually indicates anger, your own or that of a person close to you.

An eleven-year-old girl from Switzerland shared her scary nightmare about being chased and attacked by "a terrible looking beast/bird with a sewing machine beak." At the climax of this long, horrific dream, the beast with the sewing machine beak began sewing the child's hands together with a big needle. The girl "hollered as the blood ran down my fingers, and I thought I would die," until her mother woke her.

Had I been able to work with this dreamer, I would have asked her, "Who do you know who uses a sewing machine?" Her responses would have likely led to the identity of the person whose attack—perhaps verbal—the girl greatly feared.

In general, dream characters with sharp teeth as their outstanding quality represent anger the dreamer dreads. The American woman whose most frightening childhood nightmare was the one in which her mother smiled at her to reveal vampire fangs said that as a child she lived in fear of her mother's harsh words. Across the ocean in Switzerland, a ten-year-old boy told his dream that "a fakir from India with very pointed teeth like fangs grabbed me and shocked me." Someone's anger was frightening him.

Sharks, alligators, crocodiles, lions, tigers, wolves, dogs—all make dramatic, toothy, dream appearances. Almost invariably the frightening dream creatures with sharp teeth or beaks can be connected to angry words, often of a parent, grandparent, teacher, boss, or other authority figure. Numerous people have bad dreams about being chased by sharks, especially after having seen the film *Jaws*.

Sometimes you may dream of yourself as a sharp-toothed aggressor. One night after scolding his teenaged daughter severely over some misbehavior, my husband, Zal, dreamed about an alligator that was chasing his daughter. Here, he cast himself in the role of the creature with sharp teeth, as well as sharp words.

> Teeth, beaks, and claws in your dream = Anger in waking life (yours or another person's)

If you have ever been badly bitten or mauled by an animal, dreams of being pursued by a sharp-toothed beast may be partly based on your waking experience. After being mauled by a pack of wild dogs, an American boy living with his family in postwar Germany began having horrific dreams of being chased and attacked by a wolf. He told me that, after years of the recurrent wolf dream, he learned to accept the nightmare, sitting still while being devoured, knowing that he would eventually awaken safe in bed.

Usually, Chase or Attack dreams end at the critical moment, just before death or destruction occurs. In his nightmare, this child felt himself being torn apart, chewed, and swallowed and going down the beast's esophagus before he woke up terrified.

As in many traumatized victims, these nightmares were a part of the post-traumatic stress syndrome, resulting from painful waking life experiences. A natural response, they are the mind's way of trying to accept the unacceptable. Gradually such dreams lessen in frequency and intensity, until there is a kind of healing. They tend to recur later, however, whenever the person feels threatened. Methods for coping with nightmares, described in the section "Steps to Cope with Dream Aggressors," can accelerate the natural healing process.

Many people—adults and children—dream about wild dogs attacking them, without actually having undergone an attack. When dogs appear in this role, it is their wolflike nature that is being emphasized in their ripping fangs. As with images of other sharp-toothed creatures, such dreams usually reflect fear of the anger of someone in the environment rather than fear of waking physical attack, but keep in mind as you work with dreams that sometimes the dream attacks mirror waking-life experiences.

Outstanding Characteristic: Horns on the Aggressor

PERHAPS THE SHARP element that characterizes your dream assailant is horns. Like teeth, beaks, and claws, horns can be expressions of anger and weapons of attack; they also occur as a sexual symbol.

An elderly American woman described to me the recurrent nightmare she had during her twenties and thirties. "I would be in a field," she said, "when suddenly a bull would appear, lower its horns, and rush at me. I'd run frantically to climb the fence in time before it got me." Having grown up on a farm, this woman was familiar with the sight and sound of bulls. She said they were "dangerous, aggressive beasts," who move toward you with "a deep rumble in their chests." She always managed to escape the bulls in her dreams.

In the case of horns, which may be as sharp as teeth or claws, the emphasis shifts from the keenness of a cut or tear to the ability of the horn to penetrate. Given her age at the time the dream recurred, along with the imagery, we might guess the bull's horns had a sexual meaning for the dreamer. In art and vernacular slang, the penis is a kind of horn. The American slang word *horny* is often used to refer to a state of sexual arousal. Devils, too, sprout horns on their heads.

Horns on assailant in your dream = Possible waking sexual threat

---

Outstanding Characteristic: Weapons Carried by the Aggressor

THE MOST OBVIOUS thing about your dream foe may be the weapon or object used to threaten you. When trying to understand the symbolism of weapons in dreams, remember that weapons are extensions of the human body. Knives and swords are more effective nails or claws, and they extend the reach of the human hand and arm. Guns of all types are more potent punching fists; the weapon's shape and its projectile contents parallel the penis and its ejaculate, as Freud has indicated.

Almost anything can become a weapon in dreams, besides the traditional guns and knives—poison, powder, tablets, bottles, nets, ropes, chains, needles, rocks, and so forth.

Weapon in your dream = General waking threat or specific sexual one

---

Like animal attacks, weapons in recurrent nightmares may be part of a posttraumatic reaction, as they were for a ten-year-old ethnic Albanian boy. In an interview with a reporter from the Associated Press, he described his nightmares after having watched his mother and three sisters being gunned down by the Serbian police, who then set his house on fire. The only survivor of eighteen people in the house, he has been reunited with his father and is safe in Albania. Nonetheless, he is haunted by nightmares of the rifle attack and of his sister's cries for help; he awakes screaming. His experience is typical of people who have endured severe trauma; they often need therapy to help them recover.

Outstanding Characteristic: Assorted Odd Attributes of Attacker

PERHAPS YOUR DREAM aggressor has no outstanding color, size, hair, sharp teeth, or shooting weapon but has some peculiar characteristic not mentioned here? You will find a set of guidelines for exploring idiosyncratic dream symbols in Appendix A, in case answering the questions listed does not reveal the meaning of that motif for you.

COPING WITH YOUR CHASE OR ATTACK DREAMS

YOUR DREAM FOE may try to kill you or another dream character, threaten to do so, merely criticize you, frown at you, or clearly indicate anger toward you without acting on it. Aggression is common in dreams of all people worldwide.

What will these big, black threatening beasts/men do if they catch the dreamer? For children, the answer is simple: eat them. Like the wolf in "Little Red Riding Hood," the aggressive characters in nightmares seem to have one purpose: to kill and consume us. Celebrated illustrator-author Maurice Sendak, whose *Where the Wild Things Are* is a classic children's book, described his childhood terror at an overbearing relative's fond comment "You're so cute I could eat you up." Around the globe, in lullabies, bedtime tales, or jocular comments, children learn to fear being eaten alive. Small wonder such fears penetrate their dreams and last into adulthood.

In Japan, the mythological creature Baku is said to eat not the dreamer but the dream. Children are advised when they awake from a nightmare to call upon Baku, the dream eater, whose food is bad dreams, to dispose of the nightmare. He acts more as a protective spirit than as a threat within the dream. Baku is the origin of the video icon "Pac-Man," who consumes the "ghost-monsters." We need more images of figures to protect us from the terrors of the night, like the five modern "dream friends" French-Canadian dream worker Nicole Gratton created for children. Adults sometimes find their own dream guardians in positive dreams.

We've been considering the general structure of dreams about being chased or attacked and the frequent motifs that occur in them. Here's the overall pattern:

Something evil
{
A strange person
A wild animal
A supernatural being
A vague "thing"
A known person
An odd object
}
{
chases you and you run
attacks you
}
{
you hide
it finds you
it catches you
it kills or harms you
it eats you
you escape
}

Steps to Cope with Dream Aggressors

IT MAY SEEM impossible to change your behavior during a dream, but you can do it. I have done so, and hundreds of other dreamers who have tried this approach have succeeded. It can be truly satisfying to vanquish the enemies in your dreams, and you are apt to feel more confident about dealing with the person or situation the dream foe represents.

The important principles for you to become aware of are (1) your ability to vary your behavior during the nightmare and (2) your ability to change the conclusion of the dream. Here are some suggestions (partly based on the work of Paul Tholey) to guide you:

1. *Confront and conquer the aggressive dream figure by force.* Sometimes when chased by a dream foe, the best policy is to turn around and face it. (At times, confrontation alone will dispel the threat.) If it continues to threaten you, or physically attacks you, counterattack it. You can call for help, but fight alone until help comes. In apparent life-or-death situations, kill the menacing dream figure. If destruction proves to be necessary, allow the "spirit" of the conquered dream figure to continue to exist in a helpful form. When you have experienced how it is possible to triumph over a dream enemy, you may prefer some of the approaches that follow.

2. *Confront the aggressive dream figure with confidence.* Turn around, face the menacing dream figure, gaze directly into its eyes (if it has them), and challenge it. Ask, "Who are you?" "What do you want?" "Why are you doing this?" You may be surprised by some of the answers that emerge from such questions asked in a dream. Be willing to listen to reasonable responses and

discuss them. This "challenge with confidence" step, and the following steps, can also be used in your imagination before falling asleep or after awakening. You'll learn a lot.

3. *Confront the aggressive dream figure with friendliness.* Question the hostile dream figure in a friendly manner, while continuing to hold your ground and maintaining eye contact. The same questions as in step 2 should be raised: "Who are you?" "What do you want?" "Why are you doing this?"

4. *Offer reconciliation to the aggressive dream figure.* You may want to make a kind of bargain with the threatening dream figure. Befriend it. Offer to change some of your behavior if you agree that this is appropriate.

5. *Request help from the dream figure, if it has become less hostile.* Ask the dream figure to give you a "gift," solve a problem, guide your future, or grant any other request you wish to make. This may be part of the bargain in step 4. If reconciliation and dialogue prove fruitless, separate yourself from this dream figure, at least for the time being.

6. *Enter the less-hostile dream figure's body.* Can you understand what the figure wants and needs better from this perspective? Is there some quality in this figure that you could benefit from absorbing?

7. *Enjoy the formerly hostile dream figure.* Interact with the dream figure in positive, pleasurable ways, if this feels good. Swim with it, fly with it, be happy with it. You can also apply this step in your imagination, before you sleep or after you awaken.

8. *Bless the dream figure.* Surround it with golden light. Open your heart to it. Let it merge with you. Love it despite all.

9. *Seek out any hostile dream figures or situations.* When you feel confident of your ability to cope with dream dangers, then deliberately seek out and find them. Take this step only after considerable success in dealing with the hostile figures that spontaneously arise in dreams. Move from the safe, protected spaces of your dream to the dangerous ones; go from the light into the dark, from high places to low places, from the present into the past. Enter the eye of the storm; go into the tidal wave. Face the worst. You may want to carry with you special protective devices and be accompanied by a helper.

10. *Imagine a better outcome to your dream about being chased or attacked.* Simple as this step seems, just picturing a different ending to a bad dream, especially during the drowsy period before sleep, or after waking from a nightmare, can start the process of dream change.

No matter how distressing a dream of being chased or attacked is, you can always learn from it. You can understand better the nature of what is bothering you and begin moving toward improving your waking life by making changes in the troublesome dream.

Because you are acting in your own dream, you may choose to use any or all (or none) of these ten steps for coping with hostile dream figures. It's up to you. I have seen these methods eliminate nightmares that have recurred for years. I have witnessed dreamers' discovering amazing things about their inner life. Making the smallest change in a recurrent dream scenario can lead to profound life shifts for the better. You've got options, awake or asleep. Use them.

What if instead of running from a menacing figure you dream of moving toward an attractive one? At the opposite pole of Chase or Attack dreams is the delightful dream theme of Embrace or Love.

BEING EMBRACED OR LOVED

1.5 BEING EMBRACED OR LOVED

Description: You dream of being embraced or loved by some other dream character; you initiate or return the loving behavior. There are many variations to this pleasant dream: getting married or engaged, or falling in love; you may be holding hands, petting a lover, cuddling a baby, or sensuously dancing with a sweetheart. You may be having loving sexual intercourse or feeling passionately aroused(violent sexual contact is considered a Chase or Attack dream). Partners vary from romantic strangers, lovers, and mates to surprising people, known and unknown. Your love and sex partner may be a movie star, a powerful political figure, a member of a royal family, or some other celebrity. Your dream friend or lover may be an animal, a mythological or spiritual character, or an imaginary figure of your own. You move toward the dream lover or friend.

Frequency: This delightful dream is fairly common. It arises out of the basic sexual drive to procreate and the human desire to relate to others.

Usual Meaning: "I want to connect"; "I feel connected" with the figure in the dream, or with some quality that individual represents (romance, creativity, gentleness, spirituality).

These are the dreams that enthrall us—the ones we wish would never end. In the golden glow of our dreamworld we have an enchanting encounter; we cradle an adorable baby; we befriend a magical creature; we find ourselves in the arms of a beloved; we are swept away on waves of passion. No wonder we don't want to awaken. Life is rarely as beautiful as in our dreams of bliss.

INFLUENCES ON YOUR DREAMS ABOUT BEING EMBRACED OR LOVED

1. Biological

OUR LOVE AND sex dreams arise, in part, from inborn drives that guarantee the survival of our species. We are impelled—driven—by our genes to mate and produce children. Sigmund Freud was not mistaken when he claimed that sexual relationships are a primary topic in dreams. We may argue that he has gone too far, that dreams are about other topics of interest aside from sex (as they are); we may feel his approach reduces complex, even exquisite, imagery to simplistic sexual mechanics, but we cannot deny that sex is outstanding in our dream life.

Indeed, much of recent biological research has underscored and expanded the notion that sex influences our dreams. Researcher Charles Fisher and others have demonstrated that male erections take place during the rapid eye movements (REMs) that occur when we are dreaming. What every male knows from personal experience of awaking in the morning with an erection has been documented in sleep laboratories around the world. The only time erections do not seem to accompany dreams is when the imagery evokes extreme anxiety.

Since it is more difficult to measure a woman's degree of sexual arousal during dreaming, the proof that this occurs did not emerge until several years after male arousal was documented. Researcher Ismet Karacan and his colleagues were able to measure changes in the diameter of the clitoris (the female physical equivalent of the penis) when it enlarges during REM. Another investigator reported an increase of about one-half degree in the temperature of the clitoris during REM. Studies also showed that whether a woman was watching an erotic movie, masturbating, dreaming, or having an orgasm in her dream, vascular engorgement of the vagina reached about the same high level.

We can now say with certainty that both women and men experience sexual arousal during the dream state. Nipples become erect, the pulse in the genitals increases, and the sexual organs moisten and swell. Small wonder that our dreams often deal with sexual imagery. The pictures the dreaming mind conjures may be as direct as a pornographic magazine or as cloaked as an allegorical play, but sex is alive and well in our dreams.

The sexual arousal you experience when you dream is part of a general nervous system arousal that ebbs and flows throughout the night and is woven into your dreams. We know from Alfred Kinsey's work that 83 percent of males say they experience orgasm in their dreams by the age of forty-five, compared with 37 percent of women of the same age. This number may be increasing, as today's generation of women are more sexually active and more accepting of their sexuality.

As human beings we are biologically programmed to bond with others. Our attachments between parent and child, family members, lovers, peers, and the wider community are as determined as sexual drives. Our chances of survival are vastly increased when we are members of a cooperative group. Because we need to affiliate with others, we perform certain ritualized behavior that many species exhibit. For instance, kissing between human adults is thought to be a form of ritualized feeding behavior, much as other animals chew food before giving it by mouth to their infants or birds feed their mates as courting behavior. Touching another person is believed to be a ritualized grooming behavior, similar to that of other animals when they remove parasites from each other. As a living creature you share the basic needs for sex and relationships that serve you well for safety and security—needs that are expressed in your dreams about love and sex.

2, 3. *Cultural and Subcultural*

IN ADDITION TO biological needs, your dreams of love and sex are sharply influenced by your beliefs about these topics absorbed from your culture. Should a man be macho or sensitive? Should a woman be submissive or self-sufficient? Is marriage best arranged by your parents or by your heart? Who are the most desirable partners in your mind? The rich? The famous? The beautiful or handsome? The most passionate? The skinny or voluptuous? Is it desirable to dream about a lover? Should such dreams be sought or merely accepted? Are these dreams dangerous and to be resisted? Can you really connect at a deep level with another human being of the opposite sex? Or is the mate just a convenient tool for certain times? These and many other aspects of love and sex in the waking state are determined by the ideas in your dominant culture and subculture; they influence your dreams.

4. *Personal*

LIKEWISE, YOUR LIFE experiences so far will affect your dreams on the topic of love. Did you feel loved and accepted by the opposite sex parent? Did a parent abandon you? Have you ever felt completely in love, holding back nothing? Have you felt truly and completely loved by another person? Were you hurt in a love affair? Have you ever been sexually assaulted? Have you ever been brutally rejected? Has a good friend ever betrayed you? All these situations, and many more, will affect how you personally symbolize love, sex, and friendship in your dreams.

Last, any deviation from your usual sexual pattern results in dream changes. A period of personal deprivation—a mate away on a lengthy trip, the death of a loved partner, a separation forced by war or other crises—can temporarily increase your dreams of desire and longing for love. Our bodies become accustomed to a certain pattern and intensity of sexual interaction, as well as to physical touching of a less sexual nature, such as affectionate squeezes, hugs, kisses, playful pokes and tugs. When you deviate from your usual pattern, your dreams are likely to supply the desired missing elements, sometimes complete with orgasm.

Any period of heightened stimulation, such as being immersed in a new and intense love affair, is also likely to increase your love and sex dreams. When your body is stimulated more than usual, it responds by registering the waking increase in more dreams of this sort, echoing your waking preoccupation with the affair in progress.

UNDERSTANDING YOUR DREAMS ABOUT BEING EMBRACED OR LOVED

WHEN YOU DREAM about making love in a dream, the lover is usually clearly pictured. Unlike in dreams about being chased or attacked by a stranger or "men," the dream lover almost always has a face and body. Instead of running to put as much space as possible between you and the pursuer, you want to get as close as possible to the lover. The pattern is reversed: instead of fleeing for your life, you are attracted to the figure for love.

Meeting Your Dream Lover: Connecting with a Desired Quality

WHO IS YOUR lover in a particular dream? He or she is apt to be one of these characters:

A lover in your current waking life

A former actual lover

A total stranger

A person you know casually (with or without any actual interest to you)

Someone you know who is completely inappropriate (such as a family member)

A famous person (politician, movie star, music or sports celebrity, member of royal family, other)

A transformed animal (bird, fish, jaguar, other) or even a plant

A spiritual being (angel, figure of light, other)

Any of these types of lovers may appear in your dreams. Each category suggests a slightly different connection. Feeling romantic or making love is a favorite dream for men and women, although they usually express it differently. Women are more likely to emphasize the sensual and loving side of a dream encounter, whereas men more often focus on the sexual or passionate elements. Both men and women claim that they occasionally experience dream orgasms that are more powerful than any waking experience. No wonder it's a happy dream!

Whatever shape your dream lover may take, your dreaming mind is expressing a desire to be connected with either the person from the dream or the quality this person represents.

Making love in your dream = Wish to connect with waking person or quality of that person

---

You may know at once why you dreamed about a certain lover and who or what that person means to you. But often people find their dream lovers puzzling, asking, "Why in the world would I dream about him (or her)? I don't even like that person!" Or they may like the dream lover well enough but not want that person for a mate. What do such dreams mean? We'll try to find the answers.

Questions to Ask Yourself About a Dream Lover

YOU CAN HELP reveal the meaning of the dream lover, the connection that you desire to have or that you feel currently exists, by asking yourself the following questions:

1. Who was my dream lover? (Describe fully in your dream journal.)
2. Can I name three outstanding traits of my dream lover?
3. Are these qualities or characteristics that I want more of in my life?
4. Does my dream lover's name contain a pun?
5. Does my dream lover's name or appearance suggest someone I know?

Try describing the person you dreamed about in a single sentence, as if to a child (a method first suggested by Jung, which he taught to his patients). Notice what you emphasize about that person—some personal attribute or an aspect of his or her name, appearance, rank, or influence. There is something about the person in the dream that you desire in your own life now. What is it?

Meeting Dream Celebrities: Connecting with Power

YOU MAY BE one of the many people who choose celebrities for their dream lovers. If you find yourself making passionate love to a movie star, political figure, or member of the nobility, it's important to detect his or her meaning for you. Don't just dismiss a dream of being seduced by Tom Cruise or wildly kissing Julia Roberts as plain wishful thinking.

Meeting a celebrity in a dream = Desire to connect with a quality the celebrity represents

Making a Spiritual Connection

A MIDDLE-AGED WOMAN in one of my workshops said she often had romantic encounters in her dreams with Charlton Heston. When I asked her, "What kind of person is Charlton Heston?" she assured me that he was "very spiritual." Another woman might have said, "He's superconservative," or "He's the president of the National Rifle Association," or "He played religious roles in overblown epics." To this woman, Charlton Heston's biblical roles had conveyed the notion that he is spiritual in actuality, a quality she hungered for in her own life. By making love with him in her dreams, she felt she was blending with this spiritual element.

Making an Artistic Connection

THIS SAME PRINCIPLE, of course, holds true when the lover is not a movie star. An American man in his thirties was obsessed by dreams of making love with his high school sweetheart, who had married someone else. Asked to describe what kind of person she was, he told me she was "very creative, sensitive, artistic." This man went so far as to travel to his home state and arrange a meeting with his former sweetheart. She no longer appealed to him as a lover, he found, but he realized that it was his own artistic, creative ambitions that he was yearning to rekindle.

Whatever attributes attract you to the star or to a former lover are the qualities you sense missing in your current life — or want more of in your life.

Making a Punny Connection

MANY YEARS AGO, when I was feeling discouraged about a project, I dreamed of kissing Bob Hope. Now, this is a star who has zero appeal for me as a man, yet I chuckled to realize that the impulse behind the dream was the desire to "be kissed by HOPE," an emotion I needed badly at the time.

An American woman in her thirties who had just entered a love affair with a man named Jack dreamed of gambling on a coin-operated machine when she "hit the JACKpot." A great gushing of coins poured out. Freudians would point out that the machine was "eJACulating" in her dream. She felt that by gambling in the game of love, she had hit a winner.

Another American woman in her thirties, unmarried but living with a boyfriend, began having sensuous dreams of making love with an old boyfriend named Art. When I discussed what Art was like as a person, it emerged that he had little attraction as a male. Art as a creative pursuit, however, was something she very much missed and had neglected since getting into her current relationship. Her dream said, I want more ARTistic activities in my life.

An elderly American woman who had seen the film *The Horse Whisperer* was greatly attracted to Robert Redford. That night she dreamed of meeting a family friend who wore a bright RED hunting jacket and looked happy, impish, and appealing, "more exciting, not so humdrum." She seemed to be pining for a little more excitement in her love life.

Always consider whether there is a pun involved in the name or in the appearance of your dream lover.

Making Other Connections

WE CONSORT WITH the famous in our dreams, whether they are movie, theater, or media stars; politicians; heads of state; or royalty. In one subcategory of Being Embraced or Loved, we are not necessarily making love, but we have a pleasant encounter with the famous. I particularly liked the example of a British male journalist who interviewed me. He told me his dream of having tea with Queen Elizabeth, in which she played a violin for him. For him, the dream represented emotional warmth (the quality he perceived in the violin music) combined with ultimate good taste (his view of the queen), the two qualities he would like his writing to have.

Famous People in Dreams as Metaphors for Power

QUEENS, KINGS, PRINCES, princesses, media stars, and other celebrities have always been a target of dream interest. In part, these not-quite-mortal beings carry our projections of the ideal mate, the Prince Charming. When the lovely Princess Diana was tragically killed in a car crash in Paris, she became a figure in the dreams of people around the world. Likewise, when the handsome John F. Kennedy, Jr., died in a plane crash off Martha's Vineyard, dreamers responded. When lives of the young, good-looking, and powerful are cut short, dreamers feel as if a part of their own possibilities have diminished. When you choose a famous person as a lover in a dream, or simply meet him or her as an equal, you may feel you are contacting the potency and possibilities for a good life that you want in your own.

Meeting Dream Animal Friends: Making New Connections

YOU MAY DREAM about encountering a mythological, magical, or speaking animal in your dreams. Adults, as well as children, have this dream, although boys and girls report it more often. These dream encounters are usually nonsexual exchanges with enchanted beasts, although at times animals may become specific lovers.

When you happen upon a precious tame, talking bird, or some other highly idiosyncratic dream image, you are probably meeting a newly evolving part of yourself.

Meeting a marvelous animal in your dream = Something new is evolving in you

---

Encountering a magical animal friend also suggests a wish to connect with an element that animal represents for you. The night before her seventh birthday, an American girl dreamed "A friendly unicorn played with me all night." A boy from India dreamed "Birds flew beside me in the moonlight," and an American boy said, "I flew with the birds and they spoke to me in their language and did acrobatics with me." A French-Canadian woman dreamed "I made love with a crocodile"—since she enjoyed the dream, perhaps she was connecting with her own anger or strength.

The positive roles animals in our dreams play vary from friend, to helper, to rescuer, to mate. Each expresses a different aspect of the dreamer's needs and wishes.

I treasure some of the delightful meetings with dream animals that I've had. Years after the dream, I remember following a snake who wore a golden crown. This was not an image I read about in mythology or legend or fairy tale, but one that emerged from profound sleep. It was probably related to a newly found sexual happiness.

In a dream not long ago, in my mid-sixties, I "sent out a call" while standing on a dream beach, much as I have read that the ancient Hawaiian *kahunas* (shamans) did when "calling" dolphins. After a while, some great fish came swimming into the bay by the beach in response to my call. One was huge, with black and white stripes. I watched in wonder, thinking, "I always knew it was possible," that is, if I "called" them mentally, they would come to me. This dream was related to my wish to connect with some special aspects of the deep dreaming mind.

Our dream animals can be as unusual as those in legends. In fact, dreaming might be the origin of many of our classic myths.

Your Dream Animals

WHEN YOU MEET with a dream animal on friendly terms, it is a precious experience. If you've already had such an encounter, you know how mysterious, even awesome, these dreams can be. Simply observing your special dream animal is amazing, but it's important to explore its significance. Here are some questions and activities as a guide:

1. What was my dream animal like? (Describe it in your journal.)
2. What makes this animal unique, special? What does it look like? Sound like? Feel like? What does it do? How does it live?
3. What differentiates this animal from all other similar animals?
4. What personal experiences have I had with such a creature? (Describe.)
5. Does my dream animal possess any attributes that the actual creature does not have? The animal's characteristics encode its meaning for you.
6. Set your writing material down and rest comfortably in a chair or recliner. Close your eyes. Take three deep, slow breaths, in and out.

In your own time, visualize your dream animal as you saw it. Picture the details as clearly as possible—shape, color, style, every part of the animal's appearance. Do you have an impression of its texture? Its scent? Its sound?

7. In your imagination, ask the creature, "Who are you?" and listen to the reply. Ask, "What do you want? How can I help you?" and hear the response.

8. Now picture yourself merging with the creature. For a moment, enter into the animal in your imagination. What do you feel? Sense what life is like for this creature. What does this creature desire? Ask again, "What do *you* want?" Is there some quality the dream creature has that you would like for yourself? If so, ask it to share this.

9. In your mind's eye return to your own being. Visualize yourself relating to your dream animal in some pleasant way, perhaps as you did in the dream, or extending the interaction in other ways. Put your feelings into a short phrase. Remember.

10. Open your eyes, and when you feel ready, add to your notes anything you have learned from this imaginary encounter with your dream animal.

Our dream animals have much to teach us about our inner needs and our desires to connect with something beyond our everyday selves.

Hybrids in Your Dreams: Combinations

YOUR DREAMS ABOUT animals may seem especially puzzling when you encounter one that is composed of different creatures, or a beast that is half human. I once dreamed of watching a "cat-bird" flying. This was not a kind of bird, but a combination of the two creatures, more like a cat with wings than a bird with whiskers.

To sort out the meaning of such an image to you, you first need to contemplate each creature separately. So, asking myself to describe a cat, I said that "a cat is a sensual creature who enjoys being petted, and purrs with pleasure; I've often noticed that in my dreams cats have a sexual meaning, probably from the slang term for the female genitals." When I asked myself about birds, my reply was "A bird has the near-magical ability to fly; in many cultures, birds represent the soul." Combining these two descriptions, it became apparent to me that my cat-bird would be an ideal combination of the sensual body and the ability to move into spiritual realms.

In an earlier dream, when I was about forty, I saw a "princess with the head and naked upper torso of a shapely woman, her lower body that of a delicate fawn." She was snow white—skin, fur, and long, flowing hair. At the base of her white fur-skin throat was a circlet formed from drops of scarlet, and upon her head grew a crownlike arrangement of small rounded horns. Alongside her flank huddled four small children that she embraced with an outstretched arm.

For me, the "fawn-princess" dream had echoes of Snow White, from my loved childhood fairy tales. But she was more than a princess who is saved and awakened by her prince (as I felt myself to be in a second, happy marriage). She was partly her animal self, partly a protective mother (it's no coincidence that there are four children in my life), and partly a royal personage, a descendant of divinity with growing powers of her own. There is more symbolism to explore here, in the colors of white (purity for me) and red (passion, life's blood), but you get the idea.

When you dream of a hybrid animal-person, ask yourself the following questions:

1. How would I describe each aspect of the creature separately? (These descriptions are unique for each dreamer.)
2. What would such a creature be like if it had these attributes combined?
3. Would this combination help me at this moment? Is it a goal for my future?

"Magical" animals in our dreams, like the mythological creatures in fables and folktales, have much to teach us about qualities and potentials in ourselves. They shimmer with wisdom of our innermost selves. Embracing them is the right thing to do.

Metamorphoses in Your Dreams: Transformations

AN UNUSUAL BUT very powerful type of connection with a dream lover occurs when the lover changes from an animal or bird into a human being. Such dreams seem to have a transcendental quality for the dreamer. One American woman described a dream of making love with an "enormous bird," who, wings flapping, swooped down onto her body where she lay on the grass. As they made love, the great bird's blue heron–like feathers "shapeshift and melt into his skin and he becomes inch by inch a man," all except for his pterodactyl-like bird head. The dreamer wondered as she awoke whether the man was under a spell. As the Greek mortal Leda might have been, when Zeus made love to her in the form of a swan, this woman felt transported.

The reverse transition, from human being into beast, is quite rare but does occur. Such dreams tend to be negative, as was that of an engaged woman who dreamed of talking with her fiancé in a bar where they usually met after work. In her dream he said he was not going to marry her after all because he thought she was ugly; as she watched, her fiancé turned from a man into a horrible beast-monster. This, of course, is how she would have thought of him if he had betrayed her trust in this way. Her dream turned out to be pure wedding jitters, and the couple were soon agreeably married.

Some women who felt trapped in unhappy wedlock have described to me dreams of their husbands with the head or mask or form of a rat. Here the slang expression "He's a rat" has become literal in the women's dreams. Others have related dreams in which their husbands are cast in the unfavorable role of a troublesome bear.

There is no hard and fast rule—the change of form from human to dream animal may be positive. I once dreamed of shape-shifting into the likeness of an earthworm. Fully aware that I was dreaming, I felt the plump movement of my earthworm hips as I sashayed across a carpet, looked out through my earthworm eyes, and felt the fuzzy pile of the carpet tickle my belly. This dream was strange, indeed, but not the least unpleasant. Surely, I was feeling "earthy" at the time.

Meeting Divine Dream Lovers: Connecting to Spirit

YOU MAY FIND yourself meeting heavenly lovers in dreams. Some women describe dreams of making love with angel-like men. An American in her thirties said she had recurrent dreams of hearing the doorbell ring and answering it to find a Greek god. Once he took her for a walk in a forest. Often he would take her dancing, and she would waltz in a full gown, whirling over the floor, her feet not touching the ground. At the time, this woman was unhappily married, so her dreams of dancing with a Greek god provided a welcome respite.

Another American woman in her thirties dreamed of making loving with a man who was "composed of golden light"; their movements were "incredible," her orgasm "cosmic." At other times she dreamed of making love with a man whose penis was made of shining light; his ejaculation was a shower of sparkles. These heavenly lover dreams reflected a joyful waking union. Besides positive associations to the man involved in her waking life, such dreams suggest a connection with something "illuminating." Dreams with divine lovers may be metaphors for the woman's feeling of being united with spiritual powers; they also leave her with a sense of feeling profoundly loved.

Divine lover in your dream = Connecting with your spirituality

---

Weddings: Uniting Aspects of Self

WHEN A MAN or woman is planning to get married, dreams about weddings are often anxiety dreams. If you're about to get married and have some alarming dreams about it, you're reacting in a perfectly normal manner. Making a commitment seems to bring out the dream jitters in a lot of engaged couples. Joyful wedding dreams are relatively rare when an actual ceremony is being planned.

People fairly often dream about weddings to symbolize a connection that is important to them. For instance, an American woman had a significant dream in which her spiritual teacher married her design teacher. Their wedding took place in a beautiful teahouse with a Japanese-Filipino-African flavor that seemed lovely to her. Shortly after this dream, the woman began to design jewelry that has an exotic quality, like the teahouse structure in her dream. No one element can be clearly identified, as the designs are a blend uniquely hers. Before this dream, she had divided her energies between her artistic and spiritual interests; now she was able to see the possibility of "wedding" the two. The dream union yielded a product line in the waking world that gives the woman much commercial success as well as supreme personal satisfaction.

When you dream about a wedding (when you're not about to get married), you are apt to be expressing a union between aspects of yourself. You are anticipating a change in your life.

A wedding in your dream = Union between waking aspects of yourself

---

An inner bond is taking place when you have a happy dream about getting married. Here are some possibilities:

- You may be finding the way to integrate your intellectual and emotional sides.

- You may be becoming more able to unite your career and homemaker roles.
- Perhaps you are improving at blending your masculine and feminine parts.
- You may be linking your business and romantic sides.
- You may be discovering how to wed your artistic and spiritual selves.
- You may be merging your sensual and higher selves into a whole.

Jung regarded dreams of marriage, especially those involving the wedding of a royal couple, or that of a brother and sister, as pivotal images in the process of becoming a unique individual, what he called "individuation." He thought that wedding dreams could be a "transforming symbol."

A puzzling aspect about dreams of getting married is that they are sometimes associated with death. The ritual of marriage marks a change from one state of being to another. People approaching death sometimes dream of weddings. You'll find several examples of this connection later in the book, especially in the last chapter. When my ninety-one-year-old mother was very ill, near death, she began hallucinating that she was going to be married, asking for her wedding gown from the closet, and greeting visitors with the statement that they were just in time for the ceremony.

For older or ill people, the wedding ceremony, in dreams or hallucination, seems to represent another kind of union, perhaps the reconnection of the individual's soul with the vast spirit of the cosmos.

Meeting Adorable Dream Babies: Connecting with Newness

WHEN YOU HOLD an enchanting child in your arms, your dreaming mind may be expressing a number of different meanings. Much depends upon your stage of life, current activities, and wishes.

The desire to birth a child is one of our basic biological drives. Worldwide, male or female, we have an inherent need to reproduce, to have our genes and our names live on when we are gone. So it's no surprise that our dreams prompt us with charming dream children. Studies have shown that women are most likely to dream about babies during the first half of their menstrual cycle, when the possibility of becoming impregnated is greatest. If you are a woman in your childbearing years, or if you are a man who has not yet sired a child, your dreams about babies may be simple biological impulses to do so. However, your dreams about babies also may have an underlying symbolic significance. Many people refer to their pet projects as their "babies." Like a newborn infant, a newborn idea requires nurturing and tender care.

The babies in our dreams often represent some project, mission, or activity that is precious to us—a book concept, a new musical composition, an idea for a painting series, an advertising campaign, a "newborn" romance, even a new house, and endless other absorbing activities. Whatever engages your mind, and especially your heart, can take form as a vulnerable and valuable baby in your dreams.

Adorable baby or child in your dream = Deep desire of your heart in waking life

---

Even the language we use to describe a baby and an idea shares a vocabulary: we get the "seed" of an idea; we "conceive" a plan to carry out a project; we "labor" over bringing it to fruition; we "give birth" or "breathe life into" a completed mission.

Of course, when bad things happen to our dream babies, our project-information is under threat. Forgetting the baby, losing the baby, neglecting the baby—these are common anxiety dreams when you've been too busy or distracted to attend to the "baby" project in your care. (These dreams are discussed in the next chapter.)

Good dreams about babies are less common than alarming ones, but they are special experiences that can nourish us and help us move toward our goals. For example, when I was working on this book and "conceiving" the idea of making a visual language that could be used to depict dreams for residents of many different countries, regardless of the spoken language, I had an impressive dream. In it, I watched a woman put her ear to the belly of a pregnant woman, trying to hear the heartbeat of the unborn child. I awoke with the idea of the visual language more fully formulated in my mind.

Anyone who has tried to hear the heartbeat of an unborn child knows it's not easy to do—one must become very still and listen intently. I was pleased to listen to the message of this dream—that the idea is growing well and is capable of being born.

Writers and creative artists in many fields compare their work to birthing a child. Watch for your creative projects shaped into dream babies.

Dream Babies as New Relationships

DREAM BABIES ARE not always creative projects. When a married American woman was about to start a love affair, she dreamed of "holding a tiny new baby against my shoulders and snuggling it." Many characters in the dream had come to celebrate the birth of this "love child," who was dressed in pink overalls and sunbonnet and was lovingly cared for. The dreamer was embracing the notion of the new love affair.

Questions to Ask About Your Dream Baby

IF THE CONNECTION between your dream child and your waking life is not apparent, here are some questions to consider:

1. What's special about your dream baby?
2. What differentiates your dream baby from all other babies?
3. Can you describe the baby in detail? (Write it in your journal.)
4. What waking life activity has some of these same qualities?
5. How can your dream baby help your waking "baby" thrive?

Dream Babies as Newly Developing Aspects of Self

JUNG THOUGHT THAT dreams of a child with special abilities was an archetype. He saw the "divine child" in a dream as an expression of the birth of a new potential within the dreamer, the possibility of wholeness, the Self, the unity of opposites. In various mystic systems, alchemy, and Taoist meditation, the goal is to produce the spiritual "golden child." Jung likened this to the "divine child" that may appear in dreams when inner development is under way.

A miraculous dream baby may appear when you are discovering new abilities in yourself. A young American woman who was not yet a mother dreamed just before her birthday that she gave birth unassisted to a baby that was "so smart. She has her full intellect in four days. I am so proud of her." Awake, the woman felt that her life was changing in significant ways at the time of her dream; her bright baby reflected her own inner growth and her pride in it. A few months after my daughter Cheryl had given birth to her son, she dreamed she looked into the bedroom in a girlfriend's house, where she saw a baby girl lying on the bed playing with her toes and counting them, "One-two-three-four-five. They don't know I can talk!" Cheryl was discovering new capacities within herself in her new role as mother.

The mystic child who speaks to you in your dreams, who solves riddles, or imparts wisdom, is the harbinger of healthy new potential. Whether you are male or female—pregnant or not, mother or not—a dream of a miraculous child speaks of new life within.

Your dreams of being embraced and loved take many forms: making love, meeting fascinating human or animal characters, getting married, tenderly caring for an unborn or newborn child. In each variation, you are reaching toward some person, a newly developing aspect of self, or a newly shaped waking life project. As you embrace the dream image, you welcome your new ventures and newly evolving self. Greet your dreams of loving embrace wholeheartedly—they will serve you well.

2

Being Injured, Ill, or Dying

Versus Being Healed, Born, or Reborn

2.0 INJURY, ILLNESS, OR DEATH

Description: You or another character (often a loved one) is injured, becomes ill, or dies in a dream, or there is serious risk of these events. The cause is accidental. In no case is a villain identified—injury, illness, or death just happens. There is a car accident; you fall and get hurt or contract a fatal illness. (Car accidents without injuries or death are classified with Car Trouble; falls that don't involve injuries or death are classed with Falling dreams.) Injury includes the common dream that your teeth crumble.

Frequency: This nightmare is moderately common and frequent. It sometimes occurs at the onset of an actual illness, such as a fever.

Usual Meanings: "I feel emotionally hurt"; "I feel damaged"; "I'm wounded"; "I fear I will be hurt"; "I'm coming apart." This dream may be a warning about a physical risk you or a loved one are taking. When another dream character dies, it may mean "That part of me (represented by the person) is *as if it were dead.*" At times it means "I wish that person would go away" or "I am afraid I will lose that person."

These are the dreams that leave people feeling uneasy or alarmed. To dream of yourself or a loved one having a serious accident, becoming sick, or dying can fill you with dread that the dream might come true. Since these dreams sometimes do occur just before the onset of an illness or injury, we learn to fear their imagery. Nearly 50 percent reported it.

Most often, however, these dreams are warnings to slow down, to take it easy, to change your course of action; otherwise some accident or illness will result. At times these dreams warn you of dangers to loved ones and help you to be more cautious in their care. Heeding the warnings in these dreams may allow you to prevent the misfortunes or destruction depicted in the dream.

INFLUENCES ON YOUR DREAMS ABOUT INJURY OR DEATH

1. Biological

AS HUMAN BEINGS we are biologically programmed to survive. When you or a loved one becomes ill, gets injured, or dies in a dream, you are mobilized to fiercely defend yourself and the people you wish to protect. Every instinct to protect your mate, to safeguard your children or other loved ones, and to survive, is aroused in dreams about being injured or dying. No wonder these nightmares create anxiety. Understanding the messages in such dreams gives you the basis to change your behavior in waking life, and so reduce the possibility of dire events and your concerns about them.

2, 3. Cultural and Subcultural

PEOPLE AROUND THE world have widely varied ideas about dreams of death and injury. In some cultures, people believe that a dream that a specific person gets hurt or dies is a certain prediction of that event. A woman in India confided that she was terrified of dreaming, since she had on several occasions dreamed of the death of a relative, who soon thereafter actually died. This experience is rare.

Since dreams sometimes do provide warnings about actual dangers, it is wise to take precautions that are reasonable and feasible. It is always worthwhile to listen to your dreams at a realistic as well as a symbolic level. At the same time, don't neglect to look at the possible symbolic meaning of an injury or death that happens in your dream.

4. Personal

ALL YOUR LIFE'S experiences come into play with this universal theme: when and how your parents, children, or other loved ones became ill or died, whether there are actual babies and children in your waking life, what your personal history of illness and injury is, whether there are genetic illnesses in your family that may affect you in the future, and so forth. If you happen to be pregnant, this condition profoundly influences dreams, as we will see.

Naturally, if you are ill or seriously threatened with a disease that could be fatal, you are more likely to dream about the topic. In such a case, dreams about dying can actually help you to cope with preparations that may be necessary. They can spur you to make appropriate farewells and other arrangements. Some studies, such as those done by physician Robert Smith with patients hospitalized for heart disease, showed that those who dreamed about death and journeys were, indeed, the ones who had a higher mortality rate. If you dream about these topics when you are well, it does not have the same implication; the dreams are more likely to stand for a current change in your life.

If you should have recurrent dreams about an injury to a particular area of your body, in which you feel pain during the dream, it may be advisable to have a checkup. People sometimes dream of wounds or other injuries in a specific area of the body when a disease process is under way in that location. One man who had a powerful dream about natives thrusting spears into his throat, causing severe pain, found that he was suffering from cancer of the thyroid gland. A woman who had recurrent dreams that wolves were tearing at her stomach, giving her excruciating pain, was subsequently diagnosed with cancer of the stomach. Experiencing pain *during the dream* is one clue that there may be something amiss in the dreamer's physical body. Usually, when we are in a healthy waking state and we dream of being injured or dying, we do not feel pain in the dream.

For most of us, dreams about injury, illness, and death are usually more symbolic than literal. They tend to express your emotional response to some waking event. We'll explore how to sort out the meanings of your dreams about death first, then look at those about injury.

UNDERSTANDING YOUR DREAMS ABOUT DEATH

WHEN YOU OR another dream character dies, the first question to consider is Who is the victim? Dream deaths often involve one of the following:

- Death of a famous person ("John F. Kennedy dies")
- Death of an elderly parent ("My mother gets sick and dies")
- Death of a youngster ("My child is hit by a car and is killed")
- Death of a parent ("I attend my father's funeral")
- Death of a sweetheart or mate ("My lover is killed in a plane crash")
- Your own death ("I'm dying of cancer")

The men and women of all ages whose dreams are quoted were expressing a range of meanings; the same range is likely to appear in your dreams. Each has a different shade of meaning.

You Dream That Someone Else Is Injured, Is Ill, or Dies

IN GENERAL, WHEN you dream about the accidental death of any person, that person's death symbolizes something in you that is no longer functional. Some aspect of you isn't "alive" at the moment; it's become inoperative, as if it were "dead."

Accidental death in your dream = Waking aspect of yourself is currently inactive

You'll see how this works in the following examples.

You Dream a Famous Person Dies

WHEN A FAMOUS person dies in your dreams, it's important to ask yourself who is (or was) this person and listen carefully to *your* answer—not what someone else says or remembers about the person, but your specific reaction. The American man who dreamed John F. Kennedy was dead described him this way: "He was a political idealist." Needless to say, other dreamers with the same dream would give quite different answers—"He was the first Catholic president," "He was a womanizer," "He was assassinated," and so on—each comment true, but emphasizing what the dreamer considered paramount or reacted to most strongly. This dreamer, a man with an active political background himself, was able to recognize that his own "political idealism" was "as if dead." By confronting this feeling, the dreamer is offered a chance to let the "dead" part remain dead, or to revive it in his or her life.

If you dream that a famous person died, ask yourself the following questions:

1. Who is X (the celebrity who died)?
2. What is or was this person like? In your dream journal, or aloud, describe this person in a brief sentence or phrase. Name three of his or her outstanding qualities.
3. How do you feel about this person?
4. What attracts you or repels you about this individual? Do you feel a personal connection with some aspect of X?
5. Do you want to leave this part of you inactive?
6. If not, what can you do to revivify this aspect?

It's especially important to notice what qualities or attributes of the celebrities in your dreams give you a feeling of personal connection with them. For instance, I occasionally found myself dreaming about Grace Kelly, long before she gave up her movie career to marry the prince of Monaco and prior to her tragic death. It took me a while to realize the connections: her middle name is Patricia, the same as my first name, and she was from Philadelphia, where I grew up in the suburbs. These slender similarities were enough to suggest to my dreaming mind that she could play the role model of a successful, pretty woman in my ambitious dreams. When she was in danger in my dreams, so, too, did I feel myself to be.

Celebrities aside, the misfortunes in our dreams often portray people we know intimately.

You Dream an Elderly Person Dies

WHEN YOU DREAM that an elderly relative or friend dies, you may be anticipating his or her actual death, or the dream may be symbolic, in that the older person may represent certain attitudes of your own. The American woman who dreamed that her elderly mother fell sick and died was, in a way, preparing herself to accept the inevitable loss of a person close to her. By anticipating her mother's death, the dreamer was spurred to keep in closer contact with her parent and have the needed conversations while there was still time.

The aged will, in the natural course of the life cycle, die. These dreams are rarely predictive, but even when they are, they help us prepare for loss. If the death is not imminent, we can be inspired by such dreams to make the most of the time that remains. Rather than becoming inundated with feelings of sadness, we need to take the dream warning to heart, have the exchanges we need to have now, and find ways to cherish the qualities of the person we want to keep alive in us.

Don't overlook the possibility that the dream may symbolize the death of what the elderly person represents in you. This might be some old-fashioned ideas or ways of doing things. You may be glad to have that part of you cease to be active. On the other hand, the elderly person may stand for some positive values or ideals that you feel have been lost in your life. Here is where your answers to the question What is or was this person like? and to the other questions will help guide your understanding. And remember, elements that die in a dream are not dead and gone forever. Your dream shows you how you feel at the moment. You can bring back to life those aspects of the person that you want to survive in you.

You Dream a Person of Middle Years in Good Health Dies

WHEN YOU DREAM that a parent or other person of middle years dies, as did the American man who dreamed of attending his father's funeral, you are not likely to be expecting his death. Such a dream is often distressing, for fear it may be predictive, but more often it is symbolic, related to your relationship with the parent.

When dreamers tell me this dream, I always ask questions 1 and 2: "What kind of person is X (the person who died in the dream)? Describe him/her to me in a sentence." If the dreamer's answer does not make the dream meaning clear, I will ask further, "What makes this person special? What's unique about the person?" If you have this dream, ask yourself the same questions. Your answers will be significant; for example, when an American woman who dreamed her father died told me, "He is the warmest, most loving person I've ever known," she was expressing a sense of loss of warmth and love at the moment in her own waking life. She went on to say that she had recently broken up with her boyfriend, whose presence she greatly missed. A man who dreamed of his father's funeral said, "He is always cold and withholding, very focused on money, and cares nothing for people." This man was expressing rejection of that aspect of himself, a refusal to let that quality "live." The dream imagery was the same in both cases: my father died. The meaning was opposite.

In dreams about death, always explore the nature of your relationship to the person who died in the dream, and what that person is or was like. You'll begin to see the connection to what you want to have active or inactive in your own life.

You Dream Your Child Dies

IF YOU DREAM that a waking life child is injured in an accident or killed in one, and such an unhappy event has never occurred in waking life, you will probably be distraught. Such dreams are often a torture to parents. Parents who have actually lost a child or had one severely injured in an accident sometimes replay the event in recurrent dreams about it. Dreams after a waking life trauma (posttraumatic stress syndrome nightmares) are an effort that the mind makes to bear the unbearable. Although extremely painful, they are the mind's attempt to heal. Eventually the dream imagery begins to change and the healing process moves forward.

For those parents who have not experienced the injury, illness, or death of a child, the dream imagery may be a warning about an actual child in danger, or it may be symbolic of the danger to the child within you—sometimes both. Only you will be able to judge. Consider the following questions:

1. Who died or was hurt? What's special or unique about this child?
2. How did I feel about the accident in the dream?
3. Is my child engaged in some dangerous activity?
4. If so, what can I do to improve the situation?
5. Is there a goal, something essential to me, that having a child seems to prevent?
6. Is there some situation in which I feel as vulnerable as a child?
7. If so, what can I do better to safeguard my inner child?

The American mother who dreamed that her child was struck and killed by a car took precautions to ensure that her child was complying with safety rules when going to and from school. She also realized that she was feeling extremely anxious about herself and her loved ones, more than seemed reasonable. That, combined with the fact that her marriage was in trouble, led her to the conclusion that she should get some therapeutic help before she— like the child in her dream—was damaged beyond repair.

Some parents find themselves in the painful situation of wanting to be free of a marriage or passionately desiring a career that a child's presence makes difficult. When we wish for the removal of a person—child or adult— who frustrates us in fulfilling our needs, dreaming that the person dies is not a wish for actual death. It is, rather, a wish to be free, to have the obstacle between the dreamer and the desired goal removed. If you suspect your dream is of this type, it is a good idea to focus on small steps toward meeting your goal. There is always something we can do to move closer to our desires without sacrificing what is already part of our life and responsibility.

If you are not a parent, to dream that your child has been hurt or killed is certainly symbolic. Consider what part of you is feeling wounded or totally inactive. Think about what you can do to care for this part. Do it. Cherishing and protecting your dream children are as important as performing the same activities in waking life.

You Dream a Lover or Mate Dies

WHEN YOU DREAM a lover or mate is hurt, gets sick, or dies, the meaning depends upon the nature of your relationship at the moment. The American woman who dreamed that her lover was killed in a plane crash was highly anxious about the survival of their relationship. She felt that it might be "about to crash." To her, for her lover to die would be more tolerable than for him to leave her. Her dream suggests her realization that the relationship felt unlikely to survive.

Dreams about lovers or spouses in danger may represent realistic dangers to them, especially if they are ill in waking life or have had some serious threat to their health. The dream may express concern about the loved person's ability to recover from a current condition. Any precautions that seem wise should be taken.

When your lover or mate is not ill, and your relationship with him or her seems secure, examine your dream from the symbolic point of view. Asking yourself the same questions outlined earlier will guide you to understanding what qualities or parts of you seem in danger. Additional useful considerations are the following:

1. What is unique about this person?
2. What is special about our relationship?
3. How can I preserve the qualities I admire in this person in myself?

Remember that dead in dreams is not dead in waking life. Your dream warning gives you time to think about the situation, to assess your feelings, and to take action to keep the love flowing during your hours awake.

You Dream That You Are Injured, Are Ill, or Die

WHAT DOES IT mean if you, rather than other persons, are dying in a dream? This variation of the Injury or Death dream was the most common among the first five hundred survey respondents on my website.

Wounded or Killed in an Attack

WHEN YOU DREAM about dying, it's most likely to be part of a Chase or Attack dream. Multitudes of people described dreams about injuries or death sustained in the course of an attack.

If you are a person who wants to classify your Universal Dreams, injuries inflicted by a foe would be considered primarily a Chase or Attack dream, with the motif of Injury or Death. Especially common were dreams of this sort that included being stabbed, like that of the English man who was pierced through the chest by an African warrior's spear or the Estonian woman whose head was cut off with a sword. Other dreamers were shot, like a man from the Czech Republic. Still others were wounded in dreams of being attacked by a supernatural being, like a Canadian woman whose hand was bitten by a vampire. On the whole, if you have this type of dream, you are implying that you have been emotionally hurt or wounded by someone in your environment.

> You are hurt or wounded in a dream attack = Feeling emotionally hurt
> by a waking person

Wounded or Killed in a Fall

YOU MIGHT ALSO dream you get hurt or die as part of a falling dream. Many dreamers do. Such dreams are basically Falling dreams, with the additional motif of Injury or Death. The typical falling dream is simply dropping through space and awakening before impact.

When other dream characters ignore the dreamer's suffering, as they did that of a Canadian woman who fell off a Ferris wheel and slowly died while others stood around laughing, that detail implies indifference to the dreamer's emotional wounds by people in his or her waking environment.

Classic Injury or Death Dreams

YOUR DREAMS THAT are the classic Injury or Death type are those in which

- you are dying of a disease
- you are accidentally injured by an inanimate object
- you suddenly drop dead
- you are accidentally hurt or killed in an accident, by a car or some other object

A Serbian woman dreamed "Mushrooms grew on my feet and palms—it's some disease I got from my grandmother." A Malaysian woman dreamed "I'm just lying there and I think 'My time's up' and I slowly fade away." An American woman dreamed "I had cancer just like my cousin who died of a brain tumor." These women from different parts of the globe were expressing various concerns. When someone you know and care about dies or comes down with a disease, it's natural to react with fear for yourself, especially if you are related. You wonder whether shared genes may cause a similar illness or death.

If, however, you are not reacting to the death or illness of someone you know, you are probably portraying a sense of personal limitation.

You die in a dream = Some waking part of yourself needs attention to survive

---

Ask yourself the following questions:

1. Am I feeling numb or disengaged lately?
2. Do I feel as if some waking situation is "killing" me?
3. Am I engaged in self-destructive behavior?
4. Is there a childish part of me (or some other negative quality) I need to let go?
5. What can I do to restore my vitality? How can I rekindle my enthusiasm?
6. What do I need to change in my waking life to feel fully alive again?

When you dream that you are dying, something is not working well in your life. One young American woman who was a heavy smoker dreamed that she and her sister were looking at X rays taken of their lungs, which looked black. She woke up feeling dreadful and quit smoking. Another woman smoker dreamed of seeing a cube of smoky glass, inside which was a slab with her, dead, a chest X ray hanging over her head. She had not yet stopped smoking when she told me her dream. I hope she listens to its warning.

If you have a dream in which you see yourself injured, dying, or dead, you'll want to consider your behavior, reassess your options, and make changes that are desirable. Find the way to restore the sparkle to your days. Your dreams will respond to your new behavior.

Injured or Killed by an Object or Activity

DISEASE IS NOT the only cause of death in this Universal Dream theme. You may dream of being accidentally injured or killed by some inanimate object, as was the Mexican man who was hit by a car or the American man who was crushed by a train. You might dream of feeling suffocated, as did a woman from Malta, or of being blown away by the wind, as did an American woman, or of collapsing after strenuous effort in a dream, like the American man who expired after saving family members from a burning building.

In these nightmares, the dreamers felt they had no control over what was happening to them. They felt life impinging on them in harmful ways, without fully understanding why they were hurt and how to stop it. If you are troubled by similar dreams, changing your life circumstances may be important; you'll also want to become active in your dream. Get help. Do something to improve the dream situation. You'll be helping your emotional survival.

If you dream of dying after helping others, you'll want to reassess how you are handling what's happening in your waking life. Are you giving too much of yourself? Are you taking unreasonable risks that endanger you in order to assist someone? Are you hazarding your health? Make appropriate changes.

UNDERSTANDING YOUR DREAMS ABOUT INJURY OR ILLNESS

THE PART OF your body that is injured in a dream provides clues to the meaning of your dream. Remember the rat with the golden curls? The dreamer didn't mention where the rat bit her, but it was probably on her hand, perhaps on the ring finger, since at that time she was angry that her boyfriend had not proposed marriage. Ask yourself the following questions:

1. Where in my body is the dream wound or illness located?
2. What is the nature of the illness or injury? What are its symptoms?
3. What is the result of this wound or illness?

Each type of injury or illness has different effects and different implications.

Type of Dream Injury or Disability

IF YOU DREAM about an injury to your leg (and it does not relate to an actual injury), you are apt to be expressing a limitation in your ability to move effectively in life at the time of the dream. For instance, an American woman who dreamed she broke her leg was injured in the part of her body that enables her to move around, to walk, dance, and freely do things in life. Her dream injury lamed her, hobbled her, slowed her down, and hindered her ability to fend for herself. Something in her waking life was making her feel similarly hampered.

If you dream about blind people (when they are not part of your daily life) or of being blind, you are probably unwilling to look at, or see, something in the waking state. Dreams about deaf people (when they are not part of your life) or of being deaf imply some waking situation that you are not listening to. If you dream about wounds in your mouth or things stuck in your teeth, you are apt to feel unable to speak out in anger, or you are leaving some other emotional words unsaid.

Injuries in your arms relate to your ability to do things, to act in the world, to accomplish what you wish. I am right-handed, and, more important, I write with my WRITE-hand. When I dreamed that I had a grandfather clock pressing on my right hand, I recognized the "time pressure" that was weighing down my ability to write. When I dreamed that a horse bit my right hand and clamped down, I got it to release in the dream by putting papaya into its mouth with my left hand. Awake, I understood that I had to use some sweetness (symbolized by the luscious papaya) to get out of a situation that was hindering my ability to write. These dreams made me smile, and I got back to work. An American man who dreamed his arm was paralyzed was having a period of impotency—a situation Freud would have quickly recognized.

Whatever area of your dream body is injured or ill, or that of other characters in your dreams, is related to the meaning of the dream for you. Nonfunctioning or wounded parts of the dream body correspond to some lack of ability at the time of the dream.

Nonfunctional or wounded body part in your dream = Waking reduction of some ability

---

Odd Body Distortions

WHAT DO YOU make of dream changes in your body size, distortions impossible in waking life? An American boy told me that whenever he had a fever, he dreamed he expanded to fill the room. In fact, whenever an area of the physical body is hot or swollen, it is apt to appear in dreams as larger than it actually is, or it may float in the dream. Fever in the body may appear as dream images of fire or sunburn. When you are injured or ill in the waking state, your dreams frequently depict the sensations in the body areas that are experiencing symptoms. Constricted blood flow may appear in dreams as cold or ice touching the body part where the circulation is limited, as it did for a man with restricted circulation in his legs who dreamed about walking barefoot on snow.

You might change size completely in a dream, as did an American boy who shrank so small he got stepped on and squashed flat. This boy was physically well but emotionally had a very "low" ego. He felt in danger of being totally "flattened" in a difficult family situation.

Dream changes in your body's size or shape, in warmth and cold, in getting wounded or ill, speak of changes under way in your emotional state (when they are not associated with changes in physical health). As you understand your dream images better, you will be growing in ability to cope more effectively with the waking life problems these dream pictures represent.

Your Teeth Crumble

YOU ARE ALMOST certain to have dreams about injury to your teeth. Nearly everyone does. The dream is so commonplace I suspect it has a physical origin—perhaps in gritting or grinding teeth during sleep.

Freud suggested that dreams of teeth falling out are related to fears of castration. Perhaps at times this may be so, but women have this dream as often as men do. I suggest, instead, that dreams about trouble with teeth are related to anger, in addition to being prompted by the physical stimulus of the dreamer's clenching his or her teeth. This would make sense on all counts, as people often grit their teeth when they are holding in angry words or emotions. We bare our teeth when we snarl, as do most enraged animals.

Teeth falling out or crumbling in your dream = Probable waking emotions of anger

---

We have already discussed how dreams of being chased or attacked by an animal, or person, or supernatural being with sharp teeth are often connected with cutting and biting words uttered in the waking state. These angry words may originate with the dreamer or be directed toward the dreamer.

When our own teeth disintegrate, they become less effective natural weapons. If you dream about your teeth falling out or crumbling to bits, you may be having trouble expressing anger that you feel. You may also feel you are coming apart or aging. An American woman in one of my workshops composed a haiku based on her dream about tooth trouble that ran, "Gum stuck in mouth, trapped in places not wanted, words left unsaid."

If you suspect that your dream about teeth falling out or crumbling is associated with angry feelings you have, you'll want to find the way (1) to relax your jaw awake or asleep and (2) to give thoughtful voice to any resentments you may be holding in.

Your Dream Baby in Peril

AROUND THE WORLD, babies are a source of pride and anxiety for the parents who strive to clothe, feed, bathe, carry, soothe, and protect these fragile beings. Since they are so important in daily life, babies become a powerful symbol in dreams.

In the last chapter we saw that babies in your dreams often represent your heart's deepest desires. What's going on when your dream baby is forgotten, lost, neglected, hurt, or dying? Such dreams are potent warnings to you.

Your Dream Baby Damaged or Dead

IN THE MOST extreme cases, you may dream that a precious baby is irretrievably injured. Remember, these dreams contain no deliberate villain— any damage is accidental.

If you happen to be pregnant when you have such a dream, the imagery can be particularly distressing. Some pregnant woman, especially first-time mothers-to-be, have anxiety dreams about the coming child. Fortunately, most of these frightening dreams are simple expressions of anxiety. Facing an unfamiliar major life event, we may question our ability to perform well; as we become parents ourselves, any unsolved conflicts with our parents also arise in dream imagery. Alarming dreams are so common among pregnant women and first-time parents that we know they are normal.

One American woman, for instance, who had recently birthed a boy, dreamed she was "holding my son in the shower and dropped him and he shattered." In other alarming dreams she "broke parts of him just by dressing him or changing him." For this new mother, her dream baby was not only her waking-life son, but the entire role of parenthood; she feared that she would fail at being a good mother. It's a concern many new moms and dads share the world over. Their fearful dreams about damaging their newborns express waking concerns as new parents struggle to master baby-tending skills and become adequate parents.

Although this type of first-time parent or parent-to-be dream is common, it can be worrisome. If you have a dream about a baby's being injured or dying, it's important to recall that "dead" in a dream is not dead in waking life, nor even permanently "dead." You or other dream characters can be reborn stronger than ever in dreams. Dream dead can be revived or reborn, the injured given magical potions, the broken and shattered made whole. Rather than being paralyzed by distress in your dream, resolve to take action within it to improve the situation. Remembering to *take action* is important in any nightmare. Our best chance of resolving a dream problem is the same as in the waking state. Do something about it. Enlist allies. Try different solutions.

Meaning of a Dream Baby Shifts over Life Span

"WHERE'S THE BABY?!" This is the agonized cry of numerous dreamers when they realize that a child has disappeared. Like a harassed waking-life parent who has packed all the essential baby equipment in the car, then driven off without the infant—or who has left it on the top of the car— dreamers are devastated to discover that the baby is gone.

Your dream babies are likely to represent different aspects of your life as you age. Their meaning varies because the images are multidimensional, rich, and full of connections. Your best strategy for understanding your dream babies is examining what the baby does in your dream and how you feel about the infant. As your life experience expands, so will the meaning of your dream baby.

I will try to demonstrate this shifting, evolving nature of the dream baby by briefly showing how the image has altered over my fifty-year dream diary. During my teenage years, before I had experienced intercourse, and then after marriage but before I was pregnant, my dreams about babies often referred to actual babies—a strong desire to have one, or a fear that I might be pregnant, depending upon the mood of the moment. Sometimes the dream babies were my more vulnerable self, at risk in some relationship or situation.

Later, after I had given birth to a daughter and was in the process of developing a career, babies more often represented a precious new relationship. When I was subsequently divorced, joyfully remarried, teaching psychology in college, and writing books, dream babies became a clear symbol of my "newborn" projects, offspring of my heart and mind. When they were in danger, so was the new idea or work in progress.

Now, in older years, I find that my dream babies may still carry any of their earlier meanings, but a new symbolism is emerging. Last winter, when my then seventy-nine-year-old husband was stricken with a bad case of influenza, I found myself dreaming frequently about babies in danger. In one such dream, I saw someone backing up a car in a garage. The person came mighty close to hurting a baby, who was sitting as if in a high chair behind the car. I cried out, "Watch the baby!" The car stopped in time, but I wasn't sure the baby was okay. I noticed a hanging skeleton in the garage. This dream cast my ill husband in the fragile role of the endangered baby. The skeleton suggested fear of death dangling nearby.

These husband/baby dreams were not all negative. In one I carried a small baby boy, wrapped in a cashmere blanket, all cozy as he fell asleep. This dream arose when my husband's fever finally began to go down.

In other dreams during this same period, my dream baby continued to be an obvious symbol for my current book project, as it was in the dream I mentioned earlier, in which an Asian woman, a mystically oriented friend, was listening to the heartbeat of an unborn child inside another woman. On the night of the day I had worked on a proposal for this book, I dreamed that a neighbor woman (who was pregnant in waking life) brought a basket of food to share with me. The child in the womb of each of the pregnant women in my dreams was my own growing idea, soon to be born. These dreams and many others of this sort paralleled the good progress, or frustrating struggle, with my project as it developed.

When working on an earlier book, I had a vivid dream about being in a department store when I got on an elevator with a baby carriage; as the lift descended, I looked into the carriage and saw with shock that it was empty. I suddenly remembered I'd left the baby on the sixth floor and hurried back, hoping to find it. This dream came at a time I had ceased intensive work to attend to one of life's inevitable distractions. I recognized the missing baby as my neglected book project but was puzzled at first by the image of the sixth floor—why sixth? When I realized that it was my sixth book I was working on, I laughed.

Sometimes my dream baby poops and makes an awful mess. These dreams are more likely to occur when some particularly "messy" waking life event has occurred.

From this short survey spanning more than fifty years, you can see that a dream baby may represent several different feelings.

A baby in your dream = Possibly your desire to have a waking life baby, or

= (If pregnant) the infant in the womb, your waking hopes and fears about it

= (If pregnant or a parent) your waking feelings about being a parent

= A newly developing precious relationship in waking life

= A newly developing idea or project in waking life

= A loved person in waking life in need of "being babied" at the moment

---

Your life situation will clue you as to the shade of meaning your dream baby depicts. Contemplate the following questions:

1. What did my dream baby look and act like?
2. How do I feel about my dream baby?
3. What does my dream baby need or want?
4. Does my dream baby require special care at this time?

Your Neglected Dream Baby

FORGETTING TO FEED your baby is a special form of the motif of babies in peril. Hungry and starving children in our dreams need immediate care to survive. If you suddenly discover in a dream that a baby has been unfed or uncared for, the discomfort can be intense. If you have this dream, ask yourself the following:

1. Who was responsible for feeding the baby?
2. Who didn't do the job?
3. What's needed to restore the child to health?

A wide range of neglected babies crawl through our dreams. An American woman in her sixties confided, "I awoke to the sound in my head of a baby crying, actually wailing, 'Wah-wah-wah!' I wonder if it is the baby inside me that is crying its head off. Is it unhappy again? Am I not listening to its needs? Have I abandoned her in the crazy busyness of getting Christmas ready?" This dreamer, who takes great pride in making an elaborate festive holiday for her family and friends, felt her dream to be a warning that she was overlooking her inner self, which needs nurturing.

Your forgotten dream babies may represent neglected projects, important and precious goals, lost and mourned. Dreams in which you experience the distress over their absence can activate you, startle you into awareness, and help you to reaffirm your determination, to search for and find your "baby." Forgotten or neglected in a dream is not lost forever. Bring back your wounded dream baby and tend to it. In nourishing your dream child, you are nurturing your future.

Your Dream Pets and Other Animals in Trouble

BABY ANIMALS ARE often stand-ins for human babies in your dreams, just as they are in children's stories. While I was pregnant and planning to nurse the newborn, I dreamed several times, "I see dozens of tiny starving kittens. I wonder desperately how I can feed them." Like human babies, kittens feed on milk. My waking concern about my ability to nurse successfully was no doubt behind the many hungry kittens in my dreams. Somewhat overwhelmed with becoming a mother, I had little confidence in my coping skills. I was grateful to find that these fears were unfounded, and I nursed my newborn daughter with pleasure for her first year.

We saw in the last section that your dreams about neglected babies may symbolize your neglected special projects and activities. Neglected pets play a similar role. The scenario usually goes like this: You become aware that some pet animal, usually one for whom you are responsible, has been neglected, often to a state of near-death. Sometimes the pet is in a cage or otherwise enclosed. The creature is found to be without adequate care, which can take the form of being deprived of water or other liquids, food, air, petting, or affection. You are shocked to discover the situation. The neglected pet may call attention to its dire condition by some means such as flying or flapping about, pleading or whimpering. You then provide or intend to provide the missing item or items and sometimes vow to give constant care in the future.

This motif of the neglected pet is not as common as the dream motif about neglected babies. In a period of about thirteen months, I had only ten neglected pet dreams. They can be, however, extremely powerful and, I believe, sometimes represent deeper issues than the neglected baby dreams, perhaps spiritual ones.

You need to assess what is going on in your current waking state, and what the dream imagery tells you about your area of need. Starving cats can portray concerns about adequate ability to nurse or can express a hunger for sexual interaction. By examining your neglected pet or neglected baby dreams, the wounded and dying who cry out to you, you will better understand your deep needs and be more able to attend to them before they escalate.

WORKING WITH YOUR DREAMS OF INJURY AND DEATH

I SUGGEST YOU begin by giving your dream an action title. By this I mean titling your dream with a phrase that summarizes its essence, including an active verb. Instead of naming a dream about a neglected goldfish that flew near my ear to plead for juice "The Flying Goldfish," "The Starving Goldfish," or some similar title, I chose words that included verbs of action. The name "Neglected Goldfish Flies and Declares Need" helps me remember the dream in more vivid detail. It also identifies the major motif of the dream, a neglected pet, which is more helpful than a simple descriptive title. Some dreamers name their dreams at an interpretive level, using labels like "Bliss" or "Freedom," which do not contain the main image of the dream, nor the action involved. Years later, it's difficult to impossible to recall dreams with vague titles of this type. Here are some steps to help you understand your dreams about neglected pets or babies (also useful for any dream):

1. **Title your dream.** Include (a) the name of the key image, and (b) the main action.
2. **Look for the three main parts in the dream:** (a) the introductory situation, (b) the crisis, and (c) the resolution.
3. **Identify the three parts in the dream.** Draw a line between sections. Not every dream has all three, but many do.
4. **Search for the contrasts in the crisis section.** For instance, in many neglected pet dreams, the following contrasts occur:

Being unaware of need	versus	becoming aware of need
Neglect	versus	providing loving care
Being confined in a cage	versus	being free to move
Being in need, lacking	versus	being nurtured, having abundance
Remaining neglected	versus	calling attention to need
Withholding care	versus	providing missing need
Giving inconsistent care	versus	vowing constant future care

In your dreams about neglected pets or babies, you are telling yourself what part of you needs attention and what kind of attention will fulfill you. By listening to your dreams, you will become more able to provide sustenance to the parts that hunger and thirst for your attention and care. You are both the neglecter and the neglected in these dreams, which can help you become aware, give loving attention, bring back to life, free, provide abundance where needed, and prevent further neglect. Realizing the situation, you can move from a state of deprivation or lack to one of fulfillment.

You are likely to find similar contrasts (between lacking or needing something and being abundantly nurtured) in your other dreams about Injury or Death. Help yourself move from the negative extremes in the left-hand column to the positive, healthier alternatives in the right-hand column. Your dreams of Injury or Death, in their many variations, are messages to yourself. You are expressing

- where you hurt
- why you hurt
- what part of you feels nonfunctional or wounded or neglected

The opposite pole from dreams of Injury or Death are those dreams in which we are Healed, Born, or Reborn. These dreams speak of the reemergence of qualities in you that were formerly inactive.

BEING HEALED, BORN, OR REBORN

2.5 HEALING, BIRTH, OR REBIRTH

Description: You or another character is healed, gives birth, or is reborn in a dream. Activities leading to these events may be depicted. The mood in these positive dreams is always upbeat, even joyful.

Frequency: A relatively rare good dream. It may accompany some new start in your waking life or occur just prior to the onset of a waking-life improvement in health. The good fortune may just happen or may be the result of another dream character's advice or help.

Usual Meanings: "I feel hopeful"; "I feel better"; "I feel renewed"; "Something is stirring to life." When you or another dream character is healed or gives birth, the dream often means "I'm improving" or "Something new [represented by the baby] is born in me." If, in waking life, you are pregnant or have a pregnant spouse, the dream may refer to your hopes for the expected baby. If you are grieving, the birth imagery may refer to hopes for a new life for the deceased loved one.

If you dream about being healed, about giving birth, or about a deceased loved person's being reborn, you'll probably wake up happy. These dreams express a delicious sense of renewal in different realms. Depending upon your circumstances, such dreams may herald a significant improvement in health, give suggestions for improving health, or depict the unfolding of a new and welcome change in your life. Dreams about giving birth or witnessing rebirth may symbolize the reemergence of some element that was formerly part of your life but became inactive until near the time of the dream.

UNDERSTANDING YOUR DREAMS ABOUT BEING HEALED

YOUR DREAMS ABOUT Being Healed are at the polar opposite of dreams about Being Injured, Ill, or Dying. They signal a change for the better. If you are currently experiencing some physical malaise, have an illness, or are convalescing from an injury, dreams about being healed are reflective of what is happening in your body. If you are bereaved, dreams about being healed may be part of your recovery from the loss of a loved person. If you are well, and not grieving, any dreams you have about being healed are apt to be expressions of an emotional healing currently taking place in your life.

I have said that injuries and disabilities in your dreams often represent emotional wounds or waking limitations you are feeling at the time of the dream. Dreams about being healed refer to emotional repairs or to the restoration of abilities.

Being healed in your dream = Restoration of a waking ability or emotional repair

Your personal experiences with ill health, sickness, operations, accidents, and recuperation, as well as the health of your loved ones, will influence your dreams about being healed. Of course, your health-related activities and interests, as well as your hopes and fears for future health, will also have an impact on your dreams.

As with all Universal Dreams, your cultural beliefs influence your dream content. If your culture accepts that healing is possible and that it may come in a dream, you will be more receptive to such experiences. In ancient Greece, temples built to the healing god Asklepios were sanctuaries that were the goal of pilgrimages. There, amid the natural beauty of these temple settings, after purification baths and rituals, pilgrims prayed for healing dreams. They slept in special dormitories, where they anticipated a visit from the god in their dreams. Many people believed that they received immediate healing for their woes or were given advice that led to their healing in the dreams they had while they slept in the incubation dormitories. Stone tablets, *stelae,* attest to these dreams, citing the pilgrim's problem and the cure received in the dream.

You may live in a part of the world where beliefs of this sort still exist. Several "dream incubation" temples remain operative in far-flung locations. There are said to be an active dream-incubation temple in Taiwan and others operating in Eastern Europe. If you are part of a culture, subculture, or religious group that accepts these possibilities, you are more likely to have such dreams yourself.

Even dreamers who do not have these backgrounds report experiences of profound healing that occur during a dream. In recovering from surgery on a badly broken wrist that was misdiagnosed as sprained, and had to be rebroken and reset with a plate and pins to restore use, I noticed how my dreams paralleled the stages of my mending. Often a restored ability would surface in my dreams just prior to the recovery of the same ability in the waking state. For instance, during the nine months of physical therapy that were necessary to regain use of my arm, I dreamed one night that I was doing a fluid tai chi movement in which I reversed my position (my stance). In the same dream, I was suddenly able to scratch the middle of my back with my injured arm—a movement impossible in the waking state at that time. Yet, within the next day or two after the dream I was easily able to perform the previously impossible movement. I had, in fact, "reversed my position" from serious limitation of movement with my injured arm to greatly expanded range and ability to move.

As I studied the dreams of various men and women who had been injured or become ill, along with scrutinizing my own dreams as I recovered my health, I discovered that dreams during healing share several elements. When a person is physically damaged, dreams picture wounded and dying animals, destroyed plant life, disintegrating buildings, and other images of destruction. As a person begins to heal, the opposite type of imagery emerges: dreams contain healthy and vigorous people, often playful children and newborn babies, blossoming trees and plants, newly constructed or remodeled buildings, new clothing, and new cars. The contrasts in dream content are dramatic.

Human beings have an impulse toward healthy well-being, one that is active in our dreams. We need to listen to it. You can help stimulate this inner healer by imaginative exercises prior to falling asleep. Consider the following questions:

1. What does my ideal healer look like? Act like? Sound like? Picture him or her in vivid detail.
2. What advice might he or she be likely to offer?
3. Is this rational counsel? If so, how can I implement it? If not, wait for better advice.

Endless numbers of dreamers have confided to me their dreams of meeting a physician or healer or religious figure who told them what to eat, drink, or put on their bodies to help themselves heal. Do people make actual contacts with a healing presence? Or do we shape our own intuitions into the form of advice from a traditional healer in a dream? Whatever the source, we sometimes dream a connection with a healing power that can turn around poor health and lead to renewed vigor. Of course, you must use common sense when awake, but you may find that the "inner healer" is able to provide a suggestion or solution to restore the gift of vibrant good health. If you have such a dream, consider the advice carefully.

Dreams that urge us to undertake activities or renew them may be the very thing we need to spur our behavior in the right direction. One American woman dreamed "If I don't dance, I will die." She decided it was a good idea to get back to the rhythmic movements that had given her pleasure in former years. If you receive advice of this sort in a dream on any topic that was a past interest, or one that you suspect would be good for you, listen to it.

If you dream that you encounter a curative figure—physician, surgeon, nurse—who offers suggestions, you may want to follow them if they make sense in the waking state and will cause no harm to you or others. You may even have the extremely rare dream that a religious figure blesses you or cures you; those who have had such dreams felt their lives were changed thereafter.

UNDERSTANDING YOUR DREAMS ABOUT GIVING BIRTH

WHEN YOU DREAM that you or another dream character gives birth, examine your life for the newly emerging thing just born by asking yourself the following questions:

1. What's new in my life?
2. Who or what has come into being or is coming into being in my world?
3. How can I welcome and nourish this newborn part of me?

I have said that dreams about accidental death represent a waking aspect of the dreamer that has become inactive. Dreams about giving birth stand for some aspect of the dreamer that becomes active again.

> Giving birth in your dream = The awakening, or reawakening, of part of you

Birth-giving dreams may be straightforward and readily understandable. In an earlier section, we saw that a newborn baby in your dream may have many meanings, such as portraying a newly developed project. Dreams about giving birth may be "pregnant" with mysterious elements that take years to untangle, as with a dream of mine about a queen who birthed twins, a girl and a boy sheathed in cauls that had to be torn off quickly so the infants could breathe.

Of course, if you or someone close to you is pregnant, your emotional involvement with the baby—your hopeful expectations or fearful worries—affects your dreams about childbirth. Pregnant dreamers, particularly in the third trimester, are undergoing mild contractions of the womb, called Braxton-Hicks contractions, that are a sort of exercise or preparation of the womb for the hard work of "labor" it will soon be performing. These mild contractions occur during sleep and dreams, as well as during the daytime. The pregnant woman's dreaming mind senses these physical contractions and often incorporates them into dreams about giving birth. Such dreams are not always pleasant, but they are always helpful in terms of preparing the pregnant woman for the forthcoming delivery, and some studies have shown that anxiety dreams about childbirth may lead to shorter and easier labor. Blissful dreams about childbirth are among the pregnant woman's delightful memories.

UNDERSTANDING YOUR DREAMS ABOUT REBIRTH

YOUR CULTURAL beliefs about the possibility of reincarnation will influence your dreams about the topic. Rebirth dreams are fairly rare in the American culture, yet when I made a local study of the dreams of grieving men and women, I was surprised to find several reincarnation dreams. A similar study in India would yield even more dreams of this type because belief in reincarnation is widespread there. In the final chapter, you will find several examples of rebirth dreams.

On one level, if you dream about rebirth, you may be dreaming about your hopes for a deceased loved one. You may also be hoping for your own "rebirth."

Someone is reborn in your dream = Waking hope for renewed life for loved one or self

---

Dreamers who are bereaved often dream about the person who has died. Depending upon the nature of the death, and the quality of the relationship between the deceased and the dreamer, dreams about the person who died can be agonizing or uplifting. Some grieving people who dream about the deceased's being reborn count these dreams as precious, hope-filled messages.

If you dream about someone's being reborn, ruminate on the following questions:

1. What is being renewed in my life lately?
2. What was absent for a long time but has now reemerged?
3. How can I best support this reborn part of me?

Remember that to be reborn is to be renewed.

Dreams about Being Healed, Giving Birth, or Being Reborn are ones that can be true gifts. As you learn to unwrap these gift-dreams and cherish their contents, you'll be opening yourself to new possibilities.

3

Car or Other Vehicular Trouble

Versus Pleasure

3.0 CAR OR OTHER VEHICULAR TROUBLE

Description: You dream of being in or near a car or other vehicle that is out of control or has some other problem. Circumstances vary: no brakes, a steering wheel that won't work, low gas, going off the road, over a cliff, through a red light, crashing, and so on. You may be in the driver's seat, the passenger's seat, or the back seat. Vehicles vary: you may be at the control panel of an airplane, pedaling a bicycle, on a leaking ship, or on some other transport with problems. You may or may not try to regain control.

Frequency: A common nightmare among all people and ages, whether or not the dreamer actually drives. May occur frequently. Usually arises when the dreamer feels that events in waking life are under poor control.

Usual Meanings: "I've got no control" (no brakes, hard to steer); "I feel powerless, no energy" (low or no gas, motor cuts off); "I can't go forward" (obstacles on road); "I may collapse" (about to crash, go over the edge of cliff).

Throughout the centuries, people have harnessed animal strength to help them pull and push heavy objects: pack asses, elephants, reindeer, camels, oxen, and so on. People traveled from place to place on horseback or in carriages or carts pulled by horses. These "horse-powered vehicles," or the horse itself, were often topics for yesterday's dreamers. In fact, the automobile was first called the "horseless carriage," and the train "the iron horse."

Tomorrow's conveyances may make our cars seem as old-fashioned as a buggy with a fringe on top. We may be jetting to other planets in spaceships or going to work with personal-sized strap-on nuclear-powered wings.

Today, dreamers often picture themselves having difficulty with their cars. Even children too young to drive and people who do not drive at all dream they are driving out-of-control vehicles in their nightmares. They also have difficulties with an aircraft they are flying, or they are on ships with hulls ripped open by rocks. At times they dream of riding a bicycle that gets a flat tire, or of being on a bus that arrives at a road block, or of being in a train that derails. Nearly 40 percent of website respondents had it.

What is going on? Tonight if you dream of recklessly careening in a car without brakes, you are sharing the dream road with sleepers in France, China, Saudi Arabia, and anywhere else that men and women wrestle with the issue of control in their waking lives.

INFLUENCES ON YOUR DREAMS ABOUT CAR OR OTHER VEHICULAR TROUBLE

1. *Biological*

ALTHOUGH WE ARE not biologically programmed to drive or to travel, as humans we are hard-wired to protect our lives. When we begin to feel that events are out of control, our survival instincts kick in. We try to regain some power over what is happening in our lives, in efforts that often show up in dreams about out-of-control vehicles.

As humans we are also genetically inclined to explore, to try different things, to move around, to experiment—it's what makes us able to solve problems.

2, 3. *Cultural and Subcultural*

WHAT ARE THE vehicles available in your life space? Do you ride camels or horses on a daily basis? Are there tanks and military vehicles in your environment? Do you often travel by subway or bus? Are semitrailers and tractors part of your waking life? Whatever types of transport surround you, the ones you operate or ride in are the ones most likely to appear in your dreams. What sort of conditions exist in the use of these vehicles? Are the trains overcrowded and unsafe, or are they swift, clean, and carefully regulated? The normal conditions of the transportation systems in your environment influence how they appear in your dreams—as usual or oddly altered.

Is your country at war or undergoing attack? Are you coping with a natural disaster? Whatever general situation you are facing in your life space at the time shapes your dreams about level of control. People often have nightmares about devastation when it is part of their daily experience at the moment. All nightmares, including those about trouble with vehicles, are attempts to cope.

4. Personal

WHEN YOU FIND yourself in a situation in which you have little or no ability to affect what is happening, you are likely to dream about vehicle trouble. If you are physically ill, if you have been badly injured, or if your loved ones are experiencing severe stress, you may dream of damaged vehicles. It is when things seem to be coming apart, when we are under extreme tension for any reason—mental or physical—that we are most troubled by nightmares about reckless driving, crashes, or other difficulties with vehicles.

In addition, your personal history regarding cars or other vehicles is relevant. What cars have you owned in the past? What did your parents drive? Your friends? How do you feel about large cars? Sports cars? Luxury cars? Old jalopies? My sixty-year-old brother recently acquired an old blue Chrysler convertible that filled him with pleasure, an emotion carried over from happy teenage days of tinkering with old junkers for hours after school. Although he already owns two family sedans and two motorcycles, none gives him the lighthearted joyful lift of that convertible. Your experiences with cars and other conveyances, your attitudes and ideas about them, any past accidents you've had, or serious injuries resulting from them will find their way into your dreams.

UNDERSTANDING YOUR DREAMS
ABOUT VEHICULAR TROUBLE

YOUR DREAMS ABOUT Vehicular Trouble are apt to fall into one of the following six variations:

- Car Trouble
- Truck or Other Large Land Vehicle Trouble
- Bicycle or Other Small Land Vehicle Trouble
- Trains, Buses, Subways, or Other Public Land Transport
- Airplane or Other Flying Vehicle Trouble
- Ship or Other Water Vehicle Trouble

Because these variations have many features in common, we'll look at Car Trouble in most detail. Then we'll see how the variations differ from it.

Car Trouble

WHEN YOU get into a car you have a purpose: going somewhere and doing something. Because cars have become a routine and seemingly essential part of daily life in modern society, they play a significant role in our dream lives as well. You may dream you are simply driving a car, riding in one, or parking it as part of your natural activities; dreams in which a car is merely mentioned as part of ongoing events are emotionally "neutral" and cause no problem.

Driving a dream car has become a metaphor for how things are "moving along" in our waking state. Thus, when things are going well, when we are traversing our life space with special ease or accomplishment, we may dream about driving smoothly and skillfully. It's when things are going badly in the waking state that we are apt to dream about a car in crisis.

Your Dream Car as a Metaphor for Your Body

THE WORD AUTOMOBILE derives from the Greek word *autos*, meaning "self," and the Latin word *mobilis*, meaning "movable." Automobiles are self-moving, in a way that makes them ready metaphors for our self-propelled bodies. Like organic bodies, autos require an energy input of fuel and have a residual output of exhaust, processes that parallel our functions of eating food and excreting waste. Like bodies, cars require maintenance to function well; they may break down or have an accident; go too fast, too slow, or just right.

When you dream about a car, you are emphasizing the degree of control you feel you have over your body and its movement through your life space at the moment. Here are some common correspondences between cars in dreams and the dreamer's body:

Automobile Part	Body Part or Function
Body (outer shell)	Body surface, skin
Steering wheel	Degree of control, mind-set
Brakes	Ability to control activity level
Headlights	Eyes
Windshield, rearview mirror	Ability to see ahead, what's coming up
Horn	Voice
Fuel	Energy level
Engine, concealed parts	Inner organs
Tires or wheels	Legs, mobility

In dreams, you use many metaphors to portray how you feel about your body and what is happening to you in waking life. A vehicle, a building, an animal, a tree, a garment, and a machine are common metaphors expressing your body's condition, its functioning, or your emotions about it. Each dream image pictures exactly what is important for you at the moment, while downplaying other aspects of the image. The type of car trouble that arises in your dream relates to the problem that exists for you in the waking state.

I studied one hundred dreams that mentioned cars from an eighteen-month period of my dream journal, assigning them to one of three categories (Car Trouble, Car Mention, or Car Pleasure). I found that 70 percent of these dreams involved a problem with a car (e.g., "I nearly collide with a crashing car"); 27 percent of them contained neutral mentions of a car (e.g., "I park my car"); and in 3 percent of the dreams I had positive experiences with a car (e.g., "I drive downtown a new way, impressing my husband").

I also carefully coded the surveys submitted by five hundred visitors to my website that included dreams of car trouble, as well as dreams from direct interviews with various men and women. My analysis of these sets of dreams yielded nine clusters of problems. By far the most common Car Trouble motif worldwide is that of having no brakes or poor ones. You've probably had that bad dream at least once.

"Help! The Brakes Are Gone!": Diminished Control

IF YOU DREAM about driving a car and suddenly find that the brakes are gone, you are likely to feel frightened and agitated. Anyone who has had the experience in waking life—as I once had as a passenger—knows how terrifying the situation can be. Hurtling down a freeway, looking for an exit ramp, trying to avoid crashing into others, blowing the horn in warning, and searching for a place to slow the car to a stop without causing severe damage are alarming experiences. Even without having experienced loss of brakes while awake, people the world over dream about its happening to them. Why?

Whenever we lose command over something that is usually responsive to our authority, we feel stressed. In a car, the brakes are the major means of applying control. We can regulate our speed and bring the car to a stop with them. When we lose our dream brakes, we have lost control over some situation in our waking life.

Lost brakes in your dream = Reduced control in waking life area

If you find yourself "going too fast" in the waking state, perhaps working too hard, pushing yourself to complete a project, trying to take care of too many things before a deadline or to handle a family crisis, you may dream of driving recklessly and losing your brakes. Such a dream warns you to slow down, to be more careful, so you don't risk "crashing." It is when we are under most stress that we are, in fact, most likely to have accidents of any kind. We need to reassert our hold on the direction and destination to which we want to go, to keep our speed under check, to "put the brakes on" before we get into serious trouble and make matters worse.

If you dream of losing the brakes on your car, two courses of action are advisable. It won't hurt to be sure the brakes on your actual car, if you have one, are sound. Dreams are sometimes warnings about actual waking life situations, ones that we may have dimly noticed while awake, that reemerge in dramatic action during the dream state. The greater probability is that your dream is symbolic. In that case it's important to recognize that, regardless of the situation you find yourself in, you will not improve it by collapsing. Take some deep breaths, slow down, and reassess.

"The Steering Wheel Came Off!": Decreased Ability to Direct

BESIDES LOSING THE brakes on your dream car, you may lose control in other ways. Have you ever had trouble with the steering wheel of your dream car? This, too, is a common motif.

Like brakes, steering wheels are a major control on actual cars. With them, we steer ourselves in the direction we wish to go; we make turns right or left or completely around. If your steering wheel is not working, you are like a ship without a rudder; you can only drift at the mercy of fate.

> Loss of your steering wheel in dream = Decreased ability to direct waking life situation

The motif of a broken steering mechanism may occur in a dream of any vehicle that has a means to steer it by direct control of the driver, as it did for the young Latin-American man who dreamed he was riding his bicycle when he realized there were no handlebars.

If you lose the steering wheel to your dream car, the handlebars to your dream bicycle, or the helm to your dream yacht, it's time to pay attention to how you are trying to handle a waking life situation. You need to reconsider your direction and take better charge of your means of getting there.

"Someone Else Is Driving the Car": Reduced Control

ANOTHER WAY YOUR dreaming mind may express a sense of loss of control over your life is by picturing someone else at the steering wheel. The dream driver may be a person known to you, a total stranger, or an imaginary character. This motif occurs when you feel that someone else or some other aspect of you is directing your life at the moment. Who or what is it? Ask yourself the following questions:

1. Who is at the steering wheel of my dream car?
2. What kind of person is the driver?
3. How would you describe him or her in a phrase or brief sentence?
4. Where are you seated in the car? Passenger seat? Backseat? Rumble seat?

Your answers to these questions will tell you what quality seems to be "driving" you at the moment. An American woman of middle years dreamed that a five-year-old girl she knew was driving her car. When she asked herself these questions, her answer included the comment "She's the ultimate spoiled child." Amused, she realized that recently she had been acting in a childish way regarding a waking life situation. Understanding that she felt the "spoiled child" part of her was in charge at the moment, she was able to alter her behavior accordingly.

When I once dreamed that a strange male, "an Italian," was at the steering wheel of my dream car, I was puzzled at first. Describing an Italian to myself, I thought of the housekeeper I had newly hired who was Italian and incredibly strong. She was able, in the course of a few hours, to make pasta from scratch; clean the entire house; wash, fold, and put away the laundry; and have freshly cooked lasagna with the rest of dinner on the table by evening. The impression she gave me of hardiness and capability cast her compatriot into the role of a strong driver in my dream. A strong sexual drive of my own was operating at the time.

Remember, it's *your* associations to the dream driver that determine the meaning of the dream. When I used this example of the Italian man at the steering wheel in a dream workshop, participants guessed that the dreamer was "probably dieting because Italian food is fattening," "probably involved in some shady activity because Italians are associated with the Mafia," or "might be in a passionate love affair because Italian men are very sexy." These suggestions, of course, are what the imagery would have meant for the participants if it had been their dream.

On the occasion that I traveled to London with my then-fourteen-year-old daughter to find a flat for our family before my husband joined us two weeks later, I slept in the same room with her for the first time since she was a baby. Our days were filled with frustrating—and mostly futile—searches for a good place to live. It was a miserably cold, rainy mid-April, and my lack of familiarity with the city and customs made our task more difficult. One night I awoke to my sleeping daughter's cry, "I can't even say it— Folly!" she shouted. Over tea and crumpets in the morning I asked what she was dreaming last night. She relayed a tale of being in a crashing car with a crazy woman at the steering wheel. I didn't need to be a dream psychologist to recognize that I was the "crazy driver" who had taken her to a strange country where she felt life was totally out of her control.

Person at steering wheel in your dream = Quality of self (or other person) in control at the time

---

Another American woman's daughter put a "witch" at the wheel of her dream car. In this case, her mother had recently become furious at the nurses in the hospital where the girl was being treated for pneumonia. In the child's eyes, her mother had turned into a witch.

When someone else is in charge of your dream car, he or she is usually not doing things the way you wish. I have rarely encountered an automobile dream in which a driver who is not the dreamer is doing a great job driving, and the dreamer is content to let the other person take control.

If you dream that someone else is driving your dream car, determine what that person represents for you by answering the previous questions, then consider, Who or what would I prefer to have at my dream steering wheel? Think about how you can put a more appropriate part of yourself back in authority. Perhaps you would be better off to seat yourself at the steering wheel. When you drive your own dream car, you are in far greater control of your destiny.

"I'm in a Dangerous Location": Surrounded by a Threatening Situation

DREAMS ABOUT TROUBLE with your car often begin in a risky or borderline place, such as driving in or near woods, along the edge of a cliff, or in or near a perilous part of a city. When you find yourself in a risky environment in a dream, you are apt to feel that something about your waking life space—your "environment"—makes you uneasy.

> Your dream car is in a dangerous area = Current life situation feels threatening

Driving in a risky area may be complicated by being in bad weather conditions or in increasing dark. "I'm at an intersection in a woodsy area at night," began the dream of a middle-aged American woman. Although no problem had yet arisen, this initial situation conveyed an atmosphere of impending malice, which occurred later in her dream.

"The Road Is Dangerous": Complications on Life's Path

SOMETIMES RAIN CAUSES slippery dream roads, makes the road muddy, full of puddles, or gorged with ruts. Slick or wet, icy roads are hazardous in waking life and seem to become more so during dreams. Rain, snow, or fog may obscure vision while you are driving your dream car. "Whenever I drive in dreams my vision gets strange. It's as if there's a terrible fog blocking my sight," said a young American woman.

The condition of your dream road may be dangerous without weather problems, as it is for many dreamers struggling with curvy, twisty dream roads or going steeply uphill or downhill. You may find your way blocked by obstacles or other hazards, such as huge tires obstructing the road or a stoplight knocked down. Other vehicles may create a hazard for you, such as heavy traffic on a freeway that comes too close to your car or other cars that crash, burn, or explode as you drive along. Although you are doing nothing wrong, your well-being seems at risk from the chaos around you.

> Bad condition of your dream road = You feel waking environment is a problem

An American woman in her sixties described a dream about driving along a castlelike fort on the left (near where she used to live, an actual castle that once was a college but had been converted into apartments). The road itself was fourteen miles of elevated rock with a sheer drop on the right, hardly wide enough for her car. The left wheel was off the road. She realized how easy it would be to run off the road on the right and drop into space. "I must be careful," she told herself as she awoke.

If you dream about being near a dangerous drop-off, or negotiating a narrow passage, or driving on treacherous mountain roads that twist and turn, or trying to see your way through blinding rain, or being pelted with snow, or cruising down gloomy, unsafe city streets, you'll want to give yourself the same warning—be careful! You're on dangerous turf.

"My Car Will Hardly Move!": Reduced Energy Level

SO FAR, THE Car Trouble situations that have been described involve the dream car in movement—going too fast, having poor control, driving in dangerous areas, in poor weather or road conditions. But many problems with dream cars arise when the car is barely moving or is at a full stop, as they did for a woman who was parked on the wrong side of the road and was struck head-on by a truck.

The speed of your dream car may be too slow, instead of too fast, for your safety or purpose. You may find your car stuck in a park mode when you want it to go. The car's motor may shut off just when you intend to drive forward. Your car may barely creep when you rev the engine, or it may simply coast.

If you dream that your car battery dies, or that you are low on fuel, or out of it, or in any of the "too slow" situations, the problem the dream represents is apt to be with your waking energy level. When dreamers seem to have little or no power in their dream cars there is some constriction in available energy.

One young American woman said her dream car sometimes reverts to a "Flintstones" car, which she has to operate by running. Old-fashioned "leg power" is helpful but doesn't provide much oomph for operating a car, awake or asleep.

Low power in dream car = Diminished energy in waking life

A dream car that is in "idle" may have two different meanings. The car may be in idle because you don't feel any zip in your waking life; you may be at a low physical ebb and need to renew resources before being able to continue your journey through life. In this case, paying attention to your health and building it up is a wise route to take.

On the other hand, you may simply be "idle," not because you lack the energy required to operate, but because your interest in a project or other activity is not sufficient to stimulate you to act. In this case, you need to reassess whether or not you want to continue to follow this road. If you do, get to work! Leaving cars in idle—dream cars or actual cars—puts you at risk of having your car stolen by someone else. If you have lost interest in a project and, after considering the situation, decide you don't want to go on with it, turn off the motor, study the map, and pick a different route.

"I Hate This Kind of Car!": Attitudes

YOUR DREAM CAR may work properly; the road conditions, weather, and location be satisfactory, but you may dislike the vehicle itself. Certain models or brands of cars are totally unacceptable to some people. An older woman of my acquaintance would not under any circumstances drive a sedan. "They're too stuffy," says this woman in her late seventies; only a coupe provides the sense of freedom and fashion she requires. Her husband, in his early eighties, will drive nothing but a Cadillac; he wants a spacious interior. Other dreamers I have interviewed despise this brand of car, and when they dream of driving a "big, American gas-guzzling car like my mother used to drive," they are expressing distaste for more than a car. One dreamer's luxury car is another dreamer's inefficient gas hog.

Of course, it is *your* associations, and even your attitudes toward the environment, that define the role a particular type of car plays in your dreams. Ask yourself the following:

1. What model of car appeared in my dream? (sedan, coupe, convertible, other)
2. What make of car was it? (Domestic? Foreign? Specify the brand.)
3. What's special about this model and this brand? (snappy, good brakes, ugly, and so on)
4. What do I like or dislike about it? (sporty, fun, hard to park, guzzles gas, other)
5. How do I feel driving such a car? (awkward, snobby, carefree, other)
6. Is there any pun involved in the name of the car?

Always stay alert for possible puns in your dream images. I have had dreamers describe driving a Volvo, then tell me they always thought the name sounded like *vulva*, suggesting a sexual association for these people when driving such a car in a dream. Many people, of course, may drive a Volvo daily without such a connection, saying it's the safest car on the road. When car manufacturers name their products, they try to stimulate positive associations, such as giving them names of powerful animals, like Jaguar.

Model and brand of your dream car = Your waking life attitudes and emotions

---

"My Car's in Terrible Shape!": Reduced Physical Health

REGARDLESS OF the style or brand of your dream car, a problem may exist with its condition. You may find yourself having to drive a car that is too old or decrepit for your needs. Parts may be missing or broken, or the vehicle may be entirely dilapidated.

If driving a dream car is a metaphor for how you are moving through life, the car's condition is a metaphor for the state of your body. An automobile in run-down or deteriorated condition in your dream is a vivid declaration of your run-down or deteriorated physical or emotional state. One website participant reported a dream that his car's radiator overheated and exploded after he had lost his temper in the waking state.

Condition of your dream car = You feel your body (or that of a loved one) is in a similar condition

---

Your dream most often refers to your own physical or emotional condition, but it may sometimes express how you perceive the condition of a loved person. When my then-seventy-nine-year-old husband had severe influenza one winter and was struggling to regain his health, I dreamed of various old cars in bad shape. One had been "a great little car that was too worn-out to repair." It's important to remember that dream images tell us how we feel emotionally *at the time of the dream*. They do not depict a static or unchanging state of affairs. My husband recovered, but I have learned to feel uneasy when that old, beat-up car occasionally drives through my dreams.

Another elderly American man, the one who prefers to drive a Cadillac, told me a dream about a dilapidated Cadillac in a used car lot. The back window was cracked and the vehicle was confined to running back and forth on tracks. He didn't want the car in this shape. A formerly active man, a vigorous tennis player and competitive swimmer, he had undergone a hip replacement just prior to dreaming that his favorite car was severely restricted by being limited to tracks, confined with other "used cars" that were ready for the junk heap.

You don't need to be elderly to dream of cars in bad shape: any temporary physical impairment may emerge in the form of damage to an auto or of some impediment caused by the shape or size of the vehicle.

"This Car Is Too Big to Drive!": Increased Body Size

WHEN I WAS pregnant, I dreamed of driving a car and at the same time carrying the spare tire around my waist. Awake, I found it obvious that the "spare tire" was my expanding midsection. My movement through life at the time of the dream felt exceedingly clumsy.

Pregnant woman often picture themselves in dreams driving trucks, buses, or other vehicles that are more difficult to maneuver than cars; these images of bulky vehicles reflect their current sense of awkward movement. Such dreams begin early in pregnancy and may continue throughout the term.

Without being pregnant, women who have gained weight describe a similar kind of dream imagery. "I was driving a wide-bodied truck," said one middle-aged American woman who had never driven a truck; she had, however, recently put on some excess poundage. When you dream about being at the steering wheel of a big conveyance (unless you usually drive a large vehicle), you are apt to be expressing some difficulty maneuvering your body in the waking state.

Driving a bulky vehicle in your dream = Waking feeling of awkward movement

---

If you find yourself having trouble driving because your vehicle is hard to manage, consider whether you need to trim down your waking body. If you're pregnant, the natural course of events may take care of this situation. If you're coping with a waking life situation that makes movement awkward—a broken leg, a hip replacement, or some other condition that hampers you—dreams of driving awkward vehicles are natural, until you return to your usual level of functioning.

Occasionally dreamers say they are in vehicles that are too small and crowded. If you have such a dream, consider whether you feel that you have too little space in some area of waking life. Contemplate these questions:

1. In what part of life am I unable to work properly?
2. In what way do I feel hampered?
3. How can I open things up and move more freely?

"Where Do I Turn?": Trouble with the Route

PERHAPS YOUR CAR Trouble is not the car's condition or operation, or the state of the road, but rather a problem en route. Many dreamers find themselves at a crossroads, an intersection, or a fork, not knowing which path to choose. A middle-aged American woman who dreamed of being at an intersection in a woodsy area noticed a traffic light had been knocked down at the side of the road. In the other direction was a stopped car full of officers, perhaps navy or army men, who were also unsure what to do. The broken stoplight was still green, but traffic was at a standstill.

Dreams of being at a crossroads tend to occur when the dreamer is contemplating choices in waking life and is unsure of which direction to take. If you experience such a dream, it's important to make a choice. Don't simply "stand still." Decide; move ahead.

Being at a crossroads in your dream = Contemplating waking life choice

---

Sometimes dreamers see themselves taking a wrong turn or missing a turn; they might even travel in the wrong direction altogether or have to back up when they want to go forward. A Malaysian teenager reported, "My car is going backward," as did many dreamers who slid downhill. Like Sisyphus, who was condemned in Hades to push a rock to the top of a hill only to have it slide back down, they find their efforts to make progress are futile.

Each car problem corresponds to something in your daily life. If you dream of missing a turn, notice what situation you have not paid adequate attention to; if you dream of taking a wrong turn, you'll probably be able to identify where you went astray while awake. Do you dream of reaching a "dead end," "going off the end of a pier," as one American man did, or over a cliff? You're probably feeling unable to proceed safely in some waking situation.

Confusions over the route you are traveling in a dream indicate uncertainty about waking methods you are using to reach your goal, perhaps a feeling that you've made a mistake. You may dream of being unable to link with the road you want, or of having inadequate or misleading directions, or of getting an incomplete or erroneous map. Perhaps the dream route you are traveling is exceedingly complicated, with difficult or impossible connections. In such cases, reexamine your plans. Your dream suggests something is missing from what you need to know.

> Confusion with dream route = Unclear plans and methods in a waking
> activity

Rethink where you want to go, and how you need to proceed to get what you want in waking life.

"Someone Is Attacking My Car": Someone Else Causes Problem

YOUR DIFFICULTY WITH a dream car may be an attack by people or animals outside or inside the vehicle. If people try to steal your dream car or damage it with sticks or other weapons, the imagery suggests a different meaning from problems that emerge from your own actions.

Your dream road may be obstructed by men and women who block it. You may dream an animal suddenly enters your car and distracts you, as did a middle-aged American woman when a peacock flew into her open car window and tapped on her sunglasses. Your passage may be impeded by a collision with an animal or person outside the car, or the problem caused by other people may be subtler, such as a passenger who criticizes your driving or the route you take.

> People or animals make problem in your dream = You feel others cause
> waking problem

In these dream cases, you are apt to feel that it is others, rather than you, who is responsible for difficulties in waking life. Indeed, the feeling may be accurate. We can always, however, find some way to negotiate our life path better. The middle-aged American woman who dreamed that her road was blocked by two huge tires got out of the car to examine the situation. Up close, she could see that there was still room to maneuver around the obstacles, even though her way looked totally blocked from the car. Awake, she recognized that the "tires" she thought were obstructing her way represented two large "rounds" of house guests that had "tired" her. Her dream clearly said that she had more room to move than she thought and that she could proceed.

"I Can't See!": Reduced Clarity

I HAVE ALREADY mentioned that the driver's vision may be impaired by bad weather and road conditions, such as fog shrouding the rearview mirrors, rainwater, or snow clouding the windshield. People report that at times they simply can't see well in dreams about driving vehicles. In addition, dream drivers sometimes find their vision obscured by material hanging over the windshield or some other odd hindrance. These dreams suggest lack of clarity about some waking life situation.

Obscured vision in your dream = Trouble seeing waking situation clearly

---

Occasionally, you may be attempting to drive from a weird position, such as lying down, or trying to steer from the backseat. Or the driver, you or someone else, may have an abnormal condition, like being sick, drunk, crazy, or unbearably sleepy. When you dream of being in a particularly clumsy or hazardous driving position, you can be sure that you are trying to do things in the waking world from an awkward angle.

Bicycle Trouble (or Other Small Land Vehicle Trouble)

BICYCLES, TRICYCLES, WHEELBARROWS, carts, wagons, skateboards, and other such conveyances have problems that are mainly connected with their wheels and being vulnerable to puncture, damage, breakage, and so forth. They share problems with dreams of Car Trouble when they have mechanisms to steer the vehicle, as happened with the young Latin-American who lost the handlebars to his bike, or when the vehicles are equipped with brakes that can fail.

Difficulties with the terrain apply equally to bicycles and cars, as they did for a young Italian woman who dreamed of riding along a narrow mountain road when her bicycle slipped from under her and she rolled to the bottom of a ravine, where she lay badly hurt.

The major difference between Bicycle Trouble dreams and those of Car Trouble is that the bicycle is under more direct control of the operator. It is the dreamer's own power that moves the vehicle forward, or a sense of loss of power that contributes to problems. These small land vehicles go more slowly and require more physical effort than motorized ones.

If you dream about problems with a bicycle, your dream is likely to involve a large investment of personal effort (even if bike riding is part of your daily life), but you may also find that you have greater control over the outcome of any problem that arises than you have with a car.

Small motorized land vehicles, such as motorcycles, share the majority of problems in dreams with those of cars. Additionally, the dreamer has less protection on a motorcycle than in a car and therefore may feel more vulnerable at high speed. At the same time, the driver of a motorcycle may feel an increased ability to squeeze through small spaces and to be more flexible in response to adversity. As always, it's *your* associations to the vehicle that will determine the ultimate meaning of the dream.

If you dream of operating a small land vehicle, determine the nature of the problem that occurs, look up the corresponding motif under Car Trouble in Appendix B, and make adjustments according to your associations to, and emotions about, the vehicle.

Truck Trouble (or Other Large Land Vehicle Trouble)

IF YOU DREAM of having difficulty with a truck, tractor, trailer, semitrailer, or similar land vehicle, you will probably find that the trouble closely matches that which arises with cars, cabs, and other smaller motor conveyances.

The main difference between these variants of Vehicular Trouble is that with large land vehicles you are dealing with greater size and reduced ability to maneuver. If you drive large vehicles on a regular basis, dreams of doing so may be more neutral than nightmarish. For those people who do not drive large vehicles, doing so in a dream is apt to suggest increased problems in moving easily through your life space, as with weight gain, pregnancy, or a leg cast.

Bus Trouble

YOU ARE NOT likely to dream of being at the wheel of a bus unless you drive one as an occupation, in which case dreams of operating a bus may be emotionally bland. For people who do not habitually drive a bus, doing so in a dream is likely to be traumatic, as it was for the man from New Zealand who tried to drive a bus from the rear seat. In these cases, the problems that occur closely parallel those of Car Trouble; the difference is that problems are related to greater size and reduced ability to manipulate the vehicle, as well as more responsibility for other people. Fellow passengers on a bus or other public vehicle often represent members of the dreamer's family or colleagues in a work setting.

Dreams involving trolleys introduce problems with tracks and electrical connections. Ambulances, police cars, fire engines, and other emergency vehicles add the element of crisis. Dreams about problems in subways add the possibility of being trapped underground, collapsing earth, risk of insufficient air, suffocation, and so forth.

Many dreamers see themselves as passengers traveling by bus, jitney, van, or a similar vehicle when a problem arises, just as it does with Car Trouble. Yet, in the case of vehicles normally driven by other people, the dreamer is apt to perceive himself or herself as having less control over the route and destination. When you dream of being a passenger in a bus or a similar vehicle, you probably feel that you are being carried along, rather than deciding for yourself where and how you want to go.

An American man in his early sixties dreamed of riding in a bus downtown during rush hour. He was sitting in a front seat of the very crowded vehicle. People were lined up outside waiting to board while many inside were trying to get off. The dreamer was running late and began to get anxious when a major problem arose. Suddenly he noticed that people outside were moving to the rear, behind the bus on which he was seated; people inside were getting off, then walking behind the vehicle. When the dreamer asked a bus supervisor what was going on, he was told to get off and board one of the buses in the rear. No general announcement had been made, and the dreamer was one of the last passengers to get the word. By the time the he got off and to the rear, all the other buses had pulled out.

At this point, the action became a classic Missing the Bus motif. The dreamer concluded, "I was furious, angry, and frustrated and screamed at the driver. I was incensed that no one had told me about the new buses in time. I was livid." In this man's dream you can observe the sense of inability to control what is happening, which is more exaggerated in Bus Trouble dreams than in Car Trouble ones. There was some situation in the dreamer's waking world that felt out of his control. For all the problems that may arise with cars, you will still feel more able to affect the outcome because the vehicle is under more personal control than a public transport.

Train Trouble

DREAMS OF DIFFICULTIES that occur when you are the passenger on a train share the feeling of lessened ability to affect outcome that characterizes dreams of trouble with buses or other public vehicles. In addition, specific dilemmas arise in Train Trouble dreams that do not arise in dreams of problems with other conveyances, such as difficulty with the train tracks and snarls with switches, signals, crossing gates, conductors, tickets, and so forth. In Europe, crossing borders in trains is often the source of concern in a dream, as it was for a Swiss woman whose young boyfriend had suddenly, unexpectedly died. She dreamed of meeting him at a border station and riding together on a train. At a certain place, the passengers had to disembark, and only her boyfriend was required to continue traveling. The distraught dreamer appealed to the highest authority for permission to stay on board, without success; she must return to the city. After a tender, tearful farewell with her lover, feeling numb, she searched endlessly for the right train, running from station to station. Finally she got on a crowded train with people who frightened her, and there was no room for her to sit. She ended up traveling between two train carriages. She awoke completely exhausted.

The border in this young woman's dream symbolized the boundary between life and death; only the deceased could pass it. This deeply bereaved woman said, years after the dream, that it had saved her life; it was decisive in turning her back to face the world.

In my study of dreams of the bereaved, I found that the motif of journeys was characteristic. Many dreamers in mourning saw their lost loved ones leaving on trains, on airplanes, or traveling on alone; others pictured themselves saying good-bye at airports and bus terminals.

We'll be examining dreams about trains in greater detail in a later chapter. Meanwhile, if you dream about having trouble while traveling by train, make careful note of the motifs that occur.

Airplane Trouble (or Other Flying Vehicle Trouble)

SEVERAL OF THE problems that arise in dreams of operating an airplane are identical to those that occur in dreams of driving a car. My husband, for instance, when he was in his sixties and was due to have a hernia operation, had a vivid dream of "piloting an old-fashioned airplane going to or from combat." In the dream, it felt adventurous until he saw that the needle of his fuel tank indicated less than half-full. He thought he probably had enough fuel for the trip but felt concerned.

Since my husband rarely remembers a dream, I knew he was deeply concerned about the upcoming operation. Discussing it, we realized that the half-full fuel tank corresponded to his sense of depleted energy. Also, in his sixties, his life's journey was "less than half-full." The old-fashioned vehicle represented his aging body. The surgery went well and he was soon back to his peppy self.

Airplanes, obviously, introduce the element of air into dreams, with the accompanying possibility of falling through the air to earth. Another American man in his early sixties told me that he often dreams about piloting airplanes. He says they are usually positive dreams in which he is flying skill-fully, going under low wires, and making good progress. But once in a while, he will find his dream plane losing power before it plummets to a collision with the ground.

Other unique features that may emerge in dreams of Airplane Trouble include the airport, departure gates, security checks, tickets, choppy weather conditions, landing fields, signal towers, and similar elements characteristic of air travel.

People sometimes portray themselves or loved ones traveling in space vehi-cles that zoom far beyond the range that most of us experience. A young American woman dreamed that her father met her on a spaceship some-where out in space. He told her that he had to leave her, but that he would always be with her, then hugged her good-bye. She was so overwhelmed with feelings of love, she "passed out." When she came to, still in the dream, she saw the spaceship flying deeper into space. The young woman awoke, shaken, and received a telephone call later that her father had suddenly died a few hours earlier—the time of her dream—of a massive heart attack. He had been relatively young and completely well to all appearances. The dreamer felt she had had a true visit from her father's spirit, and it comforted her in her loss.

Such a dream suggests that spaceships and other vehicles that probe high altitudes (deep space) may symbolize contact with the spiritual realm, cross-ing the border between life and death.

Most of the time, aircraft are of the familiar types in our dreams. If you dream you are piloting an airplane or riding in one that develops a difficulty, your dream is probably saying that you feel you've got a serious waking life annoyance. Who or what is causing you to feel harassed or in danger?

Ship Trouble (or Other Water Vehicle Trouble)

AS WITH GROUND vehicles, ships have numerous features that allow you to compare troubles with them to Car Trouble. If you dream of standing at the helm of a ship, for instance, it is analogous to sitting at the steering wheel of a car. Similar problems with the engine, fuel gauge, possible collisions, explosions, fires, and other hazards occur.

However, dreams of all boats, ships, and other watercraft, of course, intro-duce the element of water and the risk of drowning in it. Additionally, prob-lems with a rudder, a compass, sonar, winds, storms at sea, lighthouse beacons, buoys, harbors, sails, rigging, lifesaving gear, oars, and other parts of watercraft equipment or weather appear. As the tragic collision of the *Titanic* with the fatal iceberg made clear, ships are vulnerable to the conditions of the ocean and its contents.

Large vessels are complicated to conduct. Unless you operate a large ship, you are more often apt to cast yourself in the dream role of a passenger of a seagoing craft than as the helmsman. For example, an American man in his fifties dreamed that he and his wife were passengers on a pleasure cruise ship, moving along a beautiful flower-lined canal like those in Amsterdam, looking at people's decks and living spaces. The passageway grew very narrow. The ship began moving toward someone's house with a low overhead. He thought, "We'll never clear the doorway," and sure enough they were soon stopped. He and his wife jumped to the dock, almost not making it. Suddenly the ship began backing up, faster. They ran. He could have jumped aboard, but he waited for his wife. At this point his dream became a classic Missing the Boat dream. The ship left without them. He ran down white plastic stairs that ended in the canal, to no avail. The ship disappeared, leaving him frantic.

Later in his complex dream he was on another ship trying to find the captain. "Below," a girl said, but he found that his way below deck was blocked by ropes and a guard. The dreamer pushed through and found the captain, who agreed to help him get back to the first ship. He had a map, but the dreamer didn't know where the original ship was going. Next, the unhappy dreamer tried to find his wife, running up and down the corridor screaming her name. Finally reunited, they returned together to the captain's quarters. When he turned to his wife, she transformed into an old, wise black woman.

Without going into detailed analysis of this intricate dream, I'll mention that the aspects of the dream that parallel Car Trouble are the progressively narrower passage that could as well be a road that grows too narrow, finally blocking the dreamer and preventing forward movement. Also, the dreamer was unsure of where his ship was going; unclear destination is a typical Car Trouble motif. The person and the ropes that blocked the dreamer's way are characteristic of obstacles in the road that plague dreamers in Car Trouble.

The elements of this dream that are particular to ships are the canal in which it was traveling, the interior corridors of the ship, and the captain. The most interesting aspect is the transformation of the dreamer's wife from a white woman in her fifties to an old, black wise woman. This is a case in which black color implies mystery, not danger Here, it seems, the dreamer has contacted some inner aspect of himself, what the followers of Jung call the *anima*, that could provide the wisdom he needs to find his way again. Working with the most unusual element of a dream is a good place to begin to unravel its secrets. For now, notice the parallels to Car Trouble, and the special qualities of Ship Trouble dreams and their motifs.

When you dream of being on a ship or other watercraft, watch for these same elements. You'll become familiar with the universal motifs in this type of dream and be in an excellent position to pursue your dream's unique images.

Working with Your Dreams About Vehicular Trouble

WITH EACH VARIANT of Vehicular Trouble:

1. First assess what is universal about your dream.
2. Identify the typical motifs that are present, whether you dream of driving a truck that breaks an axle, piloting a plane whose engine cuts off, paddling a canoe that strikes a rock, or whizzing along a highway in a car without brakes.
3. Underline each motif in your dream journal or make a separate list of them.
4. Then, using the Dream Key in Appendix B, look up the most probable meaning of that dream motif. Read more about it in this book. Your dream may be crystal clear without further scrutiny.
5. If not, turn to your dream's unique features.

In the chapters to come, you will see how to unlock these images for a more complete understanding of your personal motifs. Your stresses and crises, as well as your periods of delight, are mirrored in your dreams. They sound warnings or provide crucial clues to make your life better.

VEHICULAR PLEASURE

3.5 VEHICULAR PLEASURE

Description: You dream of being in or near a car or another vehicle that has some delightful element. The most characteristic motif arising in this dream theme is freedom: being able to move in the direction of your choice and to set any goal. Whereas Vehicular Trou-

	ble dreams typically contain loss of control, Vehicular Pleasure dreams entail increased control.
Frequency:	An occasional pleasurable dream among all people and ages, whether or not the dreamer actually drives.
Usual Meanings:	"Things are going well"; "I have power and energy"; "I can move however I wish"; "I can fly"; "I can transform difficulties."

You'll have no trouble recognizing Vehiclular Pleasure dreams—they are fun. One of my all-time favorite dreams is of this type. The opening scene in my dream seemed to be an ordinary, pleasant day with me driving through the city, but something—perhaps the wind I felt—clued me to the fact that this was no waking event. Realizing I was in a dream, I was able to command, "Up!" and my body lifted from the ground into the air, leaving the car behind. I continued to hold on to the steering wheel, which expanded until I lay across it, flying through the air. Everything became sharp and bright, a characteristic of lucid dreams. I felt gloriously happy as I whizzed along before awakening.

I had this dream when I had just finished writing my first book, *Creative Dreaming*, and was busy with plans for its publication. Reactions by reviewers to the prepublication copies were enthusiastic, and I had been scheduled for a month-long publicity tour. On one level, the dream was a symbolic expression of satisfaction with the way I was "steering" myself through life. I felt as though my new career was headed "up," as indeed it was, when the book became a best-seller.

On another level, when I had the dream of "The Great Steering Wheel," I was just beginning to taste the heady power of conscious dreaming— becoming aware within the dream that I was dreaming. The sensation that the dream evoked was one of pure enchantment. I had flown upward deliberately and drank in the flight through every pore. I yearned to explore the fantastic space further. It was the start of some remarkable adventures, ones I've recounted elsewhere. The important point here is that I changed the direction I was going from earth travel to air travel by *choice*. This ability of the dreamer to choose where and how to move through the dream space seems to be a major motif in pleasant dreams about vehicles. You don't have to be lucid (aware that you're dreaming *during* the dream) to do it.

UNDERSTANDING YOUR DREAMS ABOUT
VEHICULAR PLEASURE

Choosing Your Dream Direction and Goal

YOUR DREAMS ABOUT Vehicular Pleasure may not be as intense as the one described, but they may well contain the main feature of improved ability to choose your course. In one of my recent Car Pleasure dreams, one that was not lucid, I drove downtown by a new route, impressing my husband. This is a less vivid but nonetheless similar variation of the motif of finding your own path.

A French marquis in the mid-nineteenth century had a dream with the same motif as my dream, "The Great Steering Wheel," only his "vehicle" was a horse. The dreamer, Hervé de Saint-Denys, saw himself "riding on horseback on a fine day"—a situation analogous to my driving my car on a beautiful, sunny day. Suddenly he became aware of his "true situation": that is, he was asleep and dreaming and had some control over the images. "I want to gallop, and I gallop; I want to stop, and I stop. A fork in the road appears before me." Saint-Denys first chose the right-hand path, then decided that the left one would be more interesting, and he followed it, later exploring the manor house to which that path led. Again, the greatest source of pleasure for the dreamer seemed to be the option—the freedom—to choose the direction in which to move.

An English psychologist, Morton Schatzman, translated from French the book that Saint-Denys had written about his dream adventures, *Dreams and Ways of Directing Them*. While doing the translation, Schatzman had a dream with a parallel motif. His dream about riding his bicycle also began on a beautiful day, but he almost lost control. By "shifting his weight" he was able to regain the path. At that point, he became aware that he was dreaming and that he could go anywhere, steer any direction, and see anyone he wished. Once more, the ability to choose one's direction and purpose gave pleasure.

Conscious choice of direction in a dream = Increased ability to affect waking destiny

---

A middle-aged American man dreamed about driving his car along his usual route home, traveling north. As he passed a farm, he saw the farmer "laying down a double line of red earth to celebrate his favorite authors." The dreamer found this "exciting." At first he continued on his customary way, but then he turned his car around and went back to check out the new road. He and another dream character followed the double line of red earth, thinking it might go "all the way to the Grand Canyon."

The dreamer said he associated the Red Road with the Native American concept of the road of trials and sacrifice. Yet he felt that south, the direction the road led, was a symbol of the unconscious. Red is a marker used in this man's work, something he specifically searches for. He thinks of the Grand Canyon as a sacred place of the Earth goddess, containing a lot of red rock. In effect, his dream seemed to be saying, "The road to your unconscious is one of trial and sacrifice, yet it is worthwhile, as it will lead you to a grand destination, a place of deep wisdom." Notice that the dreamer did not continue in his customary way: he *turned his car around to check out the new road*. The message of his dream is that he found a new path he wanted, and he set his sights on the goal.

Your dreams about Vehicular Pleasure may well develop the same motif of conscious choice, if it's not currently present. Watch for it. Being able to choose your direction in a dream indicates a feeling of increased ability to influence your waking life paths and goals.

Other Motifs in Vehicular Pleasure

"An Adorable Guy Was Driving My Car": A Positive Part Is in Charge

DREAMS ABOUT VEHICULAR Pleasure occasionally involve a highly desirable driver. A middle-aged American woman dreamed that the driver of her car was a jovial man who kissed her palm as he drove. She enjoyed this ride; she felt that a happy and loving part of herself, or of a person close to her, was in charge of her life at the time of the dream.

Attractive driver in your dream = Some positive waking aspect is in control

---

If you should dream about a driver of your dream vehicle who is good, or kind, or loving or has some other positive trait, you can be fairly certain that you are pleased with the way your life is being managed at present.

"I've Got a Great Car": Satisfaction with Physical Condition

WE HAVE SPOKEN about the meaning of broken-down cars and other vehicles in decrepit condition. When the car in your dream is superb, it may be just what you would love to have or plan to own. Sometimes such dreams are pure wish fulfillment, or part of a waking plan. At other times they reveal an increased feeling of being in good shape or "finely tuned."

A middle-aged American woman dreamed about seeing a car with a shining disk at the rear go down the road; it charmed and intrigued her. Another, in her sixties, confided a dream about a "classic car," old but well-tuned, restored and lovingly maintained. I understood that she felt happy with the way she had "maintained" her figure. "I'm the same weight I was when I graduated from high school," she told me with a touch of pride. Such feelings are not necessarily vanity or smugness; they may simply reflect self-esteem.

Car in first-rate condition in your dream = Waking satisfaction with
body shape

If you dream about a superb car, you may be hoping to acquire such a vehicle in the future, you may feel that your body is in great condition, or you may feel especially content about your appearance at the moment.

Riding My Magic Carpet: Satisfaction with Life

THE VEHICLE MAY be some fabulous one that never existed or never will. A recent dream of mine involved "a magic carpet that I could hop on and travel anyplace in the world." By now, you'll recognize the motif of freedom to choose direction that this dream contained.

I had the Magic Carpet dream soon after I had set up a website that contained a survey on the subject of Universal Dreams. Soon people from around the world were visiting it and contributing samples of their dreams. I was quite amazed that the purpose of the website was actually being achieved. It seemed a kind of "magic carpet" by which I could touch the lives of people in far corners of the world—and they could "fly" their responses through the air back to me.

Good Dream Roads and Smooth Sailing: Satisfaction with Circumstances

IN THE SAME manner, you may dream you are driving easily, flowing in and out of tight situations, managing well under difficult conditions, always able to solve whatever glitch arises. Your dream ship may sail over calm waters under clear skies. When the dream medium you move through (earth, water, or air) and the path you travel on (road, track, shipping lane, or air route) are in fine condition, so, too, is your view of your waking situation. When the atmosphere is bright and sunlit in your dream, instead of dark and stormy, your emotions are apt to be sunny also. Such dreams suggest that your environmental conditions and your mood are currently favorable, as they were under the circumstances of my dream about the gigantic steering wheel.

Good weather and conditions in dream = Favorable waking circumstances

---

TRANSFORMING YOUR VEHICULAR TROUBLE INTO VEHICULAR PLEASURE

IT MAY SEEM that you have little chance to alter bad things that are happening in a dream. In reality, you can make a powerful positive impact on them. Here's how some dreamers accomplished a metamorphosis of their nightmares.

The Natural Healing Pattern Involves Restored Control

"I Went over the Cliff but Landed Safely": Increased Ability to Cope

MANY DREAMERS DEPICT themselves on the edge of a cliff when they feel they are in a precarious waking position. If you should have a dream like this, remember that the cliff's being there doesn't mean you have to go over it. The dream is warning you that danger is present. Take precautions.

Even if you should go over the edge, you can still exercise dream skills to bring yourself to a safe landing. An American man who was involved in an extramarital love affair dreamed that he was driving his car as it went over the side of a steep cliff. "With consummate skill," he told me, "I guided it to a safe landing at the bottom." This man had considerable confidence about his ability to guide his destiny through the difficulty. In fact, he negotiated a divorce and eventually married the woman of his choice.

You don't have to be an adult and a driver to experience the exhilaration of controlling your dream vehicle. An eight-year-old American girl described her dream of riding a tricycle in Disneyland, at the climax of which she was pedaling down a steep hill on her trike, pulling seven carts containing the seven dwarfs, when she lost control. Distressed, she saw that they were going to crash into a tree. Suddenly her tricycle transformed into a car, she turned the steering wheel, and they were saved. The dwarfs gave her a rousing cheer. Being able to take action within the dream is the difference between a nightmare and an adventure.

Skillful driving in your dream = Increased control in waking life

---

In Dreamland, If You Believe You Can Do Something, You Can

AS A GUEST on a radio show during one of my book tours, I explained how it was possible to change dreams while they were happening. In particular, I mentioned that people who dream about cars that are out of control can actually steer the vehicle to a safe landing rather than letting it crash.

To my surprise, the next day a woman called in to another show on which I was appearing, to thank me for yesterday's remarks. She had been plagued for years by nightmares of driving off a cliff. The previous night she had experienced that familiar bad dream, but this time as the car hurtled through the air she told herself, "Dr. Garfield says I can land safely." Responding to this inner advice, she said that she was able for the first time to direct her crashing car to the ground without damage. She was bursting with pleasure at her accomplishment.

Since that time, I have encountered similar descriptions from dreamers who changed their nightmares because I said they could. But it is important for people to realize that it is not my authority or ability that is transforming their dreams. The dreamers *themselves* are the ones who change their behavior within the nightmares. When they feel able to do so, dreamers can make magic in their own dreams. So can you.

"I Was Able to Stop in Time": Increased Ability to Control

WHEN YOU ARE able to convert an ongoing nightmare into a dream with a satisfactory or even joyful conclusion, you are using a skill that is part of the natural healing process. I learned this when I was recovering from a badly broken arm. As I mentioned earlier, my broken arm had been misdiagnosed as a sprain, and it was almost three weeks after the accident before the multiple fractures were discovered. I had to have surgery under general anesthetic to rebreak the bones that were healing in the wrong position, have a plate and pins inserted, and have the bone reset. The process involved months of physical therapy to recover use of my arm. In the hand therapy clinic I heard tales of horrific nightmares from other patients and gradually learned how their dreams changed as they healed. As they began to dream about new growth, healthy plants, newborn baby animals, buying new clothing, driving solid cars, and other pleasant images, they were changing not only their dreams. The uplifted mood and confidence their dreams engendered carried over to improved performance in the waking state.

A young American man among the patients in the physical therapy clinic had had his left arm badly mangled by a machine. His median nerve and nine tendons were severed, and the bones in his wrist chipped. He suffered nightmares in which the machine that had injured him was inflicting worse damage, mauling his right hand as well as his left. An important turning point in the recurrent dreams about his trauma occurred when he had a dream about driving a car on a mountainous road.

In this dream, the machine was again going wild, but this time instead of being without protection, as he usually was in his nightmares, the dreamer was driving a BMW. He was descending a twisting mountain road (often a symbol for difficult conditions) and had to swerve to avoid the machine, almost going off a cliff. But the brakes on his car worked so well, he was able to stop at the edge without plummeting over it. He explained to me that a BMW is "a good stable racing car—one you can win with. It handles better than other cars." This car gave him better "HANDling" ability, making it a strong asset in his ability to cope with convalescence from his injured hand. His dream announced that he had a chance to "win" over his wound. His psychological scars were beginning to mend, as well as the physical ones. Although his dream was not pure pleasure, it represented improved protection and increased control. He was still partially "hung up" on the edge of the cliff, but he had begun to cope more effectively. The improved control in his dreams led to greater control in his waking state.

Transforming your dream crisis = Greater ability to solve waking problem

---

Any improvement in your ability to drive in a dream, any dream in which you are seated at the steering wheel of a car that you feel is adequate for your needs, is a dream to celebrate. You are "getting a grip" on your waking problem.

Skillful driving through your dreamscape stands for increased satisfaction as you move through life in the waking world. Take charge of your dream steering wheel. Direct your dream car to where you wish to go. Enjoy the ride.

House or Property Loss or Damage
Versus Improvement

4.0 HOUSE OR PROPERTY LOSS OR DAMAGE

Description: You dream that your house or some other building is damaged or destroyed. The loss may result from a number of causes, including fire or water damage. (Destruction due to Natural or Man-made Disaster is classified with disaster dreams.) You may feel frightened, make efforts to escape, or try to save others. Your entire house or parts of it may vanish. Variations include dreams in which some valuable possession, such as a wallet, purse, keys, wristwatch, precious records, books, or artwork, may be stolen, lost, or damaged. (Car damage is considered separately with Car Trouble dreams.)

Frequency: Loss or Damage Dreams are fairly common. You may have one when you feel that some valuable aspect of waking life is at risk, including threat to your body or emotional well-being.

Usual Meanings: "I feel damaged"; "Things are deteriorating"; "My identity is threatened" (loss of purse or wallet); "I've lost time" (wristwatch); "Something valuable is crushed" (jewelry, art, and so on). Meanings vary according to the specific property at risk of loss, and how it is damaged.

When you dream that your purse or wallet has been stolen, or that you discover rotting floorboards in your house—variations of the Loss or Damage dream—you are apt to feel extremely uncomfortable. You may be angry or resentful in the dream, and a similar mood carries over to the waking state. Your dream may picture some ongoing deterioration within your physical body or express the worsening of some emotional relationship. Your dream may forecast dangers ahead unless action is taken promptly. Dreams that your property is lost or damaged are stern warnings: "Trouble under way. Take heed." Thirty percent of people in the survey reported it.

INFLUENCES ON YOUR DREAMS ABOUT LOSS OR DAMAGE OF PROPERTY

YOUR DREAMS IN this category are perhaps less affected by genetic programming than in other themes, yet there are some inborn reactions to the situations represented by your dreams about loss or damage.

1. Biological

IN GENERAL, YOUR dreams about Loss or Damage reflect a basic need to defend your territory. "Every man's home is his castle," goes the old English saying. We might paraphrase the adage to "Every dreamer's house is his body or lifestyle." Your dream house and dream belongings are an extension of your physical body and your emotional relationships. When your dream house is under threat, you rally to its defense. Indeed, you may be protecting your physical health by attending to any loss or damage to your dream house and taking precautions.

2, 3. Cultural and Subcultural

THE EXTENT THAT your culture influences how you feel about your valued belongings will determine the frequency of dreams about Loss or Damage. Among people to whom material goods are less important, few of these dreams are likely; among those to whom property has high value, such dreams will be more frequent. All of us have belongings that we treasure. Any cultural expressions or puns that are part of your daily language, as usual, may become literal images in your dreams.

4. *Personal*

HAVE YOU EVER had your home burglarized? Have you experienced having your purse or wallet snatched? Have you lost precious jewels on a trip? Has your home been damaged by an accident, fire, or other cause? Has your garden or lawn been damaged? Your personal history will be present in your dreams about Loss or Damage. You may be reminded of a specific event in your past the next time you sense a threat, producing dreams about the previous loss or destruction.

In addition to actual incidents from your past, your current health becomes an element in dreams of Loss or Damage. Whatever physical problems are present in your body often are expressed in dream pictures of broken or deteriorating objects. There were some ancient dream theorists who believed that each organ of the body finds a voice (or image) in our dreams. Certainly, I observe that when people get hurt or become sick, their dreams depict their deteriorating health; when people begin to heal, their dreams likewise reflect the improvements in their condition.

As we explore this correlation between dream images and physical health, keep in mind any physical problems that you have or suspect you have, as well as your past experiences with loss and damage to actual property.

UNDERSTANDING YOUR DREAMS ABOUT LOSS OR DAMAGE OF PROPERTY

SINCE THE DREAM theme we are considering covers such a broad range of material objects, we must limit our discussion to the few that appear frequently. However, any belonging that is valuable to you may be lost or damaged in dreams. If you follow the general principles described, you'll be able to apply them to any property in your dreams. Dreams about damage to your car or some other vehicle are considered separately in the chapter on Car or Other Vehicular Trouble.

Your dreams about Loss or Damage of Property are most likely to involve damage, destruction, loss or theft of:

- your dream house
- your purse or wallet
- your jewelry
- other valuable belongings

Your Dreams About Loss or Damage of Your House

YOUR HOME MAY or may not be your castle, but it is a personification of you. A multitude of things may go wrong with it in dreams. Since these malfunctions often relate to the dreamer's physical condition, we'll look first at the parallels that may exist between your dream house and your body.

Your Dream House as a Metaphor for Your Body

HOUSES HAVE AN inside and an outside. They have sections that usually include a foundation, framework, basement, ground and upper floors. The building contains pipes to conduct heated or cooled air, ducts to transport hot and cold water, and wires to carry electrical energy from one section to another. Windows and doors may be open, closed, or locked. All these structures are analogous to parts of the human body in shape or function. When something goes wrong with your body, it often appears as a problem with part of the house in your dream. Here are some typical correspondences:

House Part	Body Part	Parallel Function
Basement, foundation	skeleton or bones	support structure
Staircase	spine, throat, vagina	long, slim passage
Climbing of stairs	intercourse	rhythmic movements
Windows	eyes	open, shut, provide view
Front door	mouth or vagina	opening in front
Back door	anus	opening in rear
Furnace	stomach or womb	process energy
Pipes	blood vessels	carry fluids
Wires	nerves	conduct impulses
Room	inner space or vagina	contain space
Balcony	breasts	extend outward
Chimney, tower, turret	penis	extend upward

This inventory shows the ways some dreamers have depicted their bodies; your way may be different, so notice the condition of your dream house. Ask yourself the following:

1. Is my dream house too small, or is it spacious?
2. Is it shabby, dirty, or messy, or is it neat and clean?
3. Is some part broken, disconnected, or disintegrating, or is it in good repair?
4. Is it decorated in a repellent manner or a harmonious one?

5. Is the foundation shaky or strong?
6. Are there spaces, new rooms, or openings I never saw before?

Your physical body may appear as a house, skyscraper, cottage, castle, or other building—or a part of it. An entire dream building may represent a part of the body, as when a "high-rise" (skyscraper) or a silo stands for an erect penis; or a barn containing animals may symbolize a woman's womb with unborn children. In these cases, there is a metaphorical comparison of the dream building and a body part that has a similar structural shape.

We have seen how you use various vehicles to express feelings about what is happening to your body or your lifestyle in the waking world; the emphasis is on how your body is *functioning*, and how you are *moving* through your life space. With dream houses, the emphasis is shifted somewhat to the *structure* of the your body and lifestyle.

Notice, in particular, which *area* of the dream building is in danger of damage:

- Is it the basement? Your foundation may be shaky.
- Is it the living room? Your general relationships may be in trouble.
- Is it the dining room? Your social relationships may be at risk.
- Is it the kitchen? Your source of nourishment may be involved.
- Is it the bedroom? Your sexual and loving relationships may be in peril.
- Is it the attic? Your thoughts may be troubled.

These are only rough guides. You always need to question yourself, asking the following:

1. What do I use this area of the house for?
2. Why is it important to me?
3. What happened here lately?

"My House Is a War Zone!": Violent Invasion of Private Space

LIKE PEOPLE WORLDWIDE, you may dream that your house is invaded and damaged. There can be numerous reasons for this dream. One meaning of dreams about invasion and damage to a dream house is recent physical trauma. For example, a young American woman dreamed that her house was a "war zone": the stairwell and hallway were covered with arty graffiti; she was furious at a tenant, bit his arm, dumped his clean laundry, and tried to evict him; "a pack of mad lesbians" were driving a bulldozer on the front lawn; the garage door was missing, replaced by cardboard; and her car was stolen.

On a physical level, this young woman had recently had an abortion. The defaced stairwell and hallway (representing her vagina), the damage to her front lawn by the bulldozer (the abortion), the missing garage door (invaded private space), and the stolen car (the lost fetus) aptly symbolized her sense of bodily intrusion and damage. The "mad lesbians" seemed to stand for her sense of reduced femininity.

On an emotional level, the woman was in the midst of a bitter divorce. Her anger toward the tenant in her dream symbolized her fury toward her soon-to-be-ex-husband (who, before he left the house, had slept in the area the tenant now occupied). The artlike graffiti in the stairwell were also a reference to her then-husband, who was in the art field. Altogether, this woman's body and her life space felt like the "war zone" they became in her nightmare.

Extensive damage to your dream house = Waking turmoil and/or physical damage

---

With a dream as blunt as this, the connections among dream image, body damage, and emotional response are readily apparent. Your dreams about Loss or Damage may be more subtle, involving minor deterioration to just one section of your house.

"My Bathtub Was Ripped Out!": Missing Mobility

AN AMERICAN WOMAN in her late seventies dreamed her bathtub was torn out; only white crumbles were left. She was irate, thinking perhaps the maid had removed the tub.

Her fury puzzled me because I know she prefers to shower rather than take a bath. As we explored her dream, I began to understand. This older woman recently underwent knee surgery. She was no longer able to bend over to pick up something on the floor; hoisting herself out of a bathtub was particularly awkward. Finally, she used the word that made the dream's meaning clear: "I feel like I'm *crumbling*," she said. Now the "white crumbles" that were left when the tub was ripped off the wall in her dream made sense; they signified her crumbling self. Her resentment over the stolen bathtub was her indignant feeling over the physical limitations she was experiencing.

Missing part of your dream house = Reduced waking function, physical or emotional

---

If you dream of finding a part of your house missing, it's important to explore what that section or object means in your dream language. Consider the following:

1. What is X? (Define the missing object or part.)
2. What's important about X?
3. Why do I need X?
4. How do I use X?
5. What's changed in my use of X?

By answering these questions, you'll begin to decipher the meaning of the lost or damaged dream object for you.

"My House Got Towed Away!": Stolen Youth

YOU DON'T HAVE to be in your latter years to have resentful dreams about bodily changes. A middle-aged American woman dreamed that a couple came to dinner in her home; when they left, they towed her house away with them. The dreamer was furious. Later, visiting her former house, she disliked the décor and felt annoyed. Finally, the thieving couple burned her house down to a pile of ashes.

This dreamer connected her damaged dream house to bodily changes as she ages. She feels angry about them, as though she's left with nothing but "a pile of ashes." She feels her youth has been "stolen."

If you should have such a disturbing dream, you need to take action to improve your situation. We cannot stop the process of aging, but we can change our feelings about it. This dreamer, in her fifties, could find much joy in her life yet—if she listens to the warning in her dream. You may dream, as a Canadian woman and others did, that people move into your house and claim it belongs to them. This dream suggests something is making the dreamer feel displaced.

"My House Is Being Crowded Out": Limited Opportunities

YOU MAY FIND that it's not your dream house, but the surroundings that are spoiled. A middle-aged American woman who is a lawyer in a prestigious firm woke up weeping from a dream. In it, a favorite childhood home was surrounded by high rises, isolated, with an ugly school yard covered in concrete nearby. In her mind, the dream house was perfect, with a yard and garden, "just the way houses should be, traditional." But instead of being located in the South, as it actually had been, the house in her dream was placed in a city she dislikes. She described it as a spot where "there is nothing old; there's no history. It's the grossest place I can think of." The dreamer said concrete was "hard, cold, impersonal, and unapproachable; no grass can grow on it." For this dreamer, her favorite house with all its beautiful flowering trees was stuck in a cold, sterile environment, isolated. The house itself was not damaged, but its environment had badly deteriorated.

As we discussed her dream, I learned that the woman's law firm consisted mainly of men, and only males were partners, no doubt symbolized by the "high rises" in her dream. Although she was a long-term member of the firm, her rank was lower than it should have been. Metaphorically, she was a small house competing with high rises for space. Here the size difference conveyed the dreamer's sense of unimportance. The "concrete" that surrounded the area represented the poor conditions for growth in this position. As a result of her dream, the woman realized how unhappy she was with the situation at work, and she determined to be recognized or change firms. Whatever she did worked. Within a few months she received a raise, and shortly thereafter she was made a partner in the firm.

When you have a dream about Loss or Damage of Property, watch for the connection between what is lost or damaged in the dream and what feels lost or damaged in your waking space. It may be your physical body; it may be some aspect of your life space. Notice how you feel about it in the dream and what you do about it in the dream. Once awake, remember that you can make a change in your life when your dream points out its necessity.

Termites in the Foundation, Germs, Bugs, and Dirt: Presence of Infection

DREAMS THAT INVOLVE insects, germs, bugs, dirt, or rot in a home can be cause for great concern. I have often noticed a connection between damage due to swarming insects in dreams and the presence of infection in the body.

A middle-aged Australian woman had an ominous dream of this sort shortly before she was diagnosed with fibromylagia and went into a deep depression. Her dream contained many references not only to dirt and disorder but also to germs and infected water that she had to drink.

Termites, germs, bugs, or dirt in your dream = Waking physical infection
or aggravation

Since the foundation of a house is the basis of its structure, any dream that involves termites destroying it, or the presence of rot, may be a serious health indicator, physical or emotional.

In English, we use the expression "I caught a bug" to mean we came down with a cold. If you should have such a dream about termites, germs, bugs, or dirt, please look to your health. Have a checkup, take precautions, and get appropriate medication, if indicated.

On an emotional level, dreams of bugs usually represent a situation that is "bugging" you, meaning you find it annoying. Many dreamers describe dreams in which parts of their houses or some other property are covered with excrement, as a way of expressing that they find a waking situation "shitty" or "a real mess." Such dreams, too, require action to deal with the waking situation that has become bothersome enough to contaminate one's dream.

Collapsing Walls and Other Structures: Things Are Falling Apart

IF YOU DREAM about a house (or part of it) that is collapsing, the dream may refer to a physical or an emotional situation. On the physical level, one mature American woman dreamed that the railing going down the outside steps of her house collapsed; as she held on to it, the spokes broke and she fell. During the day preceding the dream, she had broken several of her ribs when someone performed the Heimlich maneuver on her as she choked on an after-dinner mint. The broken ribs in waking life became the collapsing spokes of the railing in her dream.

On an emotional level, a middle-aged American woman dreamed that her "retaining wall fell down again." She lived on a hillside that required a supportive structure to prevent mudslides. After being divorced, she dated a man who profoundly disappointed her. In vivid images, her dream said that her "support structure" was giving way again: first her husband and now the current man had "let her down." Another American woman in the process of a divorce dreamed that a large pole standing next to her dream house fell over sideways and smashed it flat as a pancake; she was probably reflecting a similar feeling that her life space was collapsing. The young Mexican man who dreamed that a train ran through his house probably felt some extraordinary waking situation was crashing into and destroying his personal space. During the period that her marriage was "coming apart," a young American woman dreamed that the bookcase her husband had built was warping and separating at the seams so badly it had to be held together with clamps.

Loss of physical support in your dream = Reduced waking support

---

If you dream about your house or other property's falling apart, collapsing, or being crushed, there's a good chance that some relationship in your waking state is in peril. The expressions in our daily speech contain many images of "building a relationship" or "breaking up." In your dreams these metaphors become literal. Do you want to "patch it up" or "put it back together," "mend the damage" or "discard the whole thing" and move on? Your dream gives you the chance to decide.

"My House Is on Fire!": Anger or Sexual Arousal

YOU MAY DREAM that your house is ablaze rather than being damaged in some other way. Dreams about fire are considered in greater detail in a later chapter, but here I want to state that your dreams of fire in a house generally have one of two meanings: either you are extremely angry about a destructive waking life situation in the home or you are feeling erotically aroused; in either case, the feelings are intense.

If it is feelings of fury that are causing the dream destruction, you may feel "burned up" about some aspect of home life or "burned out" at work and sense that it is destructive to you. If it is feelings of passion that consume the dream house, you may be "on fire" for some person. A young married American woman dreamed about seeing a house near hers in flames. She tried to escape the spreading fire and to help bring it under control, but soon her dream shifted to loving embraces with a man to whom she was actually attracted. She felt that getting involved with him in the waking state would be destructive to her home and marriage, but she allowed herself to indulge in passion in the dream. In fact, this dreamer eventually chose to leave her marriage but did not end up with the man in her dream.

Fire in your dream house = Arousal of anger or erotic waking emotions

---

When dreamers express lustful longings in dreams about houses on fire, they are giving form to expressions we use in English: "He makes me hot," "I'm on fire for her," "I get a warm glow just being near him," "I stoked her fire," and so forth.

Perhaps the middle-aged woman from the Netherlands who dreamed her house was on fire, burning her mother and her cats, was expressing both types of arousal, since cats often represent female sexuality in women's dreams. Only the dreamer would know.

If you dream about fire's consuming a dream house, you alone can say whether your emotions are those of heated anger or of passionate sexual arousal, unless, of course, the dream conveys that information as well. How you choose to act on this awareness may determine the direction of your future.

Your Dream Purse or Wallet Is Stolen, Lost, Damaged, or Destroyed

TURNING TO DREAMS of Loss or Damage involving wallets and purses, we shift emphasis to the dreamer's personal identity. When I ask dreamers to describe what's important about having their wallets or purses, the answers usually contain the phrase "my identification cards." The crucial things a person needs to function in today's society are carried in the back pocket or over the arm. We have keys, money, credit cards, checkbooks, and makeup (in purses) available for use. When these things are missing, our mobility is restricted. But most important seem to be those items that prove who we are: our driver's license, our banking card, our main charge card. Sometimes passports, visas, and airplane tickets are in the same compartments. Without these personal identity papers, we are in serious jeopardy.

Loss or damage of your purse or wallet in a dream = Waking threat to personal identity

---

"I drop my belongings into a bog by the road. I, too, either fall or stumble into it. I manage to climb out, but when I turn to grab my purse, airline tickets, and other things, they have sunk beyond retrieval"—this was part of a dream I experienced after I had fallen and badly broken my arm. When I had it, I was in the hospital, awaiting surgery the following morning. I felt bereft of my personal identity, tagged and gowned, an impatient patient, not a whole person. Such dreams leave the dreamer feeling adrift. If you have one with the motif of losing your purse or wallet, you'll want to explore the following:

1. What value does the lost or damaged item have for me?
2. Do I have a sense of diminished identity in the waking state?
3. How can I reestablish a feeling of self-worth?

In my own experience with personal injury, reestablishing a feeling of self-worth meant returning to being a professional dream worker–writer. Eventually, as I underwent nine months of physical therapy to restore lost function to my damaged arm, I wrote a book about dream images associated with injury, illness, and healing—one that helped me regain a sense of self. It is important to pursue any way you can find that helps restore your feeling of self-identity.

Your Precious Dream Jewelry Is Stolen, Lost, Damaged, or Destroyed

MANY WOMEN HAVE confided dreams about damage to their wedding rings, discovering them to be misshapen or broken. Because the wedding ring stands for union, and its circular perfection represents the continuity of the loving relationship, dreams involving wedding rings are always significant. The gold, from which most wedding rings are made, adds the further symbolization of this metal—durable, valuable, and unchangeable.

Almost invariably, wedding rings appear marred in dreams when the dreamer feels there has been some temporary deterioration in the relationship with the spouse. To dream of losing one's wedding ring or some other precious piece of jewelry that was a gift from the spouse suggests the presence of risk to the marriage.

A young woman from Thailand who recently broke up with a boyfriend told me her dream about swimming underwater and finding a beautiful antique ring that pleased her, but later it was gone. The dreamer expected good luck to follow this dream, because in her country, finding a diamond is a sign that something nice will happen soon. But because the antique ring disappeared by the end of the dream, I suspect that her dream symbolized her lost relationship with her boyfriend, as well as a wish for its replacement.

Loss or damage of precious jewelry in a dream = Threat to valued waking relationship

---

You may dream of having precious family jewelry taken, as did a young woman from Australia; such dreams suggest a threat to a valuable family relationship.

You Dream That Some Other Valued Property Is Lost or Damaged

THE CATEGORY OF items that dreamers lose or find damaged is so vast that I can only give a few examples here to guide you with your dreams of this type. Dreamers who lose their contact lenses, as did a survey participant from the Netherlands, may be expressing loss of ability to see a waking situation clearly; or they may be "losing contact" with some important relationship in the waking world.

"My Guitar Was Smashed!": Damage to a Sexual Relationship

DO YOU HAVE a valued musical or artistic instrument? A middle-aged American man was disturbed by recurrent dreams of damage to his guitar, an instrument he plays. In some dreams it was merely cracked; in others he found a hole in it. Usually, he reacted to finding the damage by taking his guitar to a master craftsman from whom he had bought the instrument and leaving it for repair. Finally the man dreamed he found his guitar totally smashed; he thought he would have to replace it with a new white guitar (in contrast to the dark wood of his current waking life guitar).

A successful, busy executive, the man wondered what his guitar symbolized. At first, I thought it might represent leisure time for creativity, but his comments revealed no evidence of this. He told me that he played his guitar to relax, focusing on simple music he could gradually learn to play better. As we continued to explore the circumstances of his dreams, it emerged that there was some connection between his musical instrument and his sexuality. His relationship to his wife was sometimes rocky, and the sexual aspects were not always what he wished. Lately, he saw the possibility of a new and better relationship between them. For this dreamer, the destruction of the instrument was a prerequisite for the acquisition of an improved (white) one: new guitars for old; damaged relationships for healthier ones.

Loss or damage to your valuable property in dream = Valued waking relationship at risk

---

"My Mother's Urn Was Cracked": Loving Relationship Shattered by Death

YOUR DAMAGED DREAM object may be a special gift from a parent. A middle-aged woman from Australia told me a dream shortly after her second husband died. In it, she saw that a beautiful vase her mother had given her was badly cracked. Again, the dream reference was sexual on one level; her sexual life had ceased. On an emotional level, the beautiful relationship she and her husband shared was shattered by his death.

"They Stole My Wristwatch!": Lost Time

YOU MAY BE one of the many people who dream about having their wristwatches damaged, lost, or stolen, as did an older woman from New Zealand who decided she didn't need it after all. A young American woman described her dream of being in the backseat of a taxicab when two men climbed in, one on each side, and stole her wristwatch. As we explored her dream, it emerged that these thieves represented the two men she had been dating; she felt they both had caused her to "lose time." Neither was a suitable mate. She must look elsewhere for the right man.

Whenever you dream about loss of, damage to, or destruction of some personal property, you are expressing a reduction in an ability, a threat to your physical body, or the deterioration of a relationship in your waking world. You feel diminished, or at risk of becoming so. The waking loss may be in the physical or emotional realm, or in both at once. You need to take prompt action to protect yourself or to restore the loss. Happily, many of our losses can be restored or replaced.

HOUSE OR PROPERTY IMPROVEMENT

4.5 HOUSE OR PROPERTY IMPROVEMENT

Description: You dream that your house or some other building is being repaired or rebuilt, or a completely new structure is being built. You may dream that you find lost goods or receive even better ones. The recovery may result from your effort or from the help or generosity of other people. (Dreams about discovering new rooms in your house or finding new areas in your environment are classified as Discovering New Spaces.)

Frequency: Property Improvement dreams are not especially common. They may arise when you feel that some valuable aspect of waking life is improving. They may correspond to body repair, pregnancy, or an emotional enhancement.

Usual Meanings: "I feel improved"; "Things are getting better"; "My identity is restored" (return of purse or wallet); "I've gained time" (new timepiece); "Something valuable is available" (gifts of jewelry, art, or other). Meanings vary according to the specific property that is repaired, restored, or presented as a gift.

If you dream about the return of goods that have been stolen or lost in waking life, the dream is partly wish fulfillment. You want the items back. Some forty years after having disposed of some marionettes that my father had made and given me when I was a child, I will still occasionally dream that I find them in an antique store and am able to recover these cherished objects. At the time I gave the puppets to a charity, my parents were divorcing; they had asked me to clear out the family home. Just before the box containing them was carted away, I plucked three of the fifty or so hand-carved puppets as a souvenir and let the rest go. Since my father's death, I strenuously wish I had not parted with these precious mementos of his skill and love. When I dream of finding them again, it is probably more than the mementos I want restored.

UNDERSTANDING YOUR DREAMS ABOUT PROPERTY IMPROVEMENT

MANY DIFFERENT MOTIFS occur in dreams about House or Property Improvement. Yours are apt to include one or more of these variations:

- Your dream house is repaired, remodeled, or rebuilt.
- A new dream house is constructed.
- You find your purse or wallet.
- You find lost jewelry or are presented gifts of equal or better pieces.
- You receive or obtain other valuable property.

Your Dreams About Improvements to a House

IN THESE DREAMS, something is being done to make your house or its surroundings better. We have seen how your dream house is often a metaphor for your body, so dreams about house construction often correlate with physical growth or restored health.

Improvement in house in your dream = Growth or restored health in
waking world

"A New House Is Being Built": Baby-Building Under Way

IF YOU ARE pregnant, you may well dream about buildings under construction. Many women do so during their pregnancy, and the size of the dream buildings often expands as their bellies expand. Researchers who have studied the dreams of pregnant women observe frequent references to buildings, ranging from simple rooms to soaring skyscrapers. In her investigation of the dreams of sixty-seven pregnant women, Patricia Maybruck found that 18 percent of the more than one thousand dreams she collected contained references to buildings or other architecture. These buildings were often places where things are manufactured, such as a factory or shipyard, probably corresponding to the "making" of the baby that is taking place inside the woman's body.

Pregnant women are extraordinarily sensitive to their enlarging inner space. Maybruck's subjects mentioned dream buildings that increased in size and complexity as their pregnancy progressed. Skyscrapers were especially common as the women neared term. Among the pregnant women whose dreams I studied, one had miniature buildings in dreams in her early pregnancy; during her last trimester, the structures were the size of a restaurant or small house.

Your dream of larger objects during pregnancy is not limited to houses and buildings. Perhaps you recall that when they are pregnant, women often dream about driving large, bulky vehicles. For some dreamers, the bigger-than-usual dream objects are items of household furniture. A pregnant American woman, for instance, dreamed of receiving, via a "metaphysical delivery person," an expandable cradle worth $2,500. She had to pay less than a tenth of that cost, one she could easily manage. The cradle opened up into a dining room table (she defined this as a place for families to get nourishment, to gather around and communicate). The cradle also converted into a china cabinet (she said this was a place to keep fine things). Altogether, this expandable cradle provided the dreamer with a valuable object, one that would increase nourishment and communication (like a dining room table) and protect her fine baby (like a china cabinet). The expandable cradle seemed to be a magical gift from another time and space, since it arrived by means of a "metaphysical delivery person" and was capable of remarkable transformations.

"The Barn Was Being Reconstructed": Maintenance of Good Health

YOU SAW HOW dreams of an old house that is falling apart, rotting floorboards, breakage, and similar images suggest deterioration in or damage to the body. Many elderly persons describe dreams of this type. But not all. An American woman in her nineties had had a bout with cancer a quarter of a century earlier but was currently well and still going to work every day. In her most recent dream, she saw a house being fixed over, a kind of barn in the process of reconstruction. She explained to me that she had been an active horseback rider; that she liked barns and animals. A lively woman, she continued to exercise and was involved in learning new things. In this woman's dream language, her body was being kept in a good state of repair, able to shelter and nourish the things she valued. We're never too old, in this elderly woman's experience, to keep active and maintain the well-being of our mind and body.

Your Dreams About Grass, Gardens, and Flowers

YOUR DREAMS ABOUT property improvement may occur after physical damage. Dreams about construction are common when the dreamer is recovering from an injury or illness. The physical repair that is taking place, as scabs form and new veins branch out to nourish the wounded area, is paralleled in dreams of houses being remodeled or fixed, and new buildings being constructed. Images of healthy plant growth can have the same significance.

Gardens and flowers in your dream = Waking body repair or growth

---

"Exquisite Blue Blossoms Fill the Trees": Body Repair in Process

THE "FATHER OF medicine," Hippocrates, believed that among the dream images indicative of good health were those in which dreamers "see the earth level and well tilled, trees that are luxuriant, covered with fruit and cultivated." His thoughts, formulated over two thousand years ago, seem to hold true today. I found many images of new growth in plants and the appearance of playful baby animals as previously injured or ill dreamers began to heal.

In a dream following my return home after surgery on my injured wrist, I was encouraged by seeing positive images after having had many nightmares. I seemed to be living in a pretty, historical area of a city. From my living room, I looked out a picture window onto the grassy plot of a square. I thought how my husband and I could contribute money or raise funds to convert the grassy plot into a beautiful garden. It would complete the historical feeling and make the whole area pleasant and harmonious. The dream continued with further positive imagery.

A few days later, I dreamed I was driving past attractively landscaped grounds, with sweeping green lawns and large spreading trees. The grass was the fresh, new color of early spring, although the trees were still bare. About two weeks after surgery, I had a dream that included a scene of two girls in a garden gathering blossoms from trees. Then three weeks post surgery, I dreamed of driving through a pretty wooded countryside and seeing exquisite blue blossoms on trees, a color called "delphinium blue." Awake, I associated this color name to the Greek site of Delphi, where the oracle gave her predictions. I was predicting my own healthy recovery.

In my series of postsurgery dreams, you can see how the flowery growth increased in lushness as I moved toward better physical health. It seemed to be a literal growth from grass to abundant blossoms. These signs of a shift to sturdier health were at first interspersed with negative imagery, but as my healing accelerated, the positive images appeared more often. If you have suffered an injury or illness, stay alert for images that signal the beginning of healing. I suggest using them as a focus for meditation or sketching them. Attending to them can help you reach full flower.

"It's a Beautiful Spring Scene": Returning Health

ANOTHER AMERICAN WOMAN had undergone a painful hysterectomy. While she was still in the hospital recuperating from surgery, she had dreams about being brutally raped. She had never experienced such an attack, but the pains in her genitals felt like a violent invasion to her. I knew she was healing when three weeks after her surgery she described a dream that contains several metaphors of healing. In it, she was talking on the telephone to a woman friend when she heard noises. Going to the picture window in her living room and looking out onto her land, she saw a beautiful spring scene—a lush field, green grass, and trees in bloom. There were animals running around, "kicking up their heels." She told her friend on the telephone and called her husband to come look. A goose was chasing her favorite cat. "Like you chase me, honey," she said to her husband. All the animals were playing.

You can see in this dream the springtime revival of the woman's good health, as well as the return of her "animal spirit"—her friskiness in playing with her mate. Notice, in particular, that she was looking out a picture window in her dream, just as I was in my first postsurgery dream, which included plant growth. Scenes through picture windows are often "snapshots" of the dreamer's newly emerging state. This view was fresh and healthy for both of us.

If you have been injured or ill, watch for the return of a season of growth in your dreams. Green plants, blooming flowers, playful animals, and fun-filled sexual images—these are milestone images on the road to wellness. Celebrate them.

"Ripe Grapes Growing from My Belly": Increasing Fertility

IF YOU (OR your spouse) are pregnant, you may also dream about abundant plant growth. Flowers, fruit, and plants have long symbolized the fertility of the earth and of woman. Mother Earth yields food to feed the animals and people who walk upon her surface. Ceres, the Roman goddess of growing vegetation, from whom we get the word *cereal*, is typically pictured with sheaves of grain; her name comes from the same root as the word *create*, identifying her role as giver of life.

This fruitfulness of woman is depicted in Botticelli's famous painting *La Primavera* (Spring). The figure of Spring is pregnant, her head crowned in flowers, her neck wreathed in garlands, her body draped in a flowery print fabric, and her arms overflowing with blossoms. The trees above her are heavy with fruit; the grass below her is lush with blooming flowers.

The same fruitfulness appears in the dreams of pregnant women. Walking through grasslands, pastures, or fields; tending flowers or gardens; or growing vegetables or fruit—typical dreams of the pregnant woman. The word *nursery* means both a place where children are cared for and a place where plants are raised; it sometimes appears as a pun in the pregnant woman's dreams.

An American woman was thrilled to dream of looking down at her body, where she observed two ripe clusters of grapes swelling from her belly. In her early thirties, she had been trying for years to conceive. When she awoke from this dream, she knew that she had succeeded in becoming pregnant at last. If you think you might be pregnant, watch for images of lush, growing things in your dreams. A man, pleased about his spouse's being pregnant, might dream of fertile farms and orchards full of fruit.

Glorious Flowers: Something New Is Blooming in Your Life

OF COURSE, WOMEN dream about flowers when they are not pregnant or not recovering from an injury. Flowers are a common symbol of romantic and sexual arousal. Although both genders dream of flowers, women are more apt to do so. Many women dream about them in connection with falling in love. In this case, the new growth is a new love in the dreamer's life. A blossom is, in fact, the sexual organ of the plant, with its form and fragrance evolved to attract the creature that will fertilize it. If you find yourself dreaming about flowers (when your health is good and you're not pregnant), ask yourself the following:

1. What is special about this kind of flower?
2. How does this type differ from other, similar flowers?
3. Have I had any exceptional experience in connection with a flower of this kind?
4. Why this particular flower at this particular time?
5. What's blossoming in my life right now?

Answering these questions will help you sort out what is coming into bloom in your waking world.

Your Lost Dream Purse Is Found

"My Lost Purse Is Returned": Restored Identity

YOU RECALL THAT dreams about losing purses or wallets usually symbolize a reduction in your sense of identity. If you have this fairly common dream, you may want to try a technique my late godmother used. When this super-active woman was in her early eighties, she told me, "I never bothered about dreams until after I'd talked to you. Now I remember them all the time. Most of them are pleasant. If it's unhappy, I know it's a dream and I start fixing it up."

My godmother, Aunt Kathryn, said she started having recurrent dreams about losing her purse. She would be in a strange city (she traveled a lot) when she'd lose it. At first she wouldn't know it was a dream. Then she'd say to herself, "Now, wait a minute. I never lose my purse; this must be a dream." She would set a place in her dream where she would find it. She'd tell herself, "My purse will be behind that bush," or "When I turn the next corner, I will find it," or "Somebody will bring me my purse," and sure enough, it would happen as she planned.

Aunt Kathryn's mind was of a practical nature. If something was wrong, she just fixed it—awake or asleep. She confided to me that she only dreamed about lost purses when she felt insecure for some reason. If a woman in her eighties could learn to become aware she was dreaming and improve her dream, surely we all can acquire the dream skill of recovering lost goods. Doing so in a dream restores the confidence we need to face our daily tasks, whatever may arise.

You Get Some New Jewelry

"I Wear an Elegant Ring": Returning Health

IF YOU DREAM about beautiful jewelry when you are recovering from an injury or illness, this, too, is likely to indicate returning health. About six weeks after the operation on my arm, I dreamed about trying on magnificent jewelry made of carved rose quartz and green jade. I noticed I was wearing a lovely pink-and-green opal ring on my left hand (the one that had been injured), a gift from my husband that had actually been missing since it was stolen in a burglary. Its restoration in the dream signified the treasure of restored physical health. My body image, which had been badly shattered during the accident and aftermath, was reintegrating. By wearing a beautiful ring on the finger that had been too swollen to accept a ring for over half a year, my dreams were saying, "Look, see how well you are getting." Soon after the dream, I was able to enjoy wearing rings and a wristwatch on my healing arm in the waking state.

As do images of green growth, flowers, and new construction, wearing attractive jewelry or clothing on areas of your body that have been damaged in waking life indicates the restoration of healthy functioning. You may dream about lovely jewelry gifts when you are not in recovery. In general, such images suggest something precious is emerging for you.

You Receive a Valuable Gift: Time

"The Grandfather Clock Says It's Time to Create": Inspiration from the Dead

YOUR SPECIAL GIFTS may come from the hands of a deceased loved one in a dream. These dream gifts are discussed in the last chapter. Here I will mention the American poet Alice Evans, whose deceased grandfather was an important dream figure to her. In dreams, he showed her beautifully crafted pieces of furniture; a handmade red cherry bookcase that was empty; and highly polished, carved figurines. One of the striking images in these dreams was that of "a beautiful grandfather clock made of medium-light wood with a figured grain pattern." She believed that her grandfather, who was a craftsman, "showed me I'm running out of time. I need to do it now," that is, to create her own works, her elegant poems, to fill the empty bookcase in her dream. As we spoke, she said that her grandfather could teach her to build well-crafted things, too. The wonderful grains and patterns of the objects made of wood that he showed her in dreams reminded her of the patterns of her verses. This poet wove her dream images into an exquisite poem about her grandfather and his teaching her about how to live.

So many dreams speak of lost time, stolen time, or the pressures of time, it's a pleasure to see a dream that gives the gift of time. Perhaps you, too, will dream it's time to produce your own creative work.

Your dreams are always gifts from which you can learn, whether they are nightmares or inspirational dreams. Dreams of new construction, fertile lands, restored goods, or new gifts—these speak of healthy inner growth.

Poor Test or Other Poor Performance
Versus Fine Performance

This universal nightmare about performing poorly on a school examination, or of being in the wrong play or some other performance, is one that haunts adults long after their days in school. A physician friend who has been in practice for more than thirty years confided his version, in which he feels sure he will never graduate from medical school. Forty percent of those in the website survey reported this theme. Why do competent, capable people find themselves occasionally tormented by being back in school, fearing failure?

INFLUENCES ON YOUR DREAMS OF POOR PERFORMANCE

ALL PEOPLE HAVE areas in which they feel less confident in their abilities. As we move through life, we are continually faced with situations that challenge our capacity to perform well. These two facts—areas of lowered self-confidence and challenging situations—combine to produce the occasional nightmare that we are having a difficult time passing a test. Although we may have long finished our formal schooling, we dream of ourselves back in the setting where we first found ourselves struggling to avoid failure.

1. Biological

IN MOST SOCIETIES, we human beings have a need to achieve, as well as a need to compete. These drives are part of our equipment to meet the challenges of our particular culture successfully. When our achievement needs are threatened—perhaps by presenting a controversial paper at a conference, or by pitching a new idea to a hostile board of directors, or by performing in a difficult acting role—our anxiety rises. We feel we may be judged harshly or be compared unfavorably to others or sense that we may not "make a passing grade." These are the times we are most likely to dream about not having enough time to complete a "final" examination or of losing our voice when we get to the podium to make an important address.

If your personality tends to be sensitive or anxiety-prone, you may be more subject to dreams about test or performance failure than other people. Happily, there's something that can be done about it.

2, 3. Cultural and Subcultural

HOW MUCH EMPHASIS does your culture place on superior performance? In some societies—Britain and Japan come to mind—students' scores on tests administered at age twelve determine whether or not they may go on to higher academic training. The need to pass such tests exerts enormous pressure at an early age. Before graduation from high school, most students take the Scholastic Achievement Test (SAT) in the United States, or A-levels in Britain, to determine their readiness for college-level courses.

Advanced professional training exerts further stress on the student. In graduate school, oral examinations, called *viva voce* (the living voice) in Britain, are particularly grueling. Whether or not one makes a "first" in the final test can determine one's professional career for the remainder of one's life. The names vary in different countries—matriculation examinations, progress exams, comprehensive exams. Whatever they are called, they are exceedingly stressful for the student. Experiencing these tests serves as the model for future situations in which the graduate feels "tested" in later life.

Even getting into the "right" kindergarten can determine one's future in some societies. A recent news item described the murder in Tokyo of a two-year-old girl who had been admitted to a prestigious preschool. She was killed by the jealous mother of another two year-old girl, who was refused admission to the same kindergarten, one that is thought to put its students on the best track for future success. A mother whose child doesn't get admitted to the right preschool is judged a failure.

You may or may not have been subjected to heavy pressures to excel in school. Some subcultural groups are indifferent to marks in a school setting; others demand high achievement for acceptance as part of the group.

4. Personal

HOW DID YOU handle the pressure of your exams? How did you fare? What is the area of your specialty? What is the level of competition in it? Some professions, law, for instance, require that postgraduate board examinations be passed. The pass rate for lawyers in California is low, about 40 percent. Thus, although the graduate lawyer may have completed all the required work and passed the tests administered by his or her law school, there is still the prospect of failure to pass the board. Such experiences mark the person indelibly and influence future dreams. Your personal history of success or failure contributes to your dreams on the topic.

Also influencing your dreams about performance are the attitudes of your parents toward your achievement and how your peers fare in comparison. If you are in the performing arts—music, dance, theater, film—or in the fine arts, you face circumstances in which only a few individuals are able to become outstanding. Such odds may increase the pressure to succeed.

The final influence on your dreams about poor test or other performance is the conditions you currently confront. Have you taken on a difficult job? Are you experimenting with something new? What is your present challenge, and how capable do you feel of coping with it?

UNDERSTANDING YOUR DREAMS ABOUT POOR TEST OR OTHER POOR PERFORMANCE

YOUR DREAMS ABOUT performing poorly are likely to contain one or more of the following motifs:

- Forgetting about an exam, a class, or a project
- Being unable to find the location of an exam or not knowing where to go
- Being too late to take an exam, starting late, or having no time to finish
- Not recognizing material in an exam, not having read the required books
- Not knowing the lines of a play, the words of a song, or the music to be performed
- Not having essential equipment, books, or instrument, or loss of voice
- Feeling panic-stricken about probable failure of a test, fear of not graduating, fear of appearing stupid

We'll explore these motifs separately and see what they probably mean in your dreams, but they often clump together and overlap in any one dream.

Performing poorly is a fairly common nightmare. Among the first five hundred people who filled out the survey on Universal Dreams on my website, more than 40 percent said they had had dreams about having trouble with a performance. Twice as many women as men described having a poor performance dream. Dreamers in their middle years, between twenty and forty-nine, were more likely to speak of having this dream than teenagers or older folk.

Your Dream Test as a Metaphor for a Waking Challenge

IF YOU ARE one of the many people who dream about feeling unprepared for a test, you are apt to be expressing a feeling of being unready for some waking life situation that currently challenges you.

Taking a test in your dream = Confronting a waking life challenge

---

Each variation of test taking in a dream gives us a bit of information about the state of mind of the dreamer.

You Forget You Have an Exam: Unfamiliar Challenge

YOU ARE QUITE likely to dream about having forgotten that you had an exam. Those people who said they dreamed about Poor Performance in my survey mentioned "forgetting" they had a test or had to do a major project, more than any other motif. From Malta to America, men and women dream they forgot an exam, have to take the final "cold," or expect to fail.

In waking life, a student rarely forgets that he or she has a final scheduled in a particular course. In fact, it's usually impossible to forget that the big test is coming. Why should we have the impression of forgetting in a dream?

Most likely, we "forget" we have an examination in dreams because some situation in waking life has suddenly arisen that brings back the discomfort of feeling unprepared for a test. Perhaps you have a date with someone new and interesting whom you want to impress. Perhaps you are due in a few days to present an unusual and controversial idea to a group of clients who are likely to judge it harshly. Suddenly, you feel faced with being "graded." It's similar to being back in school and fearing failure. We must "take the test cold" or risk not passing.

Forgetting an exam in your dream = Facing a new or unexpected waking "test"

It is usually the big test that is mentioned in our dreams—the final, the end of the term. This is the examination that most closely parallels our feeling of facing an ultimate test. When you find yourself dreaming that you forgot you have an important test scheduled, notice what situation you are confronting at the moment in your waking world. Ask yourself the following:

1. Where do I feel "tested" or "judged" right now in waking life?
2. Who is assessing me?
3. What can I do to be better prepared?
4. How can I best relax and handle the situation successfully?

Remind yourself that you've taken many tests before and survived. Freud suggested that, in a sense, your dream is a sort of practice, as if you said to yourself, "What if the worst happens?" Prepare yourself as best you can for the forthcoming situation, and you will probably do well.

You Can't Locate the Examination Room: Confusion About Challenge

ANOTHER FREQUENT MOTIF in Poor Performance dreams is that of trouble finding the room where the test is taking place. Often we feel emotionally stressed when the image of hunting for the right room appears in our dreams.

There is a sense of time pressure, much as occurs in dreams about Missing the Boat. The test is due to begin and we are not yet where we need to be. In New Zealand, Hungary, and America, dreamers wander the hallways, unable to find the correct room. Some dreamers hunt hopelessly for their locker for essential supplies for the test.

If you dream about the motif of hunting for the right room, the emphasis is on your feeling of confusion. "Where am I supposed to go? What am I supposed to do? How can I find my way?"—you are asking yourself these questions in metaphoric pictures. Some dreamers speak of not knowing which class to attend or showing up for one class when a different class is taking place. This dream confusion about the right room to take the exam or the right class corresponds to some waking confusion as we confront a current or upcoming event that "tests" our capability.

Trouble finding right exam room in your dream = Confusion about
waking situation

When you dream about searching for the right room to take the exam, you need to slow down, take a deep breath, and reassess where you want to go under current conditions.

You Don't Have Enough Time to Finish the Test: Time Pressure

"IT'S THE WRONG time, and the wrong place"—the lyrics of the old Cole Porter tune fit this nightmare theme. The time pressure we experience in dream images of hunting for the right room also occurs in the motifs of arriving late for the test, getting stuck on questions, and having difficulty completing the answers within the allotted time. "It's too late to drop the course!" dreamers say again and again. They must face the final exam. When they do, there is often not enough time to do well, even though they know the material. A man from India reported a typical dream: "I am in the examination hall of high school or college, taking a science exam. I reached the room late or got stuck with some question and have difficulty completing the answers. I am running out of time."

If this motif arises in your dreams about Poor Performance, you can surmise that something about the waking life situation makes you feel as if you do not have enough time to do a good job.

> Time pressure in taking test in your dream = Inadequate time in waking situation

As usual, relaxing and calmly determining your approach to the waking life "test" are your best bet for succeeding.

You Haven't Read the Books or Don't Recognize the Questions: Unprepared

YOU MAY FIND yourself, as many dreamers do, taking a test for which you "haven't read a thing." If you haven't read the books on which the examination is based and/or have not taken the course, the material on which you are being quizzed is totally unfamiliar. A Canadian man, like many others, has recurrent dreams of having to take an exam he hasn't studied for. It's hard to answer questions when you don't have the facts.

This motif of not having read the required books reflects your lack of familiarity with how to deal with some contemporary waking life condition.

> Not having read books in your dream = Feeling unprepared to .neet waking life challenge

It's not surprising that you "don't know the material" if you are facing an unfamiliar situation in waking life. But, once again, you have passed many tests already, and the current one is not likely to be more arduous. Buckle down, "do your homework," prepare yourself in the best way you know how. You'll be surprised how much better you can perform.

Your Dream Performance as a Metaphor for a Waking Performance

LIKE DREAMS OF doing poorly on an exam, dreams about performing poorly onstage or in some other venue are expressing concern about a waking life performance. Only you will know exactly the nature of the act.

> Performing onstage or otherwise in your dream = Facing waking life
> challenge

You may be practicing for an actual performance you have to give in the near future. Or the performance in your dream may be symbolic of some other act about which you feel insecure. There are several possible motifs in this version of the universal theme.

You Don't Know the Lines or the Music: Unprepared

YOU ARE NOT alone. It's touching to see how many famous and successful people are troubled by dreams of Poor Performance. The renowned American photographer Ansel Adams, who originally trained as a classical pianist, was distressed by recurrent dreams that he was to perform some classic piece of music, got onstage to do so, and had the horrible realization that he didn't know it. American actor Sean Penn, while filming the role of a jazz guitarist in the Woody Allen movie *Sweet and Lowdown*, said he was bothered by nightmares that he was trying to play a guitar solo but his fingers "can't find the strings."

These dreams are typical of feeling unprepared for a waking life challenge. In Ireland, Canada, or America, people expecting to perform soon— give a lecture, be in a gymnastics competition, or star in a play—dream of giving a disastrous performance.

A world-class Swedish baritone confided to me one night at a dinner party that he sometimes dreams he appears in the wrong costume in the wrong opera. For him, this dream happens only when he is not feeling confident about a role. The star, who has also sung in prominent movie roles, has every reason to feel secure. But when he thinks that he has not had enough preparation and dreams of wearing an inappropriate costume (a motif we will encounter in a later chapter), he speaks to the director, cast members, and conductor to arrange for additional rehearsal. His bad dream allows him to take action to ensure a confident portrayal of his role.

Your nightmares about doing poorly in a performance should trigger the same response. You may be warning yourself that you need more preparation in order to do your best.

> Not knowing the lines or music in your dream = Feeling unprepared for
> waking challenge

When you dream about being in the wrong play, or not knowing the right words or the right music, take the hint that you are probably playing the "wrong role" in some waking life situation. Consider the following:

1. What do I want to change in my waking behavior?
2. What do I need to learn in order to improve?
3. How can I prepare myself better for the right role?

You Don't Have Essential Equipment, Books, Voice, or Instrument: Deficiency

IN THIS MOTIF, you lack the very thing that is needed to perform properly. A young woman from Australia reported dreaming of losing her voice at the crucial moment. A young woman from America described a similar dream of performing on an outdoor stage. When she began to sing, nothing came out at first, but when it did, the sound was terrible and the audience began to leave. A fine American orator mentioned his worst nightmares were of being on the podium and opening his mouth to speak, only to find nothing comes out. An American teenager said she often has dreams in which she's trying to play her clarinet (as she does in waking life) but is unable to do so, as if her ability has evaporated or she has forgotten how to do it. Her band director may scold her and the rest of the band stares at her, presumably critically. In different versions of this type of dream, she arrives at rehearsal only to discover that she forgot her clarinet. A Canadian man simply forgot his pen or pencil—how could he possibly take a test without them?

Still other people with Poor Performance dreams describe not being able to find the dress they need to go onstage or of having trouble finding their shoes. Some mention not having the right book for a class. One young American man spoke of dreaming that he kept losing his balance as he stood in line waiting to sign up for a class. For him, the essential missing ingredient was his balance. He needed to consider where his waking life was out of balance at the moment and how he could regain equilibrium.

All these variations have in common the element of being without the essential equipment to perform properly. How can you sing without a voice? How can you give a major address if you are unable to speak? You may find yourself similarly bereft of what you need in Poor Performance dreams, in either external equipment or internal ability. If so, you are apt to feel ill equipped to cope with a waking life problem.

> Lack of essential equipment in your dream = Feeling deficient in a waking situation

Questions to ask yourself when this motif arises in your dreams about Poor Performance include the following:

1. What am I missing?
2. What do I lack?
3. Where do I feel deficient?
4. How do I restore confidence in my ability to perform?

Answering these questions will set you on the way to being in the right place, at the right time, with the right things you need to achieve your goals.

You Fear Failing, Not Graduating, or Looking Stupid: Fear of Failure

PRESENT IN ALMOST all dreams of Poor Performance is the fear of failure. "I saw myself making 44 on one of my tests," said one girl. A thirteen-year-old Chinese-American told me of dreaming that "I have so much homework that I'll take years to finish! Then when I get to school, I find out I did everything wrong! I'll get in big trouble and get bad grades, then get sent to summer school to catch up." She is actually a superior student, but the pressure of performing well already shows in her dreams.

The motif of not being able to pass the final test, graduate, or become the professional that you already are indicates vividly that you feel inadequate at the time of the dream in a specific situation in waking life. In some way you feel you don't measure up. To understand the precise meaning of your dream, you need to identify that area in which you currently feel deficient or feel that you lack what you need to achieve goals.

> Fear of poor performance in your dream = Fear of failure in waking situation

Sometimes, of course, you may be worried about an actual upcoming exam. In this case, your dream is a warning that you may need to give the subject extra attention prior to the test.

LEARNING FROM YOUR DREAMS ABOUT
POOR PERFORMANCE

OBVIOUSLY, MANY OF the dreams about Poor Performance take place in school, sometimes a new school, a college, graduate school, or onstage in view of the world. These are settings that appear in our dreams when we sense that we are in some kind of learning situation during our waking hours. This is the venue where we may pass or fail, perform brilliantly for all to see, or fail miserably in the eyes of the world.

School setting in your dream = Learning situation in waking life

---

Poor Performance Dreams as a Metaphor for
Sexual Inadequacy?

GERMAN PSYCHIATRIST WILHELM Stekel was probably the first to give an interpretation of what he called "matriculation" dreams. His opinion was that they related to sexual tests and sexual maturity. Not surprisingly, Freud concurred, saying, "My experience has often confirmed his view." However, Freud also thought that these dreams take place "when the dreamer has some responsible activity ahead of him next day and is afraid there may be a fiasco." The dream says the dreamer's fear has been unjustified in the past and will be so again.

Certainly dream tests *sometimes* refer to feeling "tested" in the sexual department and fearing failure or "not making the grade." But in my opinion, sexuality is only one of several types of waking "tests" that may be represented in dreams about Poor Performance. These dreams also provide warnings to the dreamer to pay more attention to a waking situation in which he or she feels at risk of failure. The baritone who arranged extra rehearsals after dreams of this type gave himself additional security for doing a good job. We can do the same.

When you dream about Poor Performance, you feel are being tested in ways that are important to you in the waking state. Listen to the dream message. Prepare yourself more completely. Advance to meet your challenge better equipped for your future.

GREAT TEST OR OTHER FINE PERFORMANCE

5.5 GREAT TEST OR OTHER FINE PERFORMANCE

Description: You dream of doing extremely well in an examination in school or of performing superbly in some other way. There are several variations of this infrequent but delightful dream: you may be whizzing through a test with ease; you may be pleased to find you know the answers to all the questions no matter how difficult; you may see with satisfaction that you have read just the right books and feel well-prepared. In any case, you know you are doing well, will earn a high score, and are sure to pass or graduate. In other versions of the same theme, you are performing outstandingly in a play, a musical, a sport, or another event. You find it easy and fun to do. You may be accepted by, or praised by, famous colleagues who treat you as their equal.

Frequency: An occasional good dream. It usually occurs when you feel that you are doing very well in some waking life circumstance.

Usual Meanings: "I'm ready"; "I feel really confident"; "I know this role."

People have a happy time in dreams of outstanding performance. Everything goes well, just as they would wish. In comparison to dreams about Poor Performance, which are characterized by feelings of confusion and fear of failure, dreams about Great Performance leave the dreamer feeling exhilarated and successful.

UNDERSTANDING YOUR DREAMS OF GREAT PERFORMANCE

Your Dreams of Great Performance as a Metaphor for Waking Skill

YOU MAY DREAM about expertly whizzing through the final exam, "acing it," "creaming it." You may dream about skimming across the ice, executing complex twirls and jumps with facility. You may dream of hitting the winning home run in a baseball game. You may even dream of painting a gorgeous watercolor with some clever technique you've invented. This is not simple wish fulfillment. This is preparation.

Performing well in your dream = Practicing waking skills with confidence

---

Sports coaches train their athletes to practice mentally the intricate moves they need to master. For instance, competitive skiers visualize going down the ski slope, gliding through each gate with ease. The athlete mentally rehearses whatever skills are needed to become proficient. If mental practice can create success, dream practice may be even better. The sensations are more real in dreams than in imagination.

Many performers, professional and amateur, find themselves able to carry out moves in the waking world that they first performed in their dreams. "It was just like in my dream!" they say. "For the first time, I could really do it, smoothly and easily." Arnold Schwarzenegger told me he often dreamed of doing well and winning a contest the night before he was to compete. Actors and orators, too, find themselves giving magnificent presentations in their dreams, coming up with the precise words or gestures they need to convey their ideas or characters. So can you.

LEARNING FROM YOUR DREAMS OF PEAK PERFORMANCE

WHAT IS IT that you most want to do? Where in life do you most wish to succeed? Your dreams can help you get there.

Target Your Performance: Focus

MY DREAM FILES are full of examples from children who have dreamed they were Batman, Superman, Wonder Woman, or some other media hero or heroine. Others picture themselves in dreams as the star of some sports event, scoring the winning soccer goal, sinking the tie-breaking basket, playing baseball with the Dodgers or Cardinals or some other team who is currently enjoying success. Still others dream of being named Miss America, or of starring in a hit movie, or of saving the princess, getting married, and becoming king. The same topics fill their daydreams. In most cases, these dreams are unlikely to come true. Some of these dream goals are more possible, such as starring in a school musical or doing well on the playing field. Regardless of probability, these scenarios are the beginning of the small dreamers' ambitions to succeed in life, to feel important and valued.

Older dreamers, teenagers and adults, continue to dream of giving an outstanding performance. These dreams may also be unlikely, but possible, such as winning the Nobel Prize, being awarded a Caldecott Medal, or getting invited to join the Academie Française. Gradually, however, this dream theme begins to center on more realistic goals, those that reflect the dreamer's actual activities and interests or that represent existing skills that may lead to success.

Helen Keller's Dream of Napoleon: Confronting Unusual Challenge

WHEN HELEN KELLER was an undergraduate at Radcliffe College, she had a dream of a Great Performance. In it, she was Napoleon astride a fiery steed on the top of a hill, surveying her army. As the soldiers surged across the green fields to the sound of trumpets, drums, and marching feet, Helen—as Napoleon—charged. With her sword held high, she threw herself furiously into the dream battle. As she lifted her dream sword, she said, she struck the bedpost and woke.

Putting herself into the dream role of a conqueror probably depicted Helen's enormous struggle to surmount her handicaps of blindness and deafness as she worked at obtaining a college degree. Few dreamers would cast themselves as Napoleon, yet in Helen Keller's case the comparison was apt. In terms of her personal accomplishments, she was meeting unfamiliar challenges head on. There was no confusion, no unreadiness, no time pressure, no sense of deficiency or fear of failure—the motifs we see in Poor Performance dreams. She threw herself into the dream battle with the intent to win, to conquer, just as she gave herself fully to succeed despite her very real limitations. She confronted her challenge with confidence. There is a message for us all here: if Helen Keller could do it, surely we can overcome our limitations to achieve our desires.

Singing a Magnificent Aria: Finding My Writing and Speaking Voice

WHEN I DREAMED that I sang a great opera aria with extraordinary skill, such an achievement would be impossible, as I am barely able to carry a tune. Although I have sung in choirs in junior high and at church, I need a strong backing to sing out with assurance. For me, dream singing has become a metaphor for "finding my voice" in writing and public speaking. On these "stages" I can "sing" with confidence and pleasure. As you monitor your own dreams, watch for the possibility that some fine dream performance represents a skill quite different from the one portrayed.

In dreams of Poor Test Performance, you saw confusion and fuzziness. "Where is the exam room? Why didn't I drop the course?" If you want to begin having dreams of Peak Performance, focus clearly on your target. Use your dreams as a practice ground to perfect skills. Select your area. Then, in the drowsy state as you drift off to sleep, picture yourself doing what you do, making the images flow freely. Experience easy pleasure as you accomplish the movements, or the words, or the tones. Let your behavior feel good. Get ready to dream by picturing your performance in a smooth manner. You'll increase the chances of finding yourself performing fluidly in your sleep as well. And you'll be preparing yourself to do better in waking life.

Visualize and Feel the Flow of a Great Performance: Practice

THE TERMS PEOPLE most often use to describe dreams of doing well are *ease, flow, riding the rhythm, graceful, elegant, smooth,* and *creamy.* They liken the sensations of easy fluency they have in dreams to performing like pros. This feeling of fluidity contrasts sharply with the erratic movements we noticed in Poor Test Performance, scurrying here and there to find the right location, forgetting necessary equipment, and so forth.

A curving, flawless line is the mark of the true artist in any field. Watch your favorite basketball star send the ball swishing through the net. Look at the quarterback hurling the football down the field into the receiver's waiting arms. The master chef chops and minces with a marvelous assurance. The professional musician strives for *legato,* a fluid connection between the individual notes. The dancer blends the separate steps into a harmonious, graceful pattern. The French artist Matisse abstracted what he called "the line of beauty" from countless works of art. It's an elegant, arching curve—much like those on some female bodies—that he used in his own work. We can all be artists, whatever our craft.

When you dream about effortlessly carrying out some actual skill you work at developing or maintaining in waking life, *remember the sensations*. By replaying the memory of smoothness and easy rhythm when you are performing the skill in the waking world, you can recapture some of the magic of the dream act. Even test taking can become an art. Your waking execution may retain some of the same creamy texture, the sense of liberty and openness that your dream performance had.

> Easy flow of skill in your dream = Increased ability to perform waking skill

As I mentioned in the last section, you can help yourself dream about excelling in the skill you wish to develop. During the drowsy period before you fall asleep, vividly visualize the steps in your desired performance, going well of course. Imagine the details. Feel them. Sense them. Soon you'll be dancing (or whatever it is *you* wish) in your dreams.

Applause of Colleagues and Crowd: Feeling Appreciated

"OLÉ! BRAVO! BRAVA! Congratulations! Good job!" Dreamers sometimes provide their internal approval of their outstanding performances. Like the young American man who dreamed of being "high-fived" by his fellow All-Stars while playing excellent basketball—a skill he practiced weekly—most dreamers yearn for appreciation from their peers and the world at large.

The Swedish mystic Emanuel Swedenborg dreamed that his deceased father at last approved of him, when he began a work that combined science and spiritual inquiry. Indian poet Debendranath Tagore dreamed that his deceased mother congratulated him for becoming "one who has known Brahma." Many of today's dreamers report similar experiences, dreams in which a deceased loved one praises them. Most of us want to feel that we have the respect of the people whose opinions we value, even those long dead.

> Approval by others in your dream = Desire for appreciation in waking life

In dreams about Poor Performance, you saw that fear of failure is the common element the dream variations share. When you dream about giving a great performance, you are anticipating success. If you dream about being encouraged or approved of by other characters in a dream, you feel hopeful of appreciation. Enjoy the sensation. Success in your dreams is often the start of greater success in the waking world.

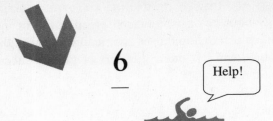

6

Falling or Drowning Versus Flying, Swimming, or Dancing Joyfully

---

6.0 FALLING OR DROWNING

Description: You dream of falling through the air, frightened. The dream may begin in a high location, such as the edge of a cliff, the edge of a roof, or the top of a building; it may simply start while you are falling through space. You may or may not strike the ground before awakening. A variation of this dream is that of anxiously sinking through the water, in danger of drowning. (Drowning associated with a tidal wave or flood is classified with Natural or Man-made Disaster dreams.)

Frequency: Falling is one of the most common nightmares among all people and ages; Drowning dreams are less common. Either may or may not occur frequently. Falling dreams usually take place when you feel insecure; Drowning dreams when you feel overwhelmed in the waking state. Falling dreams may occur in conjunction with an actual fall from bed; Drowning dreams may be associated with severe edema.

Usual Meanings: "I feel insecure"; "I have no support"; "I have no solid grounding"; or, literally, "I'm falling" (Falling dream); "I feel overwhelmed"; "Things are too much right now"; "I give up" (Drowning dream).

When you dream that you are falling, the sensations of rapid descent into certain death feel real—pure terror, followed by a wake-up jolt. People often experience such dreams as they are drifting off, "falling" asleep.

Falling is one of the most typical dreams. Several surveys of common dreams report that the theme of falling has the highest frequency, although in my survey, dreams about being chased or attacked topped it. Among the first five hundred people who filled out the survey on Universal Dreams on my website, over 64 percent of the dreamers said they had experienced falling dreams, more than those had dreamed about Being Naked in Public or performing poorly in examinations (both about 30 percent). You've probably had a falling dream at least once. Why do so many people report this jarring nightmare? What does it mean when you dream that you are falling?

INFLUENCES ON YOUR DREAMS ABOUT FALLING OR DROWNING

WE HUMAN BEINGS are forever struggling to keep our balance, to prevent ourselves from "going under." Our dream of falling through space, and its opposite, the dream of soaring joyfully through the air, deal with our assessment of how we are maintaining, strengthening, or losing our tenuous hold on our goals and on our support systems. When we dream of sinking through the water, being totally overcome by it, or dream of its opposite—swimming with easy pleasure through the element—we are dealing with similar issues of goals and support.

The dream of falling is so pervasive that many theorists think it has a genetic link. Perhaps symbolic meanings of falling are superimposed on a predisposition for falling imagery.

1. Biological

JUST AS DREAMS of being chased or attacked probably owe their origin to the dangers our ancestors faced from wild animals and enemy tribes, dreams of falling may originate from the risks these same ancestors took when climbing trees. They used high places to search for predatory animals or strangers, assess potential campsites, and survey suitable hunting grounds. Our predecessors at a primitive stage of evolution are said to have lived in the trees and swung from their branches. Since we have inherited our genes from these earlier peoples, it is not surprising that we should possess a built-in fear of falling.

Modern life has its own dangerous high places. In fact, many dreamers set their Falling dreams in these very spots—high buildings, elevators, and rooftops, along with rocky cliffs. Falling dreams may warn us to be cautious in these places, whether the meaning is literal or symbolic.

Drowning dreams, too, have a strong phylogenetic connection. Our need for air is basic. The ability to breathe is essential for survival, and anything that interferes with it will be resisted vigorously. Studies have shown that even small babies exert strong effort to prevent having their nostrils and mouths covered, demonstrating this inborn instinct. "If you can't breathe, nothing else matters," is the slogan of the American Lung Association. It's absolutely true. When, in dreams, we are inundated with water or other fluids, battling to breathe and to stay afloat, to keep our heads above water, our primal survival drive kicks in and we fight for the breath of life.

In both Falling and Drowning dreams, we feel faced with a life-or-death situation. We often awake to "escape" the danger in our dream. But there is more than our instinct to survive involved in these dreams.

2, 3. *Cultural and Subcultural Influences*

MOST CULTURES IMPART a positive association with "up" and a negative association with "down." Up is good; down is bad. When you are happy, you are said to be "up," to feel "high," to be "floating on air." When sad, you are said to be "down," to feel "low," to be "in the depths of despair."

The symbolism connected with ascending and descending, with rising and falling, is extremely rich. Moral, social, and monetary status is portrayed in these ups and downs. There are upper classes and lower classes. There are seraphim and a fallen angel (Satan), high-class women and fallen women (Adam appears to be the only fallen man, as one analyst points out). In the Judeo-Christian tradition there is the original sin, "The Fall" of Adam and Eve, as a result of yielding to the serpent's temptation to eat from the Tree of Knowledge, leading to the first couple's expulsion from Eden.

The ancient Greeks cautioned that a person could rise too high through pride and consequently fall to extinction (the sin of hubris illustrated in the myth of Icarus, who flew so close to the Sun that the wax holding his wings melted). Falling suggests, in addition to loss of moral or social or financial status, loss of control. One "falls out of favor," gets "knocked off his or her pedestal," "falls from grace," and "hits rock bottom."

Freud thought dreams about falling were to be interpreted as a loss of morality: "If a woman dreams of falling, it almost invariably has a sexual sense: she is imagining herself as a 'fallen woman.'" He also thought dreams about falling were memories of being tossed in the air and caught by playful parents. Later psychoanalysts concluded that dreams of falling represent a more general loss of control.

The ideas and views your culture has about any dream topic are sure to influence your own dreams, but these beliefs are always tempered by your individual experiences.

4. *Personal*

YOUR CURRENT AGE and physical condition have an impact on your dreams about falling or drowning. The young, the old, and the ill are especially prone to physical falls. Toddlers who are striving to acquire walking skills repeatedly tumble as they learn to maneuver in their environment. Small children, too, may endure numerous falls while playing. Older persons often become frail and unable to support themselves easily. They totter, lose their balance, and injure their brittle bones. For these populations, falling is a matter of greater risk and so may emerge to a larger degree in their dreams.

Other groups with certain physical conditions are at greater risk in a fall than the general public. If you have osteoporosis or any other condition that makes you more vulnerable to breaking bones, falling seems riskier than for most people. Those people with multiple sclerosis and certain other ailments have difficulty walking; falls may figure more prominently in dreams of this population.

People with heart conditions or other physical problems that create edema in the lungs are thought to be more subject to dreams of drowning. In these cases, there is an actual fluid accumulation in the lungs that gives the sleeping person a sensation of drowning. One friend, when she was suffering with pneumonia, dreamed she was in an upside-down submarine, gasping for breath. Even a passing cold can lead people to dream about drowning.

An older American man who participated in my website survey said that his condition of multiple sclerosis (MS) resulted in an increased need to urinate at night, as well as in trouble walking. He finds his dreams about water, sometimes with showers or mountains streams, "very useful" because he does not feel the urination urgency until he's standing. His dreams of water presumably clue him to awaken in time to get up and go to the bathroom.

Of course, your entire personal medical history, any serious falls, and any experience you may have had of near-drowning, are certain to affect your dreams about these subjects. Recent traumatic events in these areas may replay in alarming dreams.

As we turn to the symbolic meanings that emerge in the common dream of falling, then look at the symbolism in the less common dream of drowning, keep in mind your own current physical condition, as well as any personal experiences in the area.

UNDERSTANDING YOUR DREAMS ABOUT FALLING

Your Falling Dreams as a Metaphor for Feeling Helpless

WHEN YOU DREAM you are falling, by definition, you plummet from a high place to a low place. Typically, the dreamer says something like, "I'm suddenly falling through space, never hitting the ground, but I get a funny feeling in my stomach and a sudden shortness of breath. Then I wake up with a jerk." Your dream will probably contain one or more of these motifs that share the common element of rapid movement from high to low:

- falling through space
- falling from a high object: a cliff, a roof, the top of a building, an amusement ride, a roller coaster, a ferris wheel, a swing, a bridge, a ladder, a piece of equipment or machinery
- falling into depth: down an endless pit, down an elevator shaft, into water (river, lake, pond, pool, ocean), through blackness
- falling during a flight
- waking before you strike the ground
- falling until you strike the ground, with or without injury

In general, when you dream about falling, you are picturing feeling helpless in the face of impending change for the worse. The precise meaning is in the details.

Falling in your dream = Feeling helpless about impending waking life change

---

Falling from the Edge of a Cliff: Impending Danger

WHEN I REVIEWED the many dreams about falling in my collection, I was surprised to see how often they began at the edge of a cliff—"I fell from a cliff"; "I stepped off a cliff"; "I fell off a high cliff"; "I Rollerbladed over a cliff"; and so forth. A teenager from Poland described a typical scenario in his dream, that "I'm walking between a rocky wall and a chasm. I suddenly realize that I don't have anyplace to put my feet. I fall down and wake up." Why do we set our dreams about falling at the border of rugged rocks?

First of all, the rim of a cliff is a notoriously dangerous place to be. In the Bay Area of San Francisco, the daily news occasionally carries an item about the latest person to slip from the Marin Headlands overlooking Golden Gate Bridge, a spectacular view that tempts people to draw too close for safety. Or there may be the report of a miraculous rescue of someone who has ventured too near to the margin of the rocks in the Seacliff area of San Francisco and has slipped over, to hang precariously above the pounding surf until rescued.

Metaphorically, our language is filled with expressions about the danger of being at the limit of boundaries, such as "I'm on edge," "I'm on the verge of trouble," "I'm on the brink of disaster."

So if your dream about falling begins by going over the edge of a cliff, your dream language is shouting, "Look out! You're in a dangerous place! Watch your step or you'll go over!" You need to listen to yourself and act for your self-protection.

On the edge of a cliff in your dream = On the brink of danger in waking situation

---

Rooftops, Tops of Buildings, and Bridges: Too Near the Edge

BEING AT THE edge of a roof, atop a tall building, or on a bridge, is a situation almost as dangerous as standing at the edge of a cliff. The fall may be shorter, but it could be equally lethal. Several dreamers set their Falling dreams in these risky places.

What is one to make of the English saying "falling off the roof" to refer to a woman's menstrual period? How this was derived I'm not sure, but some female dreamers may use this expression as a pun in their dreams to refer to the onset of menstruation.

Rooftops, building tops, and bridges are conveniently high locations that are sometimes chosen by would-be suicides. Therefore, the element of depression may be present in dreams of going over the edge of such spots. On the bright side, many dreamers have described to me using rooftops, a location high enough to provide lift-off, as a launching pad for Flying dreams.

If you should dream about falling from any of these elevated places—cliffs, roofs, building tops, or bridges—take special care. Your dream has alerted you to the presence of danger. Don't "fall into it"; deal with it instead.

Get help, reestablish your support system, "get your feet back on the ground," make contact.

Falling from a high place in your dream = Losing a sense of waking
support

Falling from an Amusement Ride: A Change in Circumstances

A GROUP OF dreamers set their Falling dreams in amusement parks or fun situations. Some said they dreamed that a roller coaster they were on went off the rails and they fell out. One told of falling from a ferris wheel, presumably striking the ground, and slowly dying "while others stood around and laughed." Another described falling headfirst from a swing that suddenly went higher than normal.

Dreams that begin in places of pleasure and then turn disastrous suggest that the dreamer anticipates a change for the worse. If you dream about falling in a setting like this, you are saying in dream language, "Look here, this is all fun at the moment, but things could go seriously amiss." Sometimes waking events have already taken an unfortunate turn when you have a nightmare about falling.

Falling from an amusement ride in a dream = Pleasant waking situation
turns threatening

The Roman emperor Caligula dreamed, on the night before he was assassinated, that he was in heaven, standing beside the throne of Jupiter. The god kicked him "with his great toe" and sent him tumbling back to earth. A fall from heaven—the highest place—to earth is a prime example of change in circumstances, a mighty fall in status. Caligula, who had declared himself a god, must have sensed the growing hatred among his former supporters, a threatening shift that led to his assassination the next day. Caligula's dream suggests he may have felt some guilt for his many crimes. His "fall" in status became literal.

*Falling from Elevators, Ladders, Equipment, or Machinery: Unreliable
Support*

ALL FALLING DREAMS contain the element of danger that the dreamer senses is present in waking life. In cases of falls from equipment or machinery, the dream has a somewhat different emphasis. Danger is still present, but the means of ascent (or safe descent) has become impaired. The dreamer who was riding in an elevator when the cable broke and he was plunged into fearful darkness was "let down" by the very thing on which he was relying to get him where he wanted to go. The man who had recurrent dreams of falling from a ladder was also depending on some means of ascent that proved unstable. Perhaps a person he depended upon had let him down, or a method he was using to achieve his goals proved unreliable.

The Black Pit: Obscured Solution

YOU MAY FIND yourself falling through black space in a dream. Plummeting down an elevator shaft, dropping through an endless pit—whenever dreamers describe being faced with darkness in a dream, it symbolizes the difficulty they currently have in seeing their way through their trouble.

> Blackness in your dream = Difficulty seeing your way clear in a waking situation

"I felt myself falling into an abyss of enormous depth, at the bottom of which I saw flames, so surrounded by thick black smoke as to seem almost black themselves. I was stifled and afraid," wrote a nineteenth-century French marquis.

The black space, if it appears in your dream, may add to the feeling of fear as you fall, but it is also often simply a way of expressing how hard it is to see what to do about a waking situation. Blackness in dreams may also represent "black" feelings or mood, characteristic of periods of depression or discouragement. As you begin to cope with whatever your predicament is, the light will return.

Striking the Ground: Shocked into Awareness

THE EXACT POINT at which you awaken from a Falling dream is important. Many dreamers violently propel themselves awake, to avoid striking the ground. "Hitting bottom" in a dream is something most people dread, probably because they have heard the old folk saying "If you hit bottom in a dream you will die." Believing you will die if you hit the bottom is enough to waken anyone with a start. In dreams, to believe it is to experience it. Yet, the saying is simply not true. I have landed safely many times from Falling dreams. So can you.

What does contact with the ground symbolize in dreams? As mentioned, psychoanalysts suggest that when a woman dreams of falling she is picturing sexual intercourse, becoming a "fallen woman." They see hitting the ground as equivalent to orgasm. For some dreamers, these meanings for a Falling dream may apply. But today's women are far freer and more experienced in the sexual realm than were the women in Victorian days, when psychoanalysts rightly identified repressed sexual feelings. And what of men who dream they are falling, with or without striking the ground? Many men in my collection report dreams with this imagery.

The French marquis Hervé de Saint-Denys, who was able to become aware of dreaming during his dreams (what we call lucid dreaming), deliberately threw himself off the top story of a house in one of his dreams, to experience falling safely. His dream shifted to the image of a courtyard, where he stood in a crowd who had gathered to watch the body of a man who had thrown himself from a tower be carried away. The dreamer's imagination had difficulty allowing him to experience directly the dangerous landing. Yet, contemporary lucid and nonlucid dreamers have managed to land safely from dream falls, as we'll see in the next section.

There is also a school of thought that suggests that dreamers are falling back into their bodies after an out-of-the-body experience and that the thud of hitting the ground is the reconnection of the soul with the body. We have no way of proving such a theory, but we can suggest the symbolic meaning of hitting the earth.

I suggest that striking the ground in a Falling dream represents shocking contact with reality. The impact we feel—and fear—as we strike the earth calls our attention to the need to attend to the situation the dream is reflecting. When you dream about fearfully falling through the air and striking the ground, you are being sharply "brought back to earth."

Striking the earth in your dream = Shocking awareness of a waking situation

---

When you have a dream about falling, ask yourself the following:

1. What situation have I "fallen into" that needs my attention?
2. Who or what do I feel has "let me down" recently?
3. What can I do about the situation? (There's always something.)
4. How can I restore my balance?
5. How can I lift myself "up" again?

Regardless of the area of the "fall"—whether it is your social standing, a moral misstep, a financial dip, or a loss of control in other areas—you are capable of making changes that can improve the situation. You can start by changing the dream itself. Then perhaps you can restabilize a relationship that has momentarily "fallen through," "fallen down," or "fallen out."

TRANSFORMING YOUR FALLING DREAMS

Falling Gently and Landing Gently: Relax into Awareness

ALTHOUGH WE HAVE a set idea of what Falling dreams are like—an anxious rapid descent from which one awakens with a start—it is possible for us to alter these stereotyped dreams.

In my book *Creative Dreaming,* I describe how the Senoi tell their children, "Falling is one of the best dreams you can have. The earth spirits love you; they are calling you." They instruct the children to relax. "Let yourself fall gently and land gently. Go and find the wonderful things that are waiting for you there. You can see the different people or animals, learn their songs and dances, their masks and costumes, and bring them back to share with us."

Instead of allowing yourself to fall helplessly, you can convert the dream of anxious falling into one of joyful flying. Next time you dream of falling, remember—you can fly. Turn the passive role of falling into the active one of flying. Fly someplace interesting, learn something, remember it, and take it back to the waking state.

Teaching these methods to adults as well as children has resulted in some remarkable dreams. Sometimes the dreamer comes up with an ingenious solution to a Falling dream. An eleven-year-old American boy dreamed about falling over a cliff and almost hitting the rocks on the bottom. At the last minute, he converted his dream into one of flying, and he soared into the sky with the eagles. Even though his dream introduced the danger of colliding with an airplane at the end, he enjoyed the freedom of his flight. An eight-year-old American girl who dreamed of falling through a gutter found diamonds and other precious gems at the bottom. Her dream suggested that there was something precious to be learned when she let herself go.

RE-DREAMING A FALLING DREAM: CONVERTING THE FEAR

THERE'S NOT MUCH you can do to prevent Falling dreams that accompany an actual fall from bed, other than cushion the floor at the bedside. I've mentioned my own childhood dream of crashing in a small plane when I fell out of bed. Other Falling dreams in my collection that were associated with actual falls include falling down a mountain, falling off the Empire State Building, and being in a rocket that took off into space. A teenager from Wales dreamed she was Alice in Wonderland, when "I fell down the hole, after the rabbit. I ended up falling out of bed, in reality."

However, whether your dream was associated with an actual fall or not, you can help dispel any discomfort over a Falling dream by visualizing it differently. I sometimes ask traumatized dreamers to "redream" their experience. If you want to try this method, get yourself settled comfortably in a quiet and safe place. Close your eyes. Bring back the imagery of the dream as vividly as possible. See it. Hear it. Feel it. Sense your emotions. Now picture it differently from the way it was. Change the action in any way you like. Make it better. See the new scene as clearly as the original one. Examine it in your mind's eye until it feels right. Then open your eyes. If you wish, you can make a sketch of the transformed dream.

A thirteen-year-old American girl found this technique helpful in coping with what she called her worst nightmare. In it, she opened a door, walked through it, slipped, and fell into "totally nothing, just space, pitch dark." In her re-dream, she closed her eyes, recalled the imagery of the dream as vividly as possible, then imagined its changing. Afterward she drew a picture of her re-dream that showed a gigantic cushion set where she would have landed, to catch her and soften the fall. Such a simple process can make a big difference in the dreamer's level of comfort with a nightmare. It can also start the process of altering the life situation that the dream represents.

In the chapter on Car or Other Vehicular Trouble, I recounted the dreams of many adults who transformed their nightmares of driving a car off a cliff into dreams of steering themselves to a safe landing.

Whenever you have a Falling dream of any kind, remember that you can fall gently and land gently. You can convert a dream of falling into one of flying, as a young woman from Canada did. For her, "It's usually black and I can't see the ground but at the peak of my terror and anxiety, I suddenly swoop up and begin flying upwards; the anxiety almost immediately changes to this unbelievable rush of euphoria that begins in my chest and spreads through my body." As she and many others have, you can re-dream a better dream. You can change your waking life through your dreams.

UNDERSTANDING YOUR DREAMS OF DROWNING

IN THIS SECTION we'll take a brief look at the symbolism underlying dreams about drowning, especially in connection with falling. Drowning dreams are explored further in the chapter on Natural or Man-made Disasters, with which they are often classified; Drowning dreams that are not associated with disasters are included here.

We have seen how there is a strong genetic component to the desperate need to breathe in dreams of drowning, and how the dreamer's physical condition may play a role in those dreams. Here we focus on this dream's symbolic layers.

Drowning as a Metaphor for Feeling Overwhelmed

WE CONSTANTLY USE metaphors in waking life that include references to the dangerous aspect of water, such as "I'm in deep water"; "I'm going under"; "I'm sinking"; "I can't stay afloat." We use these expressions in a variety of situations, ranging from a disastrous love affair to financial burdens. One dreamer spoke of a Drowning dream in which "I am thrashing around for my life but can't seem to stay afloat." She seemed to find the dream strange because in waking life she can swim well—a sure cue that her dream is symbolic.

Whenever you have a dream about drowning, it's probable that you are using the imagery to express feelings of being overwhelmed in some waking situation. A Spanish woman dreamed about "drowning" and dying under snow; some aspect of her waking situation probably felt emotionally "cold," as well as being overwhelming.

> Drowning in your dream = Feeling overwhelmed by a waking problem

The Waters of Life or Death

THE ELEMENT OF water is, like air, indispensable to life. It is the origin of life, the "primal soup" where living beings originated. As humans, we must have water to survive. Our bodies are largely composed of water. We need it to drink and to clean ourselves. We swim in it for refreshment and sail over it in travel.

Yet water can kill us as well as save us. Most of mankind's myths contain stories of the primal waters and the catastrophic great flood. They also tell of the aqua vitae (the water of life) and its precious life-restoring qualities.

This ambivalence is present in our dreams of drowning. Water can be life-giving or life-taking. Jung believed that "water is the commonest symbol for the unconscious." Certainly, the dangers we confront in dreams about drowning are aspects of our inner life.

If you dream about drowning, and the situation that is making you feel "inundated" is not immediately obvious to you, question yourself about the following:

1. What situation in my waking life makes me feel overwhelmed at present?
2. Where do I feel inundated with too much to do?
3. What's causing a hopeless and helpless reaction in me?
4. What can I do about this problem?
5. How can I improve the situation?

Afloat on an Endless Sea: Feeling Hopeless

A DUTCH WOMAN who was undergoing a divorce dreamed of lying on her back in an endless sea, paralyzed with fear that she would drown. There was no land in sight, no airplane or ship she could signal for help; she awoke in fear.

This woman explained to me how at the time of the dream she was tormented by her husband's request for a divorce. The couple continued to live together for several years, but she felt lost, totally unable to carry on with her writing profession. She readily connected her feeling of helplessness in the dream and her daytime feeling of hopelessness about her future.

As we discussed the symbolism of her dream, the woman said, "If I had started to swim I might have seen land, an airplane, or a ship." It was her passive acceptance of drowning that terrorized her. The idea that she should have done something in the dream seemed to dispel her waking sense of paralysis. The day after her dream, she began to write again. Although the divorce eventually went through, the woman felt stronger. She entered therapy, got help that restored her vitality, and was able to rebuild her life. Even distressing dreams can guide us to a brighter future.

As in most alarming dreams, taking action can alleviate the dreamer's distress. This woman acted after she awoke and contemplated her lack of effort in the dream. She took waking action to help herself. You can also profit by taking action within the dream. The same behavior that may save you during an actual near-drowning experience can be undertaken during dreams — grab hold of something that floats, clutch and climb a tree, call for help. *Do something.*

There's another possibility that some dreamers discover in the midst of drowning dreams: the ability to breathe underwater.

TRANSFORMING YOUR DREAMS OF DROWNING

Discovering You Can Breathe Underwater

AMONG THE HANDFUL of people who reported dreams of drowning in my website survey, a small percentage spoke of the delightful discovery that they were able to breathe underwater.

I have encountered this motif many times in the past. Dreamers who have had terrifying nightmares about being inundated with water suddenly realize that they are having the same scary dream again, that it is a dream, and that in dreams one can safely breathe underwater.

The skill of breathing beneath water in dreams is one that may be useful to you. The next time you find yourself at risk of drowning in a dream, remind yourself that it's a dream, and remember that you can breathe underwater without fear.

Being able to breathe underwater in a dream = Greater waking ability
to face inner depths

Some dreamers say that discovering the skill of underwater breathing has enabled them to take pleasure in dreams of great waters, to ride the waves, to explore the sea, and to gaze at the wonders of the deep. Symbolically, such dreamers portray the new insight that it's possible to face unknown aspects of one's own submerged depths and unveil the secrets that dwell there.

As you learn to move freely through water or air in a dream, you will be reflecting increased capacities in the daytime world. You'll probably find yourself flying joyfully, swimming pleasurably, or dancing with abandon in your dreams.

FLYING, SWIMMING, OR DANCING JOYFULLY

6.5 FLYING, SWIMMING, OR DANCING JOYFULLY

Description: You dream of whizzing through space, feeling the wind, sensing a delicious freedom. Flying may evolve as an escape out of some alarming dream situation, becoming a sheer delight. A similar feeling of joy may occasionally arise when you dream of moving effortlessly through water or of dancing with total abandon.

Frequency: A highly pleasurable dream among people of various ages and cultures. For many individuals, flying is their all-time favorite dream. Its frequency varies from dreamer to dreamer.

Usual Meanings: "Things are great"; "I can soar as high as I wish"; "My possibilities are unlimited"; "I can transcend difficulties"; "I am free" (with flying); "I can explore my depths with confidence" (with swimming); "I can let joy permeate my body" (with dance).

You'll know when you've had a joyful Flying dream—the pleasure seems to carry over from the dream to waking hours. The sense of incredible freedom that such dreams impart is legendary. In fact, in these extraordinary dreams, we seem to share with the shaman the skill of "magical flight." If blue ribbons were awarded for dreams, Flying dreams would win the first prize for best of show.

Many of our dreams can inspire us, lift us to spiritual heights, or fill us with creative notions, but the dream of flying stands apart from most of our pleasant dreams because of the special sensation of freedom from any restriction it gives the dreamer. We transcend our problems. All things seem possible. We have no limitations. We can accomplish our heart's desire. We can connect with the exalted heights and return to tell the tale.

Each dream in this category shares the gift of freedom. We examine Flying dreams first, in more detail, then look at the subtle shifts in emphasis contained in blissful dreams of Swimming and Dancing.

UNDERSTANDING YOUR DREAMS OF FLYING

Flying as a Metaphor for Freedom

THE COMPLEX AND richly textured symbolism we saw in metaphors and in dreams about falling, going downward, is of course, applicable in reverse when we dream about going "Up!" In English we say that we are "on the rise," "moving up in the world," "floating on air," "in seventh heaven," "on cloud nine," "feeling high," "flying high," "having high hopes"—to mention just a few of the numerous expressions that associate the direction "up" with happiness and good results.

In Falling dreams we feel helpless; in Flying dreams we feel free. We can move in the direction of our choice, which is usually up. If you already fly in your dreams, you know what rapture it can bring.

Flying in your dream = Feeling free to achieve waking wishes

Some dreamers hover in a space between falling and flying, as did the young American woman who said, "I've had dreams where I can float at will, up to the vaulted ceiling of my mother's house or over trees outside." She added that sometimes she feels guilty for having the ability to float or fearful that she won't be able to control it so she can return safely to earth. Another dreamer spoke of being able to stay aloft only for short times, having to contact the earth to push back up again. Still other dreamers worry about getting tangled in electrical wires or other obstacles in the air. These dreamers have partially freed themselves to move in any direction at the time of the dream. Luckily, they sometimes, like many others around the globe, enjoy the "rare and wonderful dream of soaring far above the earth at will."

If your dreams of flight ever turn into Falling dreams, you'll want to review the material on Transforming Your Falling Dreams, earlier in this chapter, to see how to reverse the process.

Moving Up in the World: Reaching Toward Your Waking Goal

IF DREAMS ABOUT falling are associated with loss of moral, financial, social, or spiritual status, dreams about going up are connected with gain in these areas. Flying dreams may represent our goals, ambitions, and achievements.

When we fly with pleasure in a dream it is likely to be after a sense of success. I remember the delight I felt the day I learned that my first professional paper on dreams (I had not yet produced my first book) was to be published in a respected journal. I dreamed that night of floating in air, tossing my body up and down and up again with happiness.

We spoke of a "fallen woman." Is there such a thing as a "risen woman"? We do have the concept of a "risen man." Indeed, saviors in many cultures are said to have "arisen from the dead." Perhaps this is part of the enchanting quality of Flying dreams. In them, we seem to have acquired the skill of birds, the capacity of moving in any dimension that is attributed to spirits and saints.

By itself, flying in a dream can be appreciated simply for the experience. "I fly over the countryside surveying marvelous sights," said an older American woman, adding that she once flew by sitting on a garbage can—suggesting that she was able to "rise above" some trashy material. An American teenager said her Flying dreams were like "swimming in the air": sometimes she floats on an inner tube across the heights. Perhaps the man from Japan who dreamed "I am flying effortlessly through space" is expressing his pleasure in excelling in the waking world. Yet I think there is more to learn from these highly sought-after adventurous flights. We'll look at the separate characteristic motifs, and what these variations might mean in your next dream of flying.

Rising Through the Air: Deliberately Exploring Your Heights

IN DREAMS ABOUT Car Pleasure, we saw that you are able to select your driving direction at will. Flying dreams extend that notion of choice to a wider sphere. Not only may you determine the route to take to a desirable spot, but now you may also choose the dimension. In my dream "The Great Steering Wheel," described in the section on Car Pleasure, I rose upward by choice. Likewise, a young German woman flew along a staircase, practicing her flying. But the goal of dream ascents may be far beyond hovering a few feet above an ordinary street or above a staircase.

In my collection of Flying dreams are many examples from children who sailed with the birds, swooped across Golden Gate Bridge, and climbed still higher. A contemporary Frenchman dreamed of trying to land on the Eiffel

Tower; as he flew, he was ascending into the same airy realm. And in a dream I called "The High Flyer and the Strawberry Lady," I chose to fly to the moon. At times I have flown over the night ocean, at the border of shore and sea, exulting in the beauties of the moonlight and starlight sparkling on the waves.

An older American woman shared her dream that "I am flying, soaring, over a beautiful woodland." When she realized that just by *thinking higher*, she could fly still higher, it was "a real breakthrough for me, even in the dream. This has served as an inspiration for me in real life." Such dreams can transfer some of their magic to the waking world.

In my dreams of flight, the sensations are sometimes so real as to make me wonder whether there is such a thing as an actual projection of a "second body." I feel the wind in my face and the coolness of the air. I can understand the ancient belief that when people dreamed of flying, their souls were literally traveling in spirit worlds.

Reaching Upward: High Hopes for Connection

ON ONE LEVEL, our dreams about flying high represent our ambitions, our wishes to succeed. The children who dream of flying are often expressing their wish to have special powers, to be able to save others, to do good and be rewarded. These childhood dreams of flight may represent the beginnings of the need to achieve, the desire to be recognized and appreciated. Adults who are striving upward in their careers also may be expressing a wish to accomplish a difficult task, to rise above their troubles and be outstandingly successful. To a certain extent, Flying dreams symbolize connection with worldly success.

> Flying in your dream = Climbing closer to connection with waking goal

Yet, there is something more that is involved in dream flying than straightforward ambition to rise in life. The gods and goddesses of pagan times, the spirits, the saints, have been said to dwell on high. This is true as well of the holy figures in every major religion today. Whether we speak of Heaven, Paradise, Valhalla, Elysium, the Happy Hunting Ground, or any of the numerous appellations of the domains of afterlife, in nearly every culture this ethereal kingdom lies upward from earth. This is why humankind has built its religious structures on high ground, in an attempt to get closer to the gods, on mesas or hilltops or in mountaintop cloisters. The buildings themselves often strain upward, from cathedrals, to ziggurats, to pyramids. They point up, and by climbing their towers or steps, we picture ourselves getting closer to the holy source.

So, too, in our dreams of flight I believe that we are often reaching for something higher in ourselves. By ascending in our dreams we may be yearning for more than worldly success; we may be reaching for the stars, striving to connect with the spiritual part of ourselves. This may be why Flying dreams gift us with ecstatic delight.

Flying in your dream = Possible reaching for connection with spirituality

---

When you dream about flying, consider both layers of meaning; perhaps both are applicable at different times.

UNDERSTANDING YOUR DREAMS ABOUT
JOYFUL SWIMMING

YOUR DREAMS ABOUT rapturous Dancing or Swimming share the feeling of freedom imparted in Flying dreams.

Pleasurable Swimming Dreams as a Metaphor
for Freely Exploring Your Depths

WE HAVE SEEN that dreams about drowning indicate feelings of being overwhelmed. When you move easily with pleasure through the element of water, you are expressing your confidence in exploring your inner depths. For some dreamers, it is not the element of air that enthralls them, but the skill of serenely swimming where they will, examining the marvels of the sea. A young American woman dreamed she was a dolphin, seeing and feeling the incredible beauty of the watery world. Like the young woman from Sweden who reported happy dreams of diving, something she enjoys in waking life, gliding into the waters with easy grace, she finds the delight that other dreamers get from soaring upward.

Swimming joyfully in your dream = Waking confidence to explore your depths freely

---

Remember how it is possible to breathe underwater in dreams? People who have learned to do so find particular delight in their Swimming dreams, probing deep watery worlds.

UNDERSTANDING YOUR DREAMS ABOUT JOYFUL DANCING

IF OUR HAPPY dreams of flying are movement through the element of air, and joyful dreams of swimming are movement through the element of water, fabulous dreams of dancing are grounded on the earth. These may come closest to what we can actually experience in our bodies in the waking world.

Joyful Dreams of Dancing as a Metaphor for Moving Freely Through Your Life

WE SOMETIMES DREAM of dancing in a way that is as transporting as flying or as joyous as swimming through deep waters. In my dreams through the years I have watched extraordinary dance performances, or I have become the dancer weaving incredible movements and rhythms. One of my earliest recorded dreams, in my journal at age fifteen, is a dream of dancing in a school play. In it, my father was holding my hand, then let it go as he tossed me high into the air. I swooped upward and down, to be caught in the arms of one of the boys from school, as the audience burst into applause. On one level, this was clearly a dream of awakening sexuality.

In a much later dream, an especially strange one from my forties, I was a dancer and at the same time I was also my ancestor who was a temple dancer; I seemed to feel the two realities at once. In yet another dancing dream, as I moved in rhythm I began to sing, "This is the dance that my grandma used to do—Long, long ago; long, long ago." Sometimes my dance movements in a dream become the energy that powers flying, as in the dream in which I gave a shimmy of my hips, and the movement propelled me up and through the air in dance-style flight.

Many women have shared with me dreams about ecstatic dancing. Often they dance in the arms of a waking life lover, gliding, waltzing, swirling, feet barely touching the polished dream floor. Sometimes they dream of being in the imagined arms of a lover-to-come. Remember the woman who dreamed of dancing with the Greek god? These dreams are stimulated by loving feelings, already existent or aching to be born. I feel there is a deeper desire than that for love or sex in these dreams of rapturous dance—there is a yearning to experience the fullness of life.

When I was a girl, I pulled the strings to make my father's marionettes dance across the stage. Now I let the rhythm flow and I dance, freely and easily, through my life, asleep or awake. Aside from sexuality in my dreams of ecstatic dance, there is something beyond the mere physical: there is contact with the rhythm of life. I *experience* dance. I can understand why the Indians declared that the god Shiva brought the world into being by dancing. Indeed, in most cultures, the origin of dance has been sacred.

The exhilaration in dreams of dance shares with dreams of flying and swimming an element of freedom. When you dance in your dreams with joyful abandon you participate in the basic element of life—the pulse that moves the world. Perhaps you are also making a connection with the rhythm that moves all life.

Joyful dancing in your dream = Greater freedom to participate in sensual life

---

Regardless of whether dream flying is expressive of waking goals or spiritual heights, Flying is a favorite happy dream for people of every age in every culture. Whether you choose simply to relish the dream flight, or to see your wished-for and achieved success, or to recognize your spiritual search, the choice is yours. When you dream of exhilarated Swimming or jubilant Dancing, you are gaining freedom in your waking space.

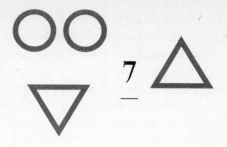

Being Naked or Inappropriately Dressed in Public Versus Being Well Dressed

---

7.0 BEING NAKED OR INAPPROPRIATELY DRESSED IN PUBLIC

Description: You dream of being nude or partly dressed in a public place. Or you may see yourself inappropriately dressed in some social situation, for instance, showing up at work in your nightgown or pajamas. Another variation of this theme is seeing some other dream character naked, or unsuitably attired, in public. Your feelings may range from embarrassment (the most common reaction) to indifference to pride. Sometimes dreamers feel especially free in a state of undress, but this is a rare response.

Frequency: A fairly common anxiety dream among all people and ages, including children.

Usual Meanings: "I feel exposed"; "I feel vulnerable"; "I have been too revealing"; "I have no protection"; "I feel awkward"; or, rarely, "I feel free, unencumbered."

When you dream about Being Naked in Public, you're most likely to react with feelings of embarrassment or shame during the dream. If you're old enough, you'll remember the advertising campaign whose slogan was "I dreamed I went shopping in my Maidenform bra." Accompanying the text was a photograph showing an attractive woman from the waist up, dressed only in a brassiere in the midst of a crowded city street or some other public scene. The campaign was extraordinarily successful, in part because almost everyone has dreamed of being naked or half-dressed in public at some time in life.

Attitudes toward nudity vary considerably from country to country and from age to age, yet the dream about Being Naked in Public has recurred over the years and continues to flicker through the minds of sleeping folk throughout the globe today. Among the first five hundred people to fill out a survey on Universal Dreams on my website, approximately 52 percent said they had dreamed of being naked or wrongly dressed in public. These responses were equally divided between men and women. The youngest to contribute a Being Naked in Public dream was a twelve-year-old girl; the oldest was a mature man (fifty-five to sixty-four); most were from men and women in their young adult years (twenty to thirty-four). People from Austria to New Zealand reported this Universal Dream. Why do dreamers picture themselves nude, partially dressed, or totally inappropriately dressed? What does it mean when you have this dream?

INFLUENCES ON YOUR DREAMS ABOUT BEING NAKED IN PUBLIC

1. Biological

ALTHOUGH HEREDITY PLAYS a lesser part in shaping your attitudes toward nudity than your culture and personal experiences, it still has a role.

Clothing provides protection and warmth. Without it, we are more vulnerable to various environmental discomforts such as cold, sunburn, scratches, attacks by insects, itchiness, or pain from objects we sit upon or walk over. To the extent that we are programmed to protect our body's integrity, to keep it at an even temperature, to prevent damage to our skin, and so forth, our biological status influences our dreams about nakedness. When your bedcover slips off in the middle of the night, for instance, you may well dream of walking through an icy landscape, perhaps without shoes or adequate clothing. Such dreams may disturb your sleep enough to awaken you, allowing you to retrieve the missing covers.

At the other extreme, if your bedroom becomes unpleasantly hot, you may dream of crossing a desert, laden with heavy clothing, burdened with layers of socks or mufflers that make you sweaty enough to awaken you, to throw off the offending blankets and open a window to cool down. Our built-in thermostatic regulator continues to operate while we are asleep and dreaming, in order to ensure our survival.

Dreams about enjoying a state of nakedness may have a different source—the sexual connection. Most animals have a genetically programmed instinct to "display" themselves to the opposite sex. Complex mating dances in birds, "presenting" the genitals in apes, and other such rituals, are ways that some animals commence courting. Humans have a similar propensity to flaunt our bodies in certain situations, with the hope of initiating sexual contact. Certainly this element is a factor in "streaking" and in exhibitionism. Some dreams about being naked may evolve from this impulse, especially those in which the nude dreamer feels free and happy.

Most dreams about nudity, however, contain an element of embarrassment, ranging from mild self-consciousness in a social setting to shame and humiliation.

2, 3. *Cultural and Subcultural*

IN AN ISLAND culture in the tropics where a state of undress is the rule rather than the exception, a dream about being undressed is apt to be unremarkable. Women on the island of Bali, for example, traditionally wore no top garment; their lower bodies were wrapped in a *pareo*, a kind of sarong. They also wore headgear. It was only when Europeans began arriving in large numbers and showed interest in and shock at the local dress that Balinese women began to cover their breasts. It was *our* discomfort that caused them to feel ashamed.

Likewise, when the missionaries arrived in Hawaii, they were appalled at the natives' state of undress. Soon local women were forced to cover their bodies with hot, high-necked, full-length gowns, instead of the open short skirts that left breasts and limbs exposed to cooling breezes. Perhaps both these peoples—Hawaiian and Balinese—began to have dreams about being self-conscious when not wearing European-approved clothing.

People in some countries today find public nudity much more acceptable than Americans or Europeans do. In Japan, for instance, public and family bathing is commonplace. I was startled myself when many years ago I hired a Japanese housekeeper. A lovely young art student who had recently arrived in the United States, she thought nothing of entering my bedroom while I was fully or partly nude to put away folded clothes or perform some other household duty. However, if my husband gave me the lightest kiss on my cheek in her presence, she went into gales of embarrassed laughter, hiding her mouth, turning red, and looking most uneasy. Public nudity was okay; public affection was not.

Whatever your culture's attitudes toward being naked in public are, they are certain to impact how you regard it in your dreams. People in nudist colonies are likely to view a state of nakedness more positively than most of us. In contrast, some cultures are far more severe in their judgment about public displays of skin. When my husband and I traveled through the Middle East, I soon learned that there were many churches, mosques, and other public buildings where naked arms were regarded as unacceptable. To enter, a woman visitor had to wear a long-sleeved top, preferably high-necked, and a long skirt (never shorts or a miniskirt); often one had to remove one's shoes. The head usually had to be covered. Mere hand holding was considered highly disrespectful. Local women were mostly required to wear a dark covering in public, called a *chador*, or *burka*, that fell from the top of the head to the feet, with only a small netted opening for the eyes. In certain cultures, a woman's hair must be completely covered in public at all times. To dream about Being Naked in Public in such an environment would be a nightmare indeed.

Religious strictures are often the source of attitudes toward nudity. Society urges the wearing of clothing partially as a means of controlling the powerful sexual urges that are feared will be released by nudity, causing chaotic behavior. Nakedness and what is considered to be proper, "decent" clothing are two topics strongly influenced by the culture of the dreamer.

4. Personal

WHAT WAS YOUR immediate family's attitude toward undress? Was it considered all right to walk around the house in underwear or nightclothes? Have you ever been in a group of strangers in which no one was clothed? Have you ever been accidentally or deliberately observed while naked, without your consent? All these and other personal experiences with nudity will influence your dreams about it.

How you feel about your body at the time of the dream is also relevant. Do you consider yourself too fat without your clothes? Too skinny? Do you think your stomach sticks out too much? Or that your breasts are too small? Do you feel especially fit? Are you pleased with the sculpting of your muscles? Do you think your legs and breasts or other body parts will be admired? Your body image at the time of your dream about Being Naked in Public is important to the dream's meaning.

UNDERSTANDING YOUR DREAMS ABOUT
BEING NAKED IN PUBLIC

WHICH VERSION IS closest to your dreams about nudity?

- You are totally nude in public
- You are partially nude in public
  wearing an item of underwear that shows
  missing a garment that covers the top of your body
  missing a garment that covers the lower part of your body
  missing all underwear
  lacking shoes when they would be appropriate
  lacking headgear when it would be appropriate
  wearing an odd item (e.g., gloves) and nothing else
- You are wearing pajamas or a nightgown in the wrong setting
- You are wearing the wrong clothes for the occasion (e.g., a clown outfit at a wedding)

Each of these variations has a different shade of meaning in your dreams.

Your Nudity in Dreams as a Metaphor for Feeling Emotionally Exposed

SURPRISINGLY, BEING TOTALLY nude is not the most common form of the Being Naked in Public dream. People more often dream about themselves as partially nude. (Because dreamers so often feel nude dressed only in their pajamas or nightgown, we will discuss wearing bedclothes with dreams of being partially nude.)

When we dream about Being Naked, we are stripped of the usual trappings that cloak us as we face the world. Our social mask, our "persona," no longer conceals us. The clothing that conveys our rank in the social ladder is gone. We feel vulnerable, sometimes inept or inadequate. As Adam and Eve were said to have been when they became aware of their nakedness after eating from the Tree of Knowledge, we may feel deeply shamed and long to hide. But there are rarely fig leaves handy in our dreams. Although we don't fear exile, we feel concern about the reactions of other dream characters. To be undressed in a dream is to feel emotionally exposed.

> Public nakedness in your dream = Waking feeling of overexposure in some situation

Settings for Naked in Public Dreams:
Your Waking Arena of Concern

IF YOU DREAM about Being Naked in Public, the setting is important for understanding the meaning of your dream. For instance, if you dream of being naked in bed in a passionate embrace with a lover, your dream will have different implications than if you are nude at the supermarket. The context of your dream is crucial to its meaning. Ask yourself the following questons:

1. Where am I? (in school, at work, at home, outside)
2. Who notices me? (no one, classmates, colleagues, family, strangers)
3. What part of my body is exposed? (top, bottom, genitals, other)
4. How do I feel? (mortified, ashamed, embarrassed, self-conscious, indifferent, rather pleased, proud)
5. How do observers react? (laugh, point, and so on)
6. What do I do? (try to hide, wake up immediately, reveal more)

When you dream about being completely or nearly naked, you may be revealing more about yourself than you intended in the same waking setting; the location of your dream provides a clue to its significance.

> Setting for nudity in your dream = Possible site of waking emotional exposure

Naked at School

SEVERAL OF THE men and women who filled out my website survey about Universal Dreams mentioned that their dreams about being fully or partially naked took place at school. In this context, obviously, the people most likely to observe the dreamer are teachers and schoolmates. "Estando desnudo en el colegio" (I am standing naked in college), said a young man from Guatemala, describing the typical dream.

A middle-aged American woman dreamed she was naked, taking a bath in her eighth-grade English class. By specifying such an exact location years after she was in that environment, the dream suggests that some event took place during eighth grade that left this dreamer feeling overexposed or full of shame. When we have had an intense childhood experience that leaves us mortified, that event becomes a symbol for other events later in life in which we have a similar feeling. Then we are apt to dream of ourselves back in the old situation, suffering the same embarrassment.

School is a setting that evokes discomfort for many people, judging from the frequency of Being Naked in Public dreams that take place there. Here's a few more samples: A young man from Canada dreamed he was arriving at school when he realized he had no clothes on; a middle-aged American woman dreamed she was teaching a class in her pajamas; a young man from Switzerland dreamed of going skiing with his class and suddenly being completely naked and cold; an American took her finals undressed.

If your dream about Being Naked in Public takes place at school, when you are long past attending classes, cast your mind back to what was happening during the time when the dream was set and recall how you felt. Ask yourself the following questions:

1. What happened when I was in X grade?
2. What happened when I was X years old?
3. How did I feel about it then?
4. How do I feel about it in retrospect?
5. What situation in my current life evokes similar feelings to those I felt when I was back in X grade (or when I was X years old)?

If you are currently a student, consider what in particular evokes feelings of being vulnerable or overexposed in the school environment.

Naked at Work

PERHAPS YOUR DREAM about nudity took place at work, as it did for the middle-aged American woman who tried to hide between the photocopier and a column. "I was sitting at a desk only dressed above the waist," dreamed an older woman from New Zealand, along with many others. When dreams about nudity occur in a work setting, dreamers are often expressing anxiety about a situation in the office in which they feel vulnerable.

If your dream about Being Naked in Public took place at work, you can assume there is some current circumstance in the office that is causing you to feel overexposed or inadequate. In this setting, you are most likely to be noticed by workmates, bosses, or your own staff, suggesting that your discomfort is associated with something you'd rather not have them notice or something about which you feel vulnerable to their judgment. You may feel concerned that you are not handling some project properly or that your lack of knowledge of some important topic will be revealed.

Naked on the Street

YOU MAY DREAM of walking down the street, or some other outside setting, in a state of undress. This environment provides the opportunity for all sorts of strangers to observe your nude, or half-nude, condition. Many dreamers describe walking down the street or running around the street in their underwear. Others speak of going outside in a state of undress—no trousers, in a slip, and so forth. "I was partially dressed out in the street," dreamed a middle-aged Dutch woman. Another dreamer said she left home nude in order to run. "I knew I was naked but didn't become self-conscious about it until I was across town." As in Hans Christian Andersen's fairy tale "The Emperor's New Clothes," it may be only when someone points out our state of undress—"But he has on nothing at all!"—that embarrassment sets in.

On the other hand, we may be well aware from the start that we are in public without clothing. A Chinese girl in a convent grade school in Shanghai had recurrent nightmares about walking around naked, wearing only a pair of white gloves. This child's dream was a result of her discomfort with the strict dress code that required her to wear the complete school uniform to classes. It consisted of a blue serge blazer, matching skirt, white shirt, dark blue tie, and white gloves. Since the girl continually lost her gloves, they were undoubtedly a source of reprimands. Already intimidated by her poor command of English in the convent school, where most students were English-speaking, the youngster was bullied by her classmates. Her nightmares about her white gloves supplied her with the item of clothing she was often lacking but replayed the shame and inadequacy she felt at that time in comparison with her fellow students. Eventually, as recounted in her memoir *Daughter of Shanghai*, Tsai Chin went on to win the lead in the school play and in adult years became a skilled actress in Europe and the United States. Now she is much admired by strangers around the world who see her on the stage and in films.

If you dream about being totally or partially naked on the street, you can surmise that you feel overexposed generally, more than if your vulnerability is confined to school or the office.

Naked in a Public Bath

NATURALLY, WHEN WE take a bath or shower, we remove our clothing. Several of the Being Naked in Public dreams were set in a bath or shower in a house with no walls, or in front of the dreamer's house, or in a public setting like a store or movie theater. In these cases, behavior that is usually engaged in privately is made into a public display.

If your dream about nudity involves bathing in public, you probably feel that some waking situation is too revealing about your intimate concerns.

Naked on a Beach or in a Swimming Pool

BEACHES, SWIMMING POOLS, and similar settings are places people often feel aware that their bodies are less than perfect. Being Naked in Public dreams are sometimes set in such spots, as was a young woman's from the Netherlands: "I was in a swimming pool wearing a threadbare bathing suit." The worn-out quality of her swimsuit might be reflecting a feeling of inadequacy about her body, since clothing in dreams typically reveals the emotions of the dreamer.

I have already mentioned that some dreams about nudity do not carry the embarrassment that is usual in these dreams. "I was naked, walking around like it was a natural thing," a young Canadian woman said of her dream of this sort. A young American man told me a version of this dream in which he sauntered "buck naked" along the beach. Although people pointed fingers and laughed, he felt quite comfortable in the dream. He didn't attempt to conceal himself or wake up with discomfort. "I knew my muscles looked good," he said. On awakening, he felt a little odd about his behavior in the dream but still was proud that he "had the guts" to walk naked down the beach. His dream suggests a satisfaction with how his body appeared at the time of the dream, as well as a desire to have it appreciated and admired by others.

Some dreamers made comments to the effect that "people don't usually seem to notice that I'm naked or inappropriately dressed. I'm only mildly embarrassed." Others took a positive pride in the bare condition of their bodies and spoke of the sense of freedom, or "fun, being uninhibited by clothing," they had as a result.

Your Reactions to Overexposure

Hiding

WHAT DO YOU do when you realize that you are naked or partly dressed in a dream? Some men and women making this discovery immediately try to conceal their nudity. Like Adam and Eve reaching for fig leaves when they became aware of their nakedness for the first time, after having eaten from the Tree of Knowledge, these dreamers seek out the nearest thing to shield their bare bodies.

The young Canadian man who dreamed of being naked at school hid behind a piano in the room. The young Swiss man who was naked in ski class tried to hide and then make his way back home in the cold. The middle-aged American woman who was naked at work tried to block the view of her nude body by positioning herself between a photocopy machine and a column, as well as "veiling" herself with a stream of talk she hoped would distract her coworkers from her condition. A young American woman, in a dream of being naked outside, "ran from bush to bush trying to get home without anyone seeing me." An Englishman in the nineteenth century, who dreamed he was naked on a hotel stairway where a couple observed him critically, made a dash for his room but was hampered by not remembering the room number. What is it that we want to hide when we find ourselves in dreams defying public propriety? Our nakedness reveals something we do not want publicly scrutinized. It may be our bodies; it may be some aspect of our behavior. Or we may be reacting to the behavior of someone else.

Demanding a Change

WHEN MY MOTHER-IN-LAW lived with my husband and me for about three years, I had difficulty. In her mid-eighties, this elderly woman, whose mind had been exceptionally keen and whose consideration for others had been outstanding, became demanding and troublesome. Muddled, she would pick up the telephone in the midst of a media interview I was doing or appear at awkward times in disarray when guests or professional colleagues were present. I tried to carry on with my usual life while providing for her needs, but there were numerous awkward situations. One night I dreamed that she was going to attend a lecture I was giving at a local college in her pajamas (her favorite and almost constant attire). "You must *change!*" I screamed at her in the dream. In the dream, this meant that she must take off her pajamas and put on normal street clothes. Awake, it was obvious to me that I wanted her to change more than her pajamas. Sadly, her condition worsened, especially after she fell, broke her hip, and had to be hospitalized.

The only good thing to emerge from this "change" was that my patience was restored when I did not have to cope with the situation constantly, and we were able to have many loving and supportive exchanges before she died.

In retrospect, I was embarrassed by my mother-in-law's deteriorated condition. My dream of resenting her wearing pajamas to my public performance was partly a wish to conceal her deterioration, or at least not to display it to the world at large. When you dream of Being Naked in Public, what is it that you would rather not reveal?

> Attempting to hide or change nakedness in your dream = Wish to conceal waking weakness

Acceptance or Enjoyment

DREAMERS SOMETIMES SIMPLY accept nudity or inappropriate dress, rather than attempt to hide it or change it. When a French marquis dreamed that his painting teacher arrived at a country manor with a young female model who was completely naked, he thought his dream was perfectly natural because this was how he had originally seen her in the artist's studio. Nakedness was the expected—and probably greatly appreciated—condition of the pretty young woman.

When you dream that someone else is naked, rather than you, you are distancing yourself from your own feelings about nudity. Most dreams of Being Naked in Public involve the dreamer's nudity.

As mentioned, dreamers sometimes enjoy being nude. If your response to being naked in a dream is to find it pleasant, if it gives you a sense of pride, or if it confers a delight in the freedom from clothing, you may be taking pride in some usually hidden ability or strength. You may want others to see you as you want yourself to be.

> Enjoying nudity in your dream = Wish to reveal a waking capacity

Your Dreams About Being Partially Dressed in Public

SECOND-CENTURY GREEK DREAM expert Artemidorus said that dreams about "short, indecent costumes signify losses and unemployment." He also thought that being naked in a dream "signifies the loss of everything that pertains to the embellishment of life." Although I think his view is extreme, I do notice that people who have bad dreams about Being Partially Dressed feel especially vulnerable in the areas that are revealed.

What part of your body is on display in your dreams of half-dress? For women, baring the breasts usually evokes strong feelings of vulnerability. Both men and women feel ashamed in dreams when they notice that their lower parts, legs, buttocks, or genitals are exposed. Nineteenth-century English novelist Thomas Hardy said he had recurrent dreams of being chased, in which he escaped by rising above his pursuers, only to feel agitated by "a paucity of underlinen." Today's dreamers have the same problem. "I'm partially dressed, no shoes, bare bottom, only underwear," said a teenaged girl in China. A Spanish teenaged boy reported, "Sometimes I forgot my trousers, other times the shoes."

Area of body revealed in bad dream = Feeling vulnerable in same area while awake

---

At first, I found it puzzling that several people mentioned they felt uncomfortable in dreams about being barefoot or without socks. Since being barefoot, or partially so, is a motif that arises for many dreamers, it's important to understand its significance.

Barefoot in the Snow

A MIDDLE-AGED AMERICAN man dreamed he was in the cafeteria in college on the first day of class (he's no longer a student). He suddenly realized "I have left my shoes up by the classrooms and am barefoot. It's wintry outside, and cold, and I wonder how I can get to my shoes and why I took them off."

The wintry conditions and coldness in his dream suggest that the man felt his current waking conditions were arduous and somewhat harsh. He had taken off the very thing that would provide protection. Although he generally likes to go barefoot, as it makes him feel "simple, carefree, and somewhat sensual," in this dream he felt exposed and vulnerable.

The area of your body that is revealed in a dream about partial nudity may stand for a part of you in which you feel deficient or one that seems especially defenseless at the moment. If you dream of being shoeless, perhaps you feel your tender "sole/soul" is exposed.

Exploring Your Dreams About Being Partially Dressed in Public

IF YOU DREAM about missing an article of clothing, be it your top, your bottom, your headgear, or your footwear, answer the following:

1. What does X (the article of clothing that's missing) do for me?
2. What's good about X? What's useful about it?
3. What's bad about X? What does it hinder?

4. What will obtaining X allow me to do?
5. In the context of my dream, is X primarily negative or positive?
6. What does X remind me of in my waking life?
7. How can I restore what is missing?
8. What would I rather other people not see or become aware of about me?

UNDERSTANDING YOUR DREAMS ABOUT BEING INAPPROPRIATELY DRESSED IN PUBLIC

Dreams of Being Inappropriately Dressed as a Metaphor for Conflicting Roles or Emotions

SO FAR WE have considered dreams in which you are fully or partially nude. Pajamas and nightgowns are a borderline case, both putting the dreamer in a state of partial undress and being inappropriate for public appearances. What does a dream mean when you are dressed in the wrong outfit for the occasion? Or when some other dream character is in weird garb that you find embarrassing?

Many dreams about Being Inappropriately Dressed arise when the dreamer is to be involved in a wedding ceremony in waking life. Men and women seem to feel enormous pressure about participating in a marriage ritual. Insecurities, conflicts, and doubts about the commitment to a specific partner find form in odd clothing in dreams.

Inappropriate Wedding Attire

AN AMERICAN BRIDE-TO-BE who dreamed her groom appeared at the altar in a "cross between an ethnic costume and a clown's" was vividly picturing her doubts about her fiancé. I felt concerned when she shared this dream with me three months before her wedding was scheduled. Hoping it was a passing reaction to some "clownish" behavior by her boyfriend, I said nothing about the negative implication of this image. However, when she told me the week before the wedding that her boyfriend had dreamed about "being in jail," my concern escalated.

Sure enough, two days prior to the wedding, with guests arriving from out of town, the groom did a disappearing act. Citing a fictitious emergency at home in another country, he departed, leaving the prospective bride to cancel all the arrangements.

Such events are rare but happen often enough to raise fears in many an engaged person's heart. Unpleasant as this young woman's dream was, it helped prepare her to cope with the embarrassment of calling people about the change in plans, returning the gifts, and in general facing the world as a person who had been deserted. The popular film comedy *The Runaway Bride*, starring Julia Roberts and Richard Gere, portrayed this same theme; in this case the bride was the person unable to follow through on her commitment to marry.

It's always a good idea to monitor your dreams for your reaction to some upcoming important social occasion. If you find yourself or a loved one wearing the wrong clothes, you can deduce that something about your attitude toward the event feels wrong to you.

Another American bride-to-be dreamed her fiancé took off his trousers, revealing him to be naked from the waist down. However, as her dream continued, he was willing to put on padded shorts decorated with a rainbow at her request. Her dream suggested that at least her groom was willing to be accommodating, and the rainbow implied future happiness.

Bridal gowns that are ripped, ragged, grimy, or an inappropriate color indicate that the bride-to-be feels damaged in some way. One young American woman, who was a virgin, had intercourse with her fiancé a few months prior to the wedding date. Soon afterward, she dreamed that her white wedding gown was dirty. The besmirched bridal gown reflected the dreamer's feeling of being "soiled" at the time of the dream, but her wedding went forward as planned.

A young American man who was about to be married dreamed a few nights before his wedding that he was standing at the altar in his white tuxedo, when he suddenly realized that his cummerbund and shoes were bright red, as if he were in a nightclub act. In his case, the dream suggested that his role in the ceremony felt like a "performance," a feeling many men share going through a big wedding. He, too, married.

Condition of wedding outfit in your dream = Waking feelings about self
or partner

If you are about to get married, you'll want to pay particular attention to your clothing in any dream about the wedding. It's a good idea, in any case, to observe your dream clothes. They often reveal important information about your emotions.

Pajama-Clad Wedding Guest

A MIDDLE-AGED FRENCH-AMERICAN woman who received an invitation to her ex-boyfriend's wedding was consumed with pangs of jealousy in her waking state. Although married herself, she told me she still regarded her former boyfriend as "mine." In her dream, she attended his marriage ceremony in her pajamas. Later in the dream, she was outraged to find his young bride "moving into *my* house," shifting around furnishings, including a precious sewing machine that had belonged to her grandmother (the motif of Property Damage). The dreamer was so angry she wanted to hit the young woman, and woke up in a fury.

Obviously the pajamas the dreamer wore to her young rival's wedding were inappropriate, as well as rendering her partially nude. They seemed to express angry resentment (a feeling she did not want her ex-boyfriend to see), and her feeling of inadequacy in comparison to the younger woman, as well as perhaps making her appear tempting to her former flame.

Age-Inappropriate Attire

YOU MAY DREAM about wearing inappropriate clothing in a context other than a wedding. An Australian woman in her fifties confided a dream about "trying to get into those slim-fitting minidresses, more like my son's girlfriend's size." Recently widowed, this woman had struggled with depression and weight gain. She had this dream after losing weight and returning to her normal size. In it, her conflict between what she felt was appropriate for her age and her widowed state clashed with a wish to be as shapely and desirable as a young girl. Although she "felt really stupid" as she walked down the street wearing the youthful clothing, the dream concluded with an expression of approval from an old boyfriend, someone who had always been supportive of her in the past.

In her case, the dreamer's good feeling about the restored shapeliness of her body triumphed over concern about what people might think. Her dream reassured her in graphic pictures, "It's okay to look great and to feel happy about it."

The Inappropriate Suit

A YOUNG AMERICAN businesswoman who had recently given birth to her first baby planned to go back to work six weeks after the baby was born. She found that she enjoyed being a mother far more than she had anticipated and was reluctant to return to the office. She had many dreams about this conflict. In one, a few days after her baby was born, she dreamed of struggling to put on a tight, straight skirt, the kind worn with business suits. Not only was it hard to do, it was very uncomfortable. On a superficial level, the dream portrayed her weight gain, but she already knew about that in her waking state and was working to restore her figure. On a deeper level, her dream portrayed the conflict she felt between her role as a working woman and her role as a new mother. Her dream vividly said, "The business role no longer fits. It doesn't *suit* you."

In another dream a few nights later, the same woman dreamed of wearing "a bright red knee-length muumuu and a murky green knit or crocheted poncho" while carrying a portfolio to school. These colors are ones the dreamer finds unflattering for her complexion. The portfolio (representing her business life) did not go with the casual, unbecoming outfit (more typical of at-home wear).

This woman's roles as a mother and as a businesswoman were at war. Eventually, she negotiated a compromise in which she stayed at home for the first six months, then returned to work. She continues to juggle being a high-level manager with being a mother of a teenager and maintains that balance remarkably well.

When your dream outfits are mismatched, ill-fitting, or inharmonious, they suggest you are struggling with some aspect of your self-identity.

> Inharmonious outfit in your dream = Waking conflict about body and/
> or role

Likewise, if you find yourself dreaming about wearing inappropriate clothes for some public occasion, you are torn between one role and another in waking life. Your clothes in dreams communicate how you feel about your body or about your present role in life. When they are mismatched, inharmonious, or unflattering, you can be sure your attitude is negative. In contrast, dreams about Being Well Dressed convey positive feelings, as we'll see in the next section.

Meanwhile, observe the details of any dream you have on this universal theme, mark the motifs, and write your answers to the set of questions in your journal. This information will help disclose the central meaning of your dream; perhaps you'll discover how to dream-dress in harmony.

BEING WELL DRESSED

7.5 BEING WELL DRESSED

Description: You dream of being particularly well dressed and feeling pleased about it. You may be responding to the harmony, the style, the cut, the texture, the comfort, or the attractive color of the outfit that you wear. The attractive dream clothing may be a special costume, such as a wedding gown or a ball gown. This dream often arises out of satisfaction with your body or life role at the time of the dream. It may also emerge from a desire for a special outfit, or a wish to look good on a certain occasion. In all the variations of this theme, you feel good about the way you look in the clothing, or you admire how good someone else looks.

Frequency: A fairly common pleasant dream among all people and ages.

Usual Meanings: "I feel good about myself"; "I feel attractive"; "My body is in good shape"; "I feel warm and cozy, protected"; "I feel stylish"; "I look fit, sexy"; "I want to look like this."

When you dream about being attractively and harmoniously dressed, you are expressing more than pleasure at a piece of clothing. You are picturing how good you feel about your body or your life role at the time of the dream. At times, dreams of being well dressed seem to be pure yearning for a delightful gift, as they were for the young girl from India when she dreamed her daddy returned from a trip bringing her many pretty dresses. But even in a straightforward dream like this, we can read the underlying wish to have attention from her father, and to look attractive in his eyes and eventually in those of other males. The many young boys who dream of wearing Superman outfits are longing for more than a Halloween costume. They want to be strong, to be important, to wear the garb of a hero in the eyes of their friends, and eventually of females.

One of the reasons that clothing becomes so important during the teenage years is that what we wear telegraphs who we are. Even in these days of uni-sex clothes, our garments still signify our status, usually our gender, our role, and our age. Clothing functions to tell the world who and what we are.

In dreams, your clothing has some of this same purpose, but it is exaggerated. The clothes you wear mirror how you feel about your body, and also how you feel about your current role in the waking world. When your dream clothing is harmonious, attractive, and becoming, your current attitude toward your body and/or your lifestyle is apt to be positive.

Being well dressed in your dream = Feeling good about appearance and/or waking role

---

In many of our dreams, we don't even notice what we, or other dream characters, are wearing. When we do notice dream clothing, it carries a message. Pay attention to your dream clothes. They are on display for a reason.

And don't forget about puns. The young man who dreamed about being in "fatigues" was doing more than recalling his army days; he was expressing a feeling of boredom with his current work role.

Although an entire catalogue could be written about the meanings of dream garb, we can take only a quick excursion through the closets of your dreams, to see what the modes of dress are likely to say about your feelings.

UNDERSTANDING YOUR DREAMS ABOUT BEING WELL DRESSED

IN DREAMS THAT mention clothing, you are apt to notice the following:

- You are dressed attractively for work or school
- You are well dressed for a special social occasion (a ball, a wedding)
- You look great in swimwear, casual clothes, or bedroom wear
- You are fine-looking in a costume
- You look good in an imaginary piece of clothing

Dreams of Being Well Dressed as a Metaphor for Good Feelings About Your Body

YOUR CLOTHES IN your dreams are extensions of your feelings about your physical body. Hippocrates first observed this correspondence between dream clothing and waking circumstances more than two millennia ago. He said (in *Regimen IV or Dreams*) that when people are well, "the person's dream clothing and footwear appear attractive, and in the right size, neither too large nor too small." It's true today.

Shapely Clothing

I'VE ALREADY MENTIONED that when we dream about clothing that is ragged, damaged, or dirty, the images often refer to feelings that the body has been injured or soiled. Many of the participants in a study of pregnant women dreamed about trying on dresses that were too tight or of shopping for larger clothes. A dream about clothing that is thick and restrictive is an image that often arises after excessive weight gain. People who lose weight healthfully and safely have told me of dreaming that they peeled off layers of clothing, such as a heavy, padded coat, until they reached a well-fitting outfit underneath. One woman, after the loss of twenty pounds, dreamed that she unzipped a dress and stepped out of that layer of clothing to reveal a shape-hugging dress underneath. Several women who lost weight sensibly dreamed of themselves wearing slinky bathing suits as their bodies reemerged. One woman had several dreams about a mermaid—perhaps the ultimate fitted costume.

Researchers who studied the dreams of patients who were about to have surgery reported that a young woman who was grossly overweight and about to have her gallbladder removed dreamed she received some old material to cut apart and sew into a new dress for a wedding. Her hopes for a slimmer body as the result of surgery had her anticipating a new body shaped out of her old one (the old material) and her wish that it would help her gain a loving connection.

Therefore, when you dream about wearing a well-fitted, attractive outfit that shows off your body in a pleasing way, you're apt to be feeling very good indeed about how you look or hope to look in the waking state at present.

Dreams of Being Well Dressed as a Metaphor for Recovery

YOU RECALL THAT dreams about tattered clothing can portray a damaged body; in contrast, dreams about attractive clothing can reflect restored health. I found that dreamers recovering from surgery often incorporated their healed scars as part of a harmonious outfit. It was not a question of ignoring what had happened to them: they accepted the scars as part of their new, healed selves.

The V-Cut Wedding Gown: Reintegrated Body Image

ONE AMERICAN WOMAN who had undergone a total hysterectomy and had brutal dreams about being raped while she was still in the hospital had a dream nearly a month later that told me her health was returning. In it, she was about to be married (although she already was married) and was having a special wedding gown designed for her. Describing the gorgeous gown of her dream to me, she said it had "a kind of V-cut in the front of the skirt, with gathers." As she gestured to indicate the location of the V-cut, I noticed it was placed directly above her hysterectomy scar. Still in the dream, she swept up an armful of dusty-rose colored roses (a favorite of the dreamer) to carry with the gown. Perhaps the V-cut in her dream conveyed a Victory over her surgical wound; her health restored. This kind of dream garment, along with the lush roses, indicates an acceptance of the change in the dreamer's body. It integrates the new view of self. If you are due for surgery of any sort, watch for postsurgical images of harmonious or beautiful clothing and jewelry—they are harbingers of returning health.

Wearing a Beautiful Ring: Healed Hand

ABOUT SIX WEEKS into my recovery from surgery on my broken arm, I dreamed of being in a sunny shop, selecting new clothes to try on. I chose those with luscious, warm colors, tints that flatter me: peach, cream, and a light yellow-green that enhances the green in my eyes. Later I dreamed of wearing shoes decorated with rosebuds and a wreath made from rose blossoms. I tried on fabulous jewelry, including a ring that resembled a pink-and-green opal with diamonds that I owned before it was stolen in a burglary. Wearing a beautiful ring on my injured hand was especially important, as it symbolized my reintegrating body image and the treasure of restored health. Other negative images of fragile things, in danger of breaking, still occasionally appeared at this stage of convalescence, but beauty was returning to my dreams.

The Poncho Gift: Restored Body Image

AN AMERICAN WOMAN who came from an unbroken line of women who developed breast cancer had her right breast removed in her late thirties and had surgery on her left breast a few months later. During the two weeks after her first mastectomy, she had an unusual dream gift of clothing. In it, she was on a mountainside with a Christ-like figure. He had to leave on some dangerous business and wanted her to hide for safety. She declared she would rather die and go to heaven. Then the Christ-figure gave her a gift of a fine white poncho, with turquoise and blue in the pattern. He wore it, but she knew it was made for her because it had two spaces for her breasts woven into the fabric. She reached for it, feeling very happy. The dream shifted to a meeting with an old boyfriend, down a steep and dangerous gully. Her dream ended on a sad note of saying good-bye to her mother. Clearly, this woman was feeling torn between her fear of death and her commitment to life. But soon after this dream, she began to thrive and recovered fully. Her revised body image was portrayed in the marvelous poncho she received.

Shopping for new clothing and jewelry, buying clothes, making them, and being given them—these are images that relate to the injured dreamer's hopes for an improved body, perhaps even a better life when one is fully healed. Stay alert for any image that incorporates changes in your body caused by injury, illness, or surgery. Healing often appears in dreams as new or harmonious clothing and jewelry.

Dream Costumes as a Metaphor for Feelings About Your Health

WHEN YOU MAKE or wear a fantastic or unusual costume in a dream, the clothing is particularly revealing of your feelings.

The Queen of Hearts Costume: Love of Life Triumphs

THE WOMAN WHO dreamed about receiving a poncho gift from a Christ-like figure also had a powerful dream involving a costume. About ten days after the first mastectomy, she dreamed of being in a parade for which she had to prepare an ensemble. She decided to go as the Queen of Hearts and spent the day making a golden crown with red hearts and other red hearts to attach to a black velvet dress that already had silver hearts on it. At the end of the dream she became confused whether she should be the Queen of Hearts or the Queen of Spades. But she went off to the parade just in time, adding some large red hearts to her gown.

This woman's dream revealed her ambivalence between her fear of death (symbolized by the Queen of Spades) and her desire for love (represented by the Queen of Hearts). Her final costume and the golden crown were hopeful signs, as she joined the parade of life. Her dream about receiving a poncho specifically designed to accommodate the spaces for her removed breasts followed the dream of the Queen of Hearts, suggesting that the balance of her feelings was shifting toward health.

Naturally, you'll want to examine carefully any costumes you wear in your dreams and think about whether you want to "wear" the waking attitudes they represent.

Dreams of Unique Clothing as a Metaphor for Your Special Feelings

The Caretaker Smock: Time to Take Care of Myself and Others

ONE OF MY own favorite dreams hangs in the closet of unique clothes. I called it "The Caretaker Smock." I had undergone oral surgery the day I had this dream, getting a procedure called "root resection" (you don't want to know). It was quite painful, and my face was badly swollen. That night, my first dreams were unpleasant ones, evoked by the operation. The third dream involved a baby that was unhappy. In it, I was shown something called a "caretaker smock." When I awoke, I was fascinated by the image but didn't understand its significance. I decided to make a drawing of the unusual garment, a technique that helps me focus on what's important about a dream image.

After I made a drawing of the smock, I still felt unclear about the odd garment. Then I used another process, one in which the dreamer lets the image "speak." When I let the Caretaker Smock "speak," I was startled, and touched, by the words I found myself writing. The smock "said":

I am fresh, clean, and white. I slip on easily over any clothing because I'm roomy. I have large patch pockets for carrying all sorts of useful tools wherever I go. I'm decorated with cheerful colors. The rising sun at my hem reminds the troubled person that a new day begins each morning. The flowers embroidered around my buttonholes depict bright new growth. I make people happy to look at me. I'm beautiful *and* practical. Smocks are worn by artists—*I am the art of caring.* I have been worn by many people during this difficult time. I was worn by the dental assistant who stroked your cheek during the operation. I was worn by your surgeon when he greeted you kindly. I was worn by your daughter when she petted your leg, and when she held your arm. I was worn by your husband when he read to you, although his voice was tired. Anyone can wear me. Even you.

It was the last two words I wrote that made me teary-eyed. I understood that my dream was saying I had been lovingly cared for by everyone around me. Now it was time for me—the unhappy baby in the dream—to take care of myself.

When you are puzzled over a unique article of clothing in a dream, try giving it a voice. Write as if the garment were speaking. You may be surprised, as I was, to find it has more to tell you than you expected.

Whether your attractive dream clothes are indicating good feelings about your current figure or your present waking role in life, demonstrating improvement in your health, or giving you an individual message, listen to them. Let your dream wardrobe teach you. You may find something you want to wear every day.

8

Missing the Boat or Other Transport
Versus Pleasant Travel

8.0 MISSING THE BOAT OR OTHER TRANSPORT

Description: You dream of rushing to catch a bus, train, ship, airplane, or other public transport, only to miss it, usually by a fraction of a second. The dream may involve various misadventures en route to the transport. You often feel frustrated rather than afraid in these dreams. You may be lacking vital papers, such as tickets, passport, or visa. In a variation of this theme, you arrive too late for a performance in which you are supposed to participate and find that the play, musical production, sport competition, or other event has already begun. (Dreams in which you are having trouble *during* a performance are classified with Poor Test or Poor Other Performance.)

Frequency: Missing the Boat Dreams are moderately common. Some people have them often, others rarely. They usually arise when you feel anxious about making an important connection to one of your waking goals.

Usual Meanings: "I've missed out on some opportunity"; "I'm too late"; "I can't make a connection"; "I've missed my chance" (missing the transport, arriving too late); "I don't have what I need" (missing travel documents).

When you dream about Missing the Boat or Other Transport, you often feel more frustrated than frightened. You may panic as you race to make the connection, but that panic is not usually accompanied by fear for your life, as you almost always feel in Chase or Attack dreams.

Among the first five hundred people who filled out the survey on Universal Dreams on my website, about 31 percent of the respondents said they had experienced dreams of this type. People of all ages and from a wide assortment of countries described having it. Few, however, mentioned missing a boat or ship; most described missing planes, buses, or trains, in that order. This suggests that among today's dreamers, men and women are more likely to travel by means of these modes of transportation than by ship; their dreams reflected the mode of transport they were most familiar with using.

In general, your dreams about missing the boat or some other transport portray your feelings that you are missing out on something as you journey through life; that you need to pull yourself together to make the connections you desire.

Missing a boat or other transport in your dream = Missed waking opportunity

---

INFLUENCES ON YOUR DREAMS OF MISSING THE BOAT OR OTHER TRANSPORT

1. Biological

OUR GENETIC MAKEUP has relatively little impact on dreams about Missing the Boat. Yet, there is likely to be some instinct that drives us to achieve our desires. When our goal is to make a connection, and that goal seems to be moving out of reach, there is a natural tendency to "try harder," to struggle mightily to obtain what we want.

2, 3. Cultural and Subcultural

IN MOST LANGUAGES, the words we use in everyday life include metaphors about losing an opportunity. In English we say, "She really missed the boat" to refer to advantageous opportunities that the person let slip out of her hands. This expression has a long history, since ships and boats were familiar forms of transportation long before trains, buses, and airplanes were invented. Perhaps in ancient times people spoke of "missing the caravan" or "missing the coach" or some other form of public transport that was then in common use.

4. Personal

YOUR PERSONAL EXPERIENCES with transportation strongly affect your dreams in this area. What mode of transport do you use most often when traveling long distances? Do you conduct business overseas and need to get there quickly? You're likely to fly by jet, or even by *Concorde*. Are you retired, a patron of cruises? Your dreams on this theme may center on ships and docks. Do you travel by Chunnel to the continent? Vacation on trains using a Europass? Go by bullet train from suburb to city? These transport forms will arise in your dreams. If you journey by bus, jitney, or subway for short trips, these public vehicles are apt to be featured in your dreams about Missing the Boat. If you do much international travel, your travel documents, such as passports, visas, and other papers, will be part of the dream scenario, as well as borders and boundaries. Unless you are an astronaut, dreams about missing a spacecraft are unlikely to occur, although spaceships are sometimes featured in other dream themes. Whatever transport you are familiar with using is the kind you are apt to be hurrying to catch in dreams. If you travel a lot, these dreams may be more frequent.

UNDERSTANDING YOUR DREAMS OF MISSING THE BOAT OR OTHER TRANSPORT

NATURALLY, THOSE DREAMS that involve missing various sorts of transport have several features in common. Your dreams about Missing the Boat or Other Transport, or Arriving Too Late, are likely to involve one or more of these variations:

- Missing the Airplane
- Missing the Train
- Missing the Subway or Trolley
- Missing the Ship or Boat
- Missing the Bus, Jitney, or Van
- Arriving Too Late for a Performance (musical, dramatic, sport, other)

We'll look at dreams about missing an airplane first, since these were the most frequent among the dreamers I worked with, and so may be for you. Even if they're not, you'll probably want to look through this section because so many of the motifs involved in Missing the Airplane apply to other types of this theme.

Your Dreams About Missing the Airplane

Destination and Purpose in Dream

THE FIRST QUESTIONS to ask yourself when you have a Missing the Boat dream of any type are "Where am I going?" and "Why?" Your destination and purpose mentioned in the dream will probably be related to a goal in waking life.

> Destination and purpose in your dream = Waking area of missed opportunity

To New York for Work

AN AMERICAN SALESWOMAN who dreamed about missing her plane to New York, where she was due on vital business for her company, had good reason to feel anxious. In her field there are two main sales events a year, one held in summer and one in winter. When she had this dream, she was about to leave for the winter show, an event that made her particularly anxious because bad weather sometimes prevents the plane from landing in New York. Travel could be treacherous, even if she and her goods arrived safely. Each show involves an extremely expensive enrollment fee. If she should miss her flight, she would not only lose her large fee, but also miss out on sales for the entire coming season.

In this woman's dream, she seemed to wake up, had to go to the bathroom, and did so beside the bed. Then she realized her husband and child had taken the car to the airport, and the plane had already departed. She was left to deal with the mess beside the bed. She awoke, feeling angry and frustrated.

This businesswoman's dream shows that she was coping with other issues in addition to the usual pressures of conducting business. Tension was always at its height during the couple of months prior to a show. This time she had the extra burden of having had an injury that was not entirely healed, from an accident caused by some ongoing construction. She explained to me that "there was a lot of crap associated with this accident," which took time and attention away from her creative work. Her dream suggests that she felt she was still left to deal with the problems while her husband and son were free of it. She felt resentful and deprived. Her dream seems to be saying, "Because of the lousy situation I'm stuck dealing with, I've missed an important chance to succeed in business."

The fact that the "crap" was deposited beside the dreamer's bed raises the possibility that some sexual issues were involved as well. Anytime excrement is present in dreams, it's apt to be a metaphor for the dreamer's view that a particular waking situation is "shitty."

Several dreamers reported missing a plane for an important business trip. If you dream about this topic, you'll want to consider whether you feel that you've lost out on some valuable work opportunity. Of course, there will be other "journeys" and other "planes to catch," so don't let one lost chance discourage you.

To Hawaii for Fun

ANOTHER AMERICAN WOMAN of middle years was due to go on a vacation to Hawaii. She badly needed the holiday since there were some heavy issues being dealt with at work at the time. Shortly before she was due to leave, she dreamed that she was on her way to catch the plane to Hawaii but things kept happening at work that prevented her from leaving, so she missed her plane. "Will I ever get out of here?!" she lamented. Then the woman awoke feeling jittery and distressed.

This woman's dream expressed her anxiety that she would be trapped by work, depriving her of time to relax; on another level, she was perhaps expressing concern that this particular job might be too limiting. Her dream was a way of saying, "The demands of this job may make me miss out on greater pleasures in life."

When you dream about Missing the Airplane, notice whether it is business or pleasure for which you were headed before you missed out. If you suspect that you are pushing too hard and depriving yourself of the juice of life, find ways to restore fun to your agenda.

To Meet a Romantic Partner

A TEENAGER FROM Malaysia who dreamed of missing an airplane that would take her to "meet some important guy" may have been expressing a feeling that she was "missing out" on an emotional relationship she would like to have. Her dream said she felt that something was preventing her from making the loving contact she desired.

Lacking Vital Travel Material

MANY PEOPLE WHO dream about Missing the Boat find they are without essential travel documents or equipment, thereby delaying or having to cancel their journey. Dreamers in Israel, Spain, America, and elsewhere around the globe panic when they discover they've forgotten tickets, passports, visas, or other travel papers.

On one level, dreams involving missing travel papers remind us to be careful to get all our needed equipment together prior to any upcoming flight. On another level these travel documents may represent other crucial equipment we feel we do not have together to complete some important waking task and make successful connections.

Missing documents in your dream = Feeling you lack vital waking equipment

---

Each element has a different shade of meaning for the dreamer. Tickets often represent your right to travel, your proof of payment. Passports and visas are the means to be admitted to areas you would otherwise be denied. Luggage, suitcases, and trunks usually contain the bare essentials to function away from home, but this property may also be a burden. When any of these is missing, your journey is thwarted.

If you dream about Missing the Airplane because you do not have the necessary papers, you need to do some serious assessment about what's happening in your waking life at the time of the dream. Obviously, if you have a flight planned, reviewing your documents and getting them together are in order. If not, you need to review what you are currently trying to accomplish in the waking world. Consider the following:

1. What is missing for me to do my job properly or get what I want?
2. What do I need to get together and make sure is in proper shape?
3. How can I better prepare myself for what I want to do?

Answering these questions, and acting upon them, will help relieve some of your frustration and discomfort as you proceed with your life.

Obstacles En Route

YOU MAY ENCOUNTER various problems as you race to catch the transport you intend to take. These difficulties often take the form of missing travel documents, but other hindrances arise.

A middle-aged American man dreamed he was taking a couple to the airport for an overseas flight. At first he felt fine. They arrived at the airport on time and took care of the tickets. Suddenly he panicked and asked what time the plane left; next he couldn't find the tickets. Then he discovered that they only had ten minutes to race to the plane. At that point massive problems arose. Everyone had to carry things—he had two small tables, his briefcase, and some plastic containers with melting ice cubes. After many distractions, including getting lost outside the airport and being unable to find his way back in, the couple finally missed the plane. His wife was nonplussed, but the dreamer felt devastated, miserable that he had tried so hard and failed. He awoke weeping.

Whatever was going on in this man's life at the time of the dream was highly significant. Without going into the details of his long and complex dream, you can see that he felt unable to accomplish his purpose of delivering the people to the airplane on time. His dream said he felt that events beyond his control had made it impossible to accomplish his purpose. It also showed a sharp contrast between his attitude and that of his wife, who in the dream was cheerful and nonchalant. Their divergent relationship was probably an element in the husband's nightmare.

What major chance did this man feel he lost out on? What great opportunity did he miss? He gave it his best effort and felt he failed. His dream held more than the usual frustration. He was deeply sad—his tears may have been symbolized by the melting ice cubes. When people feel frozen with resentment of some sort, it often shows in their dreams as hard ice. When these feelings "melt," the sadness emerges in dream images of flowing water. Sometimes we feel we are unable to change the harsh conditions we face, circumstances that become literal obstacles in our dreams.

Obstacles on the way to catch transport in a dream = Waking conditions that thwart intentions

---

When you dream about Missing the Boat or Other Transport because of various obstacles, notice the nature of the things that prevent you from reaching your goal. See how they relate to your waking life. Consider how you might best cope with these problems, and remember that you'll have further opportunities to achieve your aims in life.

Your Dreams About Missing the Bus, Jitney, or Van

THESE SAME TYPES of environmental frustrations occur in the variations of Missing the Boat. A young man from Canada dreamed that he was going to miss the school bus, but he had no idea where his shoes were. He felt unable to run for the bus without them. It was winter in his dream, so he felt he couldn't walk in the cold. This dreamer also thought that some outside element was preventing him from accomplishing his purpose.

When people beyond school age describe dreams about missing a school bus, there may be an issue involving learning that the dreamer regards as a missed opportunity. A young woman from America who reported recurring dreams about "missing the school bus after high school lets out" is such a case. Had she curtailed her education while her classmates "caught the bus"? If your dreams involve a motif about missing a school bus when you are no longer in school, you'll want to examine whether you would like to pursue a higher education. If not, you may have lost out on some other learning experience.

A teenaged woman from Australia who dreamed about missing the correct bus, then taking a train in the wrong direction, and finally discovering that "the direction that would have taken me home didn't exist" was picturing some confusion with her direction and goal in life. First she missed out on an opportunity, then she went the wrong way, and finally she found she couldn't get back to her home base. Where do you want to go in your life's journey? Your dreams about Missing the Boat or Other Transport will comment on your progress.

A young man from America dreamed he was about to get on a bus when the people ahead of him in line were shot. "The bus left and I had to run." The dreamer was picturing some stressful waking situation that was injurious to others. He was uninjured but stranded, and fortunately, unlike the man with no shoes, he was able to get himself out of the mess by using his own two feet.

> Overcoming obstacles to catching transport in your dream = Waking skills in coping

How do you handle the environmental frustrations that arise in dreams about Missing the Boat, in all its variations? Are you able to take action that solves the problem during the dream? Even if you don't succeed, it is important that you try. Eventually, you might make enough of a difference to catch the next dream transport and simultaneously begin solving the waking life predicament the dream represents. You'll be better prepared for the next chance life presents.

Your Dreams of Missing the Train, Subway, or Elevated

DREAMS ABOUT MISSING transportation that runs on tracks share many motifs with missing other types of transport, but they have a special flavor. Once passengers are aboard, the route is determined by the fixed tracks. There is a strict timetable. Thus, there is a certain reliability, but less flexibility. The elements associated with travel by train, such as terminals, platforms, tracks, and locomotives, are sometimes featured and have individual significance.

Stations, being places of arrival, waiting, meeting, and departure, represent a transition from one stage of life to another stage, or from one direction to another. Freud thought that dreams about missing a train were consoling the dreamer that he or she would not die yet: "Don't worry, you won't die (depart)." He based this idea on the notion that we speak of trains and other public vehicles as having a "departure" time, and also that we talk about deceased people as having "departed." It's true that one can make these associations with reaching a "terminal" (end of life) and departing, but dying is only one of life's transitions that may be represented in dreams that take place at a train station. We also "change our direction" and "get on a different track." Dreams about missing a train have many meanings.

> At a train station in your dream = Making a waking transition, changing "tracks"

"The Train Took Off with My Luggage"

TRAIN TRAVEL IS common in India, so it is not surprising that a middle-aged man from this country has occasional dreams about missing trains. As a professional, he frequently crosses international borders to attend conferences and to participate in other career activities. Sometimes his work takes him overseas for years at a time. Since travel is a part of his life, travel in his dreams is to be expected.

But, of course, dreams reveal more than our daily activities. In his recurrent dream, he gets out of the train to buy something, or do something, on the platform. Suddenly the train leaves with his luggage aboard, stranding him. Sometimes he dreams about being on a bus at an international border when the same sort of thing happens.

In his dream language, this man is depicting being bereft of the crucial belongings he needs for his life's journey, while he pauses for refreshment or some other reason. His journey is slowed but not totally prevented. He is stranded for the moment. As with the motif of "lacking vital travel documents," he is temporarily deprived of some essential equipment. However, he feels he can catch the next train or bus, and perhaps eventually retrieve his luggage.

This man tells me that he has this dream less frequently now, as his life has become more satisfying. Perhaps he senses he has gotten his career "on track." In any case, he feels better. He is catching more opportunities to get where he wants to go. If you dream about Missing the Train, remember, there'll be another train coming down the track.

Trouble Climbing Aboard

A FEW MONTHS ago I was surprised to find myself having a dream about Missing the Train. At the time, I was deeply enmeshed in writing this book. In addition, my elderly mother was having a serious, eventually fatal, health crisis that required much attention. I had begun to feel ill myself with a scratchy throat and other signs of an impending cold. It was hard to cope with all three situations simultaneously.

My dream made perfect sense. In it, I was on a journey with my agent. There was intense time pressure. I was obliged to perform something difficult — grab hold of a moving train and hoist myself aboard. I was unable to do so because the narrow door was too high and smooth, much as on a European train, where one can enter several cabins from the outside, rather than via a single door with a conductor at a wide open entry.

My dream said that I felt my goal to write under these circumstances was "too high," and I felt unable to "get on board." Yet, it was reassuring, too, in the sense that in the dream I felt sure we could pick up the train at the next stop, where it would be easier to board or the train would be required to wait for us. In my dream language, I told myself, "Don't worry it's not too late to get back on track." Indeed, with ample rest, my condition rapidly improved. I was able to cope with my mother's crisis of the moment and continue to do my job.

Catching Transport as a Metaphor for Making Desired Connections

ALTHOUGH MOST PEOPLE reported feeling frustrated or panicky as they rushed to catch a particular transport in their dream, some of them nonetheless felt able to resolve the situation. Others were able to make the connection in time.

A middle-aged American woman said she often dreams of being worried that she will miss her plane, but the dream doesn't usually get to the point where she actually misses it. An older American woman who dreamed she was going to London got to the airport on time with her passport but was without ticket or luggage; yet she still felt she could manage. If she could get on the plane without her ticket—possible if the record were in the computer, though improbable—she could buy the things she needed when she got to her destination.

These in-between cases, like mine, in which the dreamer misses or might miss the transport but still feels capable of dealing with the situation, suggest a greater degree of confidence in ability to cope with the waking difficulty.

A young woman from Yugoslavia told me she had two dreams with the theme of Missing the Boat, one involving a train and the other about a boat's leaving without her. In both of these dreams, she "frenetically" ran after the moving transports. In each case she managed to get onto the boat, and onto the moving train, at the last moment. Her dream suggests that by making enormous effort, she was able to succeed in making the connection she wished. Her confidence was running high.

Catching the transport in your dream = Waking ability to make desired connection

---

When you dream about Missing the Boat, in any of its forms, make an effort during the dream to resolve the situation. Work out alternative plans. Use your initiative. Be creative. As you solve your dream crisis, you'll begin to sort out the waking situation the dream represents.

UNDERSTANDING YOUR DREAMS OF ARRIVING TOO LATE FOR A PERFORMANCE

DREAMS ABOUT ARRIVING Too Late share some of the meaning of dreams about Missing the Boat: an opportunity has eluded you in waking life. The myriad dreams I have heard of this type often involve being without the crucial equipment needed to perform. "I forgot my clarinet, and they had begun to play without me"; "I was horrified to realize I'd left my running shoes at home, so the race started without me"; and so forth. Whether the activity is a musical, dance, stage, or sport performance seems to make little difference. (Dreams about performing poorly are discussed in the chapter on Poor Test or Other Poor Performance.)

If you dream about Arriving Too Late to participate in a performance and you actually perform in waking life, your dream may be a warning to "get your act together." You may not be adequately prepared or have your equipment in proper order.

Arriving too late for a performance in your dream = Missing a waking opportunity

---

If you have made all the necessary preparations, or if performance is not a part of your normal life, think through your other activities. What it is that makes you feel you are "too late" or that you don't have what you need to take your part on the stage of life? Then equip yourself with what's required, and get ready to join the game.

PLEASANT TRAVEL

8.5 PLEASANT TRAVEL

Description: You dream of traveling happily by bus, train, ship, airplane, or other public transport. Your dream may involve various preparations to travel or other activities en route to the transport. (Dreams in which you

---

	are enjoying travel by car or some other private vehicle are classified as Driving Well.)
Frequency:	Very infrequent. Most dreams about travel deal with complications. Pleasant Travel dreams may arise when you feel content with how life is going at the time of the dream.
Usual Meanings:	"Things are going smoothly"; "I'm making the connections I want"; "I'm pleased with this opportunity" (making the transport comfortably, arriving on time); "I have what I need" (travel documents, luggage).

We've seen that dreamers sometimes manage to "catch the boat" or train or bus they are trying to board, even though they feel frustrated or panicky as they exert effort to make the connection. (I have yet to encounter any dreams about making an airplane connection after the plane has taken off.) Here, we look briefly at travel in dreams that go well from the start. The look is brief because there are very few dreams of this type. Perhaps this is because it rarely seems that things are going without a glitch in our journey through life.

UNDERSTANDING YOUR DREAMS ABOUT PLEASANT TRAVEL

Pleasant Travel as a Metaphor for Moving Smoothly on Life's Journey

Taking the Train to Lucknow

A SIX-YEAR-OLD BOY from India dreamed that he was traveling in a train to visit his aunt during vacation. He felt happy knowing he would soon see his friends, his aunt's children. He thought about how he wanted to be an engine driver or pilot when he grew up. "A happy, fun dream," he stated. His drawing of the dream shows the coaches full of people and the engine puffing out smoke as it rolls along the tracks.

In English, the destination of the Indian boy's travel, a town called Lucknow, could be seen as a pun: luck now. The boy's aunt actually lived in that town, but the boy also speaks English, so the name of the town may have been a factor in his dream. His dream might have been his way of saying, "I'm heading toward luck, now."

When we have something to look forward to, when the wheels roll easily over the tracks to our destination, this is when we may dream of happy travel—with all the pleasure of a child.

Pleasant public travel in your dream = Feeling good about waking connections

---

The Name of Your Destination

ALWAYS BE ON the lookout for puns in the names of places, people, and things in your dreams. They often convey a level of meaning you might not notice at first. Because places or people or things actually have specific names, we tend to overlook their symbolic significance when they arise in our dreams.

I have often encountered examples of dreams about travel to towns whose names are heavy with significance. For instance, a young woman who was deeply into the study of an esoteric practice told me she dreamed about going to Mystic, Connecticut. The "mystic" aspect of life was the very thing she was seeking at the moment, although she hadn't made the connection between the name of the town in her dream and its symbolism of her desire. Another American woman, who was feeling discouraged about her work, dreamed about traveling to New Hope, Pennsylvania. The symbolism of "new hope" seemed too obvious to point out, but she did not notice it immediately. Other dreamers speak of taking a trip to Newfoundland, without seeing the meaning of "new found land."

Our dreams are rich with these associations between name and meaning. Don't be fooled by the fact that these places, people, or things may be their actual names. Watch the words that emerge in your dreams—they are tables of information for you to consult.

On Life's Journey

YOU MIGHT DREAM of traveling happily alone to exotic and interesting places, as did a man from Japan. Earlier I described (in the section on Car Pleasure) my dream of riding a magic carpet to anywhere I wished in the world, as the incredible ease of connecting with dreamers throughout the globe via the Internet became apparent. Although a magic carpet is more a private form of transportation than a public one, it is an example of the pleasures of smooth, fun travel.

You might dream of taking a journey with a loved one, a motif in the theme of Pleasant Travel dreams. Delightful dream trips with a romantic partner may replay fun spots you've actually visited or picture places that you hope to see together some day. These travels speak of sharing the journey of life together. Your destination in these dreams may represent mutual life goals.

In the final chapter, you'll see that dreams about traveling with a deceased loved one are fairly common; in them the dreamer has to leave the journey at a certain point, while the deceased person travels onward. Those journeys with a loved partner that are cut short may be nightmarish or reassuring, depending upon the content. Often, however, they leave dreamers feeling that the loved person has simply gone on ahead and will be awaiting the dreamer's arrival on a later transport. An elderly man who told me his dream about his wife's waving good-bye to him at the gate to an airplane had the feeling that she had just "caught an earlier plane"; he would soon follow, to find her there to welcome him.

A partner does not have to be dead, however, to say good-bye during a dream about travel. A recently married young American woman dreamed she was at a bus station saying good-bye to a former lover, who looked short and unwell. She was glad to say good-bye. He pressed her hand several times, and that was the end of the dream. She awoke feeling good to have seen the last of the man, in waking life and in dream life. For her, this was a reassuring dream, underscoring the right choice. Her happy state of mind confirmed her choice of one of two men.

You might dream of riding in a bus, or train, or some other public transportation with people who seem to be members of your family. Perhaps you are one of the few dreamers who find themselves taking a trip with family members that goes smoothly and is fun for each person. Sometimes group journeys on public transport stand for colleagues at work on a project together. At times, these may go well. You encounter no obstacles, or those you do are easily surmounted; you have the essential travel documents or other equipment you need; and you arrive at, or progress toward, your destination.

Getting Ready for the Final Journey: Hopes for Paradise

MANY ELDERLY PEOPLE dream of taking a journey that seems to represent their forthcoming transition from life to afterlife. Occasionally, these dreams of travel are totally delightful. I felt happy to hear the recurrent dream told me by an older American woman who lived in Paris for many years. In it, she traveled to Paris, where there was a marvelous celebration going on, a ceremony with costumes, ribbons, beautiful colors, and music. At times, her dream travel took her to London, always with a similar jubilant celebration.

This woman was devout all her life and continued to be active in charitable works. She remembered with pleasure Paris, where she was married and lived happily for many years prior to her husband's death, when she returned to the States. Her dreams were more than a widow's recollection of past happiness. She reveled in the travel to far places, the delightful atmosphere, beauty, and color swirling around her in the dreams. Knowing the depth of her religious devotion, I felt sure these travel dreams were anticipations of heavenly pleasures. She has since died, and is, I hope, joining the celebration. Perhaps eventually we'll all take part.

9

Machine or Telephone Malfunction
Versus Smooth Operation

Description: You dream of trying to operate some mechanical equipment when it malfunctions. Many of these dreams involve difficulty with a telephone: trouble dialing, getting disconnected, or making a faulty connection. Computers lose their connection with the Internet, data gets deleted, a virus destroys your files, and so forth. Other machines jam, break, or, sometimes, become actively malevolent. (For machines that attack you, consult Chase or Attack Dreams; for dreams involving mechanical problems with a car or vehicle, see Car Trouble.)

Frequency: Machine Malfunction dreams are only moderately common. Some people have them often, others seldom. They usually arise when you feel anxious about making an emotional connection; sometimes they refer to mechanical difficulties with your body.

Usual Meanings: "I can't seem to connect"; "I can't reach him or her"; "I keep losing touch"; "I can't get through" (trying to reach someone on an emotional level); "Something's not working right" (about your body).

If you dream about a telephone or some other machine that malfunctions, you will probably awaken feeling extremely frustrated. These dreams can be as maddening as the same problem in waking life. We try and try to make something work, but it simply does not function properly. We have enough difficulty in today's world operating machines as it is; why do we dream about them at night, too?

The answer is that the many machines that go awry in our waking life (computers, fax machines, home phones, cell phones, modems, answering machines, printers, scanners, and so forth) become symbols for a different kind of communication while we sleep. When we try to reach another person on an emotional level and do not feel successful in this attempt, we are apt to dream about malfunctioning machines. Sometimes when an aspect of our physical body is not operating properly, we may also dream about a machine that simply won't do its job efficiently.

INFLUENCES ON YOUR DREAMS OF MACHINE OR TELEPHONE MALFUNCTION

AMONG THE FIRST five hundred people to fill out the survey on Universal Dreams on my website, roughly 25 percent said they experienced dreams about telephone or machine malfunction. The majority of respondents who spoke of this type of dream theme were women, possibly because the mechanical skills that are more often characteristic of men make them more confident in coping with equipment in dreams. It could be that women's efforts to relate emotionally are so much more intense that they register their frustrated attempts to do so in dreams more often than men. It also could be that more women are interested in dreams and so report more of this type.

Whatever the case, some people who have this dream say that it plagues them frequently. If you are one of them, the material in this chapter will help you to understand Machine Malfunction dreams better, and perhaps benefit from them.

1. Biological

WE HAVE NO natural or biological relationship to machines. Perhaps that's why they bedevil us so often, awake or asleep. But the same drive that leads us to struggle to succeed in life, to achieve mastery over our environment, also pushes us to perform well in whatever we do, including operating machines and telephones. If machines are a part of your daily life, this impulse will be even stronger. As computers become increasingly part of our future, I expect that they will play an even larger role in our dreams. Some scientists speculate that a combination of human and computer parts is on the horizon.

2, 3. *Cultural and Subcultural*

DEPENDING ON WHERE you live in the globe and how much technology plays a role in ordinary communication in your country, machines and telephones may have greater or lesser importance. The most technologically advanced countries are permeated with machines on every level. The less developed countries still have mechanical equipment, but of a simpler structure. As the Internet becomes truly global, we meet with more and more symbols of the difficulty of staying "connected" to the important people in our lives. On one hand, the opportunity for contact is greater than ever, yet the aggravation of one's technical equipment's breaking down—the computer's being "down," or the modem's losing its connection to the Internet— provides infuriating new ways to lose touch.

4. *Personal*

MOST PEOPLE IN the modern world have experienced the irritation of being disconnected from someone while speaking on the telephone. How often have you dialed or punched umpteen numbers of area code, prefix, and local numbers, only to get the wrong party? The complications are multiplied manyfold if you do business, or have relatives, overseas. Now you need the overseas code, and the country code, the city code, the other local numbers. Don't forget your charge card or telephone calling card numbers, or telephones that will accept only debit cards, or some other restriction. Small wonder that we dream of dialing endlessly and not reaching the person we want.

Those people who work with computers and the Internet have new levels of frustration to cope with—ones that become symbols in their dreams about Machine Malfunction. Depending upon your personal work mode, these elements may or may not be an issue for you. Do you deal with machines in your daily life? Once again, your experience of familiarity or lack of it will influence whether these mechanical gadgets become part of your dream metaphor language for emotional connection.

Your personal health is also a factor. A study of several dreamers prior to major surgery revealed that in some of them the mechanical problems with their bodies were symbolized by malfunctioning machines in their dreams. If you should have a dream about Machine or Telephone Malfunction, be sure to assess your current physical state. Freud spoke of gadgets that didn't work well in dreams, relating them to malfunctioning genitals, another level of metaphor to consider. Weapons that misfire or jam are most likely to have this meaning.

Although problems with the working of your body, in general ways or in specifically sexual ones, can be an issue with Machine Malfunction dreams, the most common meaning I find for such dreams is that of trouble with making an emotional connection.

UNDERSTANDING YOUR DREAMS OF MACHINE OR TELEPHONE MALFUNCTION

YOUR DREAMS ABOUT Machine or Telephone Malfunction are certain to fall into one or both of these subtypes:

- Telephone Malfunction
- Machine Malfunction

Your Dreams About Telephone Malfunction

IN GENERAL, IF you dream about having trouble operating a telephone, you are probably expressing trouble with a waking life emotional communication.

Telephone malfunction in your dream = Emotional miscommunication in waking life

---

"I Can't Dial the Right Number"

WHEN YOU TRY to make a phone call in a dream, any number of things can go awry.

You may have trouble dialing or punching the numbers, so that the effort to communicate barely gets under way. Many dreamers find themselves frustrated by problems with dialing. A young American woman who described having this dream tried dialing different numbers, but nothing seemed to work. She said she also had recurrent dreams of trying to open a "combination" lock at school—none of these numbers worked either. "The phone dial doesn't work," said a young Canadian woman. "I was trying to use a phone, but the keypad was all rearranged, and strangely shaped," said another young

American woman. An older woman from New Zealand couldn't remember the phone number she wanted or find a phone book to consult. A young Dutch woman not only forgot the number but also couldn't find enough change to use the public telephone (not having the right change in a dream often stands for feeling unable to change waking behavior). These dreams suggest that the dreamer's difficulty in making a telephone connection in the dream represented trouble initiating the desired emotional connection in the waking state.

> Trouble dialing in your dream = Unsure how to connect in an intimate waking relationship

A middle-aged American woman who reported, "It's always an emergency. I need to dial 911 and can't get the phone to work," was symbolizing a situation that was a greater crisis. A middle-aged Dutch woman had a similar dream problem: she could dial but kept entering the wrong number for emergencies. The seriousness of these dream crises probably paralleled an urgent waking necessity to make contact.

If you dream of dialing or punching numbers fruitlessly, take a close look at what's happening in your life at the time of the dream. Ask yourself the following questions:

1. What person or agency am I trying to reach in the dream?
2. Whom does this person or agency represent? (himself, herself, another person, part of self, help)
3. In what areas of my life are efforts to connect with a person not working?
4. How can I improve my efforts to communicate with this person?

Adapt your approach to the needs of that person, as well as to your own, and you may find yourself able to "get through."

"I Don't Know How to Operate This Telephone"

ONE YOUNG WOMAN from America didn't even get so far as dialing. The telephones in her mother's office were "very old and odd," she said. "I have to call my boyfriend, but no one will tell me how to use the phones." Her dream suggested that she was missing some vital information on how to maintain an intimate relationship with the man she wanted. In her case, there was a problem in communication between the dreamer and her mother, as well as one of maintaining contact with the boyfriend. Why was she not able to learn what she needed to know? Was her mother in some sense "old fashioned and odd"? If so, perhaps the younger woman felt her mother had not taught her basic social skills for good emotional contact. She may have needed sexual guidance as well.

Another dreamer, a middle-aged American woman, complained that in her dream she was unable to hold the telephone in her hand.

> Confusion over how instrument works in your dream = Lack of waking information

If your dream about difficulty with a telephone is of this type, with essential information on how to operate the instrument absent, you need to learn some things in order to make the contact you desire. Perhaps it is knowledge about how to relate to the person of your choice; perhaps it is sexual information that you need to learn, or guidance in functioning at a deeper level of relationship than conversation over the telephone. Get informed.

"I Reach the Wrong Party"

SOMETIMES WE KNOW perfectly well how to operate the telephone, we can dial properly, and the call goes through, but for some unknown reason we get no answer or get connected with the wrong party.

This happened to a young American woman who was desperately trying to communicate with her therapist. After a distressing session in waking life, the young woman had a disturbing dream. In it, she repeatedly dialed the therapist's telephone number, but no matter how often she dialed, she got a different voice mail from her therapist's. All her efforts were futile.

Although she was agitated during the dream, when she awoke this young woman felt relieved. She said, "It was a confirmation dream for me." During the waking therapy session, she had shared her feelings of anger toward the female therapist but felt that the therapist "zoned out" on her. "My dream gave me peace, and the knowledge that I do know what is so, and it gave me the strength to confront her with her mistreatment of me—it was deliberate—and she later agreed, and said she can't handle excessive anger from her clients when it's directed at her."

For this young woman, her dream of reaching the wrong party confirmed her impression that she had indeed made sincere attempts to communicate her feelings to the therapist, who had "disconnected from me totally."

> Reaching the wrong party in your dream = Waking miscommunica-
> tion

If you dream of reaching the wrong party and feeling frustrated, you, too, may have been making efforts to connect with someone who rebuffed you. If so, you'll want to consider whether you wish to continue to try to make contact. This woman's dream gave her the strength to confront her therapist and resolve the misunderstanding.

"I Get Disconnected"

YET ANOTHER MOTIF you may experience in Telephone Malfunction dreams is having the connection become distorted by static, "break up," or get cut off completely. Such dreams can represent an interruption in an intimate relationship.

> Bad connection or disconnect in your dream = Disrupted waking com-
> munication

Of course, the person you are talking with and what you are talking about in the dream will give you important clues to the emotional relationship being symbolized and the nature of the problem that's caused the deterioration in contact.

If your dream about Telephone Malfunction includes this motif, you'll want to rethink the relationship and how best to let it go or resolve it in a positive manner. This may also involve working on your communication skills.

"The Telephone Rings, but I Refuse to Pick Up"

ANOTHER MOTIF THAT occurs in dreams involving telephones is refusing to answer. In the waking state, this is a good idea if you need to concentrate on a task and can't risk being disturbed. Asleep, it's not wise. Neglecting a phone call in a dream is equivalent to refusing to listen to important advice. Some part of you is trying to make contact. You ignore it at your peril. You may be hesitant to hear the message, but you need to listen to your inner feelings. Responding to "the call" is essential.

> Refusing to answer ringing telephone in your dream = Ignoring vital inner informa- tion

"An Asian Woman's Hand Is on the Telephone"

A SOPHISTICATED BUSINESSMAN told me a single dream image with a telephone motif that had a strong impact on him. It consisted of seeing a telephone, whose handset was grasped by the hand of an Asian woman. When I asked him to tell me the difference between Asian women and any other women, he replied that he thought of them as gentler, more graceful, and more feminine. I mentioned that dreams about telephones often refer to emotional communication, so perhaps his dream suggested a wish for a softer (more feminine), gentler emotional exchange. He heartily confirmed this meaning, saying that the current discussions with his then girlfriend were fraught with heavy, harsh feelings. He longed for the light, loving touch. Who holds the handset in your telephone dreams?

Your Dreams About Machine Malfunction

IF YOU DREAM about having trouble with a machine, you are apt to be symbolizing an emotional relationship in your waking world, or you are representing some mechanical problem with your body at the time of the dream.

> Machine malfunction in your dream = Waking emotional or physical misfire

In addition to problems with telephones, several other kinds of malfunctions can emerge in dreams about machinery. Among the ones mentioned by survey respondents on my website were forgetting how to run a computer that issues tickets, having trouble operating a fax machine at a library, having a difficult time running a movie projector, trying to use a gun that breaks down into "some technical thing," being unable to see well enough to operate a machine, and operating an automatic teller machine at a bank that turns out to be a "deadly robot poised to kill."

If you have a dream that involves a malfunctioning machine, consider the following questions:

1. What kind of machine am I trying to operate?
2. What is this type of machine used for? (Define it, even if it doesn't exist.)
3. Precisely what goes wrong?
4. What situation in my waking state does this dream problem resemble?

"The ATM Is Dangerous"

ANSWERING THE QUESTIONS will help you sort out the meaning of a dream about some machine that isn't working properly. For instance, if the young American man who dreamed about using an automatic teller machine (ATM) answered the four questions, he might say:

1. I was operating an ATM.
2. It is a type of machine that usually accepts deposits and provides cash.
3. I became aware that it was a deadly robot poised to kill me.
4. This dream might be related to my recent application for a home loan.

In his dream language, the young man was describing a situation involving financial exchange that was threatening and possibly lethal. Only the dreamer can determine the exact waking situation involving money flow that made him feel in grave danger at the time of the dream, but he was probably experiencing some sort of financial strain.

It was a positive sign that the ATM was "poised to kill" rather than actually attacking the man. In dream language, this suggested that although a threat was present and dangerous, it was not yet causing damage, but rather warning the dreamer.

The "machine as robot" is an important aspect of most dreams about machines. They seem impersonal, cold, hard, and able to attack without remorse. They are incapable of caring or feeling pain. If you have a dream about a machine that won't work, observe whether this cold, impersonal element is part of your dream scenario, and consider what person or situation it might relate to in your daily world.

"There's a Garbled Message on the Answering Machine"

AN AMERICAN MAN was initially puzzled by a dream he had shortly after his elderly father's death. His replies to the four questions were as follows:

1. There was a message on my answering machine.
2. It's a type of machine that records and plays back messages from people who are trying to reach the owner of the machine from near or far.
3. The voice on the tape was my dead father's, but it was so badly garbled I couldn't understand the message.
4. I can see a connection between the garbled message and the relationship with my father because I never did understand that man!

The man's ability to make contact with his deceased father seemed forever out of his reach upon the older man's death.

We will see how efforts to communicate with significant people in our lives continue long after the person has died.

A Machine in a Dream as a Metaphor for Your Body

I HAVE ALREADY mentioned how machines in dreams that physically hurt or try to kill you are classified with Chase or Attack Dreams. Here I want to underscore that statement. When people get injured by a machine, that is the time they are most likely to dream about machines that become evil and heartlessly inflict damage.

Many men and women have posttraumatic nightmares about machines after being wounded by one in waking life. Several shared their dreams that the same machine inflicted worse damage. A nine-year-old American boy who had some toes and the top of his foot cut off by a power lawn mower was tormented with nightmares that the mower was in a closet in the house and was going to come after him. A middle-aged American woman whose left hand was badly injured when her glove caught in the rollers of an industrial machine had nightmares that the machines at work were closing in on her, as though to devour her. She was unable to return to work at the factory. A young man almost lost his left hand when a machine he was operating at work went out of control and severed nerves and tendons. Later he had nightmares about the same machine's digging a channel up his arm and cutting off two fingers of his right hand when he tried to stop it, thus causing worse damage than he had actually suffered. Such dreamers need professional assistance to overcome the posttraumatic threatening dreams that occurred after their injuries. Happily, these dreamers got the help they needed and recovered.

Those of us who have *not* been badly injured by machines are more apt to cast them in the role of mechanical tools that break down or otherwise hamper our functioning. But you need to be aware that, in dreams, machines can turn into monsters, as well as simply malfunction. If this happens to you, review the chapter on Chase or Attack dreams.

"The Machine Won't Work"

RESEARCHERS IN A sleep laboratory studied the dreams of a small group of patients who were scheduled to undergo surgery for a variety of reasons. Before and after surgery, the investigators found dreams of defective objects, malfunctioning machines, and poorly operating cars. For example, a man who was due to have the damaged portion of a blood vessel in his leg removed to clear vascular blockage dreamed about a septic tank that was plugged up, with no way to pump it out. This caused a backup of the sewage in the tank, which overflowed and created a mess in the barnyard, getting onto fresh hay and into chicken's nests. In his dream language, the man was comparing the malfunctioning septic tank and blocked pipes to the defective circulation in his leg arteries in the waking state. He was also vividly stating that he felt the whole situation was "full of crap."

"My Computer Won't Work"

MY COLLEAGUE RICHARD Wilkerson has specialized in collecting computer malfunction dreams, as computers and dreams are his fields of expertise. Among the motifs he's observed in this type of dream are hardware problems, odd hardware appearance, operation problems, software problems, and odd software appearance. To give you an idea, here are a few examples from his collection: "A monitor I expect to be square is shaped like a pig with wings; a keyboard is all in Greek; the scanner is as big as a car; a mouse has eyes; my chat room looks like the inside of a firehouse."

Obviously, some of these categories correspond to motifs we noticed in Machine or Telephone Malfunction in dreams, but others are unique to computers. We don't know enough yet to be sure what each unique computer malfunction means to the dreamer. Future dream researchers will have much to explore.

If you dream about machines or telephones that don't work correctly, as many dreamers around the globe do, consider symbolic and physical slants to the meaning of your dream.

SMOOTH OPERATION

9.5 SMOOTH OPERATION

Description: You dream of smoothly and easily operating a machine or telephone.

Frequency: Smooth Operation dreams are fairly rare. When they occur, it is usually at a time that you feel there is an improvement in emotional connections or an enhancement of some other situation. If you are bereaved you may dream of making clear contact with a deceased parent, spouse, child, or other relative or friend. Occasionally dreams about smoothly operating machines relate to improved health. (Dreams about pleasurably driving a vehicle are classified with dreams of Driving Well).

Usual meanings: "I'm making a good connection"; "I can really reach him or her"; "I feel in close touch"; "I've connected" (trying to reach someone on an emotional level or having insight); "I get the message" (contact with the deceased); "Things are working well" (about the dreamer's body).

Dreams about smooth operation of machines are few, but when they occur, they can leave the dreamer singing. These dreams can seem to be precious gifts from the night. For the bereaved, they sometimes provide life-transforming messages. If you've had one of these dreams, you'll know the feeling.

UNDERSTANDING YOUR DREAMS ABOUT
SMOOTH OPERATION

Your Dreams About Smooth Telephone Operation

IF YOU DREAM about calling an important person in your life, and you get an open, clear line, chances are you have a waking sense of good contact with that same person. Nourish it. Keep the lines open. Stay in touch.

Smooth telephone operation in your dream = Waking communication
flowing well

Super–Long Distance Telephone Calls

IF YOU DREAM about being telephoned by a person who has died, the conversation that takes place can be highly significant. During grief, telephone calls appear in our dreams more often than when we are not bereaved. One dream researcher found a large increase of telephone calls in dreams about the deceased. When I examined dreams that I had during the two years after my father died, I also found that a considerable number of them involved telephone calls. A study that examined apparitions of the dead also documented a large number of telephone calls. What's going on?

A telephone connection can easily extend around the globe—I pick up my telephone in the suburbs of San Francisco, California, and within seconds reach a friend in Sydney, Australia. By analogy, our minds extend the existing long distance feature to the possibility of contact over an even greater distance: beyond space and time. Receiving a phone call from a deceased person appears to be a metaphor for communicating with his or her spirit. Whether or not this contact is "real" need not concern us. It is real for the dreamer. The messages exchanged in dreams about telephone calls with the deceased can heal lives and impart hope.

Receiving phone call from deceased in a dream = Sense of contact with
departed spirit

Dreams soon after a loved person died can be painful, especially if the death was sudden or violent. Bereaved men or women often endure nightmares in which the departed person is still suffering. Therefore, when positive dreams about the deceased arrive, they are most welcome.

If you are grieving the loss of a loved person, you'll find comfort in a dream about the deceased that reassures you that the person who died is all right, that he or she is well and happy: a theme I call "I'm okay." In these dreams, when the deceased appears, he or she often looks young and healthy, even radiant. Physical flaws have vanished. Hair, clothing, and face may be shimmering or luminous. But even hearing the loved voice again in a dream is consoling. The dreamer usually awakens feeling joyful and uplifted. Sometimes these dreams convince the dreamer that there is eternal life.

We'll explore these dreams in more detail in the final chapter. Meanwhile, here's a look at the form they take when dreams about the dead include telephone calls.

"They Gave Me Back My Voice"

ONE YOUNG AMERICAN woman I interviewed after her father's death was consoled by a dream of a telephone call from him. During his terminal illness, her father had his larynx removed. He spoke with esophageal speech, which produces a unique, mechanical sound. In her early dreams about her father, the young woman heard him speaking in the same distorted manner. About five months after his death she had the dream that gave her peace.

In that dream, the telephone rang and she got up to answer it. On the other end of the line was her father, speaking clearly and normally, in his "real" voice. The father reassured his daughter that he was whole again. "They gave me back my voice," he told her. He went on to say that everything would be all right, that she should never fear death, and he instructed her to communicate this fact to her mother.

When the young woman telephoned her mother four days later to tell her about the marvelous dream, her mother said, "I had the strangest dream about your father," and proceeded to describe an identical dream. Dreams like this seem to be miracles to the bereaved.

"Mother Just Called to Check In"

AN AMERICAN WOMAN of middle years told me a similar dream involving a telephone call from her deceased mother. She had been the primary caretaker during the older woman's terminal illness. When she dreamed that her mother phoned her, it seemed totally natural, as they chatted about how everything was going. She listened to advice on what to do in her life, then hung up. Still in the dream, the dreamer telephoned her sister to say, "You'll never guess. I just had a phone call from Mother." "I know," replied her sister; "she's on the other line now." The dreamer awoke smiling.

This bereaved woman found the phone call from her mother amusing and comforting. "It was just like her," she said with wonder. The dream helped reassure the woman that life would go on as normal, and that somehow, somewhere, her mother was watching over and taking care of her.

Telephone Calls in Dreams Can Convey Extrasensory Information

DREAMS THAT DECEASED people telephone the bereaved person are not the only dreams about otherworldly communication. Studies of extrasensory perception (ESP) cite frequent examples of information that is received over long distances in dreams about receiving a phone call.

I have experienced this a few times myself. On one occasion, I had lost touch with a Chinese man I had been studying meditation with, when he suddenly stopped coming to the center where he had taught. No one knew how to reach him. A few weeks later, I dreamed that the man telephoned me and told me exactly where he was now living. The information communicated in the dream turned out to be absolutely accurate, and by going to that spot, I found him and resumed the study. There was no possible way I could have learned what I did by ordinary means. So much remains to be discovered about how minds convey information in dreams. There are forces that we do not yet understand.

Telephone call with special information in your dream = Possible ESP connection

---

Be aware of any information you receive in telephone calls in your dreams. Keep the lines of communication open. See what comes through to you.

Your Dreams About Smooth Machine Operation

AS I MENTIONED earlier, dreams of smooth operation of a machine are unusual—the opposite pole of dreams about Machine or Telephone Malfunction. Unlike the dream of the garbled message on the answering machine, dreams in which machines work wonderfully well make us feel great. You recall that malfunctioning machines often symbolize some disorder in the dreamer's body or emotions. Perhaps these well-oiled machines in our dreams symbolize our minds' or bodies' functioning in top form. As with dreams about stunningly positive telephone calls, such dreams leave us amazed.

> Smooth machine operation in your dream = Waking intellectual connection, insight

"I Get the Big Picture"

A RECENT DREAM of mine is an example of this rare dream. In it, I was seated at a computer, working in a library or archive. On the monitor was a graphic image showing lions lying down in a family scene. I followed the instructions for enlarging the picture, and to my astonishment, it worked instantly. No aggravation, no trial and error, just press the buttons, and zoom—what I desired appeared.

Without going into the symbolism of all the images in this dream, I will mention that any time I dream I am at a school or college or in a library, the dream relates to some learning experience that is taking place. Many dreamers set their dreams about learning or discovering something in a similar locale. You may do the same.

The key message for me in this dream was contained in the image of making an easy enlargement. Awake, I find working with graphics, drawings, and photographs on a computer screen and scanner exceedingly complex. In my dream it was simple. I carried out the procedure adroitly, and as a result I "got the BIG picture."

I awoke from this dream feeling exhilarated. I suddenly understood how to incorporate graphics into the book I was currently working on. Not only that, but for the first time I recognized a much broader point: that dream images can be expressed in an international visual language, one that crosses cultural and language boundaries. Suddenly, the scope of what I was trying to do unfurled onto a vast scale. I could see beyond a single book project to something that might help global dream communication.

The fact that this idea may or may not prove practical or come to fruition is almost beside the point. My dream of easily operating computer graphics, of being able to open up to a big picture, symbolized the discovery of an exciting, creative notion that I want to pursue. I felt I had connected with a momentous idea *within the dream*.

If you dream about making smooth and facile connections, via telephone or machines, you, too, may be in touch with a significant idea for your life work. Stay open to the possibility.

1 0

Natural or Man-made Disasters
Versus Natural Beauty, Miracles,
or Rituals

10.0 NATURAL OR MAN-MADE DISASTERS

Description: You dream about being confronted with overwhelming natural or man-made disasters. The dream may involve a flood, torrential rain, or tidal wave. Variations include earthquakes, volcanic eruptions, lava, firestorms, lightning strikes, tornadoes, typhoons, cyclones, hurricanes, or some other desolation. Man-made disasters include attacks by atomic bombs, chemical warfare, and so forth. You are usually terrified in a catastrophe dream, as your life seems in jeopardy. (Dreams of drowning that are not connected with a disaster are classified with Falling or Drowning dreams. Dreams about getting wounded or dying that do not involve a calamity are classed with Injury or Death dreams.)

Frequency: Disaster dreams are fairly common. Some people have them often, others only in times of crisis. They typically occur when you feel that some waking life emergency is impending or has just taken place.

Usual Meanings: "This is a disaster"; "I feel utterly destroyed"; "I feel I can't survive this catastrophe"; "Things are total chaos"; "It's overwhelming."

Dreams about disasters are among the most frightening ones we experience. It feels as if the end of the world has arrived. When you are in a crisis, facing an emergency, this is the time you are apt to dream about a catastrophe. The particular cataclysm in your dream may vary, but the basic feeling is one of being annihilated. Each disaster image has its special shade of meaning that we will explore.

The word *disaster* is composed of the Latin words *dis astro*, meaning "unfavorable aspect of a star." Ancient astrologers believed that the stars had a powerful influence on the lives and destinies of men and women. If a star or planet was descending or out of its natural orbit when a person was born, it was a sign of ill portent. An ascending star or one in its natural path was said to bode good fortune. Hence we "thank our lucky stars" or "bless our stars" and hope not to be "ill starred" or "star crossed." *Disaster*, meaning a star torn from its orbit, became the English word for a sudden and extraordinary misfortune.

More than 40 percent of the first five hundred respondents to my website survey on Universal Dreams said they had dreamed about disasters. Why do so many of us suffer cataclysms of nature during our dreams? What does it indicate when you dream of some terrible upheaval of nature or a man-made catastrophe?

INFLUENCES ON YOUR DREAMS ABOUT DISASTERS

1. Biological

IN THE CASE of Disaster dreams, your heritage plays a strong part. We human beings have an instinctive fear of the powers of nature that can destroy us. Much as we may be fascinated by the energy of the storm, the crash of huge waters, the savage strength of the wind, or the destructive force of boiling lava, we try to keep a safe distance. A large part of history is the story of people's efforts to conquer nature, and thereby conquer our fears of its uncontrolled might. Yet anyone who has watched nature wreak its powerful blows feels awed at how puny our efforts are in comparison.

Each of the elements—earth, air, fire, water—is essential for our survival. Yet, in large or uncontrolled amounts, each can destroy us. Men and women have a primordial fear of the dark that is overcome in part by our mastery of fire and our ability to create light and heat by electricity, but touching fire or electrical current can maim or kill us. This ambivalent relationship with the elements is reflected in our dream imagery. Certain depictions of the elements have positive meanings, yet dreams in which they rage wildly are negative. Any fears you have about disasters are part of your natural inheritance.

2, 3. *Cultural and Subcultural*

AS ALWAYS, THE ideas and values held by your culture partly determine the meaning that Universal Dream themes have for you. Were you taught that a volcanic eruption is a punishment by the gods for sins of the people? Earlier peoples thought earthquakes were caused by the movement of the animal their legends said carried the earth; later it was believed that earthquakes were a result of divine anger or some cosmic intervention. Ancient Greeks envisioned the lightning bolt as Zeus's weapon of destruction, hurled down at them in wrath. Some modern fundamentalists hold a similar view that such a natural disaster is appropriate chastisement.

In many of the world's religious traditions and in the oldest literature of many cultures, there are stories about a monumental deluge; these accounts are now believed to have been based on historical events. It's thought that the seas of the earth rose rapidly sometime between seven thousand and ten thousand years ago, until they settled at their present level about five thousand years in the past. Scientists are not sure what caused the "great flood," but there is evidence that it existed. The literary and religious traditions in different cultures provide their own explanations for the cataclysm. The Judeo-Christian explanation, given in the Bible, says that God was punishing mankind for errant behavior. Only Noah and his family, along with the animals he took into the ark, were saved. It's strange to read of similar accounts, recorded hundreds of years before the biblical record, of essentially the same story (in writings from ancient Sumeria, for example, and in other records of yore).

Any cultural and subcultural ideas about natural phenomena and about warfare that you have absorbed will play a role in your dreams about disasters. This is also true for any concepts about the millennium that may be prevalent in your environment. If you are a person who expects widespread destruction to occur soon, that expectation will influence your dreams about disaster. Many dreamers say, "I thought it was the end of the world," when they describe a Disaster dream. Your ideas about what the end of the world might be like find their way into your dreams about catastrophes.

4. *Personal*

IF YOU HAVE lived through great earthquakes, fires, floods, hurricanes, or other cataclysms, you have vivid memories that can be reactivated when an emotional crisis surfaces in your life. If your country is or has been at war during your lifetime, you will have images of these events, too, branded into your memory.

Even those of us who have not survived natural or man-made catastrophes are well aware of their power to devastate. Open any newspaper, turn on any television news program, hear any radio news broadcast, and you will learn of people somewhere who are coping with the miseries of armed conflict or of the destruction caused by upheavals of nature. As I write, some ten thousand people are thought to have died in India as a result of the "cyclone of the century."

The area of the world you live in is likely to be more vulnerable to one sort of disaster than another. Are you a resident of an earthquake belt, endangered by seismic faults? Do you dwell in a coastal region that is subject to tidal waves and flooding? Do you live near an active volcano or an extinct one that may stir to life? Is your home built where great winds gather and form tornadoes? (The word *typhoon* is from the Chinese words *tai fun*, meaning "great wind.") Are your biggest weather problems annual snowstorms and ice storms? Whatever your local condition or special vulnerability is, it will tend to make you feature one type of disaster over another in your dreams. Just because you must sometimes confront in reality a certain type of recurrent disaster, however, it does not follow that the dream is without symbolic meaning or that your imagination might not generate other disasters less familiar to you.

The same is true of dreams about war, atomic bombs, and other man-made calamities. If you have participated in active warfare or been subject to armed conflict, your dreams have more of these images than those of people who have always experienced peace. Yet, for everyone, dreams about warfare are heavy with symbolism. In war or in natural cataclysm, the instinct to preserve your life is paramount.

UNDERSTANDING YOUR DREAMS OF NATURAL DISASTERS

MOST DREAMS ABOUT Natural or Man-made Disasters are depicting very personal problems that are raging out of control. Sometimes they are replays of actual disasters.

> Disaster in your dream = Personal waking crisis

Your dreams about disasters are likely to fall into one or more of the following categories:

Natural disasters

- Earthquakes (unstable earth)
- Floods, tidal waves, great rainstorms, rising waters (excess water)
- Typhoons, tornadoes, cyclones, hurricanes (excess wind and water)
- Firestorms, volcanic eruptions (excess heat)
- Snowstorms, ice storms, hail (excess cold)

Man-made disasters

- War, armed conflicts (excess aggression)
- Atomic bombs, explosions
- Chemical warfare

We'll look first at Natural Disasters, then turn our attention to Man-made Disasters. Although all categories share certain features, each has its distinctive tone and meaning for you.

Your Dreams About Earthquakes

CATASTROPHES OF NATURE are sudden, extraordinary misfortunes over which we have no control. They are no one's fault; nor are they the result of someone else's intent to harm us. Earthquakes are a type of natural disaster that shakes us to our cores.

Shaken Up

LIVING IN CALIFORNIA, I have experienced several small earthquakes and one rather significant one, but, although sixty-five people died in the latter, none was totally devastating to the general population. Nonetheless, it is alarming to feel the ground beneath one's feet quiver and open. All that seems stable and permanent shakes and crashes, windows break, books fall, dishes shatter, lights and heat vanish. In less than a minute, one's world has changed for the worse. The aftershocks make it impossible to relax and feel safe.

From my firsthand sample of the smaller variety, I can easily imagine the suffering that large-scale quakes cause, such as recent ones in Taiwan, Japan, Turkey, and Mexico. Most of us have seen newscasts and photographs of the resulting desolation. If you have lately gone through a destructive earth-quake, you may replay it, or some variation of it, in your dreams. This is a natural response to trauma, and a necessary step toward recovery.

Gradually the dream will change shape from what actually happened, or worse, to images of improvement. A middle-aged American woman was so badly "shaken up" by an earthquake that she kept her clothes on for several nights after the major tremor, fearing to undress. She barely slept. Finally she dreamed about looking at terra-cotta shards that she pieced together to make a beautiful pattern. A redhead, she associates terra-cotta with herself; when she dreamed of putting the pieces together, she knew she was beginning to heal from the trauma of the earthquake.

For many dreamers who have not personally experienced this type of dis-aster, an earthquake has become the symbol of major emotional as well as physical upheaval. If you have dreams about earthquakes, they are almost certain to be nightmares. They are most likely to occur when events in your waking life are in major turmoil. Such dreams indicate a huge change in your life. Often the change that is under way in the waking world seems cat-astrophic.

> Earthquake in your dream = Waking emotions in extreme upheaval

Your dream images of earth tremors are often puns for some situation in your life that is "coming apart" or "breaking up." For instance, you may dream about a crushing earthquake when a marriage or some other long-term emotional relationship is being demolished or you anticipate that it will be. The expressions we use to describe the ending of a relationship are simi-lar to those we use to describe an earthquake, such as "We're splitting up"; "Our marriage has come apart"; "Our relationship has ruptured."

The breakup may be of a working partnership, rather than a loving bond. The dream earthquake may represent the "collapse" of a business arrange-ment. Your dream may be a way of saying, "The whole thing came crashing down."

Whether the "split" is between a loving bond or a working one, the images of destruction in your dream parallel your feelings of emotional discord, of being "shaken."

> Destruction from earthquake in your dream = Waking emotional damage

Physical or Psychological Causes of Dreams About Earthquakes

SOMETIMES DREAMS ABOUT earthquakes are ominous indicators of a severe worsening of physical or psychological well-being. I have encountered cases in which dreams about ferocious earthquakes preceded the onset of drastic deterioration of the body or mind. In the case of physical breakdown, the earthquake dream is a way of expressing the feeling the dreamer has that he or she is "falling apart."

In the case of psychological breakdown, the earthquake dream can be a sign of impending mental chaos. One young man became obsessed with insisting his parents move from California because he "knew" a major earthquake was about to take place. He grew increasingly desperate in his pleas, until it suddenly became apparent that the disaster he was forecasting was his own tragic psychological breakdown and subsequent hospitalization.

Fortunately, such cases are rare. Most dreams about earthquakes and other disasters correspond to turmoil in some waking situation other than mental collapse.

Coping with Your Earthquake Dreams

IF YOU HAVE a dream about an earthquake, you will probably have no trouble identifying the waking life situation it represents. Nonetheless, it's helpful to ask yourself the following questions:

1. What situation in my waking life feels at risk?
2. What did I do in the dream to escape destruction?
3. How can I get the help I need in the waking world to stabilize the situation and myself?
4. Is there any possible benefit from the drastic change that's under way?

Answering these questions will help you begin the process of coping with dreams about earthquakes. For example, it's very important to notice whether you did anything in the nightmare to protect yourself or others, or to salvage the situation. One young American man described running to the middle of a field to avoid the falling buildings.

Taking positive action in a bad dream is a good prognostic sign. It means you are still able to find ways to deal with the waking emergency. Furthermore, taking action in your dream actually begins the process of coping that can carry over to the waking state. So, remember to help yourself as much as possible during dreams of destruction.

Not all change is bad. When life is in crisis, your world is undergoing change that usually seems horrific. Nonetheless, time may prove that what seems unbearable at the moment can become a positive element in your future. You lose nothing by looking for what might be a possible benefit of the current turmoil. Meanwhile, get the help you need to sustain you during the emergency.

Your Dreams of Great Waters, Floods, and Tidal Waves

THIS CATEGORY OF Disaster dreams was one of the most frequently reported types of Natural Disaster in my survey. If you've recently lived through a flood, you may have recurrent dreams about them for a while. As with postearthquake nightmares, this is a natural response and gradually helps you heal.

Those who have not experienced floods of monumental proportions may well dream about being in peril during a flood or other deluge when life feels as if it's "too much." Even creatures for whom water is a natural element have trouble surviving floods.

Symbolically, water is identified with the unconscious. When it floods us in dreams, it signifies feeling inundated by some situation in our waking world.

Engulfed by great waters in your dream = Feeling overwhelmed by waking situation

---

As with earthquakes, our language about floods is filled with images that become puns in our dreams. For instance, we say "It engulfed me"; "I can't keep my head above water"; "I'm flooded with sorrow"; "I'm drowning in despair"; "I'm in deep water"; "I'm in troubled waters"; "I'm swamped at work"; and so forth. A business may "go under" or be "all washed up." One's fortune may "sink" or "be lost at sea." The images of overpowering waters conjure up feelings of too-muchness. There is a feeling of no escape as the waters rise or close in on the dreamer.

If you dream about a tidal wave about to crash down on you, or of floodwaters rising to engulf you, or of an endless deluge of rain, you are likely to awaken in fright and despair. Such dreams occur when life feels overwhelming. You are apt to feel that some situation in your waking space is beyond control or hope. Surprisingly, there are things you can do to help yourself, at least in the dream, to survive great waters.

Flooded with Despair

THE DREAM IMAGES of great waters often symbolize feelings of great sadness, "oceans of tears." An American woman in her early thirties had a series
of dreams about being engulfed by a tidal wave. In these nightmares she
found herself "clinging to a tree, clinging to my life." She was terrified as the
waters rose around her last safe spot. In the final dream of the series, she spot-
ted an island. She thought that if only she could manage to swim to it, she
would survive. She told me that it was a great struggle to get through the raging waters, but she managed to reach the safe harbor of the island.

Her set of recurrent nightmares about the tidal wave occurred at a time
that her marriage was in danger. The mother of several children, she had
become aware of her husband's involvement with a number of other women.
She felt deeply sad, betrayed, angry, and alone. Imagine her despair when
her husband then committed suicide. As in her dreams that preceded his
death, she felt adrift, at the mercy of elemental passions. But, also paralleling
her dream, she found the strength to cling to life, struggle to safety, and
survive.

The enormous sadness this woman had felt threatened to drown her; in
her dreams this sorrow took form as the tidal wave; her anger was probably
expressed in the "raging" waters. If you face wild waters in your dreams, you,
too, may sense sorrow and possibly anger as well.

> Great waters in your dream = Overwhelming sorrow or despair in wak-
> ing situation

An older Canadian woman was struggling to cope with the deteriorating
physical and psychological condition of her loved husband. She dreamed of
sitting alone in her living room when rain began to pour through her ceiling,
"not in drops, but like it was raining heavily outside," she told me. The
despondency and hopelessness she felt about her husband's irreversible condition took shape in the raindrops/teardrops that flooded her living space,
where she sat alone.

People despair in a variety of circumstances, as well as in experiencing
betrayal of love, or in facing a drastic health condition. It may be the death
of a loved person that causes feelings of drowning in grief; such losses feel
like disasters. Any situation in which we feel overwhelmed may lead to
dreams of overpowering waters. Sometimes there is a physical source for
these dreams.

Physical Causes for Dreams About Excessive Water

THE HUGE WATERS in dreams often represent the dreamer's tears, shed or unshed. Sometimes they indicate a condition of edema or of excess mucus in the dreamer's body.

The idea that dreams about large amounts of water imply an unbalanced physical condition is extremely old, as is indicated by ancient Chinese and Greek records that associated surplus body fluids with dreams about excess waters.

Today's therapists agree that two conditions seem to stimulate dreams about excessive water: a person who has edema (water retention) or a lung condition that creates large amounts of phlegm or mucus is likely to have such dreams. These physical conditions may lead to dreams of drowning or of difficulty in breathing. Patients who have suffered a heart attack need to be especially alert for dreams of drowning, which may suggest a dangerous degree of water retention.

People who are suffering with an oppressive cold, bronchitis, or other condition that produces excess mucus may find themselves dreaming about surplus water. Remember the woman with pneumonia who dreamed of drowning in an upside-down submarine? When dreams about excessive waters are due to an infection, the water in the dream is often described as "murky" or otherwise dirty or discolored. Don't be surprised if you have such dreams when you are ill. They will pass as the water retention or surplus of phlegm is eliminated from your body.

Coping with Your Dreams of Great Waters

IF YOU DREAM about a flood or some other excess of water, you may know exactly what is causing it. If you aren't sure, consider the following questions:

1. What situation in waking life is making me feel overwhelmed?
2. Do I feel profoundly sad about current life circumstances?
3. What did I do in the dream to save myself?
4. What can I do in the waking situation to improve it or get support?

You may not always be inundated in tidal wave dreams. An American teenager has recurrent dreams of looking out a car window or building window to see an immense tidal wave approaching, but it does not always reach her. A young American woman reported dreaming of a tidal wave, "but no one got hurt, only a little wet." Danger that is looming nearby will not necessarily strike you.

The structure of tidal wave dreams resembles that of Chase or Attack dreams, in that you become aware of the danger, see it closing in, but often awaken before it strikes. When there is a period of anticipation in tidal wave dreams, there is time to take some action other than waking up. I have already mentioned the dreamer who realized she could save herself if she could swim to an island and the several dreamers who discovered that they could breathe underwater. If you are troubled by dreams of Floods or Tidal Waves, try to do something to help yourself the next time the dream comes along.

You may be passing through a time of turmoil and immense sadness. If so, remember how important it is to take action in your dream and in your life. Do not let yourself sink helplessly. Swim. Breathe. You can, at the least, change your dream.

Your Dreams of Tornadoes or Great Winds

WHEN YOU DREAM that you are struggling with great winds, you are likely to be having trouble staying grounded. "A tornado coming" is the theme of many Disaster dreams and was reported as often as the theme of great waters. Great winds are a very active, violent form of air. Wind was once thought to be the breath of the god, bringing things to life; in fierce forms it became the anger of the deity, causing destruction. Thunder was believed to be the voice of this supreme god in the sky, and the thunderbolt or lightning was said to be his weapon, or sometimes his phallus. The torrential rains were said to be his semen, fertilizing the land.

Ancient Greeks thought that dreams about great winds were bad omens. Artemidorus, in his famous dream book *Oneirocritica* (Dream critique), said, "Heavy rain, whirlwinds, and fierce storms portend dangers and losses." Today we are more likely to consider the emotional implication of dreams about storms, but many of these ancient observations about dreams are still relevant for modern dreamers.

Blown Away

IF YOU DREAM about destructive winds of any form—tornadoes, typhoons, hurricanes, whirlwinds—you are apt to be experiencing overwhelming emotions. These images of great winds correspond to violent passions and emotional outbursts. Our emotional stability feels threatened.

Great winds in your dream = Violent emotions about waking situation

---

Our everyday language contains many comparisons between emotional storms and windstorms. We say, "I was blown apart"; "I was swept away"; "It's been scattered to the winds"; "It's gone with the wind"; "It's an ill wind."

Your dreams about tornadoes and other great winds may represent troubles in romantic relationships, business problems, health emergencies, reactions to a death, or some other situation totally out of your control. The storm that rages in your dream is a parallel to the emotional storm in your heart.

Coping with Your Dreams About Great Winds

ASSESSING THE SITUATION in the midst of which you are caught can help reground you. Consider the following:

1. What is it in waking life that is making me feel storm-tossed?
2. What did I do in my dream to protect myself from the storm?
3. How can I improve my waking life situation?
4. How can I resolve my inner turmoil and return to a stable state?

When you see dark, threatening clouds on the horizon or the ominous shape of a tornado in your dreams, remember that it is possible to defend yourself. Can we not ride the wind in dreams? Can we not fly high over troubled waters or windstorms? The ancients thought the gods were raging in windstorms, but today we realize that we have godlike powers in our dreams to protect ourselves. By activating them within the dream we strengthen our ability to cope with the waking life situation that the dream storm represents.

Your Dreams of Fires and Volcanic Eruptions

IN MYTHOLOGY THERE are many stories that account for humans' ability to kindle fire. It was usually the task of a sun-hero to "steal" the fire from the gods, since this flaming element was thought to be a small piece of the sun. Before people learned to create fire by rubbing sticks together, fire could only be obtained from blazes caused by lightning strikes. It's understandable that people in ancient times believed the lightning bolt that brought fire was a weapon belonging to a god. One could thrust a branch into the natural flames to make a torch. This gift of fire could banish fear of savage beasts and the dark. By learning to make fire, humanity gained an advantage over animals, obtaining warmth, protection, light, ability to cook and to make pottery. Numerous cultures worshiped light in all forms, and festivals still exist to help restore the waning light of the winter sun to full strength.

Volcanic eruptions were thought to be the fury of an angry god or goddess; destructive lava was spewed as a punishment of the erring people. To burn in eternal hellfire is the extreme penalty in some religions. Some of these ideas are still valid in our dreams about fire. If you dream about firestorms or the eruptions of a volcano, your waking emotional turmoil is apt to involve violent anger rather than the sadness associated with dreams about great waters.

Fiery Feelings

FIRE IS ASSOCIATED with human passions, especially sex and rage. When we have experienced tragic fires, the memory becomes "burned" into our minds, becoming a symbol for all occasions that resemble destructive anger. In its positive form, fire can represent the light of consciousness or a transforming, purifying spiritual experience. When you dream about raging fire, you are apt to be experiencing explosive anger or powerful erotic passion.

Destructive fire in your dream = Burning anger or passion in waking life

---

The consuming aspects of fire are portrayed in such everyday expressions as "I'm burned up"; "I'm furious"; "I'm blazing mad"; "I'm going to blow up"; "I'm seeing red"; "I'm about to explode"; "He's a hothead"; "She's burned out"; "I'm on fire"; "I'm burning with love"; "She's hot stuff"; "I'm hot."

The destruction pictured in your dreams about fire often represents the emotional damage you sense as a result of anger—either your own or that of someone close to you. Did your boss reprimand you unfairly? Did someone deceive you? Is someone close to you unreasonably angry? Many situations can evoke feelings of impending explosions that consume the lives of those around them.

Fires in dreams can leave you feeling powerless, as they did a young woman from Australia, who helplessly watched "somebody being burnt raw." When we identify with the victims of the fire, as she did, it is most probable that we feel we are the targets of someone else's anger.

Sometimes the source of fire in our dreams is our own feelings of highly aroused passion that we think is dangerous. I've described earlier the dream of the middle-aged American woman who watched a house near hers burst into flames. She was passionately attracted to a man who was not her husband and perceived that her fiery feelings might be destructive to her home and marriage, as they eventually were.

Only the dreamer will be able to assess whether his or her arousal has its origin in emotions of anger or desire.

Physical Causes for Dreams of Fire

EXCESSIVE HEAT IN a dream may indicate the presence of inflammation or fever in the dreamer's body. I experienced this in a dream I had prior to surgery on my arm, as a result of a misdiagnosis. Because an orthopedist had assured me I had a bad sprain, not a break, I suffered pain for nearly three weeks. He had told me that the intense discomfort and swelling were the results of not moving my wrist enough; he forced me to move it in his office and advised me to move it at home. After almost three weeks, I insisted on more X rays. The results clearly revealed multiple fractures. With many apologies, the orthopedist informed me that my arm must be rebroken because the bones were healing in the wrong position. No longer trusting his judgment, I located a hand specialist to treat my case, who confirmed that I must have major surgery under general anesthesia; have a plate and pins inserted in my wrist; and undergo nine months of physical therapy to repair the damage the surgery would cause. I was in pain, feverish, and very angry.

In my dream two nights before the surgery, I was with my husband in a city where a huge fire was burning. Hundreds of people were panicking with the catastrophic destruction. I declined escape by airplane as I thought it would somehow trap us in the fire. Later in the dream my husband and I took refuge in an underground cave, from which we heard a gigantic explosion on the surface. I "knew" that ten million people had died, but we survived safely under the earth.

This dream conveyed in dramatic exaggeration the situation I was in. The fire in my dream represented both the inflammation present in my arm and my furious feelings toward the physician who had misdiagnosed me, thereby inflicting unnecessary suffering. The explosion was probably my pent-up anger bursting out. Yet, the circumstance was hardly a citywide catastrophe causing the death of ten million people! Dreams exaggerate. They take real situations and portray them in grand opera style, showing our emotions about what is happening. The positive prognosis from my dream was that, in it, my husband and I and a few others with us survived the tragic situation, as, indeed, I survived the surgery, lengthy treatment, and convalescence from the injury. During my recovery, I dreamed about a house that had been badly burned and was being reconstructed.

When you are injured, your damaged body part often appears in dreams, sometimes with its exact location and symptoms pictured. Excessive heat in a dream often corresponds to the presence of inflammation, fever, or congestion in the dreamer's body. A middle-aged American woman who had a severe headache dreamed that her hair was on fire, streaming out in flames. Likewise, people who suffer from migraine headaches, when asked to draw pictures of their condition, often draw flames in the head area to represent their sensations of burning pain. Victims of burns often draw pictures containing a scorching sun or a summer beach scene with hot sand. These drawings are thought to be related to the burning sensations in the patients' skin in the same way that fire in dreams is related to sensations of excessive body heat. Excess heat in the body looks like fire in dreams.

Coping with Your Fire and Volcanic Eruption Dreams

YOU'LL PROBABLY KNOW what waking situation is making you angry or aflame with passion when you dream about fire. Nonetheless, it's useful to ask yourself the following questions:

1. What in waking life is making me feel hotly aroused right now? Anger? Passion? Fever? Inflammation?
2. What did I do to cope with the destructive fire in the dream?
3. What do I need to do about the waking circumstances?
4. How can I calm my internal fire?

The fiery stream of lava at first destroys all in its path, yet later the charred area can become extraordinarily fertile ground for new growth. Destruction may precede creation. Although you may be coping with a situation that's "too hot to handle," when matters have calmed down, you may discover that you have learned something important and there is space for new, healthy growth.

Your Dreams of Snowstorms and Ice Storms

ICE AND SNOW and cold in dreams represent chilly times in your life. In some legends and folktales, frost, ice, and snow represent the freezing over of warm human emotions. In his *Inferno*, Dante assigned punishment by freezing to the deepest level of hell, thinking it worse than the fires of hell. Many stories associate ice and snow with winter, blindness, and death. Frozen states of water, which cancel its positive potential, are sometimes associated with chastity and purity, and in an extreme state, female frigidity. The rain that freezes into hail is symbolically viewed as a destructive assault, like the terrible seventh plague the Bible says was sent by God through Moses to punish the Egyptians.

People who endure violent snow storms or ice storms every year know how swiftly the freezing whiteness can obscure vision, obliterating all familiar landmarks, obstructing movement, and leaving victims adrift in the bone-chilling cold. As it did for Robert Scott and his men stranded in the Antarctic, life becomes bleak; for the explorers it became deadly. When images of ice and snow appear in our dreams, they convey similar frozen emotions or withheld warm ones.

Icy Feelings

WHEN YOU DREAM about bitter cold in any of its forms, you will often be portraying frigid emotions in some person.

> Snowstorms, ice storms in your dream = Cold physical or emotional waking state

The chilling aspects of snow and ice are pictured in such daily expressions as "I got the cold shoulder"; "I got frozen out"; "An icy tone"; "A frosty manner"; "A cold heart"; "I'm numb"; "I've got cold feet"; "I'm frozen with fear." Symbolically, cold may portray lovelessness, the absence of warm hearts and emotions. If the fire of anger consumes people within its sphere, extreme cold freezes them out. When you find yourself repelled by cold in dreams, there may be some icy person in your environment who makes you feel excluded and unloved.

In Hans Christian Andersen's classic fairy tale *The Snow Queen*, a good, kind little boy was accidentally pierced by tiny splinters of a wicked demon's broken mirror. One fell into his eye, and the other into his heart, making it "cold and hard, like a lump of ice." He became cruel and hard to his best friend, a little girl. At the end of the tale, the girl finally found her friend, who had been stolen away to the Snow Queen's palace. Only the child's hot tears falling on the boy's chest were able to thaw the ice and wash out the splinter of glass. Then he knew her again and wept until the splinter in his eye floated out with his tears. He could see clearly once more and became warm and loving. They fled the ice palace and escaped home, with bright flowers and springtime wherever they went. These old stories contain shards of truth that are universal. Men and women around the globe dream about the icy, hard feelings that chill their hearts.

A teenaged woman from Canada related her dream about being at a community dance, where the performers needed an extra dancer. As her friend got up to volunteer, she slipped on ice—although it wasn't winter—and when she got up, her whole head had turned into a block of ice.

The dreamer didn't know what this image meant but found it "scary." In fact, this kind of image is typical of emotionally cold feelings. Probably the dreamer's girlfriend had "slipped up" in some manner, and her behavior toward her friend turned icy cold. If it grows suddenly cold or icy in your dreams, suspect cold feelings—either directed toward you from a close person or coming from you.

"The Frozen River"

SOMETIMES THE ICE or snow in our dreams represents our own frozen feelings. An older American woman suffered the death of her only son from cancer when he was in his forties, followed by her husband's incapacitation by a series of strokes, and finally a health crisis of her own. About a year after her son's death, she had a significant dream involving ice, one that helped her heal.

In her dream she stood outside a house overlooking a chasm with a frozen river, with slabs of ice that covered running water. Suddenly the woman's son appeared, hugged her, and asked her to help him. She agreed, and with her son, she heaved rock after rock onto the frozen river below. After they had worked together for some time, the rocks broke through the ice and the rushing water flowed freely down the canyon. The woman asked her son why he had returned, and he replied, "Oh, Mom, I thought you needed some help to break up the ice in your heart." She awoke, stunned.

This powerful dream enabled the woman to begin living again, to reinvest her loving feelings in her grandchildren, and to return to active living. The ice in her dream symbolized her emotions, frozen stiff with grief. Breaking up the ice with her son's help represented her returning ability to let the source flow. Water is especially meaningful to this dreamer, whose astrological sign is Pisces, the fish, which needs flowing water to live. The activities that gave her joy in the past often involved water: sailing, canoeing, and living near the sea. In discussing this dream, she pointed out that "ice can melt." She felt blessed by the appearance of her son in her dream to help her break it up. She was ready to live.

If you dream about frozen land or water, you may also be in need of getting your life "unblocked" and flowing freely.

Physical Causes for Dreams About Freezing Cold

AREAS OF THE body may feel abnormally cold because of constricted circulation. When I was going through the crisis mentioned earlier with the undiagnosed broken wrist, my arm felt hot over the breaks, but because the swelling compressed my ulnar nerve, both my ring and little fingers were cold and numb. In one dream that portrayed this symptom, I was with my husband driving through a bleak area with icy trees. The bare branches of thousands of trees were covered with ice. As the wind blew through the ice-coated branches, it made an eerie, wailing sound. Suddenly the car we were traveling in lurched and jammed. I feared we'd be stuck in this cold, awful place of icy trees.

Here, my dramatic dream compared my chilly fingers to ice-covered branches. The wail I heard was undoubtedly my own inner moan, fear of being stuck in such an inhospitable environment. I later learned that images of ice in dreams are typical symbols of reduced circulation.

In the study of the dreams of patients about to undergo surgery, one of the men had vascular blockages in his legs that caused cold feet, nighttime cramping, and limited mobility. He dreamed of driving a car with great difficulty, trying to ascend an icy incline. Several references to snow, ice, and cold appeared in his dream.

Some women who were unfortunate enough to have a fetus die in the womb have reported dreams involving cold and the unborn child. One dreamed of finding her baby icy cold in a refrigerator; her child was born dead. Such cases are quite rare; the cause of dream images of ice is usually less drastic.

However, if you have recently had an injury and begin dreaming about iciness, you may want to eliminate reduced circulation as a cause.

Coping with Your Dreams of Snowstorms and Ice Storms

WHEN YOU DREAM about snow, ice, or hail or the damage these conditions cause, you'll want to think about the following:

1. What situation in my waking life might be making me feel frozen out or loveless at this time?
2. Is there any circumstance at present that makes me feel frozen with grief?
3. Is there something in my environment making me feel cold with fear?
4. How did I cope with the ice and cold in my dream? Did I take action?
5. What can I learn about my waking life situation to thaw out any icy feelings or invite warm, loving ones?

Winter, of course, is a necessary season of rest, while nature restores itself underground before reemerging in the spring. We, too, may need periods of quiet and coolness before blossoming forth again with new life. Frozen in dreams is not frozen forever. Seasons change. Life changes. Dreams of ice and snow may presage those of warmth and flourishing.

Whether the extremes of temperature are in myths, legends, fairy tales, folktales, or dreams, they convey more than physical facts. Even when the cause of a dream of extreme temperature change is physical, emotions are aroused in reaction to the physical condition. We become frozen with fear or grief, or furious (from the root word for "fire") with anger, or aflame with passion. The images of heat and cold, fire and ice, are as universal as are our dreams about them.

UNDERSTANDING YOUR DREAMS ABOUT MAN-MADE DISASTERS: WAR AND BOMBS

WHEN YOU DREAM about war you are probably expressing inner conflicts, or emotional battles raging around you. Perhaps you have been in active warfare and images of battle are seared into your memory. They recur when you face less drastic battles in daily life. Of course, if you are living in a region where there is active combat or you expect the outbreak of hostilities, war will feature more often in your dreams than if you live under conditions of peace. War dreams, however, still have symbolic significance beyond a replay or anticipation of armed combat.

The ancient myths of war gods and goddesses who do mighty battle are a portrayal of the eternal clash between the forces of light and the forces of dark: the good against the evil. These elements exist in all humankind, as well as in our own minds. When we dream about warfare, we act out the epic struggle to rise above baser elements to nobler ones. In our dreams we fight age-old demons—the flaws in us and in the people and circumstances around us.

Your Dreams About Man-made Disasters

Explosive Feelings

IF YOU DREAM about war, you are probably going through some hard times in the waking state. When heavy quarrels are under way, when people are wearied by explosive anger in those around them or disgusted with the eruption of fury in the self, these are the times we are apt to dream about war.

> War and explosions in your dream = Conflict and anger in waking situation

The damage caused in dreams about war corresponds to the emotional destruction occurring in the waking realm. "Bombs were destroying everything" is a typical comment about Man-made Disaster dreams.

Damage from explosive warfare in your dream = Waking emotional
destruction

Many of the dreamers who responded to my website survey mentioned having nightmares about being in a war zone. A young woman from Canada related dreams about nuclear bombs, along with earthquakes and fires. A middle-aged woman from Ireland described a dream that "the Germans set up camp in my back garden, where I lived as a child." A teenage man from America told one of his many dreams about witnessing an invasion of Atlantis and the destruction and devastation to the city by fire. A young woman from Yugoslavia told her dream about suddenly being in Texas, where there was a war going on, with shooting and panic. At first she was outside in the gunfire, but she managed to get inside a building and lie on the floor. The dream ends as "some lady there keeps telling me nasty things and provoking and humiliating me." Surely this woman who provoked and humiliated her was a clue to the source of the violence being expressed in her dream.

Coping with Your Dreams About War and Explosions

HERE ARE SOME questions to help you sort out the roots of a dream about War and move forward:

1. What is making me feel under angry attack at the moment?
2. What did I do in the dream to protect myself and others?
3. What could I have done in the dream to protect myself and others better?
4. How can I best resolve or cope in the waking state with the anger present in me or others?
5. What might I learn from this period of inner and/or outer conflict?

Ancient Romans believed that Mars, the god of war, was also the god of fertility. Doing battle can sometimes allow us to gather our strength into unified power. After chaos can come peace, perhaps with new wisdom.

*   *   *

The Natural and Man-made Disasters in our dreams test our mettle. But since we are given them to struggle with, like it or not, we might learn to use our inner forces to become stronger. When you are confronting difficulties in waking life and dealing with disasters in your dreams, it is a trial. Yet by gathering your powers to cope, you may begin to reduce the troubles in your dreams and eventually to deal with the destructive elements within you and in the outer world. Your inner light can triumph. You'll find yourself roaming through dreams of beauty.

NATURAL BEAUTY, MIRACLES, OR RITUALS

10.5 NATURAL BEAUTY, MIRACLES, OR RITUALS

Description: You dream of strolling through overwhelming natural or man-made beauty. The dream may involve abundant, lush flowers or vegetation and grand trees. You may bathe or swim in healing waters or be kissed by soft rain. Caressing winds may cool your face. You may be touched by warming sun rays or watch a spectacular sunset. Perhaps you will glide down ski slopes, or across the ice, feeling invigorated and happy. All the glories of the natural world offer delight, often with musical background. Beautiful structures, including cathedrals, temples, and marble halls, are sometimes the settings in these dreams. Classic courtyards with splashing fountains may invite you, feathered fans cool your brow. You may gaze into a glowing hearth, or follow the light of a candle. You may engage in mystic dances or rituals or witness miracles.

Frequency: Dreams of beauty are rare. You may have them when you follow a spiritual practice or you may be gifted with one during a crisis.

Usual meanings: "This is incredible"; "I feel utterly transported"; "Life is amazing"; "I am part of something exalted."

When you have a dream of natural or man-made beauty, you will know it. These are the dreams that leave us utterly astonished. We wonder what the source of such images and music could possibly be. They seem to emerge from another world; they are surely not part of our everyday experience. Jung called them the "big dreams." We'll glance through a few of these dreams of awe but are unlikely to comprehend them fully. Our best approach is simply to savor these dreams, which seem to be heaven-sent.

UNDERSTANDING YOUR DREAMS ABOUT NATURAL BEAUTY

Your Dreams About Colorful Flora

ONE OF THE most outstanding features or motifs found in these dreams of Natural Beauty is color. Again and again dreamers say, "The color was so incredible, more real than real, as if lit from inside." This intensification of color is an element in lucid dreams, but one does not have to be lucid to experience the luminosity of these dreams. The color mentioned most often by dreamers in this type of dream is a bright yellow-green, "the color of sun-lit grass, or newly budding leaves," as in springtime. This color is so frequently cited, there may be a physical basis for its appearance. Symbolically, it speaks of new growth, of the coming of flowers and birds, of budding happiness in the dreamer.

Other colors are also mentioned, most often as glowing and rich.

Beautiful earth, plant, or floral growth in your dream = Abundant waking happiness

---

You've seen the association of flowers and fertile growth before in dreams about falling in love, as in the young woman's dream of walking in the mountains with her arms full of flowers given by her lover. These dreams also occur for a woman when she becomes happily pregnant. Remember the woman who dreamed of ripe grapes growing from her belly? The same feeling of lush growth is present in these dreams, possibly intensified, as the dreamer strolls through landscapes of spectacular plenty. For older people, these dreams of glories seem to be prefigurations of Paradise.

"The Golden Earth and White Doves"

A ROMANIAN-AMERICAN WOMAN in her late seventies dreamed that she was lying down in a prairie, where the earth glittered like gold. She thought how lovely it would be to make a dress of the sparkling material. For this elderly woman, her dreamland glinted with gold, a treasured substance she thought of clothing herself in. Her image suggested the idea of the spiritual body, the body of light. The word *prairie* resembled the word *prayer*.

The next night, this same woman had her favorite dream. In it, several white doves fluttered against a sunlit window, with shafts of light flooding the dining room. She was careful not to open the door to let the birds out. She awoke happy and full of loving feelings. For her, keeping a bird in the house conferred good luck; the dining room was a place of nourishment. The white doves of her dream probably symbolized her spirit, one that she wanted to keep inside her body at the time of the dream. She's since died, and I hope the feelings of bliss and peace these dreams gave her fulfilled their promise of ethereal afterlife.

"The Rosy Red Earth"

WHEN MY FATHER-IN-LAW was ninety-seven, he told me a special dream about the beauty of the earth. In it, he "went on a long journey last night." Russian born, he saw himself at home in the Ukraine, at five or six years old, digging in the soil for the rosy red sand used to make a covering on the mud floor of the house for the springtime festival. "I was waiting for Mother to come." The soil of the Ukraine is beautiful, he said, the richest in the world. "The color was extraordinary. I never saw a color like that." He awoke feeling great happiness. Pop lived another five years, to the age of one hundred three; his dream of waiting for his mother while he prepared for the springtime festival touched my heart.

These are just a sample of the many exquisite dreams people have when anticipating their own death. Bereaved people often set their dreams of meeting the deceased person in a fertile natural setting, as did the woman who dreamed of digging in her potato garden in the light of a full moon when her dead mother appeared. In these earth-rich spots they feel they make contact with someone who died.

Your Dreams About Benevolent Natural Elements

IN DREAMS OF Natural Disasters, you face forces of nature that are destructive. In dreams of Natural Beauty, these same natural forces inspire and beguile. Here's a short summary of the shapes in which they appeared for other dreamers, as they may for you.

Dream Image	Waking Metaphor
Refreshing water	Renewal, rebirth
Soft, cooling breeze	Inspiration
Warm, lovely light	Understanding and wisdom
Sparkling, crisp weather	Invigoration

"The Mystic Breeze"

IF YOU DREAM of flying or have dreams in which you become aware of the fact that you are dreaming (lucid dreaming), you will probably have noticed the recurring motif of feeling a cooling breeze as you dream-fly, a clue to awareness of the fact that you're dreaming. This zephyr is a consistent feature in dreams of Natural Beauty as well. I call it "the mystic breeze." I can hear the breeze as well as feel it, a kind of tingling buzz or hum. I do not know why it occurs, but in extraordinarily powerful dreams, this delightful air marks the start of adventure. When you feel it stir in your dreams, you can mount the wind and ride it where you will, as I once did to the moon, or you can whiz above the border of the ocean and land. Anywhere becomes possible. In these dreams we seem to hover between worlds. We return rejuvenated.

A middle-aged American woman reported that she has a lot of dreams about tornadoes, "but I like them, I think they are beautiful, powerful." Her dreams about a great wind link it to awesome power rather than to destructiveness.

Your Dreams About Man-made Beauty

"I Dreamt I Dwelt in Marble Halls"

WHEN YOU HAVE a dream of beauty, if it's not set in a natural landscape, it's apt to take place in a majestic structure. Cathedrals, castles, ancient temples, grand mansions—these often form backdrops to uplifting dreams. With the poet, we may say, "I dreamt I dwelt in marble halls, with vassals and serfs at my side. . . ." Do you remember the priest who dreamed of being in a magnificent cathedral with great, soaring spaces, built into the side of a cliff overlooking the ocean? It was a prelude to one of his most powerful dreams. So, too, Coleridge dreamed of "a stately pleasure dome" that Kubla Khan decreed in Xanadu, which he described in the opening of his famous poem.

These noble structures in our dreams set the tone for the impressive action that takes place within them. Whatever size or shape your dream palaces may be, you can be sure they will be splendid. So is what you learn there.

"The Fountain of Life"

THE WATERS OF a dream fountain can transform you. In my middle years I recorded a dream of transfiguring waters that began with some negative imagery of a little old Chinese man being tied to a chair and submerged in deep water to die; it ended with the positive imagery of his being transformed into powerful, bristling life. The dream is too long and complex to recount here, but the key image in it was of a great baptismal fountain, surrounded by circular steps that spiraled upward. Women, each at a different stage of life, climbed the spiral staircase and stepped into the fountain's waters, where they dipped. One was a girl in a communion gown, another a bride in a wedding dress, another naked and beautiful. I knew that at each important event of her life, a woman must immerse herself in these waters. I watched with fascination.

What a strange afterglow this dream left behind. What ancient wisdom, nearly dead, took on new life at this stage of my life? Some inner transformation, a renewal, was under way.

Other dreamers experiencing this same renewal speak of walking through rejuvenating, misty rain or stepping under a rushing, refreshing waterfall. Unlike in dreams of disastrous great waters, you may enjoy entering the healing waters in your dreams and feel reborn.

"The Candle in the Window"

ONE OF MY mother's most comforting dreams in her latter years, before her dreams got mixed up with her waking life, was of walking in the dark toward a cottage on a hill. Through the trees she could see the bright light of a candle shining in the window. She felt happy knowing she could find her way home.

Light has been a symbol for the spiritual source in most of the tales of mankind. Those people who have had near-death experiences and those who are dying speak of seeing the light at the end of the tunnel. The gleam of "illumination," the haloes of saints, the luminosity emanating from sacred figures—these images equate radiant light with a state of "enlightenment," of total understanding of the mystery of life. These lights, of course, are more natural than man-made lamps or candles, but the illumination symbolism is the same. They may light the way to our spiritual "home."

Your Dreams About Rituals, Mystic Dances, and Miracles

THE DREAMS THAT make us marvel take myriad forms. It's only possible to give a sampling here—they deserve a book of their own. The great dreams, the archetypal ones, often include spectacular patterns of people moving in unison, chanting, singing, weaving together the dance of life. A classic example is Dante's dream vision of Paradise in the form of an infinite rose, with God glowing at the center and angels praising Him in song filling the surrounding petals. On a smaller scale, each of us has dreams of beauty.

"The Ritual Dance of Loga-Shana"

ONE OF MY favorite dreams of splendor involved a ritual dance. In my midforties, just before the end of menopause, I had this remarkable dream. In it, I descended a complex arrangement of circular stairs, constructed as though in a temple. At the bottom, I paused to embrace a family of artists. We spoke of a predictive dream I had involving an emergency with their daughter. The scene shifted to a room where I was seated as part of a circle of participants in a special group. We also discussed the predictive dream, which, it seemed, qualified me to become a member. The leader proposed a toast to two women who embodied the principles of intellect and beauty. I joined the toast, lifting a wineglass and drinking. The leader then suggested a secret ritual called *Loga-Shana*, that he said was safe for anyone. All rose, still in our circle, and followed the leader's movements. Now it seemed to be a tribute to twin goddesses. I imitated the set of graceful movements, first opening my arms to the right and uttering "Loga!," then folding my arms inward as if to incorporate her wisdom. Turning to the left, we spread our arms and invoked "Shana!"; again we folded our arms toward our bodies, to embrace her beauty of spirit. Each movement ended with a dip and slight bow. We repeated the gestures over and over as ethereal music swelled. I felt myself slipping into trance. I saw green fields with people moving. I wanted to write a description of the ritual before I forgot it, and I awoke with the effort.

This dream has stayed with me distinctly for the past twenty years. I never heard the exact words used in the ritual before, but they resemble words for "intellect" and "beauty." Wisdom and beauty of spirit are certainly qualities I wish to absorb, but I never consciously thought about doing so. Although I am an avid dancer, I never saw movements quite like those in the dream. In my inspiring dreams about the baptismal fountain, women ascended a circular stair; here, I descended a circular staircase to an exhilarating experience. There was much more symbolism relevant to my life in this dream, but a very impressive part was its consequence. Imagine my astonishment when, a few weeks later, the artist family in the dream had an emergency with their daughter that exactly paralleled my "predictive dream." Life is surely full of mysteries.

"On Top of the Mountain"

A MAN FROM Japan dreamed of being on the top of a mountain playing a circular musical instrument like an organ. "There is a religious exaltation running through me," he added, echoing the joyous feeling of dreams of beauty. Circles are often part of these dreams of beauty, as in the shape of his musical instrument or in the form of circular dances, seating arrangements, or staircases. Jung believed that circular shapes in dreams signified a centering "wholeness" for the dreamer.

People from around the world who visited my website related dream tales involving Natural or Man-made Beauty. A young Canadian woman said she often dreams of breathtaking vistas that impress her with her imaginative powers. A man from Japan has dreams of strolling through magnificent architectural spaces.

In a recent dream of beauty, I watched an incredible ritual of song and movement performed by a group of women on a high tower. As their gestures were repeated, I suddenly grasped the import of their movements, a kind of visual language. Singing, I joined the rhythmic pattern, taking my place in the dance of life.

Dreamers undergo initiations, learn esoteric information too strange to relate, and speak with figures who seem otherworldly. What causes these dreams I do not fully know. But, as they do for other people since ancient times and around the world today who feel engaged in alternate worlds in their sleep, these dreams leave an aftertaste of glory.

1 1

Being Lost or Trapped
Versus Discovering New Spaces

Description: You dream that you are lost, perhaps feeling desperate. You may be trying to find your way in a forest, in city streets, inside a large building, or in some other mazelike structure. Or you dream that you are unable to move, perhaps powerless to scream or breathe. The circumstances vary. You may be buried alive, or caught in a web or a cage, or trapped in some other manner, usually feeling terrified. (Dreams of being lost or trapped that take place in a car or another vehicle are classified with Car Trouble dreams. Dreams about losing objects are related to dreams of House or Property Damage or Loss.)

Frequency: Lost or Trapped dreams are common. Some people have them frequently, others only in crisis. They typically occur when you feel great confusion or conflict about how to act in some waking situation.

Usual Meanings: "I've lost my way"; "I don't know what to do, where to turn"; "I'll never get out of this"; "I'm confused"; "It's a puzzle" (being lost); "I feel paralyzed"; "I'm caught" (being trapped).

We are all trying to find our way through life, to get where we want to go, to do what we want to do. However different our goals may be, we share the effort to achieve them. Perhaps that's why so many people around the globe dream about losing their way or of being caught in a manner that makes them incapable of action. Nearly 60 percent of the first five hundred respondents to my survey on Universal Dreams said they had dreamed about being lost or trapped.

Despite our efforts, life does not always yield the prizes we seek, be they spiritual or material. Our path is strewn with obstacles, so much so that we sometimes feel progress is impossible. This is when we are apt to dream about being lost or trapped.

INFLUENCES ON YOUR DREAMS ABOUT BEING LOST OR TRAPPED

1. Biological

YOU MAY BE surprised to hear that dreams about Being Lost or Trapped have some biological basis. Men and women have an inborn sense of direction, what psychologists call spatial perception, which varies considerably from individual to individual. In general, males are thought to have superior spatial perception; it is often cited as the explanation for their higher performance on tests of this ability and in tasks of geometry, engineering, and other jobs that require high levels of this skill. Females are thought to be superior in verbal skills.

There is controversy over the extent to which spatial skills are a result of practice and training. Boys' sports, for instance, and males' greater freedom to roam their environment are experiences thought to enhance spatial skills. Of course, some women are very good at reading maps and finding their direction in confusing settings, and some men are poor at these activities, so there is a large degree of individual variation. Your natural inheritance of spatial skills will have an impact on your level of confidence in locating your whereabouts in any environment.

Yet, no matter how good we may be at finding our way around the waking world, we have all experienced the sensation of being lost from time to time. This is where your personal experiences also influence your dreams about being lost.

As to the sensation of being trapped or paralyzed, a large component of these dreams is biologically determined. When we are asleep and dreaming, our large muscles are literally paralyzed, a mechanism of the body that prevents the acting out of dreams. When someone is partially aroused, his or her mind may zoom awake while the body remains in a state of suspended animation. People who experience this condition often feel terrorized because they seem to be unable to move; the episode may last for several minutes, accompanied by hallucinations. The condition is technically termed *sleep paralysis.* In some studies with cats, the portion of the brain that inhibits movement during dreaming was destroyed. When the cats fell asleep and began to dream, they got up, ran around, seemed to stalk mice, hissed, and arched their backs, as though in response to enemies in their dreams. Sometimes humans break through the inhibition that prevents movement in their dreams by making a violent thrust of an arm or leg; the vigorous movement usually jolts them out of the dream.

The terrifying experience of sleep paralysis tends to run in families; it's a dominant trait passed on by the mother, particularly common among Canadian Eskimos. The condition is also frequent in persons who suffer from narcolepsy, the abnormal state of overwhelming sleepiness that may overtake the sufferer as almost an attack. Adolescent males are prone to a type of sleep paralysis that is caused by potassium depletion. If you have a meal consisting of high carbohydrates and alcohol, it may provoke an episode of sleep paralysis.

Some sleep experts believe that dreamers become vaguely aware of their bodies' being in a kind of limbo when they report dreams of attempting to run and being scarcely able to move their limbs. Many dreamers tell me of feeling as if they were trying to run while underwater or in thick mud. This means that at times your dreams of being unable to move are partially stimulated by an awareness of the inhibited movement that actually exists in your sleeping body.

2, 3. *Cultural and Subcultural*

AS ALWAYS, THE beliefs and views held by your larger cultural group and by any subcultural groups of which you are a part will influence your individual variation of this universal theme. Does your culture have a rigid caste system, or strict social structure, that you accept? What are the views held in your community about the relative values of adherence to social rules versus individual freedoms? Have you been provided with a rigid "map" of where you may go and what you may do?

Here's an example of the influence of culture on an individual dream. A young Chinese student had come from Peking to live in my home. Only a few months away from her homeland, she had initially stayed with a Chinese family, so our family was her first experience of an American home. She had lived through the Communist revolution and, although extremely bright, had been sent to work in a factory for years before being allowed to go to college. She found many things in America baffling. Among them was the lavish attention I gave my pet, a caged singing bird.

One morning, she told me that she had dreamed about my bird. In her dream, she had come down to the kitchen to find it in its cage with the door wide open. Despite the fact that it could easily fly free, it was afraid to leave the cage. As we discussed the dream, she told me that birds that were free had to struggle very hard to get food and stay warm, whereas those in cages had their needs fully provided. Outdoor birds were free to do as they wished; the caged ones were forced to do only what the owner wished. It became clear that she had begun to feel as if her former life was like that of a caged bird. If she did everything she was told under the current regime in the Chinese government, she was cared for and fed. Now that the door of her "cage" was open, she felt afraid to venture out into the world, where she would have to take care of herself and devise her own rules. Eventually, she gained the strength and confidence to "fly free."

Although following the strict rules and regulations of an oppressive system makes decision making easy, it hampers individual freedom. We cannot always change the setting we are given; we may need to accept limits to our freedom to survive. How much choice do you have in your current culture?

4. Personal

I HAVE SAID that everyone experiences being lost at some time, perhaps as a child separated from his or her mother in a department store. The moments of panic are usually soon followed by the relief and pleasure of reunion. However, some people have far worse experiences of being lost. If you are a person who lost his or her way on a mountain hike or became separated from others while skiing and had to spend several uncomfortable days and nights before rescuers arrived, your memories of the incident are likely to be evoked whenever you find yourself momentarily confused.

So, too, any incident of being ensnared produces this reaction. Many a child gets a head wedged between railing spokes or otherwise gets stuck. Any person who has been locked in a closet, trapped in a well, or confined by a cave-in is apt to have horrific memories of being "caught." These life experiences recur in dreams when the dreamer feels snared in some new "web" and is desperate to break free.

Many adults have the misfortune to feel themselves lost or trapped in their current lives. You may be one of them. Do you feel forced to remain in an unhappy marriage? Do you feel trapped by an abusive relationship? Are you caught in a dead-end job that you fear to leave? Do you belong to a rigid group that you wish to get out of but don't know how? Do you feel encircled by a hostile environment from which there seems to be no escape? Has bad health gripped you? Any of these situations, and dozens more, may lead to dreams of Being Lost or Trapped.

UNDERSTANDING YOUR LOST OR TRAPPED DREAMS

YOUR DREAMS IN which you or some other dream character is lost or trapped are likely to fit one of these categories:

- Lost in the city, in the woods, in a building, in a desert, or elsewhere
- Lost people (you lose a child or other person)
- Trapped in an opening, underground, in or under an object
- Paralyzed on a bed
- Unable to run

Your Dreams About Being Lost

IF YOU DREAM about Being Lost, you are likely to be expressing a feeling of confusion over what to do about some waking situation. Your waking confusion might involve an intellectual puzzle, a relationship, a spiritual matter, or just about any topic.

Being lost in your dream = Confusion or uncertainty about a waking situation

---

Dreams about Being Lost usually relate to some perplexing waking situation that we are trying to find our way past.

You may easily identify the circumstances that caused you to feel deprived of clear directions at the time you became lost in your dream. Sometimes, however, when we awake we feel as bewildered about why we had the dream as we felt confused within it. These questions may help you untangle the knot:

1. Where was I trying to go in the dream? Home? School? Business?
2. Where did I become lost?
3. What circumstances seemed to lead me astray?

4. What action did I take to find my way in the dream?
5. What area of life is currently mystifying to me?

What Was Your Goal in the Dream?

WHERE WERE YOU headed when the chaos of feeling lost arose in the dream? You may have been intending to go home, as many dreamers are. Perhaps you were on your way to work, as was one middle-aged American woman who could not find her painting studio. You might have been trying to get to school, or a lesson, as was the teenaged American who had recurrent dreams about getting lost on the way to her piano teacher. You may have simply been trying to get out: various dreamers from different countries tell of trying to find the right door, or hallway, to exit a building in which they are lost.

Goal in your dream of being lost = Elusive desired objective in waking world

---

Wherever you were going is often related to a goal that seems hard to grasp. A middle-aged American woman dreamed of being lost while trying to reach her old high school. During her junior year, she had been forced to transfer to another high school when her parents moved to a house in a different district. In her case, she probably felt that she had lost something important in the transfer. She never felt at home in the new school. Making new friends was hard because her schoolmates had been together for years. Her parents' marriage grew troubled. It felt to her as though something precious could never be recovered—perhaps the peace and security of her early years.

The goal in your dream about Being Lost may be related to some state of mind or being that you wish to recapture. Here are some possible connections:

Goal in Dream	Elusive Objective
Home	Safe, secure haven
Work	Ability to achieve, to create
School	Carefree, happy times
"Home"	Heavenly origin

"You can't go home again" has been the theme of many a novel. Even when we are able to return to the homestead, it's never the same. If you dream about getting lost on the way home, it suggests that something about the home situation that you desire is evading you. Most of us pine for something that we feel we have lost, possibly forever.

The poets and mystics say that the yearning for "home" is the longing for our place of heavenly origin, often unrecognized. Is there a source from which we came and to which we desire to return? Perhaps. Whatever "home" is for us, we often go astray en route.

Where Did You Lose Your Way in the Dream?

THE LOCATIONS OF dreams about Being Lost are many. Here's an assortment: a woman from Ireland was "lost in a foreign town that looked like Spain"; other respondents were "lost in an urban wasteland"; an older woman from New Zealand was "lost in a maze." Others were "lost in a deserted terrain," "lost in a nursing home," "lost going down hallways," "lost in a large building," "lost in Woodstock," "lost on the streets of Philadelphia"; a teenaged girl from Canada was "lost in a haunted house."

Of course, the dreamer's associations to the town or other locale mentioned in the dream determine much of the dream's meaning. Ask yourself the following questions:

1. What is it like to be in X (the city or place in which you are lost)?
2. Is X a nice place to be? Why? Is it unpleasant? Why?
3. What is the most vivid thing about X?

Franz Kafka described a city as a place "where the individual loses his identity." What are your associations to the city? To the countryside? To any setting in which you find yourself lost? People most often tell me that they dreamed about getting lost in a dangerous area of the city or else in a forest. In either setting, these dreamers are responding to the "danger" they sense in the environment, and their being lost portrays their confusion, or agonized indecision, about how to cope with the situation the dream represents. Dreamers who stress the barren aspect of a setting, a desert or an "urban wasteland," are conveying some bleak aspect of their waking situation.

Area in which you are lost in dream = Disturbing aspect of waking situation

---

What is it about the area in which you become lost that is most disturbing? What aspect of the environment really bothers you? Whatever your answer, it will be related to the element that is distracting you from your goals at present. Here are some frequent associations between settings of being lost and their troublesome elements:

Setting	Disturbing Element
A large city	Dangerous areas, confusing streets, dirty, foreign/strange, uncultured
Countryside	Unfamiliar winding roads, no markers, no street lights, hard to see your way
Desert, wasteland	Bleak, barren, desolate
Forest, jungle	Dangerous, wild beasts, savages
Hallways, endless corridors	Mazelike, no information, no guide
Hospital, nursing home	Fear of aging, elderly person, death

What Leads You Astray in the Dream?

WAS IT TOO dark to see well in your dream? Many dreamers who get lost speak of the difficulties of seeing in "the middle of the night" as they move through the dark. Lack of light in dreams is a metaphor for lack of mental "illumination." A middle-aged woman from Israel, a native Bulgarian, dreamed of wandering in a desert "in heavy mist, walking in circles, hardly moving my feet." She was having trouble seeing her way "clearly" out of some waking situation. She felt her efforts got her nowhere, only round and round stuck in a rut.

Darkness, mist, fog in your dream = Difficulty seeing your way in waking situation

---

Were you given the wrong directions? Was the map incorrect? Did you take a wrong turn? Whatever seems to distract you in the dream from going where you want to go is an important clue to the thing that is sidetracking you in waking life.

The American teenager who dreamed he was lost in a "deserted terrain with dark green bushes" found himself confronting a "death symbol." His dream suggested he felt the situation that was baffling him could prove lethal. It was a strong warning to find a different route than the one he was taking.

When Other People Are Lost in Your Dream

WHEN YOU DREAM that you have lost your child or children or cannot find your husband, wife, lover, or friend, the dream is apt to be depicting a sense of emotional separation from the person or persons who are missing. If you are a parent, the dream may be a warning to keep closer track of your child's whereabouts. Or you may be feeling that the child within you is lost.

If you dream about a dead person's being lost, that individual is literally missing from your environment. Dreams about losing a person who is already deceased are discussed in the final chapter. Your relationship with a person who died continues after death, so it's important to understand these dreams, too, as you will see.

What Action Did You Take to Help Yourself?

MOST PEOPLE DO nothing productive in their dreams of being lost. They simply wander, getting more and more frustrated or becoming panicky. Many, like a young woman from Australia, dream of walking in circles. If you are moving around in a dream, you have a better chance of stumbling upon the missing person, the right doorway, or the right road to get out of the maze than if you are trapped. You have an opportunity to use dreaming skills, especially if dreams of being lost recur.

Coping with Your Dreams of Being Lost

THE MYTHS, LEGENDS, art, folktales, and fairy tales of humankind are filled with images of being lost or trapped or paralyzed (spellbound). You need only think of Sleeping Beauty's castle overgrown with thorny bushes, the inhabitants entranced in time; the stories with giants enmeshed in trees; the princes trapped in the body of a frog or a swan; or the magic knots that bind the winds. These and numerous motifs like them show us how the ideas of being lost or being trapped are basic elements of the human experience. Think of the many labyrinths and mazes people have constructed: the labyrinth built in Crete for King Minos by the great architect Daedalus to house the minotaur, a savage man with a bull's head; the labyrinths built into the floors of cathedrals in France, such as at Chartres, and in Italy, for those on a pilgrimage to tread; the mazes of hedgerows in Europe. All these structures were built for a purpose, not simply to amuse or to confuse the person who walked into them. Some scholars believe a labyrinth was intended to display the journey of the soul to the center of the underworld and its return by rebirth.

To be lost implies the possibility of rediscovering oneself. How? By finding the center. Whether we look at the model supplied by story wisdom or the model given by ancient constructions, the path to take is inward, to the center. There we may find the treasure—the sleeping beauty that represents our inner self. Call it the soul, or the true self, waiting to be brought back to life. When we feel lost we feel deadened. We need to find our inner purpose, our true calling, the value that makes life worthwhile. The center may differ for each person, but we each need to find it for ourselves. Your dreams about Being Lost or Trapped offer the chance to explore deeper, to use your intuition to guide you to a freer, fuller, richer life.

When you dream of Being Lost, the imagery suggests you feel you have gone astray. You need to find the way again. How do you extricate yourself from a current maze? Begin with finding your way in the dream.

It's of primary importance not to panic. The actions that help most are similar to those that help one find one's way in the waking world. I have an almost unerring sense of direction. I can usually find my way back to anyplace I've been only once. The first time I travel it, a map of the terrain forms itself in my head. But I must pay attention to see where I am, and where I am going. So long as I attend and make a mental picture, I can replicate the route. It's almost fun to get lost because I have such confidence in my ability to find the right route. Once I find it, another portion of the map in my head fills in, so it is a process of discovery, of enlargement of the area of familiarity. When you are lost in a dream, the same process will work for you:

1. Stay calm—remember that it can be fun.
2. Recheck any directions you have.
3. Notice agreements or disagreements with your observation of the terrain.
4. Systematically try one route after another, until one way pays off.

But, you're likely to say, how can I do that in a dream? Plan to do it. Get ready to do it. You have the ability to take props into your dream to help you—a map, a compass, a friendly guide. Remember, however, as an old college professor of mine was fond of saying, "The map is not the territory." Observe and compare your map or written directions to what you see. Calmly keep trying. You will learn. In finding your way, you may be rediscovering your inner center.

Your Dreams of Being Trapped

WHEN YOU DREAM about being ensnared or paralyzed, you are probably yearning to take some action in your waking life but feel afraid to do so. Some aspect of you, or of your situation, is blocking you. You may dread the consequences. A strong approach-avoidance conflict about any waking life situation can leave you feeling unable to move in a dream.

> Being trapped in your dream = Feeling caught in conflicting waking emotions

In your dreams about Being Trapped or paralyzed, you portray the immobilizing conflict you feel about some waking situation, assuming this dream is not caused by a physical condition. Some people use the word *trapped* loosely, such as Being Trapped in a desert or in a jungle. These dreams are more accurately considered as dreams of Being Lost. By trapped, I mean those dreams in which the dreamer is barely able to move or is in a restricted space, such as the Canadian teenaged girl who dreamed of being trapped in a closet, or the teen who dreamed of being in a windowless room that was filling with water.

You may be able to say at once what waking situation is pushing and pulling you in two different directions. Yet, at times we feel puzzled by what makes us feel trapped. This usually means we don't want to face our ambivalent emotions. But we must eventually do so, and the sooner we understand what has cast a net over us, the sooner we can free ourselves of its entanglement. Here are some things to consider after having had a dream about Being Trapped:

1. Where did I become stuck in the dream?
2. What is restricting my movement?
3. How do I try to rescue myself in the dream?
4. What waking situation in my waking life does this remind me of?

Trapped in a Bad Relationship

THE NUMBER OF places people become trapped or paralyzed in their dreams is limited only by their imagination, but the situations they refer to are few. I was truly amazed at how many women described to me dreams of being "stuck" in unhappy, even miserable marriages.

One Irish-American woman, for example, had been unhappily married for more than twenty years. She planned to leave her husband eventually but felt trapped by her husband's threats to cut off all financial support for their children, including eventual college tuition, if she left him. Already emotionally divorced, she had a nightmare in which she was locked in jail, the prisoner of a man who wore a "rat hood." In her dream she tried to ascertain how to get out, but she knew that he would end up in prison, so she felt sorry for him and remained in her cell. This dream vividly portrayed the woman's conflict between her desire to leave the marriage and her sense of obligation to her husband, who had addiction problems.

In a later nightmare the woman's situation seemed worse. She dreamed that "a woman" made herself small in order to fit inside a gas oven. Totally cooperative, "she squinched up to fit in," following her husband's directions. He then turned on the gas. She told me that if the woman "keeps her breathing even, she'll survive." The small oven in this woman's dream symbolized the limited emotional nourishment she felt was available in her home life. Her prison cell had shrunk to the size of an oven. Her husband's turning on the gas in the dream portrayed her sense of being "murdered" in the marriage. Yet, the dream said, if she could breathe evenly, she could survive even this—perhaps representing her hope for a future separation.

A middle-aged American man who had recurrent dreams about being buried alive also felt trapped in an unhappy marriage of many years' standing. He struggled to free himself from the confining coffin and the suffocating earth that was heaped upon the lid. His efforts were so frantic that he tossed in bed and moaned aloud, awakening his wife, who then woke him. Eventually, he left his stifling marital situation, divorced, and remarried happily. His dreams about being buried alive vanished.

Remember the groom-to-be who bolted after dreaming about being in jail shortly before his wedding? Bad marriages or other emotional relationships are not the only situations that leave dreamers feeling ensnared, but they are a common source of dreams of entrapment.

Trapped in a Bad Work Situation

DIFFICULT WORK SITUATIONS represent another area that people say cause their dreams of being immobilized. Men and women often find themselves in a job environment where they are neither satisfied nor able to accomplish what they wish, yet they dare not leave for a variety of reasons, usually financial.

A middle-aged American man dreamed he was at a work site where "someone" had buried him and a few of his students in "sand and gravel up to our necks or deeper." He was probably picturing a situation at the college where he taught, one that left him feeling unable to act in the way he wished. Happily, his dream contained a rescue by some nature-mystery practitioners that he decided to join, suggesting that he saw a way out of his dilemma.

Trapped in a Bad School Situation

THE SITUATION IN which you feel caught may be an educational one, especially if you have no choice over where you go and what you study. A four-year-old American boy was most unhappy at the school his mother had selected for him. One day, an aggressive classmate punched the child's friend in the eye, blackening it. The boy was so alarmed by witnessing this violent act, he had a nightmare that evening in which he screamed repeatedly for his mother without being able to make a sound. Voice paralyzed, unable to move, he felt caught like Peter Rabbit in Mr. McGregor's garden. In the waking state, he felt trapped in an ugly school situation. His nightmare convinced his mother that it was necessary to move him to a different school, and she did.

If your child has a dream about Being Trapped or paralyzed, you will want to help extricate him or her from the waking situation that caused it. Similarly, you want to take action to solve whatever is making you feel trapped when you have a similar dream.

Trapped by Bad Health

IN ADDITION TO work and emotional entrapments, the source of dreams about being snared is sometimes the dreamer's poor health.

An elderly American man dreamed his head and upper body were stuck in a toilet, with his head underwater. He was beginning to feel terror and to have trouble breathing. With supreme effort, he managed to disengage one arm from the trap, but he didn't have enough strength to lift himself up. Cautioning himself not to panic, he finally managed to extricate his head, which "popped" out.

As we discussed his dream, the man explained how badly his health had deteriorated in the preceding year. After hip replacements and back surgery, this formerly active competitive swimmer and tennis player could only move slowly and rather painfully. In particular, his breathing had become restricted—this symptom was pictured in the image of his head's being underwater, an impossible circumstance for easy breathing. The dream image of a toilet as the ensnaring object was probably also a comment on how "shitty" he felt his situation to be.

His dream, although extremely frustrating, contained the positive imagery of struggling to free himself from the object that had caught him. This suggested that his efforts to cope with his disabilities and his optimistic approach allowed him to continue to get value from life.

Other Sources of Entanglement

DREAMERS ARE HIGHLY inventive in depicting objects or incidents that bind them in dreams. One young girl dreamed the ground was covered with vines so that she had to watch wherever she stepped. Surely her dream cautioned her to "watch her step" in some waking situation. A middle-aged American woman dreamed of being caught when she tried to follow two children up a loft ladder; she was "too big to get through the hole" and got wedged in it. What was making her feel trapped as she tried to follow a youthful model in her upward climb? Another woman in midlife had recurrent dreams about Being Trapped in a giant spiderweb. She felt her life was going nowhere; she felt spiritually numb.

Limbs and Voices Spellbound

PERHAPS YOU ARE one of the many dreamers who try to run to escape some danger and find their legs paralyzed, frozen with fear. We have seen how the typical sensation of difficulty running in a dream may have a physical source. "I'm running in tar," said a teenaged woman from Malaysia; "I can't move fast enough to get away," a young man from New Zealand declared. "My feet are leaden," said a young English woman. A child from India dreamed "I have to do a lot of homework, but my hands are not moving." Sometimes, like that of the boy unhappy in his school setting, it is the dreamer's voice that feels paralyzed.

Other people tell me about dreams in which they appear to awake in bed (what is called a "false awakening") and sense an evil presence in the room, such as robbers rummaging through belongings or someone watching them. The dreamer feels that the only escape from violence is to remain still as a stone, stiff with fear. The slightest motion might betray the person's awareness and draw murderous villains to the bed. Like a hunted animal, the dreamer adopts "freezing" as a defense. The person's body feels spellbound.

These comments, and others like them, may have a symbolic component as well as a physical one. If you experience a dream that contains difficulty moving your legs, consider any current conflict. In what part of your life do you want more movement? Psychoanalysts have long observed that a man who dreams that one limb, an arm or a leg, "falls asleep" or is paralyzed in a dream is often experiencing impotence; it is the man's penis that is "numb." Only you will know whether this has some application to your case. Of course, sometimes your arm or leg has actually "gone to sleep" when you dream it is numb. In this case, waking and rubbing it to restore circulation as soon as possible are advisable.

Possible Physical Causes for Dreams About a Monster or Weight on the Chest

THIS VARIATION OF a dream about Being Trapped is one of the most abhorrent. Dreamers who report it describe this dream with a degree of horror; they feel attacked by a supernatural evil spirit. The American teenager who dreamed that "a dark dog/creature is sitting on my chest about to bite off my face" is typical. He struggled and managed to throw off the creature, but it turned into his younger brother. Momentarily strengthened, he fought, but "I lose command of my body again, and am killed."

A young woman described dreaming that a huge boulder was pressing down on a group of people, including her, in a field. She said there was "no pain, but absolute paralysis, and creeping horror." Her sensation of overwhelming dread is also typical of these dreams in which there is an impression of being crushed or pressed upon by a great weight. Another dreamer spoke of getting heavier and heavier, sinking through the bed.

A surprisingly large number of people have dreams that are variations on this theme. In Europe, the creature who seems to take away our breath by sitting on our chest has been called the *incubus* or "night hag," and the dream/experience is referred to as "hagging." The term *incubus* comes from a Latin word that means "to lie upon," based on the sensation of weight upon the chest, along with the notion held by people in olden times that a demon or evil spirit has taken possession of the victim. The Swiss artist Fusili drew and painted several versions of this imaginary beast, crouched upon the sleeping form of a distraught maiden. Probably the actual source of this common nightmare is a version of sleep paralysis. The descriptions of this bad dream are so similar from culture to culture and person to person, it seems almost certain to have a physical explanation.

These dreams may emerge from a malfunction of the sleep process. In its most extreme form, some people experience several of these "attacks" a week. A prominent opera singer told me that she has this experience almost nightly and wakes everyone within hearing as she shrieks in terror with her powerful voice. This incident alarms her bed partner, whom she has occasionally wounded in her wild flailing to throw off the creature. Several adults in a study of these "night terrors" said that their attacks started during a major life change. Emotional strain seems to intensify the experience. If you are a person who often suffers from sleep paralysis attacks or "night terrors," you will probably want to seek professional help.

In addition to sleep malfunctions, other causes of the sensation of weight on the chest in dreams sometimes result from the dreamer's having a disease of the lungs or heart. The pressure in these cases is from a literal constriction or blockage of circulation in the chest. An eight-year-old American boy dreamed that a man was standing on his chest while holding the whole world; the child was suffering with pneumonia and was feverish. His dream recurred thrice before his chest began to clear and the oppressive "weight of the world" was lifted. A Russian man, who had had a heart attack eleven days earlier, dreamed he was lying in his country house, where he did not have enough fresh air. Bandits broke into his house and fought with his siblings; one bandit tried to crush the roof with a beam, which fell onto the dreamer's chest. He tried to lift it, or to scream, but could not manage to do so. He awoke in pain with a heart spasm. The weight he had experienced in his dream was caused by constriction in his chest.

Unless you have a serious chest infection or condition, or feel actual pain in your dream, a dream about a weight on the chest is probably symbolic of feeling entrapped in a waking situation. Fortunately, we can do something to make such dreams less oppressive.

Coping with Your Dreams of Being Trapped

AS WITH DREAMS of Being Lost, unpleasant dreams about Being Trapped offer us a chance to grow. When we feel entangled by mental turmoil, emotional or financial problems, and weighted down by troubles in the waking world, we need to find a way to untangle ourselves. We need to throw off the strands that confine our spirit. Dreams about Being Trapped may compel us to free ourselves in the waking state. They help us realize how tightly we feel enmeshed; they inspire us to break our bonds, to undo the knots.

Once, when I was feeling especially pressed by a troublesome waking situation, I dreamed of being in shackles. I strained repeatedly against the cold, hard metal, trying to free myself. Suddenly, in the dream, I made the astounding discovery that if I relaxed, I could simply slip out of the fetters. It was my fighting against them so vigorously, pulling and tugging, that prevented me from realizing I was imprisoned by my own tension. I relaxed, slid out of the shackles, and walked free. Awake, I smiled to see the parallel with my waking problem. If I didn't fight it, there was no problem at all; I walked away free in the waking world as well.

A young American who had developed the skill of lucid dreaming found himself stuck in a wall in one of his dreams. His attempts to get out left him paralyzed. He solved his dilemma by accepting it and "just waited it out" until he forgot he was in a dream. His dream pictured the patience that may rescue us when we realize efforts are futile. Immuring—the word literally means "walling in"—was an actual practice in olden times, when one or more persons were sacrificed by being placed inside the foundation of a building or bridge, sometimes alive, to give the structure "life." If we are immured in a dream, sometimes all we can do is wait for the unpleasantness to pass.

The repellent experience of sleep paralysis at times carries over to the waking state. If you are awake, relaxing and waiting it out may be your best course of action. You can also try wiggling a toe or moving your eyes—parts of the body that may be free of the sense of numbness. Relax. It will pass.

In dreams, if you find yourself with legs that refuse to move; or you are entangled in branches, nets, webs, ropes, chains; or you seem to be totally paralyzed, try to do the following:

1. Make an effort to move.
2. See whether you can fly—sometimes it's easier than running with leaden legs.
3. If attempts to free yourself are unsuccessful, experiment with small movements of fingers, toes, or eyes.
4. Send a "mental message" to a helper.
5. Relax and wait it out.

When we free ourselves from the traps in our dreams, we are beginning the process of clearing away the obstructions that tangle our efforts in waking life. We are moving to a more developed stage. We may be freeing ourselves from the past, releasing our inhibitions, breaking the spell, and becoming free to be who we truly are.

DISCOVERING NEW SPACES

11.5 DISCOVERING NEW SPACES

Description: You dream that you discover a marvelous new space. There are several variations to this theme. You may open a door in your ordinary house to discover a whole new room or section of the house that you had no idea was there. You may be walking in a familiar neighborhood and come across an area or a vista that you have never seen before. These new spaces are invariably beautiful, spectacular, or special in some positive way. This dream often contains a door or window.

Frequency: Discovering new spaces is a fairly unusual theme. This dream typically occurs when you feel that a new aspect of you is opening up, a potential you had not anticipated.

Usual Meanings: "I've found something wonderful"; "This is amazing"; "I didn't know this was here"; "This is just what I want"; "I want to explore"; "I feel things are opening up"; "I'm free."

If you dream about discovering a magnificent new space in the midst of the old, familiar surroundings, you are apt to feel extremely pleased. It's a natural response to the delightful realization that something novel and intriguing is quite near. This universal dream theme, the opposite pole of those dreams in which we feel lost, trapped, or paralyzed, provides a sense of hope. It frequently corresponds to some exciting new development in your waking world.

Have you met a new love interest? Are you unlocking an emotional area that you kept tightly closed in the past? Are you exploring a creative project that gives you a fresh perspective on life? Is your family growing? Is your health improving dramatically? Do you feel that you are more open to spirituality? These are typical circumstances that stimulate dreams about Discovering New Spaces.

UNDERSTANDING YOUR DREAMS ABOUT DISCOVERING NEW SPACES

IF DREAMS ABOUT Being Lost or Trapped or paralyzed involve wandering in confusion, walking in circles, or being confined in a small area such as a coffin or oven, dreams about discovering a new space involve expansion. The area of enlargement varies from dreamer to dreamer, but we share with others the effort to grow in understanding.

Discovery of new space in your dream = Waking life is expanding

---

When you dream about entering a new space or viewing a spectacular panorama, you are becoming aware of a wider horizon; your outlook broadens in scope. You may dream of going through a familiar door into vast corridors, leading to other doors to fascinating new rooms. Or perhaps you gaze out a window to see an enchanting garden filled with flowers and singing birds. Your dream may present a grand vista you never noticed before as you walk around your local neighborhood. Your reaction, like that of most people who have this dream, is apt to be amazement and delight.

Windows and Doors to New Spaces

YOUR DREAMS ABOUT Discovering New Spaces often portray doors and windows because these are the objects in daily life that, if closed or shuttered, block your view of what is beyond. When open, they may reveal sunlight, invigorating air, green trees, blossoms, and a fresh outlook. Life offers absorbing new possibilities.

Opening a door in your dream = Opening self to waking opportunity
Looking out a window in your dream = Assessing current waking situation

---

Of course, what we see or find on the other side of the door or window in our dream conveys our view of what life is presenting us at the moment. Bleak, weed-choked gardens disclose a very different attitude than a bright, lovely landscape. In dreams of Discovering New Spaces, the scene is invariably intriguing and inviting.

Psychoanalysts point out that doors and windows are feminine symbols, corresponding to the entrances in female bodies. Opening and shutting doors, from this point of view, may represent intercourse. Perhaps they are, in some dreams. But for many dreamers, the portals to our houses, the gateways to our gardens, are far more than body openings. When we step through them, we enter a new state of being.

New Spaces, New Growth

Emotional Growth

WHEN WE FALL in love, the world seems brighter. So, too, in our dreams we may gather an armful of flowers, walk down delightful winding paths, dance under twinkling stars, and drink deep the delicious nectar from the hands of our beloved.

If you dream about Discovering New Spaces when you are getting to know an exciting romantic partner, you will understand that the opportunity open to you is a special relationship. It may or may not prove to be so with time, but at the moment of your dream, the experience is real—some wondrous new space calls you.

An older American woman described a recurrent dream from her childhood in which she found herself between the walls of a house, where she climbed a magical staircase to find a wonderful treasure on the top floor, a treasure associated with her beloved grandmother. Surely the girl was finding a new space that led to valuables that would enrich her life. The magical stairway seemed to be a way for her to stay emotionally connected to her loved person.

Another woman of the same age dreamed she was going to sell her house, but when she walked through it deciding what needed to be done before the sale, she discovered a room that she had never seen before. "There were billowy white curtains and lots of open windows." The furniture was of a different style than in any other area of the house. Having discovered the new room, she realized she couldn't possibly sell the house. The dream ended with the woman and her daughter discussing the beautiful space and how they could use it. This dreamer was finding some special new potential she didn't know she had.

Psychological Expansion

PERHAPS YOU ARE experiencing a development in the area of psychological understanding. Many people who go into psychotherapy dream about discovering a new space as they explore their inner selves. A young American woman in therapy dreamed about a swimming pool in which the bottom suddenly dropped several feet to a much greater depth. She was startled, but intrigued. Awake, she was entering deeper waters as she investigated her inner depths.

Jung reported a fascinating dream he had as he was learning more about his inner self. When he was traveling with Freud for seven weeks in 1909, the two men shared their dreams. When Jung described this dream to Freud and heard the older man's comments, he drastically disagreed. In his dream, Jung was in his house (very different from the one he actually owned), looking at the pleasant furnishings of the upper story, thinking it quite attractive. Going down to the ground floor, he found an area that dated from an earlier century, with medieval furnishings. Exploring further he came to a heavy door, opened it, and descended a stone stairway that led to a cellar. Here the structure was exceedingly ancient, from Roman times. Finally he spied a ring on a stone slab, which he lifted. He descended farther yet on narrow stone steps to a low cave cut in the rock, where he found the remains of a primitive culture, including two skulls. Then he awoke.

Freud thought this dream involved a death wish, and Jung, loath to disagree with his esteemed colleague, assented. Yet, for Jung, the house was his image of his layers of consciousness. The primitive culture he discovered at the base, he saw as something "impersonal" underlying his psyche. He said, "The dream became for me a guiding image which in the days to come was to be corroborated to an extent I could not at first suspect." This dream became the basis for Jung's idea of instinctual archetypes underlying the personal elements in dreams.

You don't have to be in therapy or be a psychiatrist to discover new emotional spaces in your dreams. When you develop an intimate friendship, follow a course of learning, explore a passionate interest, or develop a creative pursuit, you may well find you are discovering formerly unknown parts that excite and delight you. Your horizons are growing wider.

Family Expansion

YOU ALSO MAY dream about Discovering New Spaces when you become a parent or grandparent. A man in his early fifties had a compelling dream shortly after his grandchildren were born. His dream was considered more fully in the section about animals, but it is the introductory passage that is of interest here. In it, he entered an incredible church or cathedral built into the side of a majestic cliff at the ocean. There were "great soaring spaces and high vaulted ceilings, and one whole side of the space was a sheer wall of glass looking out toward the ocean below." The dreamer, who was a priest in waking life, naturally worked in churches, so this was not an unusual setting for him. But the expansive space, the unique site built into a cliff that overlooked the ocean—these aspects of the dream suggest significance beyond the customary. The dream continued as the man watched two animal families that were obvious symbols of his children and their new offspring. He felt joyful and proud. Witnessing your children's children is a fulfilling experience—a glimpse of the vastness of immortality.

Increasing Good Health

PERHAPS YOU ARE one of the many people who have been injured in an accident or diagnosed and treated for a serious illness. If so, you'll want to watch for any dream that contains the theme of Discovering New Spaces. It's a favorable prognostic sign.

In my study of the dreams of people who had been injured or become ill, I found that deteriorated or destroyed buildings or damaged landscape often represented the dreamer's afflicted body. As the dreamer began to recover, some of the healing images that arose in dreams depicted repaired or remodeled buildings, with new rooms added, or wholly new structures erected. Some people dreamed of immense picture windows—ones that didn't exist in their actual houses—that opened onto views with fabulous new gardens. Other people dreamed of encountering spectacular vistas they never knew were located in the area. These changes in dream imagery reflected the ongoing restoration in their hurt bodies, as well as the "new view" they were gaining.

When I was about eight weeks past the injury that broke my wrist and five weeks beyond the surgery to rebreak and repair it, I dreamed about "a lot of construction going on to make ramps for a new freeway." In the same dream, a large light fixture that had been repaired was being delivered for installation in my house. I had forgotten the fixture but was pleased to see it again. The "freeway" was a pun for my life, which finally was beginning to smooth out once more. The repaired light suggested renewed understanding, an "illumination" of the nasty situation I had survived. The ramps were not yet finished in my dream; the light was not yet installed. But events were clearly moving in a positive direction. Part of my healing—my illumination—

involved writing a book about my experiences and those of others undergoing similar experiences.

If you have had the misfortune to be injured or become ill and dream about Discovering New Spaces, you may want to get, or make, a picture that reminds you of the openness you observed in your dream. Focusing on healing images that derive from your dreams is sustaining and may even have a curative effect.

Widening Spiritual Connection

ANOTHER AREA THAT may be opening up for you if you dream about Discovering New Spaces is that of the spiritual world. By spiritual, I refer to a sense of connection with the original source of life.

An American woman in her sixties who had been diagnosed with a type of cancer that is usually fatal made dramatic changes in her lifestyle, including her eating and exercise patterns. Against all expectation, she has survived more than five years beyond her initial surgery and treatment. In one of her recent dreams she was on a hillside, where she saw graves in disarray. Learning there was a new area, she went through a passage to find another area in the cemetery with warm-colored, pretty stones, all neat and attractive.

Whatever the future may hold for this woman, her change of attitude, as well as behavior, has brought her to a fresh, more appealing state of mind. We all, in the course of nature, must face our death. If it has positive elements in our dreamworld, our transit to the future state of being may be easier.

At times in dreams we feel as if we are in touch with that other world. A young American man described his dream—perhaps a "flashback," he thought—of being in the company of all the gods, discussing how to structure the cosmos. We may never fully understand what stimulates such dreams. But that they impress the dreamer, and sometimes impel a change of lifestyle, is certain.

In one of my significant dreams I seemed to experience a connection with a space beyond. I described it earlier in the chapter on Flying dreams. Here, I want to emphasize the opening sequence. In my dream, I was lying on a bed with a lover, as though resting. From the bed I looked out of the open window, through which a light breeze blew, lifting and wafting a sheer curtain. I could see the full moon with crystal clarity. Something clued me that I was dreaming, perhaps the stir of what I think of as a mystic wind in dreams. "Fly me to the moon!" I cried out. I stretched my arms forward and rose from the bed into the air, through the open window, climbing high into the night sky. Raising my arms above my head, I soared farther upward, higher and higher. Never before had I flown so high. I sailed still higher, approaching the gleaming globe of the moon.

This dream left a remarkable aftertaste. The sensation of flight seemed like the most intense reality. I felt as if I had touched something in a world beyond this one. I had passed into another time and space.

Indeed, at the time of this dream, many new avenues were opening to me. On a psychological or symbolic level, the dream made perfect sense. Yet, the sensation of flight, of space, of contact, was more than straightforward. My dream felt like a spiritual exaltation. Wherever such dreams come from, they are welcome.

1 2

Being Menaced by a Spirit
Versus Being Guided by a Spirit

12.0 BEING MENACED BY A SPIRIT

Description: You dream that you are being berated by someone who is deceased. You may feel terrified, guilty, resentful, or abandoned. There are a number of variations to this jarring but rare dream theme. It may range from mild admonishment to outright curse, or a sense of being haunted. (Dreams involving actual harm to you are classified with Chase or Attack dreams.)

Frequency: Dreams of being Menaced by a Spirit are unusual. Some people have them occasionally, others only in dire conditions. They typically occur when you feel guilty, responsible for a death, ambivalent about the deceased, or extremely anxious about an impending or recent death.

Usual Meanings: "I'm alarmed"; "Did I do all that I could?"; "Am I responsible?"; "How could I have helped more?"; "Did I do the right thing?"; "I'm guilty"; "I'm being punished."

Dreams of being Menaced by a Spirit are among the most uncomfortable dreams we can have. Whatever burdens of guilt or anxiety we carry after the death of a person close to us assume threatening shapes in these dark dreams.

There is a sense of supernatural doom that makes them particularly repellent.

Fortunately, dreams about being Menaced by a Spirit are rare. Only about 12 percent of the first five hundred respondents to my website survey said they had dreams of this type. Many people volunteered examples of the opposite dream theme, that of being Guided by a Spirit. If dreams about being menaced by a spirit feel like a curse, dreams of being guided by a spirit feel like a blessing; the first are dark with gloom, the second are bright with light. Despite being uncommon, both types of these dreams are considered by the dreamer to be among the most significant of a lifetime.

INFLUENCES ON YOUR DREAMS ABOUT A SPIRIT

1. Biological

AS HUMAN BEINGS, we understand that people die. We know that sooner or later we are certain to confront the death of someone we love or have mixed feelings about, as well as our own inevitable demise. We are programmed at the deepest level of our genes to resist our own death and the loss of those we care about; we have an instinct for survival and protection. This instinct may sometimes go horribly awry, as it does when a parent deliberately, or accidentally, causes the death of his or her own child. But most people, most parents, most children, fight heroically to safeguard their offspring, their aging parents, or other close, loved relatives.

When you dream about the death of your children, mates, siblings, parents, grandparents, or significant others, you are expressing concern about their well-being. Sensing a danger to a loved one can stimulate dreams about his or her death. How many mothers and fathers are startled awake from a nightmare in which their child is injured in some way, perhaps by a runaway car or a fall into a lake? These dreams provide warnings to beware, to take more precautions, to guard and watch over precious children. At times these warnings may be directed toward the "inner child," rather than a waking life child—suggesting risk to a vulnerable aspect of the dreamer. And, certainly, some dreams of this type express a wish to have a certain person out of the way. Mostly, though, I find that dreams about the death of a loved one indicate concern about that person rather than a desire for that person's removal from the dreamer's life.

When someone you love is ill and you fear that person might die, you are likely to anticipate the death in your dreams; in this way our dreams help prepare us to accept an impending death.

When a loved one actually dies, you are almost certain to dream about that person. These dreams may be disturbing at first—although not necessarily—but they are part of your grieving process. They help you (1) to accept the reality of your loss, (2) to work through the pain of your grief, (3) to adjust to an environment in which the deceased is absent, (4) to emotionally "relocate" the person who has died, and move on with your life. These are not easy tasks, but your dreams will guide you, even if they seem unbearably painful at first.

Grief counselors advise "leaning into the pain." It's a rocky route, but the quickest one, to make it through. At first the bereaved person usually feels numb with shock. This phase is followed by disorganization, with wildly swinging emotions. Eventually, the grieving person finds a way to reorganize life and reinvest in it. This does not mean that the dead are forgotten, but that the deceased has become a treasured part of the past.

Our emotional relationship with the dead is eternal. In dreams, we receive messages from the dead; we can also deliver messages to them. Conflicts left pending when the death took place sometimes find resolution in the dreamworld. Our biological instinct to survive leads us forward, often with hope for reunion in an afterlife.

2, 3. *Cultural and Subcultural*

IF YOU HAVE tormenting or consoling dreams about a person who died, you should be aware that these derive from more than your sorrow and sense of loss. Whatever culture we are part of, whatever our subculture may teach, we have absorbed ideas that involve a dread of the dead, as well as a longing to maintain contact.

Today, we rarely think of the dead as trying to harm us, unless we somehow feel we were responsible for the death. Yet, people in ancient times regarded the dead as actively hazardous to the living, an idea still present to some extent today. There was a great fear of the ghost of the deceased, especially if the person had died violently. The notion of being haunted was not a funny Halloween prank, but a serious threat.

In Neanderthal times, more than seventy thousand years ago, the dead were buried with food meant to keep their spirits happy. Their bodies were bound tightly by leather thongs, intended to keep their spirits tied to the tomb. The road from the graveyard to the deceased person's home was sometimes strewn with thorns, to prevent the ghost from following it home to the village. The worldly goods of the deceased were at times burned or buried to prevent the desire for belongings from drawing the ghost to the vicinity. The expression "Rest in peace" (or its Latin equivalent, *Requiescat in pace*) is not simply a wish for the soul of the deceased; it is also a heartfelt hope.

The ancient Greeks and Romans, like the Egyptians before them, thought it was necessary to provide for the souls of the dead. They believed that when the dead arrived in the underworld, they must cross a swampy river named Styx (meaning "hateful") in a ferryboat rowed by a sinister old man called Charon (his names means "fierce brightness"). If Charon's toll of a coin was not paid (placed by relatives on the eyelids of the corpse, underneath the tongue, or between the teeth), the poor soul would languish along the riverbank. There, with the unburied dead such as those lost at sea, they were stuck wandering, eternally lost. Some legends say that these lost souls suffer hunger and thirst that are never satisfied. Ancient Greeks poured a cupful of wine over the gravestone to "slake the thirst" of the ghost. In India, folk tradition was that goldfish were the favorite food of ghosts.

Every culture developed notions about the perils of the dead and the trials they undergo, in addition to information on how to help guide the soul through the afterlife. Each culture fashioned a notion of the realms of punishment or reward, of hell or heaven, according to what seemed most repugnant or most desirable to them. People in desert lands, for instance, picture heaven as full of greenery and flowing waters, luscious fruit, and other delectable things that are rare in their waking world.

Many of today's communities accept various ideas from bygone eras and provide "spirit food" for the hungry or thirsty ghost at certain times of the year or at festivals for the dead. The Mexican Day of the Dead is an example of this ongoing practice.

The myth of the vampire is also alive and well in the twenty-first century. Originating in ideas of vengeful spirits, the notions of vampirism have spread around the world. In the case of vampires, the dead, or "undead" as they are sometimes called, are thought to be hungry for blood, yearning to suck life energy from the living. We can't help but be exposed to these concepts in films, books, and theater. We feel their emotional impact, even if we intellectually reject the ideas.

According to folk traditions, a spirit may return from the grave (1) to complete unfinished business, (2) to give a warning, (3) to punish or protect someone, (4) to impart information that was not given prior to death, or (5) to reenact its death.

Violent deaths are said to produce vengeful ghosts: victims of murder, suicides, victims of accidents, those who die young or in childbirth, those who remain unburied. These are the spirits believed to return most frequently.

The more unhappy the dying person, the more danger from the ghost for the survivors. Correct burial rites are thought to protect the living. Mourning clothes may have originated as a warning to the public that the wearer has been contaminated by contact with the dead. The unattractive garb is also thought to evoke less jealousy from the ghost, rendering it less likely to return. Funeral pyres in some parts of the world, bonfires (from Middle English words for a fire to consume bones, "bone fires"), are thought to thwart return of the ghost.

Other folk traditions speak of a kindly spirit. The motif of the "grateful dead" refers to tales in which the hero encounters people mistreating a corpse. The hero compassionately pays the deceased person's debts or somehow stops the mistreatment. Later, a helpful traveling companion joins the hero. The unknown traveler turns out to be the grateful ghost of the dead person the hero defended. These old ideas about unhappy spirits, or kindly ones, appear in today's dreams about the dead, suggesting the universality of these ideas and their persistence over time.

4. Personal

DID ONE OF your parents die when you were quite young? Did you lose a sibling to a tragedy? Are you the survivor of a set of twins? Has one of your children been lost to illness? Did a favorite grandparent's death leave you feeling bereft? Was someone you care about murdered? Did a loved person die in a violent accident? These and dozens of similar losses have a powerful impact on your dreams.

Your memories of what the deceased person did for you or to you are elements. Does your now-dead parent criticize you and call you stupid, as one young American woman's mother does in her dreams? Does your lost parent stroke your hair and watch over you with a smile until you fall asleep, as another young woman's mother does? Every personal experience with the dead and death that you have encountered will influence your dreams about a spirit.

UNDERSTANDING YOUR SPIRIT DREAMS

YOUR DREAMS ABOUT a person who died, whether recently or long ago, are likely to fall into one of two themes, generally negative or basically positive: being menaced by a spirit or being guided by a spirit. The neutral motif may appear years after a death. These themes often consist of one or more of the following motifs:

Negative Motifs	Positive Motifs	Neutral Motif
"I'm Suffering"	"I'm Okay"	"Hi, How Are You?"
"I'm Not Really Dead"	"Good-bye"	
"You Fool!"	"Congratulations"	
"You'll Be Sorry"	"Here's a Gift"	
"Join Me!"	"Go Ahead!"	
"Stop!"	"Your Turn Is Coming"	
"Avenge My Murder"	"Please Forgive Me"	
	"I Forgive You"	
	"I'm Evolving"	
	"I'm Being Reborn"	
	"I Give You Life"	
	"I'll Always Love You"	

Since I have written an entire book on the subject of dreams about the dead, I can only give a brief summary here. (Those who would like to read about this area in greater depth should refer to my book *The Dream Messenger: How Dreams of the Departed Bring Healing Gifts.*)

When you dream about a deceased person who was close to you, the dream will probably contain one or more of the nine elements I found in the universal dream about the dead:

1. *The announcement.* You may sense the approach of the deceased person, hear his or her footstep, catch a whiff of cologne, answer a knock on the door, or otherwise anticipate "something's going to happen."

2. *The arrival.* The deceased person comes into view, often in a "border" setting, such as a hallway, beyond a gate, or at a transportation center. The encounter can take place just about anywhere.

3. *The deceased's appearance.* Age, condition, and clothing of the deceased person vary with the emotional quality of the dream. If negative, the dead person often looks haggard and ill; if positive, the deceased usually seems radiantly transformed—younger, healthier, happier, even rapturous; if neutral, appearance is unremarkable.

4. *The attendants.* The person may be accompanied by other deceased persons known to the dreamer or by a figure representing death.

5. *The message.* The deceased communicates something of significance to the dreamer, not necessarily in words. These messages are the heart of the dream and may be delivered in person, over the telephone, by letter, or in some other manner.

6. *The gift.* The deceased may give something beyond reassurance or warning, such as specific information, a flower or plant, a beautiful

artwork, or a piece of jewelry. These dream gifts are mementos the
dreamer cherishes.

7. *The farewell embrace.* The most touching aspect of dreams about the
   dead may be a loving embrace, hugging and kissing, usually with a
   vividness that seems lifelike. Some dreamers embrace mentally.

8. *The departure.* There may be a specific good-bye expressed or a simple
   fading away of the image of the deceased.

9. *The aftermath.* Dreamers often feel that their lives have been changed
   on the basis of one such dream about the dead. Faith in an afterlife may
   be restored, and the dreamer loses fear of death. These dreams can console and uplift the dreamer for the remainder of a lifetime. They can
   dissolve resentments, melt fears, give guidance, and leave the dreamer
   feeling loved and blessed.

The pattern of your dream, of course, may not contain all nine elements, but
it's likely to have a few of them. Here's an overview of the motifs found in the
messages in these dreams. (If you find the negative dreams too distressing,
skip to the positive dream section.)

Your Dreams of Being Menaced by a Spirit

IN GENERAL, THE unpleasant motifs in your dreams about being Menaced
by a Spirit are a metaphor for your feelings of fear. The specific motif reveals
the aspect that is most distressing to you.

Menaced by a spirit in your dream = Feeling fearful for the deceased
and yourself

"I'm Suffering"

INITIAL DREAMS FOLLOWING a death, especially one that is sudden or violent, can be extremely disturbing. You may see the person suffering the same
symptoms that led to death. These images may be fairly realistic, exaggerated, or profoundly distorted. In traumatic deaths, such dreams are especially
painful. If you have this common type of dream motif about the dead, you
will dream of (1) a replay of the death scene, (2) a distortion of the death
scene, or (3) some new suffering for deceased.

Several American widows described dreaming of their husband's dying
just as he had, along with their desperate but futile efforts to help. This

realistic replay is understandably harsh. An American man whose daughter was murdered had recurrent dreams about seeing her at the street corner where she was abducted and taken away; the dreams were filled with the horrific details he learned of the rape and torture that led to her death. He was in a professional grief support group for relatives of murder victims, which helped him cope and eventually led to a cessation of this awful dream. His experience was typical of people whose loved one was killed violently.

A young American woman who had stopped in to her husband's law office for a lunchtime visit encountered a crazed gunman who was attacking people. Her husband shielded her and was murdered along with several other people; she was wounded. The woman had recurrent dreams of the trauma, holding her injured, bleeding husband on the floor. About a year later, as she began to heal physically and emotionally, she dreamed of his embracing and kissing her. The trauma replay had shifted into more consoling dream content. As healing begins, this transformation in dream imagery takes place.

Some dreamers portray the death scene bizarrely distorted. A young American woman dreamed that her father's face became ghoulish, monsterlike. "His mind had started to go" as he was dying; her dream distortion dramatized this mental change by distorting his familiar face. An American woman who cared for her grandmother while she was dying of cancer dreamed that the old woman's body was covered with poisonous mushrooms that sprang up all over it. A young Canadian woman in the website survey dreamed her deceased good friend turned transparent and suffering as they walked hand in hand. A young American woman who was with her dying husband after his chest was crushed in an industrial accident dreamed of seeing his face scribbled on and erased. Dream distortions like these probably spring from watching changes in the dying person that are difficult to accept.

Some negative dreams about the dead involve new problems for the deceased. One young American woman dreamed her deceased husband rolled out from under her bed, saying he was hungry. A middle-aged American man dreamed that his recently deceased mother was "trying to get into heaven on a ball." Another man, whose twin had committed suicide by hanging, dreamed about seeing him cut his own head off with a wire. These new agonies for the deceased—as well as the dreamer—suggest that the dreamer feels that the dead person's spirit is not at peace.

"I'm Not Really Dead"

ANOTHER VERY COMMON category of negative dream about the deceased is the one in which you see the deceased and think—during the dream—that the person is not dead after all. These dreams often start out as a delightful discovery that the death has been a mistake but usually end in painful recollection of the actual death when you awaken.

During the dream, you may experience many emotions, most often that of surprise. "You're not supposed to be here! You're dead!" a young American woman said to her deceased father when she dreamed that he was coming out of a shower. "Whose ashes did we bury?" a middle-aged American woman asked her brother in a dream, after seeing their deceased father lying on the living room sofa. One woman's deceased mother replied to the query "Didn't we bury you?" in a dream, "Yes, but don't tell anyone I'm still alive. I don't want them to know."

You may be one of the dreamers whose response is anger. An older man who dreamed that he saw his deceased wife sitting at a table, chatting with her friends, was furious. "What are you doing here?! I thought you were dead. All that trouble you put me through, missing you, and you were out having a good time!" A middle-aged American woman dreamed she saw her deceased husband living in another part of town, having dyed his hair, conducting a different life without her. His death felt like a desertion to her, as deaths do to many bereaved persons. "I expected to feel sad," said an elderly woman when her mate of many years died, "but I didn't expect to feel angry at him for leaving me alone with all these problems."

Responses of surprise, delight, dismay, confusion, and anger at the sight of the deceased in a dream are common; they convey the dreamer's emotions, wishes, and hopes. Often we want the person who is gone to be back with us. Dreams of "I'm Not Really Dead" force us to give up our denial of the death. If the relationship with the dead person was formerly full of strife or hate, we may be relieved that the person is gone but be left with unresolved feelings. The emotions these dreams evoke help us work through the anguish of grief.

"You Fool!"

THIS CATEGORY OF being Menaced by a Spirit involves the deceased person's expressing strong disapproval of the dreamer. If you have such a dream about a dead person who was highly critical of you during his or her lifetime, the dream is likely to leave you feeling discouraged, downhearted, or even alarmed.

Nobody likes to be criticized, least of all by someone who is dead. Although this dream motif is fairly rare, it's too common for comfort. Everyone has mixed feelings about the people with whom they are intimate. You are more likely to have this dream when the negative aspects of the relationship with the deceased outweigh the positive ones. When we intensely dislike a person, we can dismiss him or her more readily than when our feelings are strongly ambivalent.

In past times, people who had dreams in which the deceased verbally assaulted them said an "angry ghost" had visited them. On waking, the dreamer hastened to settle the spirit of the deceased with prayers and offerings. Some tribes described people who dreamed of being criticized by a dead person as being "bitten" by an angry ghost. Sacrifices or gifts were required to appease the ghost and prevent further dream abuse.

Although we are not inclined to view dream criticism in the same way today, we still feel badly shaken from such a dream. One American woman shared her discomforting dream of this type. Her mother had suddenly taken ill, was hospitalized, and died alone the same afternoon. That evening, the woman and her siblings sorted through and divided her mother's belongings. When she fell asleep that night, the woman had a startling dream in which her mother was livid, berating her behavior. The dreamer awoke distraught. She felt her mother left the world as an unsettled spirit, with much anger and hurt between them left unresolved.

Psychologist Joyce Brothers described her poignant dreams after the death of her husband, Milt, from bladder cancer. The anger and resentment he felt during the last few months of his life were directed at his wife; after his death, the venting of anger continued in Brothers's dreams about him. In these angry dreams, he still looked "bone-thin and ravaged." A little over a year after his death Brothers had a comforting dream about her dead husband, which she called her "miracle dream" because it was like a gift, a replay of the happy days they had shared.

A middle-aged American man who was estranged from his father had a dream that prompted him to rethink their relationship. In it, he saw the face of his deceased grandmother zoom toward him, lit with bright white light and trailing a silver thread. She looked at him sternly and demanded, "Why are you crucifying my son?" Repeating this question twice, she zoomed away again. The man awoke shaken by his grandmother's "stern fearsomeness." He felt this to be more than a dream. Although he found it hard to believe his rejection of his father was not justified, he began to question it for the first time. Finally he returned to his hometown, where he learned that his father had been hospitalized, went to see him, talked things over, and was able to reconcile their differences. The shock of his dead grandmother's words in a dream led this man to an important truth. He was lucky to have made improvements in the relationship while his father still lived.

British writer Virginia Woolf was never able to resolve the conflicting feelings she had about her father, the prominent editor Leslie Stephens. After his death, when she began to experiment with fiction, Woolf dreamed of showing her manuscript to her father. In a letter to a friend in which she described this dream, Woolf said her deceased father "snorted, and dropped it on the table." When she reread her work in the morning she "thought it bad." Her dead father's dream criticism left her discouraged. Despite this, she became a successful novelist, admired for her innovative approach. Yet, she never wrote with a feeling of easy confidence and continuously feared the comments of the critics (and presumably those of her dead father).

German psychologist Paul Tholey has described a series of powerful dreams about his deceased father. Tholey's father "often appeared to me in my dreams as a dangerous figure, who insulted and threatened me." At first, when Tholey became lucid in these dreams, he would beat his father in anger. When Tholey won, he felt triumphant, but the figure of his dead father reappeared just as insulting in subsequent dreams. Finally Tholey had a dream in which he became lucid while being chased by a tiger. He pulled himself together, confronted the tiger, and asked, "Who are you?" The tiger transformed into his father, who started to order him around. This time, Tholey rejected his threats and insults without fighting him. He conceded in the dream that some of the criticism was justified and decided to change his behavior accordingly. Still in the dream, Tholey's father became friendly and they shook hands. He asked for help from his father, who encouraged him to go his own way alone, and finally his father seemed to "slip into my own body." Tholey awoke, amazed. He said this dream liberated him. His fear and inhibitions in dealing with authority figures vanished.

You can see how some of the criticism originating from the deceased person in a dream is also partly the dreamer's self-criticism. By honestly assessing the criticism, we can firmly reject those parts we disagree with and change those parts we accept as valid. If you have such a dream, it can free you to live life more fully.

"You'll Be Sorry!"

THIS RARE DREAM motif is agonizing to the dreamer, who may awake with fear and remorse. An Israeli woman who contributed to my website survey dreamed that a dead friend tried to rape her. She did not say whether her attacker had reason to be angry, but something made her feel his spirit was vengeful. If you have such a dream, consult the Chase or Attack Chapter.

Survivors of horrific trauma sometimes have a "You'll Be Sorry!" dream, especially if they feel partly or totally responsible for a tragic death. They are also the dreams of a guilty murderer.

The ancient Greeks thought there were three avenging female deities of retribution—called the Furies—who punished crimes beyond the reach of human justice. Orestes, in the classic Greek drama bearing his name, was ordered by the gods to avenge the murder of his father. To do so, he had to kill his mother and her lover. He carried out this order, but because matricide was considered a particularly heinous crime, he was pursued from land to land by the Furies, who never let him rest, until finally he was freed by the goddess Athena.

The American writer William Vollman, when he was only nine, caused the accidental death of his six-year-old sister. His mother had left the boy in charge of her at the edge of a pond in New Hampshire. Distracted, he stopped paying attention, and the little girl drowned. The profound guilt he felt from this moment of carelessness resulted in terrifying dreams. Vollman said in an interview in the New York Times magazine, "I had nightmares practically every night of her skeleton chasing me and punishing me, pretty much through high school." Much of Vollman's life as a writer has been devoted to trying to save downtrodden people—winos, prostitutes, drug addicts. His mission to help seems to be a kind of expiation of his inability to save his sister, whose "curse" haunted him in dreams.

The Roman emperor Nero, according to historians, deliberately caused the death of several people, in particular his mother, wives, and assorted relatives. Before he had his mother killed, Nero told none of his dreams. After her death, he was said to suffer appalling nightmares. In reference to the theme of "You'll Be Sorry!" Nero is reported to have dreamed that his deceased wife Octavia, whom he had tried to have strangled on a number of occasions before he had her falsely accused of adultery and executed, "dragged him down into darkness, where he was covered by winged ants." This dream, and other inauspicious ones, suggest Nero had some shred of guilt over his atrocious crimes. He eventually committed suicide to avoid public execution by being flogged to death, a penalty that was imminent, by troops in the revolt against him. The angry ghosts of his murdered victims finally got vengeance.

If you should have the misfortune of having accidentally or purposely caused the death of a person, you may find yourself likewise troubled in dreams. Coping with the curses of the dead is heavy business. Folklore and literature are full of the power of a dying person's curse, a malediction, to wreak havoc on the life of the perpetrator. If the curse is justified, repentance and atonement are crucial steps in finding emotional relief. If unjustified, forgiveness may bring ease.

"Join Me!"

THESE ARE DANGEROUS dreams because they worsen a dreamer's depression after the death of a loved one and may suggest suicide. Fortunately they are extremely rare. In this motif, the deceased person seems to entice the dreamer to a reunion in death. After a loved person dies, particularly a child or adult mate, rather than an older person, there may be deep depression and thoughts of death. The lost person may feel irreplaceable and life seem meaningless. These feelings are natural but usually abate with time. If you should have recurrent dreams, as one young American woman did of her dead lover's beckoning her to join him, you'll want to get professional help quickly. Such dreams need to be resisted.

Twins, researchers have found, are particularly susceptible to feeling the rupture of death as an unbearable separation. A psychiatrist whose identical twin died of heart trouble at forty-nine wrote about how his "ego boundaries" were vague after the twin's death, and how in his dreams he felt confused about who was who and which had died. Waking with surprise and relief, he had to struggle to separate himself from his dead twin. He said, "To be separate was to live, to be joined was to die." Gradually this man found the way to survive.

A middle-aged man I interviewed had suffered disturbing dreams about his identical twin, who had committed suicide as a teenager, after injuries from a car accident prevented his participation in sports and resulted in his being disappointed in a love affair. The man's twin had been the more dominant of the two, a sports hero. When his twin hung himself in a familiar place, where the young man found him, the tragic event marred the surviving twin's life. He said that even when he is happiest, he sometimes has a nightmare in which his dead twin's image seems to mock him for daring to be happy. Survivor's guilt is hard to shake but can be overcome.

Mates of the dead person also have difficulty reinvesting in life. An elderly man told me his dream that his dead wife urged him to kill himself. She may have given voice to his own thoughts, but this dream so disturbed the man that he was inspired to reestablish contact with the world of the living.

An older Russian woman, whose husband had died three months earlier, developed heart trouble. She was recuperating when she dreamed she was sitting on his gravestone and two bony hands reached up out of the grave, one grasping her throat and the other her heart. She tried to scream but was unable to do so. She awoke with worsened symptoms. She felt as if her husband were forcing her to join him.

These dreams about a deceased person's tempting the survivor to join him or her are allied to old ideas about demon lovers and malevolent spirits, who seduce the sleeping person and, vampirelike, drain the life juices. Legends are full of tales in which a brokenhearted lover, like Orpheus, tries to follow his beloved to the Land of the Dead to retrieve her spirit. The lover never succeeds completely. We cannot bring the dead back to life. Nor should they take us with them. If you have such a dream, resist it. Get help.

Happily, there are also dreams in which a dead loved one says something like "I'm watching over you, waiting for you; I'll be here when it's your turn." These dreams console the dreamer, especially toward the natural close of life.

"Stop!"

THIS DREAM MOTIF may be positive or negative, depending on the content and your resulting behavior. Being warned of danger ahead by a dead person may be life saving. If you have one of these rare dreams, you'll find it impressive. Like flouting an ancient taboo, whose violation can lead to misfortune, disgrace, or death, ignoring these dream warnings given by a deceased loved one is risky.

You may dream of being ordered by a spirit to separate now, this very moment. One young American woman dreamed she was riding with her dead father on an airplane. He said to her, "I'm sorry, but you'll have to get off now, as you can't go where I'm going." The plane landed in a wheat field, where she and her husband disembarked, then watched the plane continue its flight. Another young woman was following a dream path her dead mother had indicated when she was confronted by an angel (the word means "messenger of God"). The heavenly being blocked her way and said, "Don't come now. Turn back and continue walking." A woman whose sixteen-year-old son was killed in an automobile wreck dreamed a week later that he took her hands and flew up into the star-filled night sky. As they flew, she told him she wanted to join him. He replied that he had work to do; that she must continue to live until she is seventy-one. The message in these dreams, and many like them, is that we cannot accompany the dead on their journey.

You may be told in no uncertain terms to stop contemplating a particular action. A young Chinese woman who had married a man of partly Japanese heritage had such a dream. At first the couple lived together relatively happily near his family in Taiwan. Soon the husband took her to live in Japan, where life became almost unbearable for the young bride. She was completely isolated, did not speak the language, and soon discovered, she told me, "In Japan, the man is king." She bore him sons, who in that culture belong to the father. Her husband began numerous affairs, and his various mistresses telephoned her and wrote her letters, trying to drive her away. Although she had ample money, the woman was miserable. She contemplated suicide.

Finally one night after sitting up late waiting for her husband, the woman reached a decision. She would leave him and the boys and take refuge with her sisters in America. She fell asleep exhausted and had a dream that changed her life. In it, she was at the house of her father-in-law, a man she greatly admired and respected. She saw him on the lawn between the house and a river, in a white costume, with his white hair, fighting with another man. In his hands he held a leafy branch, which the opponent cut with something sharp, perhaps a sword. Yet the branch did not fall. She was perplexed, then awoke with a start.

The woman then saw before her in her bedroom a vision of her revered father-in-law in meditation, his face sharp, his eyes on hers. "I knew I did something wrong," she told me. She was certain the elderly man had come to order her not to leave his grandchildren. She promised she would never betray him. The woman explained to me that she was like the branch of the tree in her dream; even if she were separated from the base, she would be supported by her father-in-law's spirit, as long as she stayed with his descendants. The woman was true to her word. She changed her attitude completely after this dream. She studied Japanese and devoted herself to the protection of her sons, refusing to be driven away. Eventually her husband gave her permission to take the boys to America, and the couple divorced. But the woman's commitment to her promise was kept; her now-grown sons, in turn, are devoted to her.

Whether the image of the deceased in a dream is ordering us to return to life or to stop some intended action, the dreamer feels awe in these dreams. There seems to be a connection with the spirit who is providing protection for the dreamer. We need to accept the departure of the deceased. Their spirits may become a guiding force for us.

"Avenge My Murder!"

YOU ARE NOT likely to have this exceedingly rare dream motif. Yet those who have it find it impossible to ignore. Like Hamlet, confronted with his father's ghost's accusation that his brother murdered him—"If thou didst ever thy dear father love—Revenge his foul and most unnatural murder"—we may wonder whether such statements can possibly be true.

There are a number of anecdotes recorded in which a dream was said to reveal the secret burial place of a murdered person or even the murderer. In a recent case, a young homemaker in Indiana came forward to accuse her mother of killing her little sister, who had disappeared without a trace twenty-five years earlier. She did so because she felt tortured by recurrent nightmares of the pleading face of her baby sister. She had made a promise, she said, when she saw her die that someday she would find her sister's body and give her a real burial. A trial was held in 1994. The accused mother claimed her child had died naturally and her husband had secretly buried the body because he was afraid he'd be deported to Mexico. The body was never found, but investigators did locate proof of the child's existence in a birth certificate and photograph. The mother was convicted of involuntary manslaughter and faced up to ten years in prison. The grown daughter who made the accusation felt her nightmares helped her overcome her fears and seek justice for her dead sister.

You can see there is a wide range of negative dreams about a deceased person. Happily, the range of positive dreams is even broader.

BEING GUIDED BY A SPIRIT

12.5. BEING GUIDED BY A SPIRIT

Description: You dream that you encounter a deceased person who was significant in your life and a message is conveyed. There are several variations on this theme that may leave you with a feeling of wonderment, bittersweet joy, or exaltation. They may also inspire you to change your life path or give you a belief in an afterlife. They feel real.

Frequency: Many of the motifs are common; others are rare. These dreams typically occur during active grief, which may last years.

Usual Meanings: "I'm okay"; "Good-bye"; "I'll always love you"; "Go ahead"; "Congratulations"; "Here's a gift"; "Please forgive me"; and others.

Your Dreams of Being Guided by a Spirit

IN CONTRAST TO negative dreams about the deceased, if you dream that the dead person communicates one of these positive messages, you are certain to feel comforted. These dreams frequently leave the dreamer feeling uplifted. They may inspire belief in life eternal.

In these consoling dreams, the deceased looks younger and healthier, even radiant. The clothing, hair, and face of the deceased often appear luminous, shimmering, or flowing. People frequently say that unless the death was at a young age, the deceased seems to be in the prime of life, about thirty or forty. If the death involved a child or a fetus, the dreamer will see the deceased as older, grown since the time of the death.

These dreams give great solace; they often contain comforting words that seem like a benediction.

Being guided by a spirit in your dream = Feeling hopeful for the deceased and the self

---

"I'm Okay"

WHEN YOU HAVE a dream in which the deceased says he or she is okay, you will find the person looking extremely well, with physical flaws vanished. These dreams usually involve the motifs of (1) physical restoration, (2) the soul's being peaceful, or (3) a total transformation of the deceased. The guidance given in this motif is reassurance that all is well.

A young American woman, whose father had been in a wheelchair as long as she could remember, dreamed of his walking unaided. A middle-aged woman whose aunt was addicted to tobacco dreamed the deceased aunt told her she "no longer had to smoke." Another middle-aged American woman, mentioned earlier, whose father's larynx had been removed as a result of cancer, dreamed he telephoned her and spoke with his normal voice, reassuring her all was well: "They gave me back my voice."

The motif of the deceased's "soul at peace" is also restorative to the dreamer. An American woman of middle years whose nineteen-year-old son died in a fire was tortured by thoughts of his burning. Some people, like this woman, cease dreaming for a long time; the tragedy is too excruciating to allow dreams about it. Three years and much therapy later, the woman began to dream about her son. In these dreams, she saw him as a child: happy, waving, playing baseball. In a later series of dreams, in which the boy was older, he embraced her. These dreams calmed the woman. She felt her son was communicating that he was at peace, he loved her, and all was well.

Psychologist Rosalind Cartwright, whose daughter was killed in an automobile accident, wrote about a set of dreams she had in which the girl was at first a toddler in trouble. In each dream, the child grew a little older. Finally, Cartwright dreamed she was at a convention waiting at an elevator, and her daughter appeared. Cartwright said, "I'm so glad to see you. I thought you were dead." The daughter replied, "I am; I only came to be with you until you are used to the idea." Cartwright found this dream very comforting. She accepted that she could not save her daughter, and it gave her peace.

Another American mother lost a grown child after he sustained injuries in a fight over a traffic accident. She cared for him during his final months. Despite having other children and a husband, the woman felt drained and desolate, until she had a dream of seeing the dead son as a child, sitting on the grass. He laughed, looked up at her, and said, "It's all right, Mom." Many bereaved people receive such reassurance in their dreams.

A woman whose beloved mother died in Europe mourned constantly. Her grief could not be assuaged. Finally she had a dream in which she saw her mother's soul emerge from her heart and fly to the top of a very beautiful tree. She felt great wonder and peace. At last she felt able to let her go.

After her mother died unexpectedly, a young American woman was in shock. She had several dreams of finding her mother dying and of trying to save her. Eventually her dreams depicted the older woman in a usual manner, chatting in the farm kitchen. In the culmination of her series of grief dreams, the woman was kneeling in the potato garden under a full moon, when her mother appeared in a shimmering white gown, her long black hair flowing down her shoulders. She told her daughter that it was the last time she could visit her but that she could grant her heart's desire. Immediately the woman knew that what she wanted was a good education. As a result of this dream, the woman started college. Despite many hardships, she completed her studies and graduated with honors. She felt that her dead mother had pointed her in the right direction.

Instead of a series of dreams in which the deceased gradually changes from looking ill to looking supremely well, the transformation may occur within a single dream. Poet Brenda Shaw dreamed of seeing her deceased beloved father walking up a road, an old man, lame, sad, and gaunt, his rough clothes heavy. As she watched, the concrete road turned to tar, then dirt, then rough tract through forest, and finally pristine wood. She saw her father naked, young, leaping, and flinging his arms joyfully toward the sun, to disappear running through the trees. She wrote a touching poem about this dream of her father's metamorphosis.

Any dreams you have about the deceased person's looking and feeling well and being happy are certain to give you consolation, perhaps joy.

"Good-bye"

WHEN YOU HAVE a dream that your deceased loved person has come to say good-bye, you may feel touched by a spirit. In words, by gesture, or by mental communication, the dreamer understands that the deceased is taking leave of him or her. Or the dreamer may awake with the certainty that the deceased came to say good-bye. This is a common motif in dreams about the dead, often a cherished one. Don't be surprised if your dream with the good-bye theme contains references to journeys or marriages or both—they are frequently present.

Journeys as a Metaphor for Death

IN THE MYTHOLOGY of most cultures, death is depicted as a journey to an unknown land, usually in the west, the place of the "dying" sun. This imagery is very much alive in the dreams of modern people.

Caretakers of dying people report that their patients often talk about getting ready for trips. A few months before my mother's death at ninety-one, she often spoke of soon traveling to her hometown, hundreds of miles away. Dreams about journeys are usual at major life junctures (not only prior to death), such as leaving for college, moving to another home, graduating, getting married, and having children. The old life is over; the new is beginning.

You are very likely to include images of travel in your dreams about the dead. These dream journeys seem to represent our separation from the deceased. Often we dream of seeing a loved deceased person getting on an airplane, leaving in a spaceship, setting sail on a boat, catching a train, or boarding a bus. Airports, train stations, bus stations, docks, travel down a river or crossing a river—these are common settings for "good-bye" dreams.

One elderly American man dreamed he was going to the airport with his deceased wife when they reached a gate through which he was not allowed. She went onward and, at the airplane door, turned and waved good-bye to him. Shortly after her mother died, an American woman dreamed of seeing her passing on a train going in the opposite direction from the one she was on. I have already mentioned the Swiss woman who dreamed of meeting her fiancée at a train station on the border. At a certain place she was forbidden to continue, had to leave the train, then had to board another train traveling back.

When my father died of a heart attack in his early sixties, quite unexpectedly, I was devastated. About six months after his death I dreamed I saw him on a train, looking old, frail, and wobbly, not at all like him, but I knew it was he. I had to get off the train, but first kissed the old man tenderly, feeling deep sadness. This was a bittersweet good-bye. Later dreams were happier encounters.

Marriage as a Metaphor for Death

ONE YOUNG AMERICAN woman had a profoundly poignant dream of farewell. Her father, in his late fifties, was perfectly well, so far as she knew. In her dream, she met him on a spaceship out in space. He told her, "I have to leave you now." The young woman became distraught and begged him not to leave. He insisted that he must go and that he was going to marry a woman named Grace. He parted with the words "You have to remember, I won't ever really leave you. I'll always be with you." He hugged his hysterical daughter, who was overcome "by love and the merging of our spirits." She passed out in the dream, and when she awoke, still in the dream, she saw the spaceship flying off deeper into space.

This woman's dream was so real, and it disturbed her so much, she woke her roommate to describe it. Four hours later, the girl's aunt telephoned to say her father had died of a massive heart attack. His death occurred at the same time as the young woman's dream. She felt certain he had come to say good-bye. She understood that by the woman named Grace, he meant the Virgin Mary, to whom he had a special devotion. The woman said this dream changed her life; it confirmed her belief that there is no death. She felt she had experienced divine love. Wherever and however such dreams come, they are welcome.

This young woman's dream contained both a journey and a reference to marriage. Other dreamers, too, picture women in white (as in Socrates' famous predeath dream) or bridal scenes in their dreams about the deceased. Images of weddings also sometimes appear in the hallucinations of a dying person, as they did for my mother, who began asking for the wedding gown she was sure was hanging in her closet. At times she greeted people by saying, "You're just in time for the ceremony."

You may dream of saying good-bye to a deceased person anytime throughout the grieving process—weeks, months, or years later. These dreams often help you accept the reality of a loved one's death and provide a sense of completion.

"Congratulations!"

IF YOU HAVE this fairly rare dream, you'll probably feel very good. In these dreams, the deceased expresses strong approval of the dreamer. They are the opposite of the motif of criticism, "You Fool!"

Swedish philosopher-scientist-mystic Emanuel Swedenborg, in the eighteenth century, had a stormy relationship with his father, who wanted him to enter the clergy, as he had. Instead Swedenborg went into science. His father was irate, and they remained distant the rest of the older man's life. Nine years after his father's death, Swedenborg recorded a dream that his father was tying the lace cuffs that he, the dreamer, wore. At that time, only lay people wore lace cuffs, whereas the clergy wore plain ones. By assisting him in this manner, Swedenborg felt, his father had finally accepted him. Swedenborg had begun to incorporate some spiritual inquiry into his scientific work; this may have led him to feel his father would approve.

The revered Indian philosopher of the nineteenth century Debendranath Tagore had a powerful dream that his deceased mother was praising him. She said, "Hast thou really become one who has known Brahma? Sanctified is the family; fulfilled is the mother's desire." Tagore wrote, "On seeing her, and hearing these sweet words of hers, my slumber gave way before a flood of joy."

If you dream about a deceased parent's congratulating you in some way, you are likely to feel that your parent would approve of what you are doing if he or she were living. This dream often arises at the birth of children, grandchildren, and other descendants the deceased has never seen.

A middle-aged Mexican-American whose elderly father died before having a chance to see his first grandchild had a dream of this type that left him feeling blessed. After his father's death the man did not dream about him for more than two years, as happens for many bereaved who are severely stricken by a death. In his dream, he stood in a garden, "so close to my father I can smell his aftershave lotion." His son, then about one, was playing in the flowers and grass. He introduced his father to his boy. He felt happy to be with his father and feel his pleasure in his grandchild.

You, like numerous bereaved people, may find yourself dreaming of making introductions between the deceased and members of the new generation or a new mate or even showing the deceased person your new home. These visits and congratulations leave dreamers feeling happy and provide an opportunity that was denied in waking life to connect our important deceased loved ones with our current lives. These life-affirming dreams give a feeling of linking the circle of the past to that of the future.

"Here's a Gift"

MANY DREAMERS FEEL that the appearance of the deceased giving and receiving love is a gift. Sometimes the present takes "concrete" form.

A young American woman whose best friend was murdered by a serial killer went through difficult times. Eventually she dreamed of meeting her dead friend, who wore a beautiful wreath of flowers in her hair and looked radiant. She asked her deceased friend to help her; she did, making a corsage of greenery with purple flowers to wear over her heart. The dreamer awoke with a profound sense of peace. For the first time, with help, she was able to work through her anger toward the killer and to forgive.

A middle-aged American woman dreamed her beloved deceased grandfather showed her some beautifully crafted but empty bookcases. Awake, she realized she had become distracted from her ambition to write. She began to find the way to begin her own craft, to write poems, and to integrate the life lessons her grandfather had taught.

Chilean writer Isabel Allende has written extensively on how dreams of her deceased grandparents have influenced her work. She dreamed that her grandfather lay in bed dressed in mourning, in an all-black room, and where she sat beside him, reading aloud from the book she was writing. As she narrated the story, the furniture turned from black to blond, blue veils fluttered over the bed, and the sun shone through the window. When she awoke from this dream Allende knew exactly how to solve a problem in completing her first book, *The House of Spirits*.

Nowadays, Allende says, she often dreams that her clairvoyant grandmother is watching over her shoulder as she writes or that she herself is looking over the shoulder of her grandmother, who is writing a story.

Many writers state that ancestral voices guide them in their dreams to their best work. Some dreamers describe getting instructions about where to find missing things. Other dreamers tell me of receiving pink rosebushes, shapely urns, or beautiful brooches from the hands of the dead, which often represent talents or skills that await development. They are a kind of gift from the dead. You, too, may find your life enriched through dreams about your "elders." Our ancestral voices need to be heard and honored.

"Go Ahead"

IF YOU HAVE this relatively rare dream, you will probably feel greatly encouraged. An older woman whose only son died in his forties of cancer had a potent dream about him that gave her hope. I've described the dream earlier; in it she and her son were casting rocks onto the frozen river below. His statement "Mom, I thought you needed some help to break up the ice in your heart" left her thunderstruck. The dream was a turning point in her recovery.

A middle-aged American woman dreamed about seeing her deceased father, many years after his death, radiating the energy of God. She felt he was "bathing me with compassion, and speaking words of comfort that I find overwhelming." Her dream helped her continue with her work, making her feel deeply loved and encouraged at a critical juncture in her life.

A website participant from England dreamed he talked with Albert Einstein (who was dead) for hours about the secrets of life and death. Sadly, the teen couldn't recall them on awaking. Another website survey respondent from England dreamed her dead grandfather was guiding her in an old school.

My psychologist colleague Alan Siegel had a powerful dream about his grandfather a year after the old man's death. In it, he was walking in an orange grove, talking with him. Many oranges were ripe on the trees, and the grass and leaves were very green. His grandfather was encouraging him to finish school or pursue something. Awake, the young man felt his grandfather was giving him advice, as a mentor, in the way he had in life. Siegel went on to a successful career as a writer and therapist.

Another psychologist colleague, Jeffery Mishlove, felt similar encouragement after a significant dream about his deceased uncle, on approximately the same night he died. His dead uncle talked with him about many topics, including his life plans and his girlfriend. The dream ended with the young man's singing an ancient melody prayer. He awoke crying and touched. He went on, inspired in part by his dream, to a different career than he had been planning and was highly successful.

If you have a dream in which a deceased loved person gives advice about your life, you will cherish the memory of it. These dreams hearten the dreamer. Listen carefully for the voices of the dead in your dreams, as they have much to tell you.

"Your Turn Is Coming"

THIS DREAM IS a mixed blessing. On the one hand, when the dreamer is old and ill, the news that death is coming soon can be welcome. People who are dying or who have near-death experiences often dream or have visions of being greeted by loving spirits of the departed. On the other hand, being informed that you will die is not usually cause for celebration.

The Roman emperor Julius Caesar, the night before he was assassinated, is reported to have dreamed that he was soaring above the clouds and shook hands with Jupiter. This dream may not have comforted Caesar when it became apparent he would die in the Senate, but its message of welcome was better than Caligula's dream of being kicked out of heaven by Jupiter.

The writer Henry James had a sister named Alice, an invalid, who was said to be as talented as her brothers, Henry and William (a prominent psychologist). She kept a diary with entries displaying the same level of skill they possessed. She dictated entries in it to her close friend up until the last few hours before her death, aged forty-three. One of these was a dream of two deceased women friends in a boat passing from the shadow of a storm to a sunlit sea;

they looked back at her on the shore and beckoned her to join them. At the point of death, such dreams can give true solace.

Several dreamers in my study reported similar dream scenarios. Whenever our time may be, we need to accept the fact that our lives have a limited span, in order to make the best of what time we have.

"Please Forgive Me"

DREAMERS MAY BE comforted, even elated, when they feel that a deceased person who wronged them asks for forgiveness or expresses regret for some behavior before death that upset the dreamer. These dreams are also rare, but important.

If you have been alienated from a parent, you may find peace in a dream of this sort, as one middle-aged American woman did. In it, her father appeared, looking well. He put his arm around her and asked her to walk with him to the bank to settle his account. She awoke with "the most wonderful feeling of peace," even though he never apologized for some hurtful things he had said to her years earlier. She felt convinced he had appeared in her dream to apologize, to settle his emotional account.

An American woman in her seventies was able to forgive her father for some wrongs after dreaming he appeared by her bed in a bright light and smiled at her, "his big blue eyes" glowing. Without an exchange of words, she felt that he had asked for forgiveness and she had granted it.

A young American woman suffered a miscarriage a few days after going to the funeral of her brother, who had committed suicide. She blamed her brother for the loss of her child. In her dream, the deceased brother directly apologized and told her about his condition in the afterlife. The dreamer accepted his apology, forgave him, and finally felt at ease.

"I Forgive You"

IN THIS DREAM motif, you are the one offering pardon to the deceased for some wrong he or she did you, or you exchange regret for some behavior with the dead person. This is a rare dream theme but one that also gives relief to the dreamer, sometimes lifting years of resentment and guilt.

A middle-aged man from England, about ten years after his father died with issues still unresolved between them, had a dream in which he was back in the home of his youth. Entering his bedroom, he saw his father sitting on the side of the bed. The older man looked young, pleasant, friendly, and calm, instead of appearing as his former gruff self. The man was amazed at how easy it was now to talk with him. Saying good-bye after a long discussion, he kissed his deceased father. Awake, the man felt good. He let go of his resentment of the older man. He felt that his dead father was now on a spiritual path and that at last he was able to forgive him for earlier mistreatment.

An American woman whose father died quite suddenly in his fifties was deeply disturbed because he declared himself agnostic. A religious person, she felt tormented that this basically good man should be deprived of a proper afterlife. In a dream a few months after his death, she saw herself struggling in a very wide, cold river, pulling a burden toward a rocky shore. Then she saw that the burden was the body of her father on a cross. She stopped struggling and let it drift. She thought this dream represented her effort to "drag her father into heaven." By letting go, she felt she turned the burden over to a higher power.

Soon thereafter, the same woman dreamed of sitting on the ground with her legs folded, wearing a vivid blue gown, her hair hanging down. Her deceased father was lying on the ground beside her; she held his torso and rocked him. This dream gave the woman great comfort. Blue was her favorite color and the color of her father's eyes. Her hair down rather than pinned up was her "mother image." She felt able to understand her father now, to offer forgiveness and comfort to him. The "sharp, hard rocks and jagged, broken boulders" of her earlier dream had transformed into a soothing, rocking motion.

The American woman who dreamed her deceased mother scolded her for going through her things the night she died also felt guilty for not staying with her mother in the hospital. Their stormy relationship left the woman with much unresolved resentment. Over the next few months, she had a series of dreams culminating in one in which her mother died peacefully in her arms. With this dream, the woman felt an acceptance and love between her and her mother that finally released her from guilt.

For our own sake, if nothing else, it's important to forgive those we feel have wronged us or were misguided. Bitterness and resentment harm us, whereas forgiveness heals. If you are a person who holds angry feelings toward a dead person, you'll benefit from exploring ways to let them go.

"I'm Evolving"

YOU MAY HAVE this rare dream motif in which the deceased conveys information about life and activities on the other side. If so, you'll probably find this dream very soothing.

We saw how dreams soon after a death often depict the deceased in an ill or suffering condition. He or she may appear confused or not seem to be aware of being dead. Gradually, the appearance of the deceased person improves from dream to dream until seeming normal and well or radiantly transformed. You may not dream of the deceased again for a long period, but in times of crisis the deceased may reappear as a sage or guide. Later the dead person may occasionally show up as a less dramatic part of an ongoing dream, a neutral motif I call "Hi, how are you?"

Some people think that the improvement in appearance and vitality of the deceased is a development in afterlife. Are the dead evolving—learning, studying, working, moving from one level to an ever-higher level? Other dream motifs contribute to this impression. For instance, you may dream that the deceased develops skills in the afterlife, such as traveling at great speed, studying music or another subject they have always longed to pursue, or departing for further duties.

A middle-aged Chinese man dreamed of seeing his deceased father in an art class, wearing a red tie (a mark of celebration) and looking young, healthy, and happy. The dead father told his classmate to buy a book for his son, probably an art book, since his father had been an artist in life. This dream led the dreamer to explore various books his father had owned, in an attempt to know him better.

Many dreamers reported similar dreams in which the dead were studying subjects of interest or assigned to guard children in need of protection, or occupied by other pursuits. Are such dreams our wishes for the dead to be happy and continue to develop? Do we hope for these things for ourselves after death? All we know for certain is that survivors have such dreams and that they give solace and pleasure.

"I'm Being Reborn"

THIS DREAM MOTIF is extremely rare. Those who have such a dream find it extraordinarily comforting. At times they feel they have learned the place of birth and the sex of the baby who will bear the soul of a lost loved one.

One young woman whose younger brother died of an illness had a stunning dream of this type. On a bright, sunny day, walking from her porch to her mailbox, she suddenly became aware she was dreaming. As she opened an oddly folded card of three parts, she found a message from her brother, telling her that he was to be reincarnated in Mexico. She awoke with great concern for him. Falling back asleep, she dreamed of seeing her brother as a Mexican man in his prime of life, looking well dressed and cared for. He told her he had gone there to recover. When she awoke this time, the dreamer understood that her brother would find healing and recovery in a simple, healthy existence. She thought that the thrice-folded card may have represented the past, present, and future. She says that her dream gave her a lasting sense of peace.

"I Give You Life"

I HAVE ONLY encountered one example of this exceedingly rare dream motif. A middle-aged American woman who had undergone a heart and lung transplant was struggling with the possibility of organ rejection. One night she had a momentous dream in which she saw her donor. He kissed her and she felt his breath enter her body. From then on, she knew she would live. She did—and is alive and well many years later.

"I'll Always Love You"

YOU MAY HAVE one of the most satisfying of dreams of being Guided by a Spirit. In these, the deceased assures you that you will always be loved. There may be kisses, embraces, or gifts exchanged. Luckily, such dreams are fairly common. We awake feeling truly loved and deeply comforted. For some people, it is the most precious of all dreams.

The dramas, legends, and myths of humankind celebrate the strength of love beyond death—think of Orpheus and Eurydice, Dante and Beatrice, Tristan and Isolde, Demeter and Persephone, Heloise and Abelard. The same yearning expressed in these stories of past times appears in the dreams of modern people. We are fortunate to have records of such dreams from some historical figures, as well as contemporary dreamers.

The poet Novalis, a young nobleman from Saxony who lived in the late eighteenth century, fell in love with and married a twelve-year-old girl named Sophie von Kühn when he was twenty-two. The teenage bride died of tuberculosis three years later. Novalis had a profound experience when he visited Sophie's grave, where he fainted. He later described what he experienced in six exquisite prose poems entitled *Hymns to the Night*. One of these hymns describes his vision of the glorified face of his young wife in a cloud. The bitter tears he shed became "a sparkling chain that could not be broken." After this dream/vision at Sophie's graveside, he felt he was given a new life (his pen name means "new"), claiming that "ever since I hold fast an eternal, unchangeable faith in the heaven of the Night, and its sun, the Beloved."

Novalis's deceased wife became not only his muse but a guide to mystical worlds that seemed to open for him. He became astonishingly prolific over the next four years, until he, too, succumbed to tuberculosis and died. He tried to unite poetry, philosophy, and science through allegory. One of his works was a mythical romance containing the image of a "blue flower" that derived from his dreams.

Years later Edgar Allan Poe wrote the famous poem *Annabel Lee* after spending the night on the gravestone of his beloved young bride-cousin, who had died. The works inspired by the death of a loved one are many.

Dante's love for Beatrice is legendary. This Italian poet of the thirteenth century, considered one of the greatest in all literature, has recorded in his book *La Vita Nuova* (which means "The New Life") his three meetings with the girl who became his muse. After his second encounter with Beatrice (whose name means "she who blesses"), he was so overcome that he withdrew to his room, fell asleep, and had a dream that changed his life. After this dream, Dante wrote his first sonnet praising his beloved. He, like Novalis after him, felt newborn by love. He decided that his life's theme would be to write whatever was praiseworthy of "this most gracious being." Beatrice died at twenty-four, after her marriage. When Dante heard of her death, he was grief-stricken. He had several visions and dreams about her being in Paradise, culminating in one so powerful that he resolved to write no more until he could do so more worthily.

Many years later he published his immortal *Divine Comedy*, with its three sections *Inferno*, *Purgatorio*, and *Paradiso*. The epic poem concludes with the image of the ninth heaven, with gardens of angels, in the center of which is God's court, pictured as a white rose whose petals hold angels and beatified souls praising Him in unison. Here, Beatrice is in her place in the rose. Much of the imagery in this classic work is thought to be derived from Dante's marvelous vision of her.

For these men, the deceased beloved woman became muse and spiritual guide. We are scarcely likely to produce works on such a scale. Yet, our lost loved ones inspire and lead us to create. A woman dreamed of dancing with a lost brother; a man wrote a poignant song based on a dream of his dead brother; an older woman planted a pink rose garden to commemorate a dream of her husband's gifting her with pink rosebushes. I dreamed that my dead father handed me an inheritance paper and held me tenderly, saying, "I love you, baby." Dream gifts are not material gifts; they are gifts of the spirit. Many people write books, lyrics, and songs; draw pictures; or carve mementos after dreaming about the loved person lost to death. So might you.

However we express ourselves, in song, dance, verse, or prose, we give form to our emotions. These happy dreams of the spirit often contain music and dance. There is a celebratory aspect, as we cherish the genuine bond between us and the deceased that never dies. We can touch and heal others as we mend our own grief. We honor our dead with our lives—and our dreams.

Afterword

WE'VE TAKEN A journey around the globe exploring the dreams shared by all human beings. We've looked at the constant elements in these Universal Dreams and examined their local variations. We've gathered associations that the dreamers reported and assembled the most common meanings these dream motifs had. Is the collection complete? Do we have a reliable map of the land of dreams? Not yet, but it is a beginning.

This is a project that intelligent people in every area of life, not just professional researchers and scientists, can participate in. We all dream. Those of us who keep dream journals have precious material that will help the general understanding of dreams, as well as our own. The tools in this book may assist you in your personal search.

If you want to learn more about the world of dreams and people who work with them, you can contact the information office of the Association for the Study of Dreams (ASD) at P.O. Box 1166, Orinda, California, 94563. The telephone number is 925-258-1822; the fax number is 925-258-1821. You might also want to visit the ASD website: *www.ASDreams.org.*

You can find out more about the Universal Dream project on my website, *www.patriciagarfield.com.*

If you have dreams about computers you would like to share, you can contact Richard Wilkerson at *www.dreamgate.com.*

What tale will you tell yourself tonight as you sleep? Open your inner eyes, hear with a loving heart, and learn from the wealth within. And, always remember, listen to your dreams; they're talking to you.

Appendix A:
How to Unlock Any Dream Image

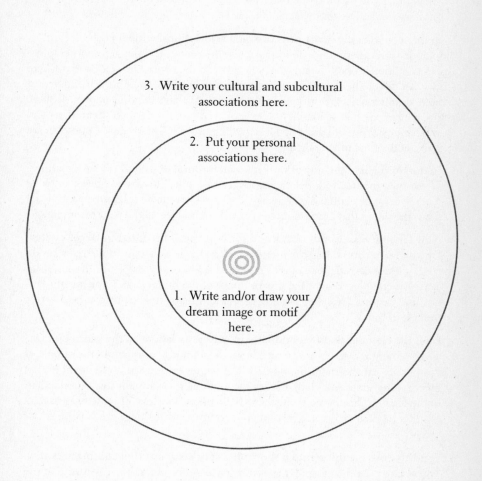

3. Write your cultural and subcultural associations here.

2. Put your personal associations here.

1. Write and/or draw your dream image or motif here.

Suggestions for Unlocking Any Dream Image

1. **Write or draw the dream image you want to explore in the center of the target.**
   This may be a motif from the Dream Key in Appendix B or it may be a completely personal dream image. You are welcome to photocopy the blank diagram in Appendix A and use it to enter your own associations to the image. You can consult the sample, Dream Image of Hungry Cat, to see how this will work.

2. **In the second circle, write your personal associations to the image.**
   Include your experience with the image in the center, emotional responses, physical condition, or past dreams that you relate to the central image. Here is where you can define the dream image in Jungian style (What is X? How is X different from all other objects or people of similar type? What's unique about X? Is there any part of me that is like X?) Give your own current personal definitions and associations; these will differ at different times in your life. Write the ones that are active at the time of your dream.

3. **In the third circle put any of your relevant cultural or subcultural associations.**
   These may include folk beliefs, myths, stories, films, television shows, or slang that relate to the central dream image. You don't have to be exhaustive. Simply jot down the things that come to mind as you think and feel about your dream image.

4. **Now let your eyes wander back and forth between the filled-in target circles.**
   Do you see a central theme emerging? This theme may cross the circles at odd angles, like a jagged piece of pie. Your dream image may have positive and negative associations, as does the dream image of the hungry cat. Look for similarities and recurrences. Be patient. Complex dream images take time for this process to "cook."

5. **Find the element that predominates in your associations to the central image.**
   This element is the core meaning of your dream image or motif. In the sample of the hungry cat the main theme is that of neglected sensuality. Remember that dreams exaggerate and dramatize, so the main theme is usually less extreme than in the dream. This theme is often a wish for "more" or "less" of something in waking life. In positive dreams, it is often a comment that things are "just right" or "great."

6. **Put this core meaning into a short phrase or sentence that summarizes it.**
   For instance, in the sample, the summary sentence could be "I realize that my sensual self feels neglected, needs 'feeding' and attention." This sentence or phrase is the main message of your dream.

7. **Decide how you want to behave in light of the message in your dream.**
   Apply the information from your dream to improve your waking life, if it seems helpful, not harmful, to you or others. If your dream is a story that you tell yourself, what does it suggest you need to do next? Altering your waking behavior will change your future dreamtales, which will in turn nourish your waking hours.

Dream Image of Hungry Cat
Motif: Finding Hungry Cat

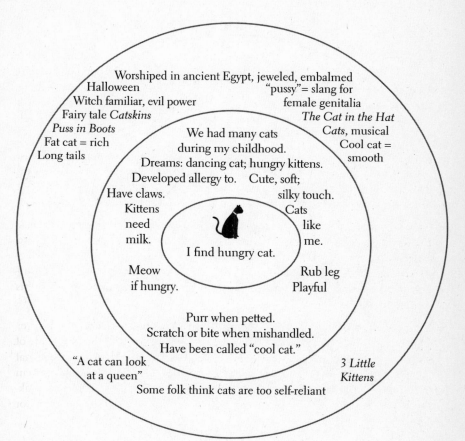

Worshiped in ancient Egypt, jeweled, embalmed
Halloween "pussy"= slang for
Witch familiar, evil power female genitalia
Fairy tale *Catskins* *The Cat in the Hat*
Puss in Boots *Cats*, musical
Fat cat = rich Cool cat =
Long tails smooth

We had many cats
during my childhood.
Dreams: dancing cat; hungry kittens.
Developed allergy to. Cute, soft;
Have claws. silky touch.
Kittens Cats
need like
milk. me.

I find hungry cat.

Meow Rub leg
if hungry. Playful

Purr when petted.
Scratch or bite when mishandled.
Have been called "cool cat."

"A cat can look 3 *Little*
at a queen" *Kittens*
Some folk think cats are too self-reliant

Blank Form

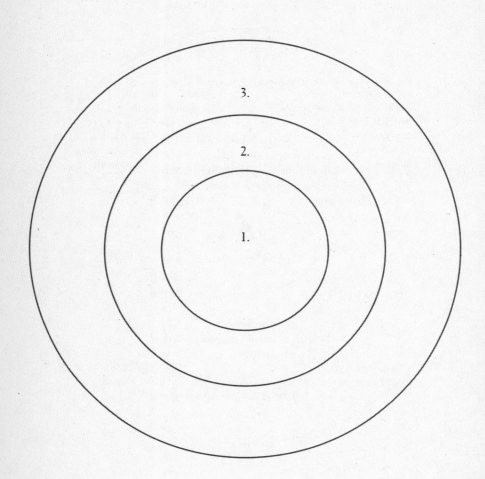

Flow Chart for Unlocking Dream Image

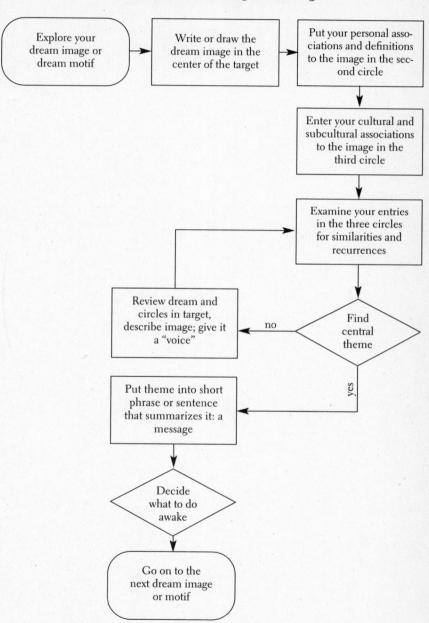

Appendix B: The Key to Universal Dreams

Suggestions for Using the Universal Dream Key

1. Consult the Summary of the Negative Universal Dreams on the next page in order to locate the dream theme closest to the one you want to explore, along with its number. For example, Falling or Drowning is Universal Dream theme number 6.0. The general meaning of this kind of dream is given on the summary.

2. Using the dream theme name and number, turn to the pages that describe this theme. Here you will see a listing of the motifs most often found in this dream theme and the specific meanings these motifs have for many people. Common variations of the motif are listed in the far right column; in many cases this column is blank. You can use the blank spaces to jot any motif variation you have had.

3. When you encounter a meaning that does not seem to fit your dream experience, work with the dream image using Appendix A: How to Unlock Any Dream Image. This will help you find your individual meaning. You can adjust the general meaning listed in the Dream Key to fit your particular case.

4. Ignore the extended numbers unless you wish to keep track of your dream motifs by indexing them in a computer. They are useful for this purpose but have no scientific or inherent meaning. I recommend using the name to refer to a motif, rather than its number; for instance, "I fell from a cliff" instead of 6.1.1.1.1. If you do want to enter motif numbers in your computer to chart your dreams, notice that each category can be extended indefinitely. Each motif has a unique number; numbers can be increased as far as necessary to code your specific motif.

5. For positive dreams, refer to the text of this book. The positive dream themes appear in the second half of each chapter; they are followed by .5 in each case. You will find a few comments about positive dreams in the Dream Key related to each negative theme (in the example, flying is the positive version of falling), but the twelve themes in the Dream Key are almost all negative, because the majority of dreams most people have are negative. Also, we know much less about the meaning of positive dreams. The comments about positive motifs are preceded by a plus sign (+). I have included one positive dream theme, Being Guided by a Spirit, in the Dream Key, since a lot of information was available to me about the meaning of this topic. Eventually we hope to have a complete positive dream key, too.

6. By keeping track of the motifs in your dreams over time, you will begin to see a pattern in the stories that you tell yourself. As you become familiar with the usual meanings of these motifs and adjust these meanings to fit your particular dream, you will see how to reach for happier endings—positive versions of the same motifs—in your dream world as well as in your waking one. May this Dream Key help guide your inner journey.

Summary of the Negative Universal Dreams

No.	Theme of Dream	General Meaning
1.0	Being chased or attacked	You feel threatened by some waking person, situation, personal impulse, or vague anxiety
2.0	Being injured or dying	You feel emotionally hurt or nonfunctional in waking state
3.0	Having trouble with a car or some other vehicle	You feel that waking life is currently out of control or unsatisfactory
4.0	House or property is damaged or lost	You feel emotional turmoil and/or physical damage, or reduction of some ability in waking state
5.0	Poor test or other performance	You are confronting a waking challenge and fear failure
6.0	Falling or drowning	You feel helpless about impending or ongoing waking life change, overwhelmed
7.0	Naked or inappropriately dressed in public	You feel overexposed in some waking situation, ill equipped to cope
8.0	Missing a boat or some other public transport	You feel you have missed an opportunity in waking life
9.0	Telephone or machine malfunctions	You are having difficulty with emotional communication in waking life or have a physical difficulty
10.0	Natural or man-made disaster	You feel you are confronting a crisis in waking life
11.0	Lost or trapped	You feel confused or uncertain about what to do in some waking situation
12.0	Menaced by a spirit in a dream	You feel concern in waking life for the well-being of someone who has died or you feel afraid for yourself

✝ The Universal Dream Key: 1.0 Chase or Attack

1.1 Aggressor in dream of chase or attack	1.1.1 Evil person chases or attacks you			
	1.1.1.1 Stranger with weapon	= you feel threatened by a potentially wounding person, situation, or emotion in waking life that you are not yet able or willing to identify	1.1.1.1.1 1.1.1.1.2 1.1.1.1.3 1.1.1.1.4	Male Soldier Female Criminal
	1.1.1.2 Stranger without weapon	= you feel threatened by a person, situation, or emotion in waking life that you are not yet able or willing to identify	1.1.1.2.1 1.1.1.2.2 1.1.1.2.3	Male Female Criminal
	1.1.1.3 Known person with or without weapon	= you are able and willing to confront the source of what makes you feel threatened	1.1.1.3.1 1.1.1.3.2 1.1.1.3.3 1.1.1.3.4 1.1.1.3.5 1.1.1.3.6	Male Female Relative Friend Workmate Schoolmate
	1.1.1.4 Supernatural, film, TV, or mythological being, with or without weapon	= you see a correspondence between some quality of the fictional figure and an aspect of what or who threatens you in waking life (identify it)	1.1.1.4.1 1.1.1.4.2 1.1.1.4.3 1.1.1.4.4 1.1.1.4.5 1.1.1.4.6 1.1.1.4.7 1.1.1.4.8 1.1.1.4.9	Devil, demon Vampire Skeleton Monster Ogre Witch Alien Film, TV figure Mythic being
	1.1.1.5 Other human or supernatural attackers			

1.1.2 Animal chases or attacks you				
	1.1.2.1 Wild animal, land	= you sense a wild, dangerous element in the waking person, situation, or emotion that threatens you	1.1.2.1.1 1.1.2.1.2 1.1.2.1.3 1.1.2.1.4 1.1.2.1.5 1.1.2.1.6 1.1.2.1.7 1.1.2.1.8 1.1.2.1.9	Bear Snake Lion Wolf Hyena Wild dog Spider Bee Ant
	1.1.2.2 Wild animal, water		1.1.2.2.1 1.1.2.2.2 1.1.2.2.3 1.1.2.2.4 1.1.2.2.5	Shark Alligator Water snake Fish Amphibian
	1.1.2.3 Wild animal, bird		1.1.2.3.1 1.1.2.3.2	Vulture Eagle
	1.1.2.4 Domestic animal	= the waking person, situation, or emotion that threatens you seems harmless, but you are unsure	1.1.2.4.1 1.1.2.4.2 1.1.2.4.3	Bull Horse Rooster
	1.1.2.5 Extinct animal	= the waking person, situation, or emotion that threatens you may be from the past or very primitive	1.1.2.5.1 1.1.2.5.2	Dinosaur Mastodon
	1.1.2.6 Mythological animal	= you see a parallel between some quality of the fictional figure and an aspect of who or what threatens you in waking life (identify it)	1.1.2.6.1 1.1.2.6.2	Dragon Sea monster

		1.1.2.7 Other animals	= any dream animal has a quality that resembles an aspect of a waking person or situation (identify)		
	1.1.3 Thing chases or attacks you	1.1.3.1 Vague "thing"	= you sense an inhuman quality in the waking person, situation, or emotion that threatens you but cannot yet pinpoint who or what it is	1.1.3.1.1 1.1.3.1.2 1.1.3.1.3	Unknown Evil force Faceless
		1.1.3.2 Odd object that moves by itself	= you sense a threat from something that seems out of your control	1.1.3.2.1 1.1.3.2.2 1.1.3.2.3	Vehicle, no driver Machine (see 9.0) Round object
		1.1.3.3 Other objects			
1.2 Action in dream of chase or attack	1.2.1 Aggressor's action = what you feel a waking person or situation does	1.2.1.1 Chases you	= you feel threatened by some waking person or situation		
		1.2.1.2 Catches or finds you in hiding	= you feel trapped by a waking person or situation		
		1.2.1.3 Wounds you	= you feel emotionally hurt (or have a malfunction in the area of dream injury)		
		1.2.1.4 Eats you	= you feel consumed by a waking person or situation		
		1.2.1.5 Kills you	= you feel almost destroyed by the waking situation		

1.2.2 Your reaction to being chased or attacked = your probable style of defense in waking life	1.2.1.6 Other actions of the aggressor	
	1.2.2.1 Run	= you try to avoid waking verbal or physical attack; you feel vulnerable
	1.2.2.2 Hide or try to	= you defend by withdrawing
	1.2.2.3 Give up, accept	= you feel helpless, unable to cope with situation
	1.2.2.3 Wake up	= you feel unable or unready to deal with situation, even in fantasy
	1.2.2.4 Defy	= you feel able to confront an attacking element
	1.2.2.5 Counterattack	= you feel able to defend yourself by action in waking situation
	1.2.2.6 Challenge, order to stop, tell "You're a dream"	= you feel able to confront verbally
	1.2.2.7 Ask, "Who are you? What do you want?" Question it	= you feel able to inquire into image meaning, symbolism
	1.2.2.8 Save self, escape	= you feel able to protect yourself

		1.2.2.9 Call for help, telephone	= you feel your need for assistance may be heard
		1.2.2.10 You are rescued by animal, hero, or person	= you feel supported by others
		1.2.2.11 Befriend, surround by light, love	= you feel capable of conceiving a new point of view toward waking situation, transforming it
		1.2.2.12 Other reactions	
1.3 Attribute aggressor has = a quality of waking life threat	1.3.1 Size of figure	1.3.1.1 Big, gigantic, very tall	= you feel a sense of overwhelming fear about the waking person or situation the image represents; + in positive dreams, large size indicates a feeling of awesome importance
		1.3.1.2 Size: multiple, small, tiny, or very short	= you feel beset by many troublesome or alarming elements in the waking state that singly seem insignificant but in mass are hard to cope with well (many small figures in dream are equivalent to one gigantic dream figure)
		1.3.1.3 Size: small but powerful	= you feel exposed to poisonous or potent waking situation or person; + in positive dreams, small but powerful may imply great value
		1.3.1.4 Other size factor	= depends on your personal definition and associations

1.3.2 Color of figure	1.3.2.1 Color of figure: black	= the waking person or situation seems dangerous or evil to you; + in positive dreams, black suggests exotic or mysterious element
	1.3.2.2 Color: white	= seems ghostly or sickly to you + may suggest purity, holiness, depending on culture
	1.3.2.3 Color: red	= seems bloody, life-threatening + may imply life energy, sexuality
	1.3.2.4 Color: green	= seems repulsive, alien, or poisonous + may imply healthy growth
	1.3.2.5 Color: other	= depends on personal definition and associations
1.3.3 Hair, skin of figure	1.3.3.1 Hair: wild, unkempt	= you sense chaotic, crazy thoughts in someone in waking situation + smooth, shining hair may imply growing ideas
	1.3.3.2 Hair: white, silver	= you have a sense of aging or evil wizardry about someone in waking situation + may indicate a wise person
	1.3.3.3 Hair: none, bald	= you sense a dangerous strength in someone in waking situation + may imply supportive strength
	1.3.3.4 Hair: bearded	= you may sense evil, danger, depending on your associations to beards + may imply wisdom
	1.3.3.5 Skin: scarred	= you sense a dangerous or primitive element + may imply healing, initiation

	1.3.3.6 Hair, skin: other factors	= depends on your personal associations
1.3.4 Natural defense of figure	1.3.4.1 Natural defense: teeth, fangs	= you feel exposed to sharp, biting words, anger in waking life + may defend you from harm
	1.3.4.2 Natural defense: claws, talons	= you feel subject to cutting, wounding actions, anger while awake + may protect you
	1.3.4.3 Natural defense: horns, antlers	= you feel that cutting, sexual, angry or wounding thoughts or actions are directed toward you + head extensions suggest expansive ideas
	1.3.4.4 Natural defense: other	= depends on your personal associations
1.3.5 Clothing figure wears (see 7.0)	1.3.5.1 Clothing: mask	= you sense deception or a hidden element in the waking person or situation
	1.3.5.2 Clothing: cloak, robe, hood	= you feel something is hidden from you, cannot see threat well + may suggest royalty or nobility; provide protection
	1.3.5.3 Clothing: uniform	= you may feel an organized group is a threat to you; depending on your associations, may identify your enemy
	1.3.5.4 Clothing: costume	= depends on your associations, may identify enemy
	1.3.5.5 Clothing: other	= depends on your own associations

8 ☙ The Universal Dream Key: 2.0 Injury or Death

2.1 Death				
2.1.1 You die in dream	2.1.1.1 You are killed in an attack	= you feel emotionally hurt and rendered inactive in a waking situation	2.1.1.1.1 2.1.1.1.2 2.1.1.1.3 2.1.1.1.4	Shot Stabbed Eaten Other
	2.1.1.2 You die in a fall (see 6.0)	= you feel emotionally wounded because of lack of support in waking situation		
	2.1.1.3 You die in car crash, accident	= you feel hurt and nonfunctional from some waking life conflict	2.1.1.3.1 2.1.1.3.2	Car crash Other accident
	2.1.1.4 You die in a fire	= you feel badly damaged from a waking situation that involves intense anger or sexual passion	2.1.1.4.1 2.1.1.4.2	House fire Other fire
	2.1.1.5 You suffocate or stop breathing	= you feel something in waking life is choking you (or you have a physical malfunction)		
	2.1.1.6 You die from overexertion	= you feel overstrained physically or emotionally in a waking situation		
	2.1.1.7 You die from other cause	= various meanings	2.1.1.7.1 2.1.1.7.2 2.1.1.7.3 2.1.1.7.4 2.1.1.7.5	Crushed Blown up Illness Suicide Just die
2.1.2 Some other person dies in dream	2.1.2.1 Type of person who dies: adult, not intimate	= some aspect of person you identify with (quality you admire or dislike) feels hurt or inactive in you	2.1.2.1.1 2.1.2.1.2 2.1.2.1.3 2.1.2.1.4	Famous Elderly Sickly now Healthy now

☼ ✤ *The Universal Dream Key: 2.0 Injury or Death (cont.)*

	2.1.2.2 Type: intimate adult dies	= you may fear loss of person or feel angry at time of dream; person may also represent quality you identify with that is no longer active in you at the moment	2.1.2.2.1 2.1.2.2.2 2.1.2.2.3 2.1.2.2.4 2.1.2.2.5 2.1.2.2.6	Lover, mate Mother Father Other kin Friend Other person
	2.1.2.3 Type: child or baby dies	= you may fear a vulnerable part of you or special project is at serious risk; you may have concern for a particular person	2.1.2.3.1 2.1.2.3.2	Child Baby
	2.1.2.4 Type: pet dies	= you feel a vulnerable part of you is at risk; you identify with an aspect of the pet	2.1.2.4.1 2.1.2.4.2	Actual pet Dream pet
2.2 Injury in dream	2.2.1 You are wounded but do not die	2.2.1.1 You are wounded in an attack	= you feel emotionally hurt in some waking situation; location of wound corresponds to area that feels less functional; if you feel pain in dream, you may have physical malfunction in that area of your body	
		2.2.1.2 You are wounded in a fall	= you feel emotionally unsupported in a waking situation; it hurts you	
		2.2.1.3 You are wounded in an accident, car or other type	= you feel emotionally hurt in some waking situation	
		2.2.1.4 Your teeth fall out or crumble	= you are having trouble with angry words or feelings in the waking state; may grit teeth	

		2.2.1.5 Your body distorts, swells, or shrinks, other	= you feel emotionally hurt in a weird way; may feel inflated or squashed; may be physically ill (fever, other)		
		2.2.1.6 Other injuries	= depends on type of emotional damage at time of dream		
	2.2.2 Other person is injured but does not die	2.2.2.1 Another person is injured by any method	= you identify with an aspect of this person; you feel emotionally wounded		
		2.2.2.2 Baby, child, pet is neglected, forgotten	= you feel that a vulnerable part of you or your project is at risk		
2.3 Illness in dream	2.3.1 You are ill (when you are not in waking life)	2.3.1.1 You have a fatal disease	= you are suffering emotionally over a waking situation and feel you may not get over it	2.3.1.1.1 2.3.1.1.2	Cancer Other illness potentially fatal
		2.3.1.2 You have an illness or disease not usually fatal	= you are suffering emotionally over a waking situation but feel you will recover		
	2.3.2 You are disabled (when you are not in waking life)	2.3.2.1 You have a serious disability	= you feel that some part of you has become limited or restricted; area of the body affected relates to restricted area	2.3.2.3.1 2.3.2.3.2 2.3.2.3.3 2.3.2.3.4	Blind Deaf Crippled Mental
	2.3.3 Other person has dream illness or disability	2.3.3.1 Other person has illness	= you identify with this person and suffer emotionally over waking situation, or you may fear for that person's health		
		2.3.3.2 Other person has disability	= you identify with person and feel restricted in a waking area		

The Universal Dream Key: 3.0 Car or Other Vehicular Trouble

3.1 Vehicular Trouble	3.1.1 Loss of control	3.1.1.1 No or poor brakes	= you feel that some waking situation is difficult or impossible to control or slow down	3.1.1.1.1 No brakes
				3.1.1.1.2 Poor brakes
		3.1.1.2 Wrong speed	= you feel things are moving at too rapid or too slow a pace to solve a waking problem; excessive uncontrolled energy (reckless driving); insufficient energy (too slow); can't get going (in idle, won't start, motor cuts off)	3.1.1.2.1 Too fast
				3.1.1.2.2 Too slow
				3.1.1.2.3 Full stop
				3.1.1.2.4 Won't start
				3.1.1.2.5 In idle
				3.1.1.2.6 Motor cuts off
		3.1.1.3 Steering apparatus gone or poor (steering wheel, helm, rudder, etc.)	= you feel unable to direct the way the waking situation is going	3.1.1.3.1 No or broken steering wheel
				3.1.1.3.2 No rudder
				3.1.1.3.3 No helm
		3.1.1.4 Missing or ruined essential parts or fluids	= you feel that your energy level or ability to cope with the current waking situation is inadequate; your energy feels depleted (no or low gas); unable to function (flat or no tire)	3.1.1.4.1 No gas/fuel
				3.1.1.4.2 Low gas/fuel
				3.1.1.4.3 Flat tire
		3.1.1.5 Wrong direction for purpose	= you feel you are slipping in some waking situation (sliding downhill); you feel you are going backward (vehicle moves in reverse); you feel it is strenuous to make progress (going uphill)	3.1.1.5.1 Go downhill
				3.1.1.5.2 Go uphill
				3.1.1.5.3 Go backward
				3.1.1.5.4 Go forward when want to stop
	3.1.2 Collisions or other emergencies	3.1.2.1 Collision, crash	= you feel that current situation is worsening into a crisis; other people are damaged, too (collide with other vehicle)	3.1.2.1.1 Into other vehicle
				3.1.2.1.2 Into other object
				3.1.2.1.3 Crash

	3.1.2.2 Fire in vehicle	= you feel worsening waking situation involves anger; you may have a fever	3.1.2.2.1 3.1.2.2.2	Vehicle fire Fire outside vehicle (see 10.0)
	3.1.2.3 Other vehicle emergency			
3.1.3 Body of vehicle is wrong	3.1.3.1 Vehicle is wrong for your purpose	= you feel poorly equipped to cope with the waking situation; may feel strange (odd vehicle); your body may let you down (old vehicle); you may feel inept (awkward); it's too much to handle (big); cramped (small); situation worse (inadequate vehicle); dislike brand or style (specify why); brand and style reflect your waking attitudes	3.1.3.1.1 3.1.3.1.2 3.1.3.1.3 3.1.3.1.4 3.1.3.1.5 3.1.3.1.6 3.1.3.1.7 3.1.3.1.8 3.1.3.1.9	Odd Too old Dangerous Awkward Too big Too small Inadequate Wrong brand Wrong style
3.2 Driver trouble (pilot, person at helm, other)	3.2.1 Driver causes problem = you feel that some quality in self or another causes current waking problem			
	3.2.1.1 Driver cannot operate vehicle	= you feel incapable of coping well with the waking situation; you feel a childish part of self or other is in control (baby or child driver); or some other aspect is in control (identify) If driver, helmsman, pilot, or operator is not you, describe person's appearance and qualities	3.2.1.1.1 3.2.1.1.2 3.2.1.1.3 3.2.1.1.4 3.2.1.1.5 3.2.1.1.6 3.2.1.1.7 3.2.1.1.8	Doesn't know how No license Sleepy Sick Drunk Crazy Baby, child Can't find vehicle

The Universal Dream Key: 3.0 Car or Other Vehicular Trouble (cont.)

3.2.1.2 Driver can't see well	= you feel unable to see how to solve current waking problem	3.2.1.2.1 3.2.1.2.2 3.2.1.2.3 3.2.1.2.4	Vision fuzzy Obstructed Odd angle Other vision problem
3.2.1.3 Driver can't find way	= you feel confused about how to cope with current situation	3.2.1.3.1 3.2.1.3.2 3.2.1.3.3 3.2.1.3.4 3.2.1.3.5 3.2.1.3.6 3.2.1.3.7 3.2.1.3.8 3.2.1.3.9	Get lost Wrong turn Miss turn Wrong way Wrong route Dead end Wrong directions Can't get to connection Can't get to goal
3.2.1.4 Other people, animals interfere	= you feel that current problem is aggravated by others	3.2.1.4.1 3.2.1.4.2 3.2.1.4.3 3.2.1.4.4 3.2.1.4.5	Invade vehicle Attack it Steal it Come too close Bother driver

3.3 Road, air, or water condition; locale trouble	3.3.1 Bad road or locale	3.3.1.1 Bad road or waterway	= you feel that current waking conditions hinder your ability to cope	3.3.1.1.1	Uphill, mountain
				3.3.1.1.2	Cliff, drop-off
				3.3.1.1.3	Narrow, twisty
				3.3.1.1.4	Rocky, sandy
				3.3.1.1.5	Rough
				3.3.1.1.6	Busy
				3.3.1.1.7	Unstable or broken bridge
		3.3.1.2 Bad locale	= you feel you are in a dangerous environment. If exact location is specified, e.g., at the corner of X and Y streets, in a certain body of water, on runway, or in a particular airspace, describe the quality of that location	3.3.1.2.1	Woods
				3.3.1.2.2	Bad area of city
				3.3.1.2.3	Shoals
				3.3.1.2.4	Airspace risky
				3.3.1.2.5	Other locale problem
	3.3.2 Bad weather or other conditions	3.3.2.1 Unstable road, water, earth, or air conditions	= you feel assailed by emotional conditions in your environment; it's hard to see what to do (dark, unlit); you feel at risk of slippage (wet); your situation feels dangerous (snow, ice, disaster); your safe passage is disrupted (broken track, bridge)	3.3.2.1.1	Dark, unlit
				3.3.2.1.2	Wet, slick
				3.3.2.1.3	Snowy, icy
				3.3.2.1.4	Storm or disaster (see 10.0)
				3.3.2.1.5	Broken track
				3.3.2.1.6	Broken bridge
				3.3.2.1.7	Other bad weather
	3.3.3 Obstacles on or near road	3.3.3.1 Other vehicles or people block or obstruct passage	= you attribute the waking problem to behavior of other people or the situation	3.3.3.1.1	Traffic still
				3.3.3.1.2	Traffic heavy
				3.3.3.1.3	Blockade

3.4 Kind of vehicle having trouble				
3.4.1 Land vehicle	3.4.1.1 Personal vehicle	3.4.1.1.1 Car	= type of vehicle operated indicates your current style of moving through life If vehicle is personally operated, you feel more control; if operated by commercial driver, pilot, other, you feel less control; you feel others are involved in situation	
		3.4.1.1.2 Taxi		
		3.4.1.1.3 Limousine		
		3.4.1.1.4 Bicycle		
		3.4.1.1.5 Small (skateboard, other)		
		3.4.1.1.6 Large (van, other)		
	3.4.1.2 Public vehicle	3.4.1.2.1 Bus, jitney		
		3.4.1.2.2 Train		
		3.4.1.2.3 Trolley		
		3.4.1.2.4 Elevated		
		3.4.1.2.5 Subway		
		3.4.1.2.6 Other		
3.4.2 Water vehicle	3.4.2.1 Personal vehicle	3.4.2.1.1 Boat, canoe		
		3.4.2.1.2 Raft		
		3.4.2.1.3 Kayak		
		3.4.2.1.4 Other		
	3.4.2.2 Public vehicle	3.4.2.2.1 Ship		
		3.4.2.2.2 Yacht		
		3.4.2.2.3 Barge		
		3.4.2.2.4 Other		
3.4.3 Air vehicle	3.4.3.1 Personal vehicle	3.4.3.1.1 Small plane		
		3.4.3.1.2 Helicopter		
		3.4.3.1.3 Balloon with basket		
		3.4.3.1.4 Other		
	3.4.3.2 Public vehicle	3.4.3.2.1 Jet, supersonic		
		3.4.3.2.2 Other		

The Universal Dream Key: 4.0 Loss or Damage to House or Property

4.1 House loss or damage in dream	4.1.1 Damage to house or building = you feel severe or moderate waking threat to your body or lifestyle	= you may feel waking turmoil from anger, sexual arousal or damage (fire); you may feel overwhelmed with tearfulness (water); at risk from wild thoughts (wind); or buried or shaken (earthquake damage)	4.1.1.1 House is damaged by element	4.1.1.1.1 Fire 4.1.1.1.2 Water 4.1.1.1.3 Wind 4.1.1.1.4 Earth movement
		= you feel your personal space is being intruded upon in waking life; you may have an infection (insects)	4.1.1.2 House is damaged by animal invasion	4.1.1.2.1 Termites, bugs 4.1.1.2.2 Snails 4.1.1.2.3 Other animal
		= you feel diminished waking support; area of house involved relates to area of waking trouble	4.1.1.3 House is damaged by collapse of whole or parts	4.1.1.3.1 Floor rots 4.1.1.3.2 Ceiling collapses 4.1.1.3.3 Walls gives way 4.1.1.3.4 Room ruined
		= you feel unable to thrive in some waking situation	4.1.1.4 Garden or yard is damaged	4.1.1.4.1 Garden ruin 4.1.1.4.2 Yard ruin
		= depends on your association to building that is damaged	4.1.1.5 Other building ruin	
		= depends on your association to type of damage; may be anger (guns, bombs)	4.1.1.6 Other types of house damage	4.1.1.6.1 Gunfire 4.1.1.6.2 Explosion 4.1.1.6.3 Tree fall 4.1.1.6.4 Car crashes into house
4.1.2 Loss of house		= you feel your personal space in waking life is being taken over	4.1.2.1 Other people take over or remove	

4.13 House is wrong in some way		
	4.1.2.2 House is sold; you may try to recover	= you feel displaced in some area of your waking life, homeless
	4.1.3.1 House is odd, bizarre	= you feel your life space has become strange
	4.1.3.2 House is too old	= your life space feels risky; you may have concern about aging
	4.1.3.3 House is dangerous	= your life space feels unsafe at the moment
	4.1.3.4 House is awkward to live in, too large, or too small	= you feel your life space is inept; too much to cope with (too big); too little personal space (too small)
	4.1.3.5 House is in undesirable spot	= you feel your waking situation is unpleasant; specific meaning depends on feeling about location
	4.1.3.6 House becomes a less desirable one	= you feel that a waking situation has worsened
	4.1.3.7 House has one room or area wrong or missing (specify area)	= you feel that a certain area of waking life is currently difficult; specific meaning depends on which room and your feelings about it; may be area of relief, cleansing (bathroom); limited emotional nourishment (kitchen, dining room); limited sexual or emotional contact (bedroom); protection (roof); solid foundation reduced (floor)

4.1.2.7.1	Kitchen
4.1.2.7.2	Bedroom
4.1.2.7.3	Bathroom
4.1.2.7.4	Living room
4.1.2.7.5	Roof
4.1.2.7.6	Floor
4.1.2.7.7	Other area

4.2 Property loss, damage	4.2.1 Property damage (Loss, 4.2.2)				
		4.2.1.1 Purse or wallet is lost or damaged	= you feel a waking threat to your self-identity, level of confidence, or ability to operate	4.2.1.1.1 4.2.1.1.2	Purse Wallet
		4.2.1.2 Jewelry is lost or damaged	= you feel a waking threat to the relationship or quality the jewelry stands for; you may feel threat to precious aspect of self, soul	4.2.1.2.1 4.2.1.2.2 4.2.1.2.3 4.2.1.2.4 4.2.1.2.5	Wedding ring Gold ring Jewel gift Inherited jewelry Other jewel
		4.2.1.3 Watch or timepiece is lost or damaged	= you feel that precious time has been lost in the waking state	4.2.1.3.1 4.2.1.3.2 4.2.1.3.3	Wristwatch Grandfather clock Other clock
		4.2.1.4 Musical instrument or tool is lost or damaged	= you feel that your creative work has been reduced in waking state; may have reduced sexual functioning	4.2.1.4.1 4.2.1.4.2 4.2.1.4.3 4.2.1.4.4	Musical instrument Art tool Work tool Other tool
		4.2.1.5 Childhood toy, family item, special antique is lost or damaged	= you feel a threat to, or reduced relationship to, your past or your heritage	4.2.1.4.1 4.2.1.4.2 4.2.1.4.3 4.2.1.4.4	Toy Inherited item Antique Other item from past
		4.2.1.6 Valuable papers, data, or books are lost or damaged	= you feel bereft of some material or information represented by the material	4.2.1.6.1 4.2.1.6.2 4.2.1.6.3	Will Book Other papers

5.1 / 5.2	Sub-entry	Definition	Code	Description
5.1 Test, poor performance: You perform poorly or have other trouble with taking a test = you feel unprepared for a waking situation and fear "failing"	5.1.1.1 You are late for the test	= you feel time pressure about performing well in a waking life situation; no access to needed equipment (can't find or open locker); hard to get started (can't find entrance or room); feel unable to face challenge (miss test)	5.1.1.1.1	Can't find room, wander hall
			5.1.1.1.2	Can't find entrance
			5.1.1.1.3	Can't find locker
			5.1.1.1.4	Miss test
			5.1.1.1.5	Wrong room
	5.1.1.2 Test is hard or impossible to take	= you feel unready to face waking challenge, lack information; challenge is unexpected (forgot class); puzzled about how to cope with challenge (never read books or read wrong ones); feel unable to cope with challenge (fail or fear failure)	5.1.1.2.1	Forgot had class
			5.1.1.2.2	Never read books
			5.1.1.2.3	Read wrong books
			5.1.1.2.4	Nervous in test
			5.1.1.2.5	Fear of failing
			5.1.1.2.6	Too little time
			5.1.1.2.7	Forgot class project
	5.1.1.3 You are missing essential equipment for test	= you feel ill equipped for dealing with a current waking challenge	5.1.1.3.1	No pen
			5.1.1.3.2	No book
			5.1.1.3.3	No schedule
			5.1.1.3.4	No thoughts
5.2 Stage, poor performance: You perform poorly or have other trouble in performing onstage = you feel unready for a waking challenge and fear failing	5.2.1.1 You are late to the performance, e.g., play, music, speech, or sport event	= you feel unprepared and confused about some waking life challenge you must meet; you feel you've missed a chance (begins without you); puzzled how to meet challenge (can't find performance place)	5.2.1.1.1	Can't find performance place
			5.1.2.1.2	Begins before you arrive
			5.1.2.1.3	Time tight

	5.2.1.2 Your ability to perform suffers	= you feel badly prepared for a waking challenge you must cope with; you feel you must do the impossible (must perform in area for which you are untrained); may be playing wrong role (in wrong play, opera, or other event); feel unable to cope (fail)	5.2.1.2.1 — No voice 5.2.1.2.2 — Poor voice 5.2.1.2.3 — Don't know words or music 5.2.1.2.4 — Forget words or music 5.2.1.2.5 — Lose skill 5.2.1.2.6 — Fumble, fail
	5.2.1.3 You do not have the equipment you need to perform well (shoes, helmet, costume)	= you feel badly equipped to cope with a current waking life challenge	5.2.1.3.1 — No or wrong costume (see 7.0) 5.2.1.3.2 — No or wrong instrument

The Universal Dream Key: 6.0 Falling or Drowning

6.1 Falling in dream	6.1.1 You fall = you feel helpless about a waking situation				
		6.1.1.1 You fall from a height	= you feel a sharp contrast in your sense of security, stability, or degree of emotional support; you feel on brink of danger (cliff, roof); you feel in transition (bridge); your situation changes from fun to fearful (park ride); you feel others are affected by the change (people cling or burden); it's hard to see what to do about situation (black void); the change is big (long fall in space)	6.1.1.1.1 6.1.1.1.2 6.1.1.1.3 6.1.1.1.4 6.1.1.1.5 6.1.1.1.6 6.1.1.1.7 6.1.1.1.8 6.1.1.1.9 6.1.1.1.10	From cliff From space Into void, pit From rooftop From bridge From ride in fun park From stairs, ladder In elevator People cling Other places
		6.1.1.2 Impact with the ground (or not)	= you feel (or do not feel) a shocking contact with some waking situation	6.1.1.2.1 6.1.1.2.2 6.1.1.2.3 6.1.1.2.4 6.1.1.2.5 6.1.1.2.6	Jolt awake Wake on impact Wake before Hit bottom, injured or die (see 2.0) Hit bottom, survive Land softly
		6.1.1.3 Your reaction to fall	= you struggle to cope with a change in your waking level of support (or do not try); you feel unable to cope at present (terror); you feel able to try to cope (scream, get help, or help self); you get different perspective (if you become lucid); you feel able to protect self (float, fly); you are aware of physical state (fall from bed)	6.1.1.3.1 6.1.1.3.2 6.1.1.3.3 6.1.1.3.4 6.1.1.3.5 6.1.1.3.6 6.1.1.3.7	Terror Scream, try to get help Try to grasp support Fall from bed Lucidity Float Fly

The Universal Dream Key: 6.0 Falling or Drowning (cont.)

6.2 Drowning in dream	6.2.1 You drown or are in danger of it = you feel overwhelmed by some current waking situation; you may have condition of edema in waking state	6.2.1.1 You drown or nearly drown in deep water	= you feel in danger of being overwhelmed by the current situation; you feel others are in danger with you (people clutch); you feel the danger is accidental or deliberate (person or animal tries to drown you)	6.2.1.1.1 In water 6.2.1.1.2 Fall into, car plunges into 6.2.1.1.3 Jump into 6.2.1.1.4 Tidal wave (see 10.0) 6.2.1.1.5 Trapped in water (see 11.0) 6.2.1.1.6 Boat capsizes (see 3.0) 6.2.1.1.7 Person tries to drown you (1.0) 6.2.1.1.8 People clutch
		6.2.1.2 Impact with water	= you feel a shocking contact with some-waking situation; situation feels life-threatening (can't breathe); unable to function (cold water is numbing); it's hard to see what to do and where to go (water muddy or murky)	6.2.1.2.1 Wake on impact with cold water 6.2.1.2.2 Wake before 6.2.1.2.3 Can't breathe 6.2.1.2.4 Water murky

The Universal Dream Key: 6.0 Falling or Drowning (cont.)

6.2.1.3 Your reaction to near-drowning or drowning	= you struggle to cope with the over-whelming waking situation (or do not try); you feel unable to cope (terror); feel able to try (try to save self or try to get help); feel hopeless (give up); futile (die); you get broader perspective (lucidity); you find you have resources you didn't realize (discover underwater breathing); accept situation (calm); feel able to cope or get help coping (save self, are saved)	6.2.1.3.1	Terror
		6.2.1.3.2	Try to yell
		6.2.1.3.3	Try to swim
		6.2.1.3.4	Give up
		6.2.1.3.5	Die (see 2.0)
		6.2.1.3.6	Lucidity
		6.2.1.3.7	Discover can breathe underwater
		6.2.1.3.8	Feel calm
		6.2.1.3.9	Save self
		6.2.1.3.10	Are saved

♠ ♟ *The Universal Dream Key:* **7.0 Naked or Inappropriately Dressed in Public**

7.1 Naked in public in dream	7.1.1 You are naked in public = you feel emotionally overexposed or vulnerable in a waking situation	7.1.1.1 You are naked in a specific public setting		= you feel overexposed or vulnerable in the same or similar setting in waking life
			7.1.1.1.1	At school
			7.1.1.1.2	At work
			7.1.1.1.3	On street
			7.1.1.1.4	In car
			7.1.1.1.5	At home in bathroom, but seen
			7.1.1.1.6	Taking bath in public
			7.1.1.1.7	On beach
			7.1.1.1.8	Other place
		7.1.1.2 Your reason for being naked		= you feel blameless for being over-exposed or vulnerable
			7.1.1.2.1	Forgot to put on clothes
			7.1.1.2.2	Remove
			7.1.1.2.3	Others naked
		7.1.1.3 Reaction of public to your being nude		= your impression of people's response to your emotional exposure in a waking situation
			7.1.1.3.1	Ignore
			7.1.1.3.2	Interest, stare
			7.1.1.3.3	Criticize, frown
			7.1.1.3.4	Mock, laugh
			7.1.1.3.5	Offer clothes or shelter
		7.1.1.4 Your reaction to public reaction to your nudity		= you struggle (or do not try) to cope with feeling vulnerable in waking state
			7.1.1.4.1	Mortified
			7.1.1.4.2	Hide, escape
			7.1.1.4.3	Find clothes
			7.1.1.4.4	Feel cold
			7.1.1.4.5	Ignore
			7.1.1.4.6	Lucidity
			7.1.1.4.7	Feel proud
			7.1.1.4.8	Feel free, fun

	7.1.2 You are partially nude = you feel vulnerable in area of waking life related to body part exposed	7.1.2.1 You are missing specific clothing or are revealing certain clothing	= you feel vulnerable in a waking life area related to the part of your body that is exposed or to specific clothing revealed; you may feel vulnerable in strength, sexuality, or maternal qualities (personal body parts revealed); in intimacy (wearing underwear only); in foundation or support (lack footwear); you may have uncontrolled thoughts (no headgear when appropriate)	7.1.2.1.1 No shirt 7.1.2.1.2 No blouse 7.1.2.1.3 No pants 7.1.2.1.4 No skirt 7.1.2.1.5 No shoes 7.1.2.1.6 No socks 7.1.2.1.7 Barefoot 7.1.2.1.8 No headgear 7.1.2.1.9 In underwear 7.1.2.1.10 Bra only 7.1.2.1.11 Slip only 7.1.2.1.12 Panties only 7.1.2.1.13 Without underwear
7.2 Wrongly or weirdly dressed in dream	7.2.1 You are wrongly dressed = you may feel you have the wrong equipment for a current waking life situation	7.2.1.1 You are dressed for one occasion while attending another type of occasion	= you feel you have the wrong equipment for a particular waking situation; you may feel your role is wrong; you may feel your behavior is too offhand (e.g., in blue jeans at wedding); you may feel you are acting too stiffly (e.g., in ball gown at barn dance); you may feel your behavior is too intimate for the situation (e.g., in pajamas or nightgown while teaching class); you may feel conflicted about participating in a waking event (e.g., wearing a bright red vest when you are a bridegroom)	7.2.1.1.1 Casual for formal 7.2.1.1.2 Formal for casual 7.2.1.1.3 Nightwear for daywear 7.2.1.1.4 Wrong accessories

| 7.2.2
You are weirdly dressed = you may have conflicting feelings about your role in a waking life situation | 7.2.2.1
You are dressed in an outfit that is totally inappropriate for the occasion | = you feel conflicted about your role in a waking life situation (e.g., wearing a clown costume when you are a bridegroom); you may feel childish in the role (dressed as a baby in diapers or as a child when you are actually a teen or adult); your role may feel too much for you or too limited (too big or too small clothing) | 7.2.2.1.1
7.2.2.1.2
7.2.2.1.3
7.2.2.1.4
7.2.2.1.5 | Weird outfit
Baby clothes
Child clothes
Too big garb
Too small clothing |

The Universal Dream Key: 8.0 Missing the Boat or Other Transport

8.1 Missing the boat or other transport in dream	8.1.1 You miss some form of transport = you feel you have lost an important chance or opportunity	8.1.1.1 Type of transport you miss	= you feel you have missed out in some specific waking situation (work, romance, health care, other) transport missed may relate to the specific situation or be your usual mode of travel (e.g., a dream of missing the school bus may relate to feeling you have lost a chance for higher education)	8.1.1.1.1 8.1.1.1.2 8.1.1.1.3 8.1.1.1.4 8.1.1.1.5 8.1.1.1.6	Airplane Boat, ship, ferry, other Bus, school bus Train, trolley, or other transport on rails Private vehicle Other type
		8.1.1.2 Reason you miss transport	= you feel blameless for missing the opportunity you had in waking life; you may feel other people prevent you or the situation itself makes it impossible for you to reach your goal; you feel ill equipped (forget or lose ticket, passport, visa, luggage); you feel you have mistimed the connection you desire in waking life (you try to take transport on the wrong date)	8.1.1.2.1 8.1.1.2.2 8.1.1.2.3 8.1.1.2.4 8.1.1.2.5 8.1.1.2.6 8.1.1.2.7	Time press Obstacle Distraction People bar Legs won't move fast (see 11.0) No essentials Wrong date
		8.1.1.3 Your goal in catching transport	= you want to connect with a waking life situation that relates to your goal in the dream (e.g., a dream of missing a plane to meet a lover relates to a feeling you have lost your desired connection to that person)	8.1.1.3.1 8.1.1.3.2 8.1.1.3.3 8.1.1.3.4 8.1.1.3.5	Romance Work School or lesson Health, to see physician, therapist Other goal

The Universal Dream Key: 8.0 Missing the Boat or Other Transport (cont.)

8.2 Undesired activity by transport in dream	8.2.1 You board transport but it acts in unexpected way	8.2.1.1 Transport goes in the wrong direction	= you feel the connection you want in waking life is going in an undesirable direction	8.2.1.1.1 8.2.1.1.2	Opposite way from your plan Some other way
		8.2.1.2 Transport goes to the wrong place	= you feel the connection you desire in waking life is ending in an undesirable spot	8.2.1.2.1 8.2.1.2.2	Wrong town Wrong land
		8.2.1.3 Transport creeps along	= you feel the connection you desire in waking life is taking place too slowly		
		8.2.1.4 Transport leaves with your belongings aboard	= you feel the connection in waking life is depriving you of something else you need; you may feel ill equipped		
		8.2.1.5 Transport crosses international border	= you feel that the connection you desire in waking life is moving you into unfamiliar territory		
8.3 Your reaction to missing or almost missing transport in dream	8.3.1 You make effort to catch transport	8.3.1.1 You struggle to catch transport but miss it despite best effort	= you feel you have lost an important chance in waking life despite supreme effort		
		8.3.1.2 You try to catch the transport and just make it	= you feel that you can succeed in making the connection you wish in waking life if you exert effort		
		8.3.1.3 You take alternative transportation (e.g., catch later transport, swim, run, hitchhike)	= you feel you can succeed in your waking goal by another route		

8.3.1.4 You hunt ticket window, departure gate, information	= you feel confused about how to proceed to achieve your waking goal	
8.3.1.5 You are stranded	= at the moment you feel hopeless and helpless about making the connection you want in waking life	
8.3.1.6 You make an outgoing transport but miss return one	= you feel you got started well on the connection you desire in waking life but feel unable to follow through	

🕿 ▢ ▦ The Universal Dream Key: 9.0 Telephone or Machine Malfunctions

9.1
Telephone mal-
function in dream
	9.11
	You have trouble while trying to use a telephone
		9.1.1.1
		Dialing difficulty
			= you feel you are having trouble getting an emotional connection that you want in waking life; you feel you can't get through to that person in emotional sense; you may lack vital information (don't know how to work phone, wrong number); or other people interfere (distraction, people bar, injury)	9.1.1.1.1
				9.1.1.1.2
				9.1.1.1.3
				9.1.1.1.4
				9.1.1.1.5
				9.1.1.1.6
				
				9.1.1.1.7
					Dial, redial
					Cannot see
					Won't work
					Odd keypad
					Odd phone
					Number is
					  incorrect
					Other dialing
					  problem

		9.1.1.2
		Connection difficulty
			= you feel you are having trouble maintaining an emotional connection you want in waking life; you feel cut off; you feel your attempt to connect emotionally goes astray (wrong party); communication is faulty (fuzzy, garbled, unclear line); you may not communicate clearly (operator doesn't understand); you may sense a negative response to effort to contact (refusal by party to answer, hang up); you may ignore message (you won't pick up ringing phone)	9.1.1.2.1
				9.1.1.2.2
				9.1.1.2.3
				9.1.1.2.4
				
				9.1.1.2.5
				
				9.1.1.2.6
				
				9.1.1.2.7
				
				9.1.1.2.8
					Disconnect
					Get wrong party
					Line fuzzy
					Operator
					  problem
					Party won't
					  answer
					Party hangs up
					  on you
					You won't pick
					  up on phone
					  ring
					Other connec-
					  tion problem

		9.1.1.3
		Urgency sense
			= you feel it's extremely important to make the emotional connection you want in waking life; you may be feeling desperate to make contact or unable to cope with some waking situation alone	9.1.1.3.1
				9.1.1.3.2
					Dial number
					  emergency
					Other urgent
					  need

☎ **The Universal Dream Key: 9.0 Telephone or Machine Malfunctions (cont.)**

	9.1.1.4 Person or party you desire to reach by phone	= you feel a wish to connect with this person, or a quality or attribute of the person or place you are trying to call	9.1.1.4.1 9.1.1.4.2 9.1.1.4.3 9.1.1.4.4 9.1.1.4.5 9.1.1.4.6	Emergency service number Lover, mate Parent Child Friend Deceased person
9.2 Machine malfunction in dream	9.2.1.1 Hardware problem (monitor and output devices; keyboard, mouse and input devices; memory storage; chip; modem; other)	= you sense trouble in making some part of your waking life function well, physical or emotional; things are difficult to understand (e.g., the keyboard is all in Greek)	9.2.1.1.1 9.2.1.1.2 9.2.1.1.3 9.2.1.1.4 9.2.1.1.5 9.2.1.1.6	Won't boot up or shut down Doesn't respond to command Pieces break Goes out of control Odd shape or appearance Other trouble
9.2.1 You have difficulty while operating a computer	9.2.1.2 Software problem (word processing program; graphics, business; search tool; virus detection, other)	= you feel things are not working well in some waking life situation; you may be concerned about your health (e.g., your program has a virus)	9.2.1.2.1 9.2.1.2.2 9.2.1.2.3 9.2.1.2.4 9.2.1.2.5	Distorts Mutates Condenses two or more programs Virus present Other trouble

The Universal Dream Key: 9.0 Telephone or Machine Malfunctions (cont.)

	9.2.1.3 Internet or virtual reality problem	= you feel you are having trouble making and maintaining connection in waking life (getting disconnected); you may feel communication has become distorted (weird look and action)	9.2.1.3.1	Weird appearance
			9.2.1.3.2	Weird action
			9.2.1.3.3	Disconnect
			9.2.1.3.4	Other
	9.2.1.4 Operator problem	= you feel you lack some vital information to make things work well in the waking state	9.2.1.4.1	Cannot see
			9.2.1.4.2	Fingers don't work well
			9.2.1.4.3	Lack vital operating information
			9.2.1.4.4	Other trouble
9.2.2 You have trouble operating another machine (for vehicular trouble, see 3.0)	9.2.2.1 Operation trouble	= you sense there is some trouble in making part of your waking life function well, physical or emotional	9.2.2.1.1	Won't start
			9.2.2.1.2	Won't stop
			9.2.2.1.3	Won't work properly
			9.2.2.1.4	Other trouble
	9.2.2.2 Operator trouble	= you feel you lack some vital information to make things work well in waking state (can't see, fingers won't work, don't know or forget how to use)	9.2.2.2.1	Cannot see
			9.2.2.2.2	Fingers don't work well
			9.2.2.2.3	Lack vital operating information
			9.2.2.2.4	Other trouble
	9.2.2.3 Machine itself causes problem (for machine threat or attack, see 1.0)	= you sense a distortion or breakdown of some aspect of your waking life; you may feel your body is in bad shape (odd shape, it comes apart, breaks, melts, explodes, parts gone, other)	9.2.2.3.1	Machine is bizarre
			9.2.2.3.2	Comes apart or breaks down
			9.2.2.3.3	Other trouble

✈ 💣 ☿ *The Universal Dream Key:* 10.0 Natural or Man-made Disaster

10.1 Natural disaster strikes in dream	10.11 You are in a natural disaster in dream = you are coping with a crisis in waking life or you anticipate one	10.1.1.1 Type of natural disaster you confront in dream	= you feel confronted with an emotional or physical crisis in your waking life; type of natural disaster in dream relates to type of trouble in the waking state; you may be feeling intense sorrow and be overwhelmed (great waters); you may have disturbed, wild thoughts and feel blown away by the situation (great winds); you may feel consumed or damaged by anger in you or others (great fire, lava, volcanic explosion); you may feel badly shaken by waking events and as if you are coming apart (great earth movement); you may feel you cannot survive (end of the world); you may be coping with intensely cold emotional behavior (blizzard, ice, hail)	10.1.1.1.1	Great water, tidal wave, flood, rain
				10.1.1.1.2	Great wind, tornado, whirlwind
				10.1.1.1.3	Great fire, lightning, firestorm
				10.1.1.1.4	Great earth movement, earthquake, avalanche, mudslide
				10.1.1.1.5	Volcanic explosion, lava
				10.1.1.1.6	End of world
				10.1.1.1.7	Famine, drought,
				10.1.1.1.8	Plague
				10.1.1.1.9	Other

10.1.1.2 Results of the natural disaster in dream	= you feel you are deeply hurt, emotionally wounded, damaged, or destroyed by the waking crisis (injury, death of self); you may feel others are being hurt by the waking situation (others are hurt, die); you may feel more a witness to emotional destruction than a victim (you remain unharmed)	10.1.1.2.1	You die (see 2.0)
		10.1.1.2.2	Others die
		10.1.1.2.3	You are hurt
		10.1.1.2.4	Others hurt
		10.1.1.2.5	Trapped (see 11.0)
		10.1.1.2.6	Unharmed
		10.1.1.2.7	Town ruin (see 4.0)
		10.1.1.2.8	Other
10.1.1.3 Your reaction to the natural disaster in dream	= you struggle to cope with the waking crisis (or do not try); you may be in shock or feel helpless (immobilized, give up); you may make efforts (try to save self, rescue); you may feel your efforts are worthwhile (succeed); not worthwhile (fail); you may be in conflict (trapped); or you may need help from others (are rescued); you may be able to get a different perspective (become lucid) or find inner resources (discover special powers in dream, such as ability to breathe underwater)	10.1.1.3.1	Immobilized or give up
		10.1.1.3.2	Try to save self, others
		10.1.1.3.3	Fail to save
		10.1.1.3.4	Rescue
		10.1.1.3.5	Are rescued
		10.1.1.3.6	Lucidity
		10.1.1.3.7	Discover special power
		10.1.1.3.8	Other

10.2 Man-made disaster strikes in dream	10.2.1 You are in a man-made disaster in dream = you confront a crisis in waking life or you anticipate one		
	10.2.1.1 Type of man-made disaster you confront in dream	= you feel confronted with an emotional or physical crisis in your waking life; the type of man-made disaster relates to the waking life problem you now confront; you may feel invaded, attacked in waking life (war, bombs); you may feel others are emotionally damaged, too (people die, are injured; property is ruined); you may feel the waking situation is catastrophic, as if you may not survive (all life gone); you may feel the waking emotional atmosphere is poisonous (gas, ecological disaster)	10.2.1.1.1 — War, armed conflict 10.2.1.1.2 — Atomic bomb, other 10.2.1.1.3 — Explosion 10.2.1.1.4 — Firestorm 10.2.1.1.5 — People die 10.2.1.1.6 — Property ruin 10.2.1.1.7 — All life gone 10.2.1.1.8 — Aftermath 10.2.1.1.9 — Other (gas, ecological disaster)
	10.2.1.2 Results of the man-made disaster in dream	= you feel the waking crisis has a profound effect; you feel hurt, badly damaged, or destroyed (you die or are injured); you feel others are emotionally wounded or destroyed (others die or are injured); you feel conflicted about what to do (trapped, imprisoned, taken as prisoner of war, other)	10.2.1.2.1 — You die (see 2.0) 10.2.1.2.2 — Others die 10.2.1.2.3 — You are hurt 10.2.1.2.4 — Others hurt 10.2.1.2.5 — Trapped (see 11.0) 10.2.1.2.6 — Unharmed 10.2.1.2.7 — Town ruin (see 4.0) 10.2.1.2.8 — Other

♣ ☀ *The Universal Dream Key*: 10.0 Natural or Man-made Disaster (cont.)

10.2.1.3 Your reaction to the man-made disaster in dream	= you struggle to cope with the waking crisis (or do not try); you feel stunned, unable to cope (immobilized, give up in dream); you may make efforts to help (try to save self or others); feel your efforts are worthwhile or not (succeed or fail to save); you feel you need help (are rescued); you may feel able to get a new perspective (become lucid) or find inner resources (you discover special powers in dream)	10.2.1.3.1	Immobilized or give up
		10.2.1.3.2	Try to save self, others
		10.2.1.3.3	Fail to save
		10.2.1.3.4	Rescue
		10.2.1.3.5	Are rescued
		10.2.1.3.6	Lucidity
		10.2.1.3.7	Discover special power
		10.2.1.3.8	Other

The Universal Dream Key: 11.0 Lost or Trapped

Lost in dream	11.1 Lost in dream					
		11.1.1 You are lost in a certain location in dream = you are confused or uncertain about some waking life situation	11.1.1.1 City area in which you are lost in a dream	= the location in which you are lost in the dream relates to feelings you have about the waking life situation that confuses or puzzles you; you feel it is risky (dangerous area); something that usually works easily is now puzzling (unfamiliar, familiar now odd)	11.1.1.1.1 11.1.1.1.2 11.1.1.1.3 11.1.1.1.4 11.1.1.1.5	Dangerous area Unfamiliar Familiar that has become strange Foreign Other
			11.1.1.2 Natural setting in which you are lost in a dream	= you feel that the waking situation confronting you has few guideposts (country); is bleak with little protection (desert); has savage, dangerous elements (forest, jungle); is stark and difficult (mountains)	11.1.1.2.1 11.1.1.2.2 11.1.1.2.3 11.1.1.2.4 11.1.1.2.5	Countryside Desert Forest Mountains Other
			11.1.1.3 House or building in which you are lost in dream	= you feel you are making no progress in solving the waking problem (many rooms with no exit); you feel you are wandering uselessly (endless hallways); the situation feels frightening (in a haunted building); you may fear aging, illness, or death (lost in hospital)	11.1.1.3.1 11.1.1.3.2 11.1.1.3.3 11.1.1.3.4 11.1.1.3.5	Rooms going nowhere, no exit Hallways Haunted spot Hospital Other structure (market, maze, other)
		11.1.2 You are lost in general in dream	11.1.2.1 Open space or void in which you are lost in dream	= you have an overall feeling of being confused and puzzled	11.1.2.1.1 11.1.2.1.2	Lost in space No setting at all
		11.1.3 Dark conditions prevail in area in which you are lost	11.1.3.1 You find it hard to see in a dream about being lost	= you find it hard to figure out clearly what to do about the waking situation that confuses and puzzles you	11.1.3.1.1 11.1.3.1.2	Pitch black, no light Very dim lighting

	11.1.4 Your goal in finding your way	11.1.4.1 You are trying to get to a specific place or person in a dream of being lost	= the specific place or person you try to reach in dream relates to an area of waking life that feels like a safe haven or is otherwise important to you	11.1.4.1.1	To escape
				11.1.4.1.2	To go home
				11.1.4.1.3	To find car
				11.1.4.1.4	To get to work
				11.1.4.1.5	To find loved one
				11.1.4.1.6	Other
	11.1.5 Your reaction to being lost	11.1.5.1 You struggle to find your way, or do not try, in a dream of being lost	= you make efforts to cope with the waking situation that confuses or puzzles you, or do not try; you feel confused, unable to cope with situation alone (don't know the way, no one will help); you feel you are not making progress (wander); you feel your efforts are unsuccessful (try, fail); you feel able to cope (try, succeed)	11.1.5.1.1	Don't know the way
				11.1.5.1.2	No people willing or able to help
				11.1.5.1.3	Wander, go in circles
				11.1.5.1.4	Try, fail
				11.1.5.1.5	Try, succeed
				11.1.5.1.6	Other
11.2 Trapped in dream	11.2.1 You are trapped in a dream = you feel a strong conflict about a confusing waking life situation	11.2.1.1 Location in which you are trapped in a dream, may be dark	= place in which you are trapped in dream relates to area of waking life in which you feel stuck by conflicting emotions or your feelings about that area; you find it hard to see what to do about situation (darkness, dimness)	11.2.1.1.1.1	In city part
				11.2.1.1.1.2	In house part basement closet wall
				11.2.1.1.1.3	In prison
				11.2.1.1.1.4	In tunnel
				11.2.1.1.1.5	Small space
				11.2.1.1.1.6	Outside / in war / in desert / in road / in sidewalk

The *Universal Dream Key*: 11.0 Lost or Trapped (cont.)

			11.2.1.1.7 11.2.1.1.8 11.2.1.1.9	Buried alive In body Other
	11.2.2 Results of being trapped in dream	11.2.2.1 You are totally paralyzed or stuck, or you are partially paralyzed in some section of your body in dream	= you feel totally unable to cope with the waking situation, stuck (complete paralysis); you feel as if you cannot get away from it (legs paralyzed or tied); you feel unable to call for help (paralyzed or weak voice); you feel your life is at risk (can't breathe); you feel weighted down by the situation (heaviness); you feel the situation is worsening (attacker, car, or other impending danger nears)	
			11.2.2.1.1 11.2.2.1.2 11.2.2.1.3 11.2.2.1.4 11.2.2.1.5 11.2.2.1.6 11.2.2.1.7	Paralysis, general In legs In voice In breathing Feel heavy, like lead, object on chest Impending danger Other
	11.2.3 Your reaction to being trapped in a dream	11.2.3.1 You try or do not try to get free in dream of being trapped	= you struggle to cope with the entrapping circumstances in a waking life situation (try to save self, others), or do not try (give up); you feel able to cope (rescue self); you may feel able to cope with help (are rescued); you may be able to get a better perspective (lucidity, discover special power)	
			11.2.3.1.1 11.2.3.1.2 11.2.3.1.3 11.2.3.1.4 11.2.3.1.5 11.2.3.1.6 11.2.3.1.7 11.2.3.1.8	Immobilized or give up Try to save self, others Fail to save Rescue Are rescued Lucidity Find power Other

✿☙ _The Universal Dream Key:_ 12.0 Menaced by a Spirit and Guided by a Spirit

12.1 Menaced by a spirit in a dream (Negative dream about a deceased person)	12.1.1 You are menaced by the spirit of a deceased person in a dream = you feel fearful or angry about the condition of a deceased person's spirit or about your relationship to that individual				
		12.1.1.1 The deceased person seems to be suffering in your dream	= you feel fearful that the spirit of the deceased person is not at rest	12.1.1.1.1 12.1.1.1.2	Old suffering New type of suffering
		12.1.1.2 The deceased person criticizes you	= you may feel guilty about some behavior, or the deceased's criticism is a continuation of a former negative relationship that remains unresolved	12.1.1.2.1 12.1.1.2.2 12.1.1.2.3	Scolds you Says you are foolish or stupid Other
		12.1.1.3 The deceased person curses or actively threatens you in dream (if deceased attacks you, see 1.0)	= you may feel continued angry resentment of or fear of former behavior of the deceased	12.1.1.3.1 12.1.1.3.2 12.1.1.3.3	Curses you Threatens you Other
		12.1.1.4 The deceased lures you toward death	= you may feel deep depression over the loss of the deceased person and fear for your survival; therapeutic help is desirable	12.1.1.4.1 12.1.1.4.2	Beckons you Suggests you die too
		12.1.1.5 The deceased issues a warning or orders you to do what you do not wish to do	= you may feel fearful of making a mistake	12.1.1.5.1 12.1.1.5.2 12.1.1.5.3	Says to stop Says to go Other

	12.1.1.6 The deceased requests revenge	= you may feel a need to act on behalf of the deceased, yet fear to do so		
12.1.2 You meet or see the deceased, who appears to be alive again	12.1.2.1 You are surprised to meet or see the deceased person; you may react with joy, anger, or fear; your feelings may change to grief when you awaken	= you may hope that the death didn't really take place, that it was a mistake or a trick; you may feel angry that the deceased caused you trouble; you may fear that the reported death was untrue, if you desired it	12.1.2.1.1 12.1.2.1.2 12.1.2.1.3 12.1.2.1.4 12.1.2.1.5	Delight Anger Fear Sorrow Other
12.1.3 Your response to a negative dream about the dead	12.1.3.1 You have a variety of emotional reactions to the dead person in the dream	= you feel strengthened or weakened in your ability to cope with the loss of the deceased, depending upon the content of the dream; you may feel deep regret over the loss (grief); you may feel the death is destroying you (you die); you may feel more able to cope with negative aspects of deceased (defy unreasonable request, protect self, forgive); feel regret for your own behavior (apologize); or feel compassion for the deceased (comfort, offer help)	12.1.3.1.1 12.1.3.1.2 12.1.3.1.3 12.1.3.1.4 12.1.3.1.5 12.1.3.1.6 12.1.3.1.7	Deep grief You die (1.0) You defy demands, protect self Forgive the deceased Apologize Comfort the deceased Offer help

12.5 Guided by a spirit in a dream (Positive dream about a deceased person)	12.5.1 You are guided by the spirit of a deceased person in a dream = you feel hopeful, reassured, or inspired	12.5.1.1 The deceased looks and acts very well, even radiant, in a dream; any infirmity prior to death may be gone; the deceased may appear transformed	= you feel hopeful, reassured, or inspired to believe that the person's spirit is at peace (looks well, is kindly); you may hope the spirit cares about your loss (says good-bye); you feel watched over and loved (will always love you, gives you gift); you may feel it's all right to reinvest emotionally in life (go on with your life); you feel satisfaction with new family members or personal achievement (congratulations, praise); or you may feel reassured there is life after death (predicts when you will die; deceased person is evolving, learning, or reborn)	12.5.1.1.1 Good-bye 12.5.1.1.2 Praises you 12.5.1.1.3 Always love you 12.5.1.1.4 Gives you gift 12.5.1.1.5 Urges you to go on with your life 12.5.1.1.6 Predicts when you will join 12.5.1.1.7 Asks pardon or accepts forgiveness 12.5.1.1.8 Is evolving, learning 12.5.1.1.9 Is reborn
	12.5.2 Your response to a dream in which you are guided by a spirit	12.5.2.1 You have a variety of emotional reactions to seeing or meeting the deceased looking and acting very well in dream	= you feel hopeful that the deceased's spirit is peaceful; reassured of caring, continued presence; inspired to believe in afterlife or rebirth; feel you can cope with your loss while being watched over and loved; or that you and the deceased will eventually reunite; you may feel connected to a greater spiritual reality	12.5.2.1.1 Reassured 12.5.2.1.2 Feel loved 12.5.2.1.3 Feel safe, protected 12.5.2.1.4 Feel forgiven 12.5.2.1.5 Forgive the deceased 12.5.2.1.6 Able to go on with life 12.5.2.1.7 Belief in afterlife

Selected References

Allende, Isabel. *Paula*. Translated by Margaret Sayers Peden. New York: Harper-Collins, 1995.

Ammann, Ruth. *Traumbild Haus: Von den Lebensräumen der Seele* [The House Dream Image: The Life Work of the Soul]. Olten, Switzerland: Walter Verlag, 1991.

Axelrod, Alan, and Harry Oster, eds., with Walton Rawls. *The Penguin Dictionary of American Folklore*. New York: Penguin, 2000.

Bell, Madison Smartt. "William T. Vollman." *New York Times Magazine*, Feb. 6, 1994.

Breger, Louis; Ian Hunter; and Ron Lane. *The Effect of Stress on Dreams*. New York: International Universities Press, 1971.

Brothers, Joyce. *Widowed*. New York: Simon & Schuster, 1990.

Bulkeley, Kelly. *Transforming Dreams: Learning Spiritual Lessons from the Dreams You Never Forget*. New York: John Wiley & Sons, 2000.

Cartwright, Rosalind, and Lynne Lamberg. *Crisis Dreaming*. New York: Harper Perennial, 1993.

Chin, Tsai. *Daughter of Shanghai*. New York: St. Martin's Press, 1988.

Domhoff, G. William. *Finding Meaning in Dreams: A Quantitative Approach*. New York: Plenum Press, 1996.

Dundes, Alan, ed. *The Walled-Up Wife*. Madison: The University of Wisconson Press, 1996.

_____. *Folklore Matters*. Knoxville: The University of Tennessee Press, 1989.

_____, ed. *Cinderella: A Casebook*. Madison: University of Wisconsin Press, 1982.

_____. *Interpreting Folklore*. Bloomington: Indiana University Press, 1980.

_____, ed. *The Study of Folklore*. Englewood Cliffs, N.J.: Prentice-Hall, 1965.

Engel, George L. "The Death of a Twin: Mourning and Anniversary Reactions." *International Journal of Psycho-analysis* 56 (1975).

Freud, Sigmund. "Symbolism in Dreams." In Alan Dundes, ed., *International Folkloristics: Classic Contributions by the Founders of Folklore*. New York: Rowman & Littlefield, 1999, pp. 177–95.

Freud, Sigmund. *The Interpretation of Dreams.* New York: Avon, 1965.

Garfield, Patricia. *The Dream Messenger: How Dreams of the Departed Bring Healing Gifts.* New York: Simon & Schuster, 1997.

———. *Creative Dreaming.* New York: Simon & Schuster, 1995.

———. *The Healing Power of Dreams.* New York: Simon & Schuster, 1991.

———. *Pathway to Ecstasy: The Way of the Dream Mandala.* New York: Prentice Hall, 1989.

———. *Women's Bodies, Women's Dreams.* New York: Ballantine, 1988.

———. *Your Child's Dreams.* New York: Ballantine, 1984.

Gratton, Nicole. *Rêves et Complices: L'Art de Changer les Cauchemars en Beaux Rêves* [Dreams and Helpers: The Art of Changing Nightmares into Good Dreams]. Québec: Coffragants, 1996. With audiotape.

Hill, Clara. *Working with Dreams in Psychotherapy.* New York: Guilford Press, 1996.

Hoffman, Curtiss. *The Seven Story Tower: A Mythic Journey Through Space and Time.* New York: Plenum Press, 1999.

Jean, Georges. *Signs, Symbols, and Ciphers.* New York: Harry N. Abrams, 1998. See Victor Turner's discussion of ritual colors, pp. 145–47.

Jung. C. G., ed. *Man and His Symbols.* New York: Doubleday, 1964.

———. *Memories, Dreams, Reflections.* New York: Random House, 1963.

———. *Modern Man in Search of a Soul.* New York: Harcourt Brace Jovanovich, 1933.

Kast, Verena. *Folktales as Therapy.* New York: Fromm International, 1995.

———. *A Time to Mourn: Growing Through the Grief Process.* Stuttgart: Daimon Verlag, 1982.

Lévi-Strauss, Claude. *Structural Anthropology,* vol. 2. Translated by Monique Layton. Chicago: University of Chicago Press, 1976.

Maggiolini, Alfio, Paolo Azzone, Katia Provantini, and Daniele Vigano. "A Classification of Typical Contents of Dreams." Unpublished paper, 1999. Maggiolini is at the Faculty of Psychology, University of Milan, Italy.

Pearson, Cynthia, and Margaret L. Stubbs. *Parting Company.* Seattle: Seal Press, 1999.

Propp, Vladimir. *Morphology of the Folktale.* Austin: University of Texas Press, 1968.

Siegel, Alan. *Dreams That Can Change Your Life.* Los Angeles: Jeremy P. Tarcher, 1990.

Stevens, Anthony. *Ariadne's Clue: A Guide to the Symbols of Humankind.* Princeton, N.J.: Princeton University Press, 1999.

———. *Private Myths: Dreams and Dreaming.* Cambridge, Mass.: Harvard University Press, 1995.

Tholey, Paul. "A Model for Lucid Training as a Means of Self-Healing and Psychological Growth." In Jayne Gackenbach and Stephen LaBerge, eds., *Conscious Mind, Sleeping Brain.* New York: Plenum Press, 1988.

Thompson, Stith. *The Folktale.* Berkeley: University of California Press, 1977.

———. *Motif Index of Folk Literature.* 6 vol. Bloomington: Indiana University Press, 1955.

Weiss, Lillie. *Practical Dreaming.* Oakland, Calif.: New Harbinger, 1999.

———. *Dream Analysis in Psychotherapy.* New York: Pergamon Press, 1986.

Index

ABOUT THE AUTHOR

PATRICIA GARFIELD, PH.D., is a world-renowned authority on dreams. A clinical psychologist who graduated summa cum laude from Temple University in Philadelphia, she has been studying dreams professionally for more than thirty years.

Dr. Garfield's first book, *Creative Dreaming*, is considered a classic. A bestseller when it was first published in 1974, it has been in print continuously ever since and has appeared in thirteen foreign languages. She also wrote *Pathway to Ecstasy: The Way of the Dream Mandala* (illustrated by the author); *Your Child's Dreams*; *The Healing Power of Dreams* (also illustrated by the author); *Women's Bodies, Women's Dreams*; and *The Dream Messenger: How Dreams of the Departed Bring Healing Gifts*.

One of the six cofounders of the Association for the Study of Dreams, Dr. Garfield served as president during 1998–99. She has recorded her own dreams for more than fifty years, perhaps creating the longest dream journal extant. Dr. Garfield lives with her husband, a psychotherapist, in the San Francisco Bay Area.